Presented by
The Worshipful
Company of Haberdashers

to J.F. BUCKNELL, ESQ.,

on the occasion of his retirement

from the Company's Solicitors and

in grateful thanks for his

endeavours on behalf of the Company.

18th June, 1996   *Master*

The History of
THE HABERDASHERS' COMPANY

St Katherine of Alexandria, the Company's patron saint, with the wheel and sword symbolising her martyrdom early in the 4th century; from the Company book of ordinances, 1505.

The History of
THE HABERDASHERS' COMPANY

Ian W. Archer

Phillimore

1991

Published by
PHILLIMORE & CO. LTD
Shopwyke Hall, Chichester, Sussex

ISBN 0 85033 798 4

Phototypeset by Intype, London
Printed and bound in Great Britain by
STAPLES PRINTERS ROCHESTER LIMITED
Love Lane, Rochester, Kent.

Contents

List of Colour Illustrations

Frontispiece: St Katherine of Alexandria

List of Black and White Illustrations

Foreword

The Court of Assistants of the Haberdashers' Company, with the concurrence of the Court of Wardens, invite me to contribute this foreword, a privilege for the first Chairman of the Committee appointed to guide the preparation and publication of this History.

The Committee decided that more than 500 years of the history of the Company must not be a dry, factual account of administration and varying fortunes, but should be a story set against the changing political, economic and social background, and that the commission should require a well researched, scholarly work which would make enjoyable reading. The search for an author who might achieve this involved wide enquiries, interviewing some of those who aspired to attempt the task, and assessing samples of their writings. The choice fell upon Dr Ian Archer, then already recognised as a rising English historian.

The Committee believe that Dr Archer has more than fulfilled the expectation that – undaunted by the sheer weight of available material and by tantalising gaps in the records – he would produce a work worthy of the Haberdashers' Company, eighth in civic precedence among the Great Twelve Livery Companies of the City of London.

It will be for the readers to judge the merits of this book; but every one of them will surely find in it subjects of special personal interest; pageantry, social conditions, religious influences, changes in fashion, gastronomy, the Company's plate, trade and protectionism, financial management, administration of charities, many facets of education; and much more.

The Company gratefully joins with the Author in acknowledging the help others have given him during the writing of this book.

Sir Maurice Bathurst
Past Master

Acknowledgements

A work which runs from the medieval button to modern educational technology is bound to saddle its author with vast debts. It gives me great pleasure to thank the many individuals and institutions without whose help this book would have been inconceivable.

The entire project would have run less smoothly without the guidance provided by the Company's Historiographical Committee. Chaired initially with a rare combination of wit and efficiency by Sir Maurice Bathurst, Past Master, its later deliberations were chaired by Mr Brian Shawcross, Assistant, who tactfully guided a sometimes dilatory author to completion. Other members of the Committee were Mr Richard Hamersley, Assistant, the late Commander Bill Miller, Assistant *Honoris Causa*, Mr Peter de Vere Beauclerk-Dewar, Liveryman, and Mr Richard Harvey, Freeman, guided with some persuasion by Captain Michael Barrow R.N. (the Clerk), who was assisted in the early stages by the late Mr Walter Greenwood, the Clerk's Schools' Assistant. It is sad that two men who provided so much encouragement and advice to the author should not have lived to see its completion. All members of the Committee read the entire work, and it has benefited immeasurably by their comments.

From the staff at Haberdashers' Hall I have met with unfailing patience, courtesy, encouragement and, not least, valuable information. Captain Barrow answered a barrage of questions about contemporary practice with an enviable clarity. The late Mr R. K. Burnett, the Company's former Archivist, gave me my initial bearings among the records. Other inquiries have been answered by Mr F. J. Oakman (the Beadle), Mr R. E. Goodwin (the Accountant), and Mr A. W. Musk (the Charities Assistant). Of the below stairs staff, special thanks must go to Mr Mick Kelson, Silverman, whose ready wit and cups of tea have made the author's sojourns in the archive more enjoyable.

Several members of the Court of Assistants have given of their time to be interviewed. To Past Masters Sir Robin Brook, the late Revd Anthony Cope, Richard Liddiard, Christopher Bostock and Monty Northcott, and Mr Barry Gothard, Honorary Assistant, I am most grateful for insights on the more recent past, and for advice on directions the work might take.

The centrality of the Company's Schools to its affairs will become rapidly apparent to any reader of this work. The Heads of all the Schools and members of their staffs have readily answered queries. It is perhaps invidious to single out individuals, but Miss Helen Gichard (Headmistress of Monmouth School for Girls) deserves special thanks for her generous hospitality, as does Mr Adrian Barlow (Director of Studies at Monmouth School) for help over photographic material.

I owe a particularly heavy debt to Mr Roy Cadman, a member of the Livery, for his help over the illustrations. Not only did he give advice over what should be included, but he also allowed several items (nos. I, V, VI, VIII, XV, XVI, XVIII, XXIII, 26 and 48) from his personal collection to appear *gratis*, as well as taking other photographs (nos. II, III, IV, VII, XIX and XX) for the *History*. Other extensive photographic commissions (cover, frontispiece and nos. IX, X, XII, XIII, XIV, 2, 4, 11, 13, 21, 23–4, 27, 29, 31–2, 39, 42, 44–5, 52, 63 and 66 were executed by Godfrey New. The photography of the silver (nos. XXIV, XXV, XXVI and XXVII) was undertaken by A. C. Cooper Ltd.

For permission to reproduce photographs, thanks are due to the following institutions and individuals: the Ashmolean Museum, Oxford (no. 7); the Bibliothèque Royale, Brussels (no. 14); the Trustees of the British Museum (nos. 8, 10, and 34); the Syndics of the Cambridge University Library (no. 16); the Corporation of London Record Office (nos. 2 and 6); the Drapers' Company (nos. IX and X); the Guildhall Library (cover and nos. 4, 11, 30–2, 38, 47); Haberdashers' Aske's Hatcham Girls' School (no. 52); Monmouth School (nos. 49–51); the Museum of London (nos. 1, 15, and 35); the Public Record Office (nos. 5 and 9: Crown Copyright material reproduced by permission of the Controller of Her Majesty's Stationery Office); the Royal Commission on the Historic Monuments of England (nos. 18 and 36); the Castle Gates Library, Shrewsbury (no. 28); Mrs Sime (no. 56); the Society of Antiquaries (no. 12); Stock, Page, and Stock Ltd. (nos. 42 and 66).

In a *History* which takes its author out of 'his' period, debts to one's fellow scholars multiply. Dr Caroline Barron, Dr Wendy Childs, Dr Vanessa Harding, and Dr Derek Keene provided help with the medieval period. Mr Geoffrey Egan and Ms Kay Staniland of the Museum of London were helpful on the history of costume and dress accessories. Mr Graham Virgo and Mr Charles Harpum resolved knotty legal issues. Dr Jon Parry and Dr Gillian Sutherland are responsible for whatever direction is present in the 19th century chapters. Other references were supplied by Dr Donald Adamson, Mr Mark Jenner, Mr Tim Stretton, and Mr Tim Wales. Many individuals from the wider world have helped on specific points: among them I should particularly like to thank Messrs Felix H. W. Bedford, Honorary Assistant, Robert Glover, Liveryman, Noel Mander, Freeman, and Henry F. Whithouse, Liveryman, John A. Christie-Miller, John Elsworth, Prebendary Peter Morgan, and Bernard M. Watney.

Charles Truman has supplied an expertise I wholly lack myself, and has written the appendix on the Company's plate.

The bulk of the research and writing for this book was undertaken during my tenure of a Fellowship at Downing College, Cambridge. My time there is drawing to a close, and I should like to record my thanks to the Master and Fellows for providing such congenial and intellectually stimulating company over the past two years.

Finally, my greatest debt is to Miss Helen Bradley, who acted as Research Assistant on the *History*, and who is now Archivist to the Company. Her labours have been prodigious, and she has shaped this work in more ways than she perhaps realises, as well as sharing in its joys and frustrations. It would have been much impoverished without her help.

IAN W. ARCHER

Midsummer's Day, 1991

List of Abbreviations

B.L. British Library
C.J. *Journals of the House of Commons*
C.L.B. *Calendar of Letter Books Preserved Among the Archives of the City of London, 1275–1498,*
ed. R. R. Sharpe (11 vols., 1899–1912)
C.L.R.O. Corporation of London Records Office
C.P.M.R. *Calendar of Plea and Memoranda Rolls Preserved Among the Archives of the City of London,*
ed. A. H. Thomas (vols. I-IV) and P. E. Jones (vols. V-VI) (6 vols., 1926–61)
C.P.R. *Calendar of Patent Rolls* (H.M.S.O., 1901 to date)
D.N.B. *Dictionary of National Biography*
G.L. Guildhall Library
Jour. Journal of the Court of Common Council
P.R.O. Public Record Office
Rep. Repertory of the Court of Aldermen
S.R. *Statutes of the Realm*
T.E.D. *Tudor Economic Documents*, ed. R. H. Tawney and E. Power (3 vols., 1924)
W.A.M. Westminster Abbey Muniments

Chapter One

Origins

The historian of the early years of the Haberdashers' Company faces a difficult task because hardly anything of the Company archive has survived from before the later 16th century. There is an early 17th-century list of freemen and their masters from 1526 onwards; the minutes of the Court of Assistants commence in 1583, and the apprenticeship registers at the same time; for the Wardens' accounts we have to wait until 1633. From the 15th and early 16th centuries all that survives are the charters (1448, 1498, 1502, 1510), the grants of arms (1446 and 1502), and a late (1505) ordinance book. Beyond this one can turn to the records of the Corporation before whom guild ordinances were registered, and where disputes between guilds were arbitrated.

It is tempting therefore to write the history of the medieval guild rather narrowly in terms of institutional development. In such an analysis attention would focus on the ordinances of 1371, the charter of 1448, and the amalgamations with the Hatters and Hurers at the turn of the 16th century. But such an approach is distorting. One of the problems of formal records such as those of the Corporation is the way they can mislead the historian into assuming the novelty of something merely because it is recorded for the first time. Thus to assume that the Haberdashers only fulfilled the functions described in the 1371 ordinances from that date would be wrong. Nor do the records of the Corporation give a representative picture of the functions of the early guild, for the Aldermen only chose to record details of its activities of relevance to their own business of governing the City. Nor can these formal records tell us much about what the haberdashers had in common nor the forces that led them to associate together in the first place, nor the economic developments underlying the institutional changes. To answer these questions a much broader range of source material must be tackled. Inventories, customs accounts, and the archaeological remains from medieval sites in the City can tell us about the nature of the haberdashers' business life; and wills can tell us something about their spiritual life. The approach adopted in these first two chapters is to use the institutional developments as a framework and to use the other sources more speculatively to provide possible explanations.

The best point of entry to the haberdashers' trade is to explore the contents of one inventory. The stock of Thomas Trewe, a haberdasher in the parish of St Ewen, was appraised in 1378. The full inventory is given below:

2 dozens of laces of red leather, value 8d.; one gross of 'poynts' of red leather, 18d.; one dozen of 'cradilbowes', made of wool and flax, 18d.; 3 'cradilbowes' made of wool and flax, 3d.; one dozen of caps, one half of which are of red colour and the other half green, 2s. 8d.; one dozen of white caps, called 'nightecappes', 2s. 3d.; 2 dozens of woollen caps of divers colours, 16s.; 6

caps of black wool, 4s.; 5 caps of blue colour, and one cap of russet, 2s. 6d.; 5 children's caps, red and blue, 2s. 1d.; one dozen of black hures, 4s.; one black hure 4d.; 2 hair camises, 12d.; one red cap, 7d.; one other cap of russet, 7d.; one hat of russet, 6d.; one white hat, 3d.; 2 papers covered with red leather, 12d.; 2 other papers, one of them covered with black leather, and the other with red, 8d.; one purse, called 'hamondeys' of sea-green colour, 6d.; 4 pairs of spurs, 2s.; one double chain of iron, 10d., and one other iron chain, 6d.; one wooden gaming table with a set of men, 6d.; 2 'permis', 2s.; one cloth painted with Him Crucified and other figures, 2s. 4d.; 8 white chains of iron for ferrettes, 8d.; one flekage of wood, 3d.; one set of beads of 'geet', 6d., one other set of beads of black alabaster, 4d.; 3 sets of beads of wood, 3d.; 2 pairs of pencases, with horns, 8d.; one pair of children's boots of white woollen cloth, 2d.; one osculatory called a 'paxbread', 3d.; 2 sets of wooden beads called 'knottes', 4d.; 4 articles called 'kombes' of boxwood, 4d.; 2 wooden boxes, 3d.; 2 wooden 'piper quernes', 3d.; 2 pounds of linen thread, green and blue, 2s.; 2 wooden 'cosynis', 2d.; 6 purses of red leather, 4d.; 4 eyeglasses, 2d.; 18 horns called 'inkehornes', 18d.; 2 pencases, 6d.; one black girdle of woollen thread, 2d.; 13 quires of paper, 6s. 8d.; other paper, damaged, 6d.; one hat of russet, 6d.; 2 wooden coffins, 8d.; 2 gaming tables with the men, 16d.; one wooden block for shaping caps, 2d.; 6 skins of parchment called 'soylepeles', 6d.; one wooden whistle, 2d.; 7 leaves of paper, 1d.; and 3 pieces of whippecorde, 3d..[1]

The sheer variety of goods is evident. There were varieties of thread; dress accessories such as beads, combs, purses, girdles, and spectacles; undergarments such as shirts; several lines in head-gear in varied colours; writing materials from parchment and paper to inkhorns and pencases; and even the paraphernalia of popular piety, pax-boards and rosaries. Not the least of the haberdasher's stock-in-trade were the various kinds of garment fastening, laces, points, pins, and buttons, although the latter two items were absent from Trewe's inventoried stock. Points were the ties made of linen or silk thread, or in the case of the poorer sort, of leather. They were tipped with aiglets or chapes, ornamental metal tags, which protected the ends of laces and facilitated threading through corresponding eyelets.[2]

It seems that originally haberdashery was stocked by mercers. This may explain why there are so few references to haberdashers in the later 13th and early 14th centuries. Only one haberdasher is named amomng the 909 men made free of the City between 25 October 1309 and 30 November 1312. William Official, 'aberdassher' was admitted to the freedom on 8 February 1312 having served his master, John Personne, for a term of seven years. Although he is alone, there were plenty of men making the kind of goods later associated with the haberdashers: Roger de Elvedene, 'mirourer', Stephen de Hereford, 'hattere', Richard Madour de Fakenham, capper, Henry, son of John le Duc de Borham, pouchmaker, and William de Fondenhale, 'chapeler' (hatmaker, Old French).[3] Where the trade ascription 'haberdasher' is given in this early period, it is used of men who were otherwise described as mercers. In 1277 William de Causton, Robert de Bury, and Roger de Bury, 'haberdashers', with others, acknowledged a debt to Matilda, daughter of Aunger the Pheliper. But William de Causton described himself in his will of 1297–8 as *mercenarius*.[4] The mercers long retained their links with the sale of haberdashery, and although specializing in linen and silk, also often imported haberdashery, and sold belts, knives, points, hats, and girdles. The stock of John Bussheye, mercer, in 1394 included beaver hats, amber and bone beads, handkerchiefs, combs, whips, silk garters, silk laces, thread, and rings in addition to linen, canvas and worsteads. As late as 1410

1. Selection of haberdashery items dating from within a few years of 1400. Two leather purses, tin buttons, amber beads, bells, tweezers, a cosmetic set (comprising earpick and nail cleaner), a pewter whistle, chapes (or points), and a boxwood comb are shown.

a Winchester mercer obtained his thread, belts, and points from John Baddeby, a London mercer.[5]

It is clear, however, that specialists in the retailing of haberdashery developed in the mid–14th century. More haberdashers can be identified on the tax assessments of the reign of Edward III than on those of his father and grandfather, and by 1371 the Haberdashers felt sufficient group identity to petition the Aldermen to allow ordinances for their guild. How then do we account for their emergence at this time? It is probable that it reflected developments in the world of fashion. The years around 1340 saw the development of tighter and closer-fitting garments which demanded more in the way of fastenings. There is also evidence that it was a more fashion-conscious age with courtiers vying for the latest in outlandish taste, creating a demand for accessories of various kinds. It is also arguable that the new tastes penetrated some way down the social scale, as more competition for limited labour in the decades after the Black Death increased the purchasing power of the artisans and led to anxieties about the dissolution of divinely ordained social distinctions, as the populace aped their betters. All these developments would have increased demand for the kind of goods haberdashers sold, thereby encouraging specialisation and the separation from dealing in expensive cloths, the main branch of the mercery.

Around 1300, garments had been similar for men and women, with long and rather shapeless body sections and sleeves attached at the top of the side seams. From about 1320 efforts were being made to make clothes fit more tightly around the arms and chest. Buttons were introduced first to the lower sleeves, and later (about 1340) as centre-front fastenings from the neck to the hip. In the 1360s men began wearing very short hip-length garments called paltoks attached to hose by points.[6] Moralists were outraged by these developments. John of Reading blamed it on foreigners. The evil could be traced to the arrival of the Hainaulters in Queen Philippa's entourage soon after the accession of Edward III. The modest, long and ample fashion of a more respectable age had been deserted for clothing that was

> short, narrow, hampering, cut all about, laced up in every part and altogether changed. With their buttoned sleeves and tippets to their over-tunics and hoods hanging down to excessive lengths . . . they are more like tormentors, or to be more truthful demons, rather than men.

Men having fallen so obviously prey to the sin of pride, it was only a matter of time before God's judgments poured forth.[7]

These changes in court fashions have been well documented through the royal wardrobe accounts by S. M. Newton. Whereas between 1327 and 1333 there are no references to buttons or any other kind of fastening on the King's garments, by 1337–8 buttons are being mentioned although it is not clear whether they were purely decorative or acted as a fastening, nor whether they appeared over the chest or merely on the sleeves. By 1342–3, however, tunics buttoning down the front appeared: they were probably still a novelty because the exact position of the buttons is described ('ante pectum'). Silk cords for tying on aiglets appear in the wardrobe accounts at this date, as well as among the purchases for horse-trappings for tournaments. The way in which changing fashions could generate large-scale demand for apparently the humblest of manufactured goods is shown by the fact that the trousseau of the King's daughter, Princess Joan, contracted to be married in 1348, included no less than 12,000 pins for her veils.[8]

The costume historians therefore provide valuable clues for explaining the emergence of the Haberdashers. Unfortunately the archaeological evidence from London sites is contradictory in that it suggests that buttons were introduced into England in the early 13th century rather than around 1330 as Newton suggests. The recent finds show that base metals were being used for buttons from the early 13th century onwards. It is suggested by Egan and Pritchard that the variety recorded indicates wide use in the lower levels of society. The problem with the approach of the costume historians is that they tend to concentrate on the upper classes who provide the documentary and monumental evidence on which their case rests. The fact that proverbial phrases such as 'not worth a button' can be dated back to the early 14th century is yet another sign of a popular market already in existence by this date.[9]

Nevertheless the archaeological evidence need not necessarily destroy the argument advanced above about the emergence of the Haberdashers as a distinctive trade. It seems reasonable to suppose that the surge in aristocratic demand for fastenings would sustain an expansion in demand for London dealers in such products. When this is combined with the fact of the increased spending power of labourers and artisans in the later 14th century, the argument seems tenable. One of the clearest indications of that rise in living standards for the humbler sections of society is the sumptuary legislation of 1363 which attempted to lay down the dress appropriate to each station in society. Servants and artificers were limited to clothing costing less than two marks apiece; people lacking 40s. worth of goods were required to 'wear no manner of cloth but blanket and russet of 12 pence and shall wear girdles of linen according to their estate'. The main motive behind such legislation was the widespread sense that 'the variety of the common people in their dress is so great that it is impossible to distinguish the rich from the poor, the high from low, the clergy from the laity, by their appearance'.[10]

Other aspects of the archaeological evidence can be used to support the notion of an expanding market for haberdashery in the later 14th century. Pritchard and Egan comment on the vast increase in the use of pins in the 14th century, reflecting changes in manufacturing methods since the 12th century. As the availability of drawn wire increased, the pin shank became finer and the head smaller, so that, rather than being used as alternatives to brooches, they could be used for fastening veils. Cased mirrors were apparently being mass produced for the popular market in the 14th century. Small bells, although found in deposits of the early 13th century, were being more widely used in the 14th century, particularly with their development as dress accessories in fashionable society (rather than merely for the collars of animals) at the court of Richard II.[11]

The first occasion on which the Haberdashers manifested themselves in a corporate capacity was on 11 June 1371 when they appeared before the Aldermen with the request that their ordinances be approved. The most important of the articles related to the control that they sought over access to the trade. It was ordained that no-one should be taken on for training in the art unless properly apprenticed, that no-one should take an apprentice unless himself a freeman of the City, and that apprentices should not serve for a shorter term than seven years. Also the right to follow the trade in the City was confined to freemen, 'for many persons who are not free of the City keep their shops and stalls open and take great profit, and bear no charges in the City to the great disparagement of the freemen of the said trade'.[12] Control over the freedom was important because of the privileges which attached to it, in particular the right to vote in elections for City officials and the right to engage in retail trade within the City's walls.[13]

It was the acquisition of control over the admission to the freedom that led to the institutionalisation of the London guilds. There was a natural tendency for men engaged in the same trade to meet together for social purposes and to discuss matters of common interest, but such *ad hoc* associations acquired the stamp of permanency in the early 14th century with the decision that no-one should be admitted to the freedom unless sponsored by men from his trade. In 1312 representatives of the good men of every mystery then existing appeared before the Aldermen to ask that

2. The formal enrolment of the Company's first set of ordinances in the Court held by the Mayor of London, 1371.

forasmuch as the City ought always to be governed by the aid of men engaged in trade and handicrafts, and whereas it was anciently accustomed that no stranger, native or foreign, whose position and character were unknown, should be admitted to to the freedom of the city until the merchants and craftsmen whose business he wished to enter had previously certified the mayor and aldermen of his condition and trustworthiness, the whole Commonalty pray that such observance may be strictly kept for the future as regards the wholesale trades and handicrafts.

At this date it was still possible for freemen from a neighbourhood to vouch for an apprentice's training for him to acquire his freedom. But Edward II's charter of 1319 included the critical provision: 'No man of English birth and especially no English merchant, who followed any specific mystery or craft, should be admitted to the freedom of the City except on the security of six reputable men of that mystery or craft'. This was combined with the provision that 'every freeman shall be of some mystery or trade'. Since the freedom was a prerequisite of the exercise of political rights within the City, this gave the City's trades and crafts a hold on its constitution.[14] As the French Chronicle put it: 'At this time many of the people of the trades of London were arrayed in a livery and a good time was about to begin'.[15] The Haberdashers were only beginning their process of separation from the Mercers at this date, but once they had emerged as a distinctive trading interest the new mechanism of control over the freedom ensured that they would soon acquire a public status within the capital.

It is significant, however, that the ordinances of 1371 made no attempt to confine the trade to freemen of the Haberdashers' Guild. This was a sensitive issue within the capital. It had long been recognised that the wholesale trades should be free, but greater controversy attached to retailing. The Common Council petitioned the Mayor in 1364 that

> it seems right that everyone who is enfranchised ought to buy and sell wholesale, within the city and without, any manner of merchandise on which he can make a profit, but he may keep a shop and sell by retail only those goods which belong to his particular mystery, which he ought to support whenever necessary. This they believe to have been the intention of their ancestors of old, but these ancient usages had been allowed to lapse, whereby the good mysteries which used to maintain the City are likely to be hopelessly destroyed, unless speedy steps be taken to guard against it.

But the petition was greeted with little enthusiasm on the part of the authorities who asserted the principle that freemen should be enabled to pursue any trade on acquiring the freedom and 'to trade in all kinds of merchandise at will without any hinderance'. Inventories from the late 14th century reveal that retailers in the importing crafts enjoyed considerable freedom. As has been shown, mercers continued to deal in haberdashery, and glovers and grocers also sometimes included haberdashery among their stock. The ruling cut both ways, of course, for haberdashers could turn to other trades. Companies like the Mercers, which attempted to assert a monopoly over the retailing of fine quality textiles, were running counter to City practice. The haberdasher who purchased a mercer's shop and complained to Chancery that he had been robbed by two mercers 'having dispyte and malice that yor besecher beyng a haberdasher shuld medill with mercery ware', had right on his side. Nevertheless it is striking that men pursuing a different trade from that of their formal Company affiliation often sought to translate (that is, transfer) to the appropriate Company which demonstrates the attractiveness of the benefits that the Company could provide. Thus in the second quarter of the 15th century there were translations into the Haberdashers' Guild by freemen of the Hatters, Hurers, Pinners, Cutlers, and Weavers. Should men not translate, the only powers the Haberdashers had over them were the rather ill-defined rights to search their goods and present defaults to the Mayor.[16]

Initially, the haberdashers seem to have been predominantly retailers. Some may have acted as wholesalers to chapmen who distributed their goods over the rest of England, but there is little sign in the 14th century of their being engaged in the wholesale importing trades. Some haberdashers may actually have been engaged in the business of producing the articles that they sold. But the fact that an apprentice could complain that he had not been taught properly by his master because the only thing he had learned was the art of making points suggests that it was expected that the skills of haberdashers should be more widely based than this.[17] Artisans engaged in the production of the goods the haberdashers sold in fact enjoyed their own guilds which appear to have predated that of the Haberdashers. The Cappers acquired ordinances in the late 13th century, the Pursers in 1327, the Pouchmakers in 1339, the Hatters in 1347, and the Pinners in 1356.[18]

There was, of course, considerable friction between the producing crafts and the Haberdashers. The manufacturing crafts had an interest in ensuring that the markets were dominated by domestically produced goods whereas the haberdashers were not choosy about the origins of the goods they sold. As early as the reign of Edward II the Cappers were mounting a vigorous protectionist campaign. Having obtained an ordinance with Parliamentary sanction in 1318 that all caps should be made from pure wool, they proceeded to destroy the imported caps stocked by 'divers haberdashers and cappers'. These foreign caps were made of inferior materials ('flock') but were cheaper and popular. The importing interests – at this date German merchants and London mercers – counter-attacked with their own charges against the cappers. They alleged that the cappers of London made false caps of flocks mixed with wool, that they sold old caps for new, and that they dyed black caps made of white and grey wool. They lobbied vigorously against the measure with eventual success, for it was ruled that the foreign caps were 'good and sufficient' and therefore acceptable on the London market. This was the first documented clash of a type which was to become familiar between manufacturers and wholesaling/retailing interests involved with head-gear.[19]

Another source of tension between the haberdashers and the cappers was the sale by the former of caps fulled by feet or, worse still, at the fulling mill, rather than by hand. The process of fulling involved beating and compressing cloth in water to shrink it and so give it greater resistance to wear and tear. Conventionally the fulling of cloths and caps was done with clubs wielded by hand, but over the course of the 13th century the fulling mill was widely adopted in England. Such an innovation was labour-saving and therefore represented a threat to the smaller scale artisans within the craft. They alleged, however, that fulling mills produced an inferior quality product and with this argument were able to secure civic ordinances against the use of mills. Such a provision was incorporated into the ordinances of the Hurers (1376) as the cappers were otherwise called by this date, and an enforcement drive followed.[20] The repetition of the ordinance in 1404 suggests that the measure was ineffective. The hostility of the cappers was not just directed at the fulling mill, but also at the fulling of caps and hats by human feet, and it was over this issue that the Haberdashers, acting on this occasion in alliance with the Hatters, clashed with the Cappers in 1417. The Hatters and Haberdashers appeared before the Mayor and Aldermen to complain about the seizure of 15 long caps from the stock of James Bowyer, haberdasher. The Cappers pointed out that the caps had been fulled under human feet. This was not disputed by the Hatters and Haberdashers who confronted the ordinance head-on, alleging that 'caps, hures and hats, both in England and also abroad, were fulled both by mills and by foot at less cost, and equally as well as those fulled by hand'. They were also annoyed by the unilateral action of the Cappers, pointing out that the search for defective products should be made by the Haberdashers and Hatters as well as by the Cappers. On this occasion the lobbying by the Haberdashers was successful for the offending ordinance was annulled and it was ordered that the search should be exercised jointly by the crafts.[21]

The Hurers *alias* Cappers did not accept their defeat readily. The journals of Common Council reveal that there was another quarrel in 1441. Although details of its nature are lacking, the survival of an undated petition to the King from the Haberdashers and Hatters against the projected incorporation of the Hurers casts light on the issues probably at stake. In short, the Haberdashers seem to have been most anxious about the rights of search which the Hurers sought. The Hurers were seeking rights of search over all making hures, bonnets, and caps within the City and had petitioned Parliament on two occasions to this effect. Rebuffed in that arena they had turned to the King for incorporation. The Haberdashers and Hatters alleged that there were fewer than 3,000 people within the city and four miles thereabouts who worked on hures, bonnets, and caps, and that if the Hurers should get their way none would be able to work in the craft but those they licensed. They would not be able to provide a tenth part of the needs of the people with the inevitable result that prices would rise, and thousands of the King's poor subjects would be impoverished. The existence of this dispute suggests that the incorporation of the Haberdashers in 1448 was part of an effort to secure their position by underlining their royal patronage.[22]

Thus far the analysis has stressed the origins of the Company in the economic needs of members and the dictates of public policy. The religious dimension to the association has been neglected. It is well known that many of the London Livery Companies originated in parish fraternities, associations of people of middling status to secure social welfare and convivial fellowship during life, and intercession for their souls after death. The trade guilds shared common features with the fraternities. They too met for annual dinners, provided social welfare for members falling on hard times, and arranged for the performance of requiem masses for the souls of the departed. Because of the tendency towards occupational zoning in the City, members of the same trade would often be concentrated in particular parishes with the result

that a fraternity could be transformed into a trade guild.[23] We do not know for
certain whether this process occurred in the case of the Haberdashers. Certainly a
study of the places of residence given in the earliest surviving wills of Company
members from the 15th century suggests that the haberdashers tended to concentrate
in two main areas: Ludgate Hill and the parishes around St Paul's Cathedral, and
in the parish of St Magnus, probably on London Bridge. Interestingly enough, it
had been around Ludgate Hill that the cappers had clustered in the early 14th
century. But it cannot be shown that the Haberdashers' guild emerged from any of
the fraternities to St Katherine in these parishes.[24] Unfortunately, the ordinances of
1371 are strangely silent on the religious and social aspects of the association. This
may merely reflect the fact that the Haberdashers only saw fit to present to the City
authorities those aspects of their activities that were of concern to the men at
Guildhall, ignoring their less public roles, however essential these may have been to
the membership. However, it is possible that the Haberdashers emerged out of the
guild dedicated to God, the Blessed Virgin Mary, St Katherine, and All Saints,
which met in St Paul's Cathedral. Among the Wardens named in the return of 1389
were Robert de Lynne, elected by the Haberdashers to the Common Council in
1376, and John Selborer, possibly the same man as the John Silbourne, elected
Master of the Haberdashers in 1384. The connection of these leading members of
the Haberdashers' Company is suggestive evidence of a close link between the trade
association and the religious fraternity.The fact that there are no later references to
the fraternity may be a result of its becoming overtly the Haberdashers' guild, and
possibly moving out of St Paul's to St Mary Staining, the later guild church.[25]

Why St Katherine should have been chosen as the patron saint of the Haberdashers is not clear. Her role as a prototype of steadfastness in faith may have been
more important than any specific affinities with the craft. St Katherine was supposedly a noble-born woman of Alexandria of high learning who protested to the
Emperor Maxentius against the worship of idols. Being required to engage in a
disputation with 50 learned philosophers, she tore their arguments to shreds, and
the furious emperor had them all beheaded; she refused to deny her faith and marry
the emperor who had her imprisoned. Her tormentors tried to break her on a wheel,
but it fell to pieces, and the flying splinters killed some of the onlookers. Such an
impressive example of christian constancy resulted in the conversion of 200 soldiers
who were immediately beheaded. St Katherine was herself inevitably beheaded, her
veins flowing milk rather than blood. The cult of St Katherine was one of the most
popular in later medieval England. At least 56 English murals of her are known to
have existed, and cycles of her life in stained glass survive at York Minster, Clavering
(Essex), Combs (Suffolk), and Balliol College, Oxford. She was also the second most
popular dedicatee of parish fraternities in London.[26]

By the close of the 14th century it appears that a separate guild of Haberdashers
had emerged with the specialisation of retailing in London as consumer demand
grew and fashions changed. The guild had acquired as one of its roles the control
of access to the freedom. Although poorly documented it probably performed the
same kind of social roles as other guilds and was developing a sense of group identity
among its members. But it was one of the more recent guilds to acquire formal

status within the City, and it remained a rather marginal force by comparison with the merchant guilds of Fishmongers, Grocers, and Skinners. That was to change, however, over the next century of the Company's development.

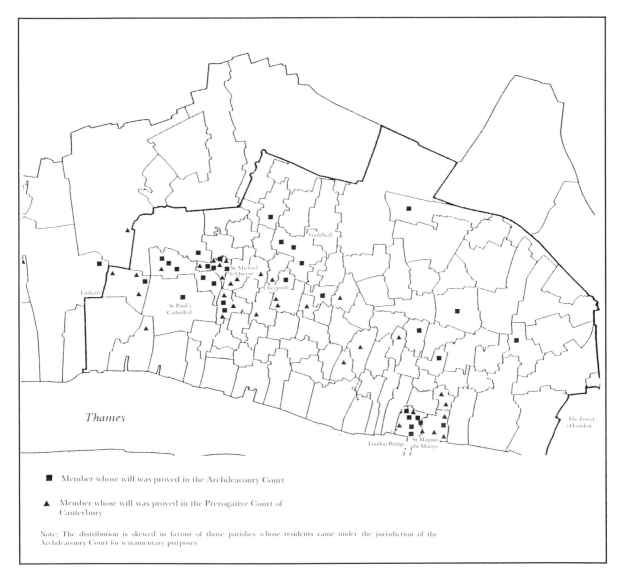

3.   Map showing places of residence of members of the Company, 1470–1550.

Chapter Two

The Transformation of the Company, 1400–1550

In the early 15th century the Haberdashers were among the more obscure of the City guilds. When the Clerk of the Brewers' Company drew up a list of the names of all the crafts practised in London in 1422 the Haberdashers were listed thirteenth. No member of the Haberdashers appears to be listed among the wealthier Londoners listed in 1436 as possessing lands worth over £5 per annum. But a century later the Haberdashers were numbered among the Twelve Great Companies enjoying the eighth position in the hierarchy, while on the list of Londoners assessed at over £50 worth of goods in 1522 (admittedly different criteria of assessment from 1436, but nevertheless regarded by contemporaries as in the upper echelons of society) there were 33 freemen of the Haberdashers' Company. These facts are testimony to the transformation in the status of the Company between about 1400 and 1550.[1]

A key sign of this greater status was the grant of a charter to the guild by Henry VI on 3 June 1448, incorporating the Haberdashers under the name of the 'Guild of St Katherine the Virgin of Haberdashers in the City of London'. This charter was among a batch granted in the second quarter of the 15th century: the other beneficiaries included the Grocers, Fishmongers, Vintners, Brewers, Drapers, Cordwainers, Leathersellers, and Armourers. From the King's point of view the motive behind these grants was to ensure that the guilds were brought into a closer relationship of dependence upon the Crown. They could now be said to exist by royal sanction and to the extent that the guilds' powers were to be exercised subject to the approval of the Mayor and Aldermen, they were locked into a tighter framework of control. This policy was articulated in a statute of 1437 which required all incorporated fraternities and guilds to bring their charters to be registered by the relevant civic authorities. From the guilds' point of view the primary motive behind incorporation was that it enabled them to hold property and gave them a legal personality so that they could bring suits corporately in the King's courts. The charters also regularised the powers of the guilds to govern themselves and to regulate the trade. Thus the Haberdashers were empowered to elect four Wardens each year, to make ordinances for the government of the guild, and to correct the faults of servants with the assent of the Mayor. The charter of 1448 unquestionably strengthened the guild's control over the trade. It provided that no-one should keep a haberdasher's shop unless free of the City and that no-one should be admitted to the freedom unless first presented to the Mayor by the Wardens or by 'four good men of the mystery'. Furthermore, the Wardens were granted powers of search over all goods relating to haberdashery, and more particularly over goods imported by aliens and sold by them within a three-mile radius of the City. The mention of the power over aliens was probably the product of a particularly vigorous agitation against the activities of alien merchants in the England of Henry VI which took its most visible form in a series of riots against them. Nor was the social side of the guild's activities neglected, for in the charter the Wardens were authorised to keep the feast of St Katherine, and provide food and drink for the members of the guild.[2]

The second mark of the Company's rising status was the acquisition of the site of the Hall in 1458. By a deed of 24 September 1458 Sir Richard Walgrave transferred property at the junction of Ingen Lane (otherwise known as Maiden Lane, and now forming part of Gresham Street) and Staining Lane to John Polhill, John Senecle, John Colred, and Robert Church, haberdashers, who were acting as feoffees for the company. By a deed of 1471 Colred, surviving his co-feoffees, entrusted the land to William Bacon and 14 other members of the guild. In 1478 they in turn released all their interest to Bacon who in turn bequeathed his interest in the property to the guild by his will. The plot was measured in 1499 and found to be 138 ft.2 ins. on the west side along Staining Lane, 136 ft.6 ins. on the east side abutting partly onto Beaumont's Inn, 71ft. on the north side, and 88 ft.6 ins. on the south side along Maiden Lane. The property had been the site of two inns in the reign of Richard II which were rented for 13 marks (£8 13s. 4d.) per annum in 1384–5. This suggests that at that date the property had a capital value of about £150. How the guild raised the money for the acquisition of the site is not known, but evidence from other better documented guilds suggests that it is likely to have been by means of contributions from members, and therefore testimony to an already strong sense of corporate identity. This supposition is strengthened by the fact that the cost of building the new Hall in 1459–61 was met by means of an assessment on the membership over a two-year period. A late 16th-century record book notes the outlines of a contract with Walter Tylney, carpenter, to set up the frame of the hall and the adjoining tenements in 1459, and says that the costs were met by assessment.[3]

We know little about what the early Hall looked like, but another contract of 1461 with Robert Wheatley, carpenter (who had worked extensively at Eton, where he was probably responsible for the design of the chapel roof), tells us that it comprised a hall, parlour, kitchen, armoury, and on the upper storey, a room called the Raven Chamber. The hall would have been used for dinners and gatherings of the membership, and the parlour for meetings of the Wardens.[4] The use to which the Raven Chamber was put in the 15th century is not known, but by the early 17th century it was associated with the meetings of the Yeomanry (the younger and poorer freemen who did not enjoy the right to wear the Livery).[5] Although the 15th-century records do not refer to them, it is also clear that the above-stairs area came to incorporate the Company's almshouse accommodation. At some date before 1543 the rooms over the kitchens were allocated for the use of the almsmen. It is clear then that the mid–15th-century developments enabled an expansion in the guild's ability to provide welfare for its members, although the rather cramped conditions at the Hall were probably not the ideal solution.[6] The loss of the Company's records before the later Elizabethan period makes it impossible to trace the development of the facilities at the Hall, but there is some evidence of considerable adornment in the Elizabethan period. William Smith, Rouge-Croix Pursuivant, in his *Breef Description of the Famous Cittie of London* (*c.* 1588), noted of the Haberdashers' Hall that 'for ye costly new wainskott [it] passeth all ye halls in London'.[7]

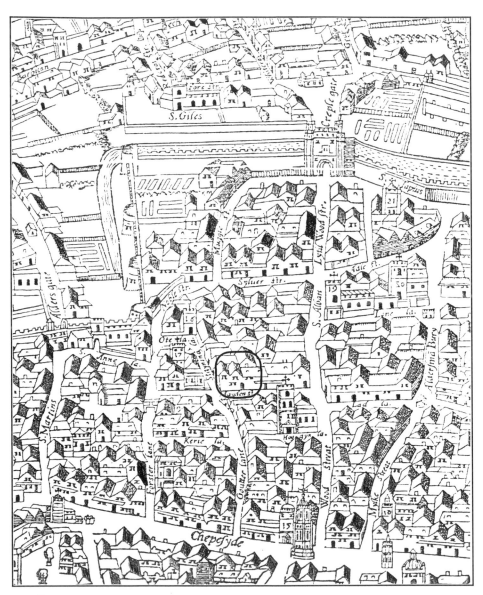

4.   Detail from the 'Agas' map of London (*c*.1565), showing site of Company's Hall.

The incorporation of the guild and the acquisition of a Hall were two marks of the rising 'honour and worship' of the Haberdashers; the grant of a coat of arms was another. The first grant of arms from Roger Legh, Clarenceux King of Arms, on 16 July 1446 actually predates the charter by two years. The arms granted were a 'f(i)eld of silver, three brosshers (brushes) of Gowlys (gules) bound of the f(i)eld between a Chevron of Asure (blue) in the Cheveron three Kateryn wheles of gold'. The patent of arms survives at Haberdashers' Hall, and is one of the two oldest patents in existence granted to Livery Companies. In the present day heraldry is often regarded as a subject somewhat remote from everyday concerns, but we should not therefore underestimate its critical importance to a society steeped in a visual culture, and well used to decoding the messages of heraldry. All grants of arms had to be authenticated and registered by the heralds under the authority of the King, although the grant of arms to the Haberdashers in fact ante-dated the formal establishment of the College of Arms by 38 years. In so far as arms were associated with the prevailing aristocratic value system, the right to bear a coat of arms gave the guild a highly privileged position. The guild lost no opportunity to sport its heraldry and thereby promote its honour. On occasions of civic ceremonial such as the procession of barges to Westminster at the Mayor's oath-taking or the reception of monarchs in London expensive banners bearing the Company's coat of arms would be displayed, while within the Hall the arms could be found in such varied forms as stained glass, carved wood and stone, and embroidered cushions.[8]

The changes outlined above both reflected and enhanced the prestige of the guild. They all required finance, and because the corporate funds were low, dependent on the income from fees and quarterage dues, the guild relied upon the benevolence of its wealthier members. To the extent that these men were underwriting the guild's new status they came to wield a greater influence over its affairs. Although it had doubtless always been the case that the wealthy wielded a disproportionate influence in the guild's affairs, the mid–15th-century changes tended to institutionalise their predominance. The charter of 1448 had authorised the Wardens to distribute a Livery among the brethren and sisters of the guild each year. There is no necessary implication here of the greater status of the Livery, but that does not prove that the division between those entitled to wear the Livery and those in the subordinate position of Yeomen had not already arrived. Certainly it was present by the time of the grant of ordinances in 1505 which refer to the admission of Liverymen by the Master and Wardens acting in conjunction with four ex-Wardens. By 1502 there were 41 Liverymen in the Haberdashers' Company out of a total membership of possibly 120. The special status of the Livery had been confirmed by changes in the City electorate. In 1475 it was decreed that Congregation, the body which elected the Mayor, Sheriffs and other officers, should be composed of the Liverymen of the companies. Freemen not in the Livery retained the right to elect the Aldermen, Common Councillors and lesser officials in the Wardmote assemblies. In this way the familiar Company hierarchy, whereby the Livery enjoyed special privileges such as greater numbers of apprentices and attendance at more social functions, came to be more firmly articulated in the course of the 15th century.[9]

The rising status of the Haberdashers was accompanied by the arrival of members

of the guild at the summit of power in the City. The first haberdasher to be elected
to the Court of Aldermen was Robert Billesdon, elected in 1471 as Alderman for
Bread Street ward, which he continued to represent until his death in 1492. Billesdon
served as Sheriff in 1473–4 and reached the pinnacle of civic greatness in 1483–4
when he served the office of Mayor. He was followed in the office of Alderman in
the closing decades of the 15th century by William Bacon (1480–3) and William
Welbeck (1492–1504), although the Haberdashers had to wait until 1532 before they
provided another Mayor, Sir Stephen Peacock.[10]

The combination of incorporation with the presence of men enjoying the political
clout of a Billesdon made the Haberdashers more attractive as a trustee for property
to secure prayers for the souls of the donors and, increasingly in later years, for
charitable purposes. The earliest example is the establishment of a chantry in the
parish of St Faith's by Alice Fulbourne, the widow of John Fulbourne, haberdasher.
By her will of 1466 she left to the 'Wardens of the art or mystery of Haberdashers'
the remainder of her interest in property in the precincts of St Paul's Cathedral
which had been leased to the Fulbournes for the term of 60 years by the Bishop of
London in 1429. In return the Haberdashers were to support a chantry priest on a
salary of 10 marks per annum who was to be present at all services in the church
as well as celebrating the anniversary of John and Alice on the Feast of St Lawrence
with placebo and dirige. More interestingly still, the priest appointed was also to
attend the Wardens of the Haberdashers on the occasion of their requiem for the
souls of departed members. Such bequests to the guild seem to have become more
common in the early years of the 16th century. Chantries were established by Henry
Somer in 1502 and Dr John Dowman in 1525.[11]

Thus we can see that in a variety of ways the prestige of the guild was much
enhanced in the second half of the 15th century. It was probably as much the
attractiveness to weaker guilds of being associated with such a powerful guild as an
aggressive desire on the part of the Haberdashers to subordinate crafts in related
fields that explains the amalgamation of the Haberdashers with the Cappers and
Hatters at the turn of the century. In 1501 the mysteries of Hurers *alias* Cappers
and the Hatters were amalgamated in the somewhat clumsily named mystery of
Hurers Hatter Merchants (in spite of the opposition of the Aldermen), and the
following year this association was amalgamated with the Haberdashers to form the
mystery of Merchant Haberdashers. We know very little of the details of the politics
of these amalgamations. Certainly the promotion of protectionist legislation suggests
that the capping industry was in trouble in the early 16th century, while the volume
of imported hats and the prominence of alien hatmakers in the capital in the early
16th century suggests that the hatters may not have proved sufficiently adaptable
to changes in fashion. There were tensions between the Haberdashers' and Hurers'
Companies in 1500 over the search of strangers, and the Wardens of both Companies
were required to post bonds to keep the peace. Perhaps the amalgamation was a
way of defusing tension. Both guilds may have calculated that their best chances of
survival lay in association with the Haberdashers whose political weight at Guildhall
and Westminster might be thought beneficial in the promotion of their case. Unwin
may therefore have exaggerated the degree to which the subordination of the crafts-

I. The Company's earliest grant of arms issued by Roger Legh, Clarenceux King of Arms, 1446.

II. The figurehead from the Company's barge; a 17th-century carved oak gilt gesso representation of St Katherine with her sword and wheel.

III. Thomas Aldersey, founder of the Bunbury charity.

IV.   William Jones, founder of the Monmouth and Newland charity.

V. William Adams, founder of the Newport charity.

VI. Robert Aske, founder of Hoxton Hospital.

men was furthered by their amalgamation with the wholesaling and retailing elements prominent in the Haberdashers' Company. An exploitative relationship between the manufacturing and wholesaling interests existed before the amalgamation; there had probably been men who specialised in wholesaling in the Hurers and Hatters (as the latter's appropriation of the title Merchant Hatters suggests); and it is difficult to see how Company ordinances, which say little about the relations of wholesalers and artisans, furthered exploitation. Exploitation was more a matter of economic realities than of institutional arrangements. Indeed it can be argued that to the degree that artisans could exploit the rhetoric of brotherhood which membership of a common organisation created their position was actually improved.[12]

It was a further sign of the Haberdashers' growing importance and pretensions that they persuaded Henry VII to incorporate them under the name of Merchant Haberdashers much to the annoyance of the Court of Aldermen. Participation in overseas trade was regarded as a more honourable occupation than the pursuit of manual crafts, and in stressing their mercantile associations the Haberdashers were seeking to enhance their prestige. It was probably a blow at the Mercers' Company which had come to value its special relationship with the Merchant Adventurers who constituted a significant proportion of its membership. The quest for further recognition is evident also in the new grant of arms of 13 December 1502 replacing the 1446 grant. The new grant was made necessary because of the Company's new constitution and charter after its merger with the Hurers and Hatters, for it was no longer the same legal entity that it had been. The new arms were blazoned 'a f(i)eld of asure (blue) and silver owndey (nebulee) a bend gowlys (gules) with a lyepard (leopard) passaunt on the bende gold armyd asur'. The wavy field of the arms, shared with the Merchant Adventurers and the Merchant Staplers, represented the sea and the activities of the merchant members of the Company, while the addition in 1570 of the leopard, one of the royal beasts, symbolised the patronage of the Crown. This is the coat of arms, with the addition of the crest (two naked arms holding a laurel garland) and supporters (two goats of India), borne by the Company today. One should not underestimate the potential for disturbance that lay in the niceties of Company nomenclature. This was a society profoundly sensitive to issues of dignity and precedence. The London Livery Companies were jealous of their status as the bitter disputes over precedence between the Skinners' and Merchant Tailors' Companies in the 15th century testify.[13]

Curiously the Haberdashers' charter, although controversial, did not generate as much conflict as that of the Merchant Tailors, granted in 1503. The name 'Merchant Tailors', the Aldermen declared, 'myght not stond neither by convenyencie of reason nor with good ordor of this cite'. The protracted battle over the Merchant Tailors' charter which followed arose not only from the name but also from other offensive clauses such as the right to recruit members without regard to other Companies and the authority to make ordinances for the government of their craft without reference to the Court of Aldermen.[14] The Aldermen's annoyance with the Haberdashers is less clearly documented, but it was present, for it was under pressure from Guildhall that they were forced to give up the title 'Merchant Haberdashers' in a charter from

Henry VIII granted in 1510. So anxious were the Aldermen that the offensive title be dropped that they instructed their Chamberlain 'to deliver and pay unto the wardens of the Haberdashers xl marks sterling towards their costs and charges sustained and made to the King's grace and his Council for their new corporation by which corporation their name is changed from the name of Merchant Haberdashers unto the name of Haberdashers'. The more tenacious resistance of the Merchant Tailors meant that the Aldermen had to admit eventual defeat in their case.[15]

Although the Haberdashers surrendered over Henry VII's charter their position among the leading Livery Companies was now assured. It was only in the course of the reign of Henry VIII that the hierarchy among the Livery Companies was formalised with the emergence of the Great Twelve. Just eight key Companies were named in 1521, but by 1538 the Aldermen recognised 'twelve head companies', and the convention was established that the Lord Mayor should be a member of one of them, and that in the event of a member of one of the lesser Companies being elected to the Court of Aldermen then translation to one of the Great Twelve became necessary. The Haberdashers held the position of eighth Company in this hierarchy which has not changed since.[16]

The Company's establishment of its comfortable position within the civic polity was accompanied in the 16th century by a huge increase in its size. Unfortunately a lack of data on freedom admissions before 1526 and on apprenticeship before 1583 makes impossible any remarks on the pattern of recruitment to the Company in the 15th century. But the 16th-century freedom register reveals that the Haberdashers shared in the enormous expansion in freedom admissions from the 1530s. Whereas 23 men were being admitted to the freedom of the Haberdashers each year in the 1530s, by the 1550s (when the fragment of the City freedom register for 1551–3 shows that the Company accounted for 4 per cent of the admissions to the freedom) the figure was 44 per annum and, by the 1590s, 98 per annum. This made the Haberdashers second in size only to the Merchant Tailors (which admitted 154 freemen each year in the 1590s). A very crude estimate of the size of the Haberdashers in the mid–1590s suggests that it may have had as many as 1,500 members.[17]

The most recent attempt to explain this phenomenon by Professor Rappaport suggests that it derives from a decision by the City in collaboration with the Crown to liberalise the conditions for access to the freedom of the City by reducing the fees necessary to secure it: this, it had been decided, was the best way to bring non-free labour under control. Thus the statute of 1531 established maximum fees of 2s. 6d. for enrolling apprentices and 3s. 4d. for admitting new members. Some Companies had been charging 20s. for the freedom in the 15th century, but whether the statute should be regarded as such a decisive turning point is questionable because some Companies had already begun to reduce their fees. Although we do not know what fees the Haberdashers were taking for the freedom prior to the statute, their fee for apprenticeship was 2s. 6d. according to the ordinances of 1505. Concentration on the Companies' role in setting the cost of apprenticeship neglects the importance of the premiums charged by masters, on which more research needs to be done. Although liberalisation contributed something to the expansion in recruitment, the chronology was probably more drawn out than Rappaport suggests, and other factors such as the growth of the London economy on the crest of the cloth export boom of the 1530s and 1540s and as a result of burgeoning aristocratic and gentry demand may have played as great a role.[18]

It is easy enough to chronicle the growing prestige and influence of the Haberdashers' Company, rather harder to explain it. The rest of this chapter attempts to establish the economic context of the Company's rise to eminence. Two forces seem to have been at work: first, the way in which a number of members became involved in overseas trade and acquired the fortunes that were essential to the bearing of civic office; and secondly, the growth of a consumer demand for the haberdashers' products. Both these developments were underway in the 15th century and rapidly accelerated in the sixteenth.

The main change in the character of English overseas trade in the later middle ages was the way in which cloth came to replace wool as the main commodity of the export trade. Exports of cloth were minimal in the 1350s, rose to 16,000 cloths per annum in the later 1360s, 40,000 by the end of the century, 60,000 per annum between 1437 and 1447, and 70,000 per annum by 1499–1500. It was not a steady rise, for the growth in exports was punctuated by periods of depression in the 1370s, the first 20 years of the 15th century, and again from 1450 to 1475. Exports of cloth may have faltered but the overall trend was upwards. The story of the wool trade was more uniformly depressing. From exports of about 35,000 sacks per annum in the 1350s, the trade slumped to an average of 13,000 sacks per annum between 1401 and 1430, and to 8–9,000 sacks per annum after 1440 for the rest of the century. The wool trade was the victim of royal fiscality. It was much more heavily taxed than cloth; the Crown developed a monopoly structure of control over the trade for the convenience of the loans the wool merchants could provide; and bans on credit sales were imposed as part of the bullionist policy pursued by government in the 15th century.[19]

The wool trade was organised through the Company of the Staple whose members enjoyed a near-monopoly of the export of wool to Calais, through which the vast majority of the trade passed. Some haberdashers were members of the Staplers' Company in the 15th century, but rarely more than two at any one time. In 1480–1 Robert Billesdon is listed among the exporters of wool; his fellow-stapler and haberdasher, William Welbeck, does not appear in the customs accounts as a wool exporter that year perhaps because he was acting in partnership with another merchant. Other haberdashers acted as middlemen in the wool trade. Thus William Bacon, prosecuted in the Court of Exchequer in 1460 for allowing too much credit on a wool sale to the Venetian merchant, Homebon Gritti, was probably linking Cotswold producers and alien exporters.[20]

The merchants engaged in the export of cloth (some but no more than a minority also being members of the Staplers' Company) initially enjoyed a looser structure. The so-called 'adventurers' exported cloth in return for a variety of commodities and voyaged widely, as far as the Baltic and Spain, although concentrating on Flanders. The London adventurers formed associations within the ranks of the Livery Companies of which they were members, the freedom of the City being important to merchants because only freemen had the right to sell to non-freemen. But most prominent among the London adventurers were members of the Mercers' Company, and it was at their Hall that the various groups of adventurers came to meet to discuss matters of common import. Thus in 1489 a meeting was held at Mercers' Hall of a 'Courte of the felishippes aventerers', where members of the Grocers', Drapers', Haberdashers', and Skinners' Companies assembled. The separate groups were drawn ever closer together by the needs of organising the cloth shipments and lobbying government, while the Crown and the City authorities found it useful to negotiate with one body. Formal recognition of the existence of the Merchant Adventurers' Company was the result of an Act of Common Council of 1486 by which the Mayor and Aldermen each year were to choose two men, one a mercer, and the other 'of sum other feleaship of the said merchauntes within the citee of London', who were to act as lieutenants to the Governor overseas with authority to summon assemblies for the making of ordinances and the imposition of assessments for the common good of the trade.[21]

Eleven haberdashers can be identified as exporters of cloth on the 1480–1 customs account. Robert Billesdon led the way with shipments of 211 cloths, followed by Richard Wethir with 209, Henry Wynger with 177, Lawrence Swarfield with 139+, and William Jeffery with 113. Those who exported more than 100 cloths were the princes of the trade: in 1490–1 there were just 39 merchants in this category who accounted for 56 per cent of the total cloth exports from London. More modest shipments were made in 1480–1 by Thomas Bate (33 ½ cloths), Nicholas Nyandezer (25 cloths 8 yards), Philip Ball (24), Richard Awbrey (18), William Welbeck (13), and Robert Aldernes (11 cloths 8 yards).[22] The customs accounts may conceal the full extent of haberdasher participation because some entries concealed the existence of partnerships. William Botyller, haberdasher, factor in northern Spain for William Haddon, draper, in the mid–15th century may actually have been a partner, for he refused to pay Haddon's executors more than half of the money received on account for cloths sold in Spain.[23]

Exports of cloth increased even more markedly in the early 16th century. From about 82,000 cloths per annum in the later years of Henry VII they increased to 118,000 in the years 1538–44. Members of the Haberdashers' Company participated in this trade in growing numbers. George Ramsay has calculated that in 1565 the Haberdashers supplied the second largest number of cloth dealers of any of the London companies. Whereas the Mercers accounted for 61 of the 243 merchants supplying the Low Countries marts, the Haberdashers accounted for 32. By the 1580s William Smith was able to allege that the Haberdashers were esteemed the greatest of the Companies and that 'no Company in London hath so many marchants in it as this of the Haberdashers'.[24]

The rate of profit in the mid–16th-century cloth trade has been estimated at about 15 per cent, suggesting that participants would have been able to double their capital every five years. It is this profitability which explains the fortunes amassed by some members of the Company and their arrival within the ranks of the civic elite. Robert Billesdon's bequests amounted to about £2,000 and he owned property in the parishes of Northweald Basset, Epping, Thoydon Garnon, Theydon Mount, Greenstead,

Castle Ongar, High Ongar, Stanford Rivers, Bobbingworth, Shelley, and Stapleford Tawney. William Marler and John Hardy, the wealthiest men in the Company according to the assessments of 1522, were both Merchant Adventurers.[25]

If increasing participation in overseas trade was one cause of the haberdashers' greater prominence by the early 16th century, the other seems to have been a rising level of consumer demand for the kind of goods the haberdashers sold. Several commentators in the early 16th century alluded to the growing prosperity of the haberdashers in the context of their concern about the import of foreign trifles which was having an adverse effect on the balance of payments. Clement Armstrong, a member of Thomas Cromwell's 'think-tank', writing probably in the early 1530s, commented that

> a thirty yere agoo a sorte beganne to occupie to bye and selle alle soche handycraft wares, callid haburdashers, otherwise callid hardware men, that a fourty yere agoo was not four or five shopes in London, wher now every strete is full of theym.[26]

Sir Thomas Smith, author of *A Discourse of the Commonweal*, the most penetrating analysis of the country's economic ills written in the 16th century, concurred:

> I have sene within these xxtie yeres, when there weare not of these haberdashers that sell french or millane cappes, glasses, Daggers, swerdes, girdles and such thinges, not a dossen in all London. And now from the towere to westminster alonge, everie streat is full of them; and their shoppes glisters and shine of glasses, aswell lookinge as drinckinge, yea all manor vesseles of the same stuffe; painted cruses, gaye daggers, knives, swordes, and girdles, that is able to make anie temporate man to gase on them and to bie sumwhat, thoughe it serve to no purpose necessarie.[27]

Evidently the 16th century was no stranger to the shrewd use of the shop display as a marketing ploy!

The main reason for the concern of Armstrong and Smith was the way in which the haberdashers' trade worked to the profit of aliens for so much of the stuff that they sold was imported. As Smith eloquently put it:

> I mervell no man taketh heade unto it, what nombre first of trifles commeth hether from beyonde the seas, that we might either clene spare, or els make them with in oure owne Realme, for the which we paie enestimable treasure everie yeare, or els exchange substanciall wares and necesarie for them, for the which we might receive great treasure. Of the which sort I meane glasses, as well lookinge as drinckinge, as to glasse windowes, Dialles, tables, cardes, balles, puppetes, penhornes, Inckehornes, toothepikes, gloves, knives, daggers, pouches, broches, agletes, buttons of silke and silver, erthen potes, pinnes, poyntes, haukes bells, paper both whit and browne, and a thowsand like thinges, that might ether be clene spared or els made within the Realme sufficient for us.

Armstrong suggested further that these goods were imported by alien merchants rather than Englishmen and therefore further boosted their fortunes. He claimed that the anti-alien rioting of Evil May Day (1517) had originated in the unemployment of English craftsmen involved in the manufacture of pins, points, gloves, and such like. Identifying the foreign goods sold by the haberdashers as the problem, the artisans

approached them for redress, but the shopkeepers pointed an accusing finger elsewhere:

> Such haburdasher adventurers shewid to the pore peple, it was not they that brought so moche
> in to the reame, but straungers, that brought it over and lay in the citie thorowt the yere and
> solde it to all haburdashers, as in very deede French men and Flemyngs ever kepith warehowsis
> and selers at the water side of all such haburdash wares and sellith it to theym at all tymes
> thorowt the yere . . . So the pore artificers in London, being distroyd by occupieng into
> Flaunders . . . murmuryd and grudgid, that so putt into ther heddys straungers was the cause
> therof, so begane they to rise upon straungers.

Although prospering, the haberdashers were viewed with little enthusiasm by the
economic thinkers of the day. Smith was devastating: 'As for haberdashers . . . I can
not se what they doe in a towne, but finde a livinge to v or vj houwsholdes, and in
steade therof impoverishethe twise as manie'.[28]

Not surprisingly, schemes for economic revival came to turn upon encouraging the
native manufacture of the goods the haberdashers sold. Elizabeth's Lord Treasurer,
William Cecil, Lord Burghley was deeply affected by the thinking of the common-
wealthmen and he was a vigorous supporter of projects to revive or establish industries such as the manufacture of pins and paper. Modest successes were scored: alien
immigrants seem to have revived the native pin industry which had folded under
Dutch competition in the early 16th century, and by 1608 it was claimed that
between 2,000 and 3,000 were employed in making pins in London and the suburbs.[29]
A supplementary strategy was the banning of the importation of the offensive foreign
trifles. A statute of 1563, secured on the petitioning of girdlers, cutlers, saddlers,
glovers, pointmakers, and others whose interests chimed with official objectives,
banned the import of (among other things) girdles, daggers, knives, gloves, points,
leather laces, and pins. Although the act was regularly renewed through Elizabeth's
Parliaments it seems to have had little practical effect.[30]

How accurate were contemporary commentators in their assessment that the
haberdashers had become more prosperous in the decades around 1500 as the
beneficiaries of the fashion for foreign trifles? The customs accounts suggest that
they grasped an important truth although they appear to have telescoped the chronology of the phenomenon. It is striking that the Elizabethan statute banning the
import of enumerated foreign commodities is paralleled by another almost exactly
a century earlier. In 1464 an act was passed in response to the 'piteous complaints'
of London artificers concerning the 'grete multitude of dyvers chafferes and wares,
perteyning to their Craftes and occupations, being full wrought and redy made to
the sale' which were being imported by aliens and denizens, and thereby causing
their impoverishment. Parliament therefore laid down that no alien or denizen
merchant should import a wide range of manufactures, many of them associated
with the haberdashers, including woollen bonnets, hats, laces, ribbons, dice, tennis
balls, points, purses, gloves, girdles, shoes, knives, daggers, playing cards, pins,
rings, sacring-bells, brushes, and wool cards. A similar act was passed in 1484
adding some commodities and dropping others from the list of prohibited goods.
But little effort seems to have been made to enforce either act.[31]

The signs are that the large-scale import of haberdashery was a development of the 15th century. If we turn back to a customs account of 1384 during the reign of Richard II we find that some of the items sold in haberdashers' shops were being imported then. They included mirrors, beads, points, brushes, and razors. Some of these goods were imported in apparently already prodigious quantities: thus the account for 1 July to Michaelmas 1384 records the import of no less than 10,192 looking glasses.[32] But in no way can the goods be said to match the range, variety, and volume that was to be the case a century later. Whereas in 1384 glass beads alone are recorded, the customs account of 1480–1 includes beads of bone, boxwood, coral, glass, and jet. During the period 1 July to Michaelmas 1481, in other words a period equivalent to that covered by the 1384 account, at least 10,691 looking glasses were imported by *aliens* alone. Other haberdashery being imported into London at this date included aglets, artificial flowers, bells, bonnets, brooches, brushes, candle snuffers, caps, chalcedony, clasps, combs, daggers, ear-pickers, girdles, hats, ink-horns, knives, laces, mirrors, paper, pins, pen-cases, pen knives, pincases, pins, playing-cards, points, pouches, puppets, razors, rings, sacring-bells, spectacle-cases, spectacles, tennis balls, thimbles, wool cards, and writing tables. The *Leonard* of London, a typical ship, included in her cargo, delivered at London on 13 November 1480, 28 gross of boxwood beads, 9 gross of glass beads, 13 gross of small glass beads, 2 gross of mistletoe beads, 16 gross and 7 dozen knives, 6 cases of pot knives, 17 gross of papers of points, 8 gross of leather laces, 24 pounds of counters, 3 gross of wire girdles, 10 dozen of latten girdles, 23 gross of girdles of other types, 10 gross of playing cards, 60 dozen of the so-called 'coppyn hats' (being those of the fashionable sugar-loaf type), and 2 chess boards.[33]

The continuing anxieties of the government about the scale of imports of haberdashery led to the compilation of statistics on the matter at Burghley's behest in the early Elizabethan period. Imports of hats in 1559–60 were valued at £7,915, pins at £3,297, paper at £3,304, wool cards at £2,837, tennis balls at £1,699, laces at £775 6s. 8d., looking glasses at £667, and so on. Imports of thread, often sold by haberdashers, amounted to £13,671 13s. 4d; inkle (linen tape) was valued at another £8,412, and crewell (a worstead yarn used in making fringes) at £3,038. Adding to this the values given for bells, brushes, buttons, girdles, hat bands, knives, needles, and points, haberdashery appears to have amounted to £49,365 or 7.1 per cent by value of total imports of £692,800. A detailed analysis of the London port book of 1564–5 reveals something of what these figures meant in terms of scale of imports and the level of consumer demand they implied. In that year 111,132 combs, 97,488 packs of playing cards, (representing at least one comb and one pack of playing cards for every man, woman, and child in the capital), 67,500 thimbles, 19,620 ink-horns, and 87,342,070 pins were imported at London.[34]

By the early Elizabethan period it was at least no longer true that this trade was dominated by aliens and denizens in the way it had been in 1480–1. Indeed it is clear that some merchants free of the Haberdashers' Company specialised in the import of haberdashery wares. Thus Richard Patrick, who traded mainly to Rouen but was also a member of the newly founded Russia Company and served as a customs official in the port of London, exported cloth, cottons, and wax in return

5. Extract from the London customs record for 1480, showing haberdashery imported by foreigners on the *Margaret Stokker*. Among the goods listed are glasses, pouches, rings, caps, hats, brushes, laces, points, pins and buckles.

for haberdashery ware. In 1564–5 Patrick imported goods worth £895 11s. 8d. He was responsible for 20 per cent of the playing cards imported at London in that year, 39 per cent of the combs, and no less than 56 per cent of the ink-horns, and 57 per cent of the woolcards. Other merchants free of the Company specialising in the import of haberdashery at this date were Thomas Awder, Henry Beecher, Henry Billingsley, Richard Billingsley, James Canon, James Challinor, Rowland Erlington, Richard Harrison, William Hobson, John Hutton, John Newton, and John Taylor. However it would be wrong to suggest that the degree of correlation between membership of the Company and specialisation in the import of haberdashery was strong, for only 13 of the 61 merchants free of the Company specialised in this way, and there were several merchants free of other London Companies, such as Humphrey Brown and Thomas Dauncer, girdlers, John Eliot and Hugh Offley, leathersellers, who were heavily involved in this branch of the import trade.[35]

Inventories of the contents of haberdashers' shops provide another route into the nature of their business and the consumer demand that sustained it. The most comprehensive inventory from the later 15th century comes from a member of the Leathersellers' Company dealing in haberdashery, but it may be taken as typical of the stock to be found in the shops of the men condemned by Armstrong and Smith. John Skyrwyth, whose goods were valued on 18 May 1486, actually dealt in animal hides and mercery, selling chamlets, satin, linen, and fustians, as well as haberdashery. His goods include many of the items covered in the 1480–1 customs account, but they were not all of overseas manufacture. The inventory distinguishes between goods 'of London making' such as worstead girdles, coarse pins, forcers (chests), and thread lace, and the corresponding imported goods such as the blue thread from Bruges, knives from Brussels, and pins from Flanders. What is particularly striking is the way in which customers were offered a variety of the same type of product at different standards and prices. Thus there were 'raysors fyne prys', 'raysurs off the medyll sortt', and 'rassours course', 'pouches with doble rings', 'pouches mydyll', 'pouches coursse', 'pouches febyll', and 'small pouches for chyldern'. Beads were sold in great variety – so-called 'bugyll' beads, glass beads 'of dyvers colours', bone beads red and black, box beads, mistletoe beads, and jet beads were available. They were supplemented by other ornaments, glass gawdies (brightly coloured ornaments), some of counterfeit jasper, and others speckled blue. Skyrwith was a large-scale dealer whose total stock of haberdashery amounted to approximately £65, only a portion of his total stock which included mercery and animal hides. Although he sold hatbands, there were no hats or caps in Skyrwyth's shop, a sign of the developing specialisation between the haberdashers of small wares and the haberdashers of hats.[36]

Other haberdashers came to specialise in parchment and paper. The parchmyners had sold their wares through the haberdashers, and with the increase in paper consumption that followed the introduction of printing, haberdashers came to take on the marketing of this costly import. An example is found in the case of William Stede, citizen and haberdasher, whose goods were appraised in 1522. He dealt in a variety of stationery, his shop containing five bales of white paper (valued at £5), 19 bundles of brown paper (used for wrapping and valued at 9s. 6d.), 54 rolls of parchment (£6 6s.), 24 dozen ynke pennars (10s.), 5 dozen 'horns for pennars' (5s. 10d.), as well as several dozen paper booklets ('bokys redy made') of differing numbers of quires. His total stock amounted to £17 6s. 10d.[37]

The inventories of haberdashers' stock from the late 16th and early 17th centuries to be found among the cases for debt in the Mayor's Court show a still more vigorous and sophisticated consumer demand. To the kind of goods we have already been considering were now added toys and cheap musical instruments. An example is provided by Gregory Dey (1633). In addition to the usual range of haberdashery (pins, needles, thimbles, bodkins, girdles, looking glasses, small chests, purses, brace-lets, rings, ribbon, thread, tape, buttons, toothpicks, spectacles, spectacle-cases, artificial flowers, combs, inkhorns, brushes, money boxes, and so on), Dey stocked a variety of toys. Dolls were being made in Nuremberg as early as 1413, and by the later 16th century large quantities were being imported from the Low Countries, giving rise to the rhyme:

> The children of England take pleasure in breaking
> What the children of Holland take pleasure in making

The crudest dolls in Dey's shop were available from ½d. each, and dressed dolls from 2½d. At the top end of the market were more sophisticated examples with moveable limbs costing anything from 1s. 6d. to 2s. 6d. each. Other toys included model coaches at 3½d. each, horsemen at 14d. per dozen, and horses on wheels at 16d. per dozen. There were hobby horses at 16d. per dozen, shuttlecocks at 5d. per dozen, and 'froggen sticks' at 2s. 6d. per dozen. The musical tastes of the young were catered for with Scottish harps ranging from 3d. to 6d. per dozen, fiddles at 1½d. to 2d. each, trumpets at 3d. each, drums at 2½d. to 5d. each. Nor were educational needs neglected, with globes available at 5d. each, and horn books at about ½d. each, as well as prayer books.[38]

We learn relatively little about the interior of the shops from the inventories. Skyrwyth's shop included 'a flatt chest for ware & a layn chest with ij lytyll chestes & other lombre prys of all xxs'. Nicholas Troute's early 17th-century shop (1604) had 'a waynscott presse with cupboordes' valued at 12s. Dey's shop was decorated with painted cloths valued at 14s. and furnished with presses and drawers . . . with two counters and a settle bed' valued at £10 in all. In addition to the display on to the street, Dey had a back shop and a warehouse. These arrangements represented a more sophisticated set-up than the shop-board pushed down into the street which characterised most medieval shops. Some shopkeepers showed their loyalty to the Company by displaying its coat of arms. Thus James Heyward's shop (1603) had 'the haberdashers Armes in a frame'.[39]

The evidence of the kind of goods haberdashers sold and the volumes in which they were imported gives some credibility to the notion of an expanding consumer demand from the mid–15th into the 16th and early 17th centuries. The problem with the concept of the 'consumer revolution', of course, is that, like 'the rise of the middle classes', it is something the historian is likely to find once (s)he starts looking. Joan Thirsk identified the emergence of a consumer society in the late 16th and

6. Extract from a late Elizabethan haberdasher's shop inventory, including snuffers, thimbles, pinpillows, needles, brushes, combs and cittern wire.

early 17th centuries as the large-scale production of consumer goods got underway through the sponsorship of projects such as those in which Burghley expressed interest. Margaret Spufford's work on the probate inventories of the later 17th century suggests improvements in domestic comfort and the wider availability of consumer goods in that period. But it is the conclusion of this chapter that the rise

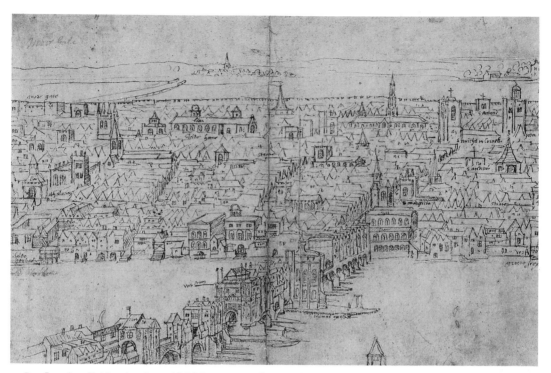

7.   London Bridge in the mid-16th century, from a drawing by Anthony van den Wyngaerde.

of the Haberdashers to prominence within the city reflected a remarkable increase in consumer demand for their goods from the mid–15th century.[40]

To some degree the market for haberdashery goods reflected the extraordinary demand of the aristocracy, much of it channelled through London. It has been calculated that the 15th-century aristocracy disposed of about half a million pounds a year, more than ten times the budget of the state in peace-time.[41] Although the wares that haberdashers sold were often too trifling in value for them to be itemised in household accounts, that is not to say that aristocratic demand was insignificant. Occasional payments to haberdashers can be traced such as the 17s.7½d. paid to Walter Lucy, haberdasher, by Thomas of Lancaster, Duke of Clarence in 1418.[42] During the 1570s the children of Sir Henry Sidney each received an allowance of 3s. worth of pins to last them six months. As Joan Thirsk points out, that was the equivalent of nine days' wages for a male labourer at 4d. per day.[43] The aristocracy depended on the pins, points, buttons, and girdles of the haberdashers to keep their clothes fastened, and they festooned themselves with the accessories such as ribbons, purses, and bells that the haberdashers sold. The Elizabethan woman-about-town could be satirised for her obsessive attention to the full panoply of accessories:

Give me my girdle and see that all the furniture be at it. Look if my cizers, the pincers, the penknife, the knife to close letter with, the bodkin, the ear-picker and my seal be in the case. Where is my purse to wear upon my gowne? And see that my silver comfet box be full of comfets. Have I a cleaane hankercher? I will have no muffe for it is not cold, but shall I have no gloves? Bring me my mask and my fanne . . . [44]

Aristocratic demand is most visible in the documents in the case of hats. The letters of the aristocracy to their London agents are replete with instructions to secure the latest in London fashions, a statement as true of the Pastons in the 15th century as of the Lisles in the early 16th century. John Hussee, London agent of the Lisles, is found insisting to a displeased Lady Lisle that the caps he had procured for her in 1537 were 'the very fashion that the Queen and all the ladies doth wear'. Elsewhere Hussee complains about the truculence of the London haberdasher from whom he was arranging for a new cap for James Basset against his wedding day: 'I have had no time to provide his cap, for where I thought assuredly to have had the same trimmed ready at William Taylor's, when I came for it Larke can tell how he handled me and disappointed me. Your ladyship's honour reserved, he is the veriest knave that ever I met withal, and I put Larke to be judge. But I shall not fail with the next that goeth to send both cap and feather'. It is worth pointing out that Tailor was also employed by the King's wardrobe to whom he supplied hats and caps in the 1530s. When one reflects upon the aristocracy's notoriously dilatory payment of their tradesmen's bills, perhaps Tailor's truculence becomes more understandable.[45]

But the availability of cheap versions of so many of the goods the haberdashers sold suggests that there was a substantial popular demand. Already in the 14th century haberdashery had acquired its role in popular courtship. Chaucer's friar was well aware of the usefulness of some of the haberdashers' stock-in-trade as the way to a woman's heart:

> His typet was ay farsed ful of knyves
> And pynnes, for to yeven faire wyves.[46]

That popular demand was growing in the 15th century is plausible because the rising real wages of the post-Black Death decades and the prosperity of the cloth producing districts meant that the spending power of the humbler sections of society was growing. Because lower labour costs meant that foreigners produced so many of these consumer items more cheaply than the English, the increased demand worked particularly to the haberdashers' benefit as the wholesaling interest. Whereas in the 14th century much haberdashery could be bought direct from the native manufacturers (as the existence of pouchmakers, agletmakers, pinners, mirrorers shows) over the course of the next century it became more usual to turn to the general dealer.[47] Although economic conditions changed in the 16th century, nevertheless it is likely that consumer demand was sustained. Although the growth in population without commensurate increases in output resulted in the impoverishment of the labouring poor, it boosted the incomes of the middling groups in society who were in a position to benefit from rising property values, and contemporaries are agreed

8.   Shop interior of the later 17th century, showing shopkeeper, customer and chapman.

on the rising standards of domestic comfort they enjoyed. The demand that they represented was sufficient to compensate for the loss of demand from the very poor whose propensity to consume was probably less. It was only in the later 17th century that the poor began to participate more fully in the consumer society as their incomes began to rise once more with the stagnation of population and the growth of economic opportunities.

The haberdashers of London were responsible for supplying most of the kingdom with haberdashery through their contacts with the petty chapmen who toiled through the villages of rural England bearing their sacks full of trifles. A 15th-century tract identifies 'men as march with fote packes . . . [who] owe to buy all maner of peny ware, also pursys, knyvis, gyrdlys, glassys, hattes, or odyr peny ware . . . and farthyng ware'. The chapman becomes a familiar figure in literature from the mid–16th century. John Heywood's representation of his stock may be taken as typical:

> . . . gloves, pins, combs, glasses unspotted,
> Pancardes, hooks, and laces knotted;
> Brooches, rings, and all manner of beads;
> Laces round and flat for women's heads;
> Needles, thread, thimbles, shears, and all such knacks,
> Where lovers be, no such things lacks;
> Sipers, swathbands, ribbons, and sleeve laces,
> Girdles, knives, purses, and pincases

Their activities are best known in the 17th century as a result of work by Margaret Spufford: inventories show London haberdashers supplying chapmen active in Norfolk, Hertfordshire, Lincolnshire, Buckinghamshire, and Hertfordshire, but this was doubtless already a long-established pattern.[48]

There is perhaps rather more evidence of direct involvement by the haberdashers in provincial trade in the 15th century than later. For the haberdashers seem to have broken with the policy of others engaged in the distributive trades of forcing provincial dealers to come to London for their goods. The haberdashers acquired a rather unsavoury reputation within the City for their willingness to haunt provincial fairs, thereby siphoning off trade which otherwise would have come to London mercers and grocers. In 1477 the Mercers resolved that their ordinance against members serving fairs should be repealed on the grounds that:

Forasmoche as that alle or the more parte of all felyshipps in this Citie be at theyre libertie and many of them accustumed and gretely use fayres and markethes owt of this Citie thurgh which many persones abydyng at hom be gretely hurt in losyng of their Custumers that used and cam unto this Citie and here bought their Ware that nowe be served of the haberdisshers and other hauntyng such ffayres and markethes etc. and no remedy therfor Wherfor many and in speciall yonge men in oure felyshipp that be ther with gretely greved and as they say sorely hurte by the mean of non comyng of their Custumers and other Chapemen to towne mony a day.[49]

The willingness of the Haberdashers to break with the policy of other guilds in this regard provides another reason for their advancing prosperity in the 15th century.

The transformation of the status of the Haberdashers' Company in the 15th and early 16th centuries was a result, therefore, of an expansion in consumer demand combined with large-scale imports of haberdashery and the growing involvement of Company members in the distributive trades to the provinces. This development was accompanied by the growing participation of members of the Company in overseas trade, the profits of which account for the involvement of haberdashers in City government and the growing political clout of the Company.

Chapter Three

Reformation Changes

The regulation of the trade was but one side of the Company's activity, for it also served to cater for the spiritual needs of its members. At the heart of the Company's liturgical year was the election of a new Master and Wardens on the feast day of St Katherine, the Company's patron saint, when all Company members were required to attend mass and offer a penny before the ceremonies surrounding the election of the new officers at the Hall, where a dinner was held. Another mass was celebrated every year on 1 May at which attendance was again obligatory on pain of a 6d. fine.[1] Such occasions provided a demonstration of brotherhood as well as giving a spiritual sanction to the rulers. Spiritual brotherhood was important to the achievement of salvation in so far as it provided another valued source of prayers to ease the passage of the soul through the pains of Purgatory. Hence the insistence of members on securing the attendance of their fellow Companymen at their funerals. Such attendance may well have been more widely practised at the upper levels of the Company hierarchy, for it was only at this level that attendance appears to have been obligatory. The ordinances of 1505 prescribed that, when a man who had served as Warden died, four brothers of the craft were to be assigned to carry the body to church, and all those in the Livery who had not been Wardens were to accompany the corpse to the grave on pain of 3s. 4d.[2] Some members so valued the presence of their fellow Companymen that they provided incentives to secure attendance. Alderman Robert Billesdon provided 6s. 8d. for each of the six 'honest men of my craft' who were to carry his body to the grave. William Symondes (d. *c*.1532) requested that 4d. be given to each of the Liverymen bringing his corpse to the church and attending the dirige and mass. Robert Raven requested in his will of 1543 that the Livery of the Company should 'helpe to bringe my boddye to the earthe' and attend a requiem mass the following day. In recognition of their pains he added that £4 should be spent on spice bread, cheese and comfits overnight, and on a 'recreation' to be provided at the Hall on the following day.[3]

The Company also acted as a trustee to fulfil the pious wishes of its former members, in managing the resources they left to provide intercessory masses for the benefit of their souls. Thus Henry Somer (d. 1502) left to the Company a tenement in St Dunstan in the East on condition that from the income they provide an obit (an anniversary mass) on his anniversary day in the church of St Mary Staining. The parson was to receive 12d. each year for performing the dirige and requiem mass, and the other priests and clerks of the church 4d. each. Somer reflected the general belief in the peculiar efficacy of the prayers of the poor by requiring that 12 poor members of the craft attend and each receive 12d. for their pains. The responsibility for seeing to the observance of the obit was given to the younger Wardens of the Company, who were to receive 12d. each, and to the Beadle who was to receive

Extract from the will of Robert Billesdon, haberdasher, typical of pre-Reformation élite piety, showing bequests of ecclesiastical vestments to the churches of St Augustine by St Paul's, London and Queniborough, Leicestershire.

8d. After attending the service at St Mary Staining the Wardens and Companymen were to retire to the Hall where bread, cheese, wine and ale to the value of 13s.4d. was to be provided, and those assembled were to say the psalm 'de profundis' and 'the orisons thereto according'.[4]

The Chantry returns of 1548 reveal that the Haberdashers then sponsored eight obits in several City churches, St Michael Hogan Lane, St Katherine Cree, St George Botolph Lane, St Martin Ludgate, St Andrew Undershaft, and in St Paul's Cathedral, as well as providing support for three priests to sing daily masses in Reading and again at St Paul's, a modest level of religious provision compared to the nine priests and 20 obits supported by the Merchant Tailors. The services were primarily endowed by Company members, but the most lavish, which involved an expenditure of £22 per annum on two priests and an obit, was endowed by Dr John Dowman, Archdeacon of Suffolk and Prebendary of St Paul's Cathedral, to provide prayers at the altar of St Martha in St Paul's.[5] The perpetual nature of the corporation of a London Livery Company, and the obligations created by its spiritual brotherhood, offered obvious advantages to those wishing for prayers to be said for their souls to the end of time.

As far as we can tell, the piety of haberdashers in the decades preceding the Reformation was entirely conventional.[6] Almost invariably they entrusted the fate of their souls to the intercession of the Virgin Mary and the saints. Bequests to the high altars of their parish churches for forgotten tithes were likewise almost universal. They expressed much concern over the place of their burial:

> 'at thende of the Aulter of seynt Erasmus under the pictor of seynte Jerome over the southesyde in the parishe church of seynt Mighell le Querne in London', 'in the churche yerde of the parisshe churche of seynt Botulphe besyde Byllingesgate of London on the South side of the Crosse in the same churcheyerde where the bodies of Alice and Alice that were my wyves lyen buryed', 'as nygh to the place where my master Edmond Smewen lyeth as convenient be', 'in the body of the chirch of the freers prechours of London be fore the Image of Saint Erasmus ther on the north syde of the same chirche as nyghe unto the wall ther as it maybe'.[7]

Loyalty to parish churches is shown by the bequest of the torches and tapers which burned about their corpses at their funerals to favoured altars with the intention that they should burn at the elevation of the host. Alderman Robert Billesdon (d. 1492), for example, left 24 torches and four tapers 'concurrent to my degree' to burn in the church of St Augustine Watling Street.[8] Billesdon also left to this church a set of vestments 'of blue velvet embroidered with flowers and spangles of silver gilt'. Others bequeathed plate to their churches.[9] Sir Stephen Peacock gave a pix, chalice and patten to the church of St Martin Ludgate, Thomas Gale a silver cross and a statue of Mary and John to St George Botolph Lane, and William Jenkys 40s. towards the projected renewal of the cross in St Mary Colechurch.[10]

In their wills the pre-Reformation haberdashers show a determination to secure intercessory prayers. Typical of the wealthier members was Robert Billesdon. He left 240 marks to the Company to provide a priest to say daily mass at the altar of St George in St Augustine Watling Street, on a stipend of 10 marks a year, and an obit which the Livery were to attend costing 2 marks a year. Rather surprisingly, given that the cash was sufficient to provide for masses in perpetuity if invested in land, this was to continue until the money was exhausted at the end of 20 years. He also requested that his soul be recommended to the prayers of the faithful by the preachers of the sermons at Paul's Cross and at St Mary Spital for the same period, each preacher being paid 4d. for his pains. Cash bequests totalling £13 13s. 4d. were made to a panoply of religious institutions about the capital, the Hospitals of Bethlem and St Bartholomew's, the Priory Hospitals of the Elsing Spital and St Mary Spital, the lazar houses of the Lock, Kingsland, and St Giles, the brotherhoods of the Priests of the Pappey and of St Nicholas of the Clerks, the four orders of Friars (the Augustinians at Austin Friary, the Carmelites at White Friars, the Dominicans at Black Friars, and the Franciscans at Grey Friars), and the Friars of the Holy Cross at Crutched Friars. In each case he requested that the recipients should 'pray for me', and the friars were requested to sing a trental of masses on the day of his death. The same desire for intercession lay behind his bequests in poor relief to the poor of St Augustine, St Faith, and St Michael le Querne, who were to receive 20 quarters of coal at Christmas for 20 years, to the London prisons, and to the poor householders of his craft.[11] Humbler members could not hope to match pious largesse on this scale, but they nonetheless eagerly sought access to salvific intercession by whatever means lay in their grasp. John Byfold (d. c.1473) requested that a trental of masses be said for his soul at the Charterhouse on the day and morrow after his death, and requested his wife to distribute every Friday during her life five half pence to the poor 'in the worchyp of the v wondys off owre lorde Jhesus cryste', and three half pence every Sunday 'in the worchyp off the blessyd trinitie'.[12]

Of the 22 wealthier haberdashers whose wills haved been traced in the registers of the Prerogative Court of Canterbury in the period 1470–1540, only one was able to afford the endowment of a perpetual chantry, but 17 left money either for obits, trentals of masses, the singing of daily masses (for periods of between one and three years), or the friaries. Of 44 haberdashers of usually more modest circumstances whose wills were proved in the Commissary Court of the Bishop of London in the same period, 12 made bequests for these purposes. Bequests to the poor were made by 15 (68 per cent) of the wealthier testators, and by eight (18 per cent) of the poorer ones.

Another means of securing intercessory prayer was through membership of a religious fraternity. These parochially-based guilds existed to provide masses in commemoration of former members as well as providing a variety of social facilities such as poor relief and the sense of identity that a shared feast entailed.[13] It was to such institutions that Chaucer referred in the Prologue to the *Canterbury Tales*:

> An Haberdasshere and a Carpenter,
> A Webbe, a Dyere, and a Tapycer,
> And they were clothed alle in one lyveree
> Of a solempne and a greet fraternitee [14]

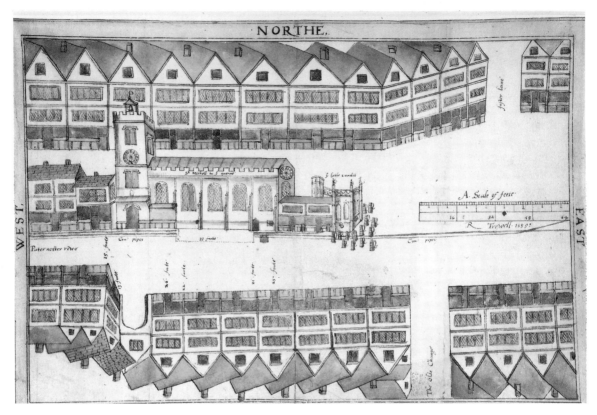

10.   The church of St Michael le Querne, a popular beneficiary of early Haberdasher wills; from a
watercolour drawing by the surveyor, Ralph Treswell, 1585.

With their usually modest membership dues they were open to a wide range of the
City's inhabitants. From the evidence of their wills at least one third (eight of 22)
of the wealthier members of the Company, and one quarter (12 of 44) of the poorer
members enjoyed membership of a religious fraternity. Some like Thomas Osborne
(d. *c.*1538), a member of both the fraternities of Our Lady and of St Katherine and
St Erasmus in St Michael le Querne, enjoyed membership of more than one.[15]
Haberdashers record their devotion to fraternities as varied as those of Our Lady
and St Thomas and of *Salve Regina* in the parish of St Magnus, of Our Lady and St
John the Baptist in St Botolph Billingsgate, of Our Lady and St Michael and of St
Christopher in St Martin Ludgate, of Our Lady and St Stephen in St Sepulchre
without Newgate, and of St Katherine in St Mary Colechurch. The most popular
were inevitably those located in the parishes in which most members of the Company
lived, that is St Martin Ludgate, St Michael le Querne, St Magnus, and St Botolph
Billingsgate.[16] The wealthiest members of the Company, like Ellys Draper, John

Browne, and Robert Raven were sometimes members of the prestigious guild of the Name of Jesus, refounded by John Colet in 1504, and which met in the Shrouds of St Paul's Cathedral.[17]

Although there were more fraternities dedicated to St Katherine than to any other saint apart from the Virgin Mary, there was no particularly marked tendency for haberdashers to prefer membership of guilds with her as patroness to others. However there are other signs of devotion to the saint in the wills of Company members. Thomas Cherell wished to be buried in front of the chapel door of St Katherine under the rood loft in the parish of St Magnus, and he wished for a priest of good name and fame to say mass in her chapel for one year after his death, praying for the souls of himself, his wife, his mother and father, and all Christian souls. Likewise, Sir Stephen Peacock, a former Lord Mayor and a member of the brotherhood of Our Lady and St Christopher in St Martin Ludgate, nevertheless wished to be buried in the chapel of St Katherine in that church, and instructed that masses be celebrated there for three years. Thomas Sonnyff also wished to be buried in the same church before the image of St Katherine.[18] Some left money for the maintenance of the lights which burned in front of images of the saint. Thomas Digill and John Standish both left 12d. to the light of St Katherine in St Augustine's, and John Byfold 20d. to her light in St Michael le Querne.[19] Others left plate which reflected their dedication to the Company's patron. Nicholas Nyandezer left to his son William his cup with St Katherine in the bossell, and Ellys Draper left to the Company a gilt cup with St Katherine's wheel in its base.[20]

At the heart of the Reformation lay a challenge to the theology of salvation by works and intercessory prayer which underpinned traditional piety. So deeply embedded were the London Livery Companies in this religious culture that at one point it seemed as if they might themselves be swept away in the whirlwind. Protector Somerset, influenced by the evangelical chaplains who filled his household, in 1547 embarked on the full-scale assault on chantries which had eluded the Henrician government, whether through the religious scruples of the late King, or the prudential considerations of the outrage it was likely to provoke. However, the government's initial proposals were more radical than those which eventually passed, for the original bill presented to Parliament in December 1547 would have expropriated all chantries and all guilds and fraternities, even those whose functions, like the London Livery Companies, were largely secular. As it was the bill provoked a storm of Parliamentary opposition, and the government backed down, amending its proposals to cover only endowments made for explicitly 'superstitious' purposes.[21] The properties supporting the chantries were seized over the course of 1548, and only recovered by the Companies on payment at 20 years purchase to the Crown. Thus the Haberdashers handed over £810 3s. 4d. to recover their lands. The lack of survival of accounts from this date makes it impossible to determine how the Company raised this sum, but the experience of others suggests that it was probably necessary for the Haberdashers to sell other properties, thereby endangering their long-term financial position.[22]

The assault on the cult of saints at the Reformation was reflected in the diminishing importance of St Katherine to the Company. It is less commonly referred to as 'the

fraternity of St Katherine the Virgin of the Haberdashers of the City of London',
but more usually as 'the fraternity of the art or mystery of Haberdashers in the City
of London' as the Company was incorporated by the charter of 1578.[23] References
to St Katherine had rather surprisingly been removed from the arms granted in
1502.[24] Although the garlands of purple velvet with scutcheons of St Katherine given
by George Tadlowe (d. 1557) continued to be used by the Yeomanry, the use of
patronal imagery was generally much less prominent.[25] The election of the Master
and Wardens continued to be associated with the festival of St Katherine, but less
specifically than in the past. By the terms of the ordinances of 1567 the election was
to take place on the feast of St Katherine or within eight days thereof; those of 1629
specified that the election should take place on either the Saturday before or the
Saturday after St Katherine's Day, and that the Publication ceremony should be
held on the Tuesday following 'commonly called St Katherine's Day'.[26] Possibly the
traditional ties with St Katherine were re-emphsised in the 17th century, when they
lacked the same emotive force as during the fraught later 16th century decades while
the evangelisation of England proceeded: certainly there are references to the saint
in the surviving texts for the pageants on the Lord Mayor's day.[27]

How rapidly did haberdashers adopt reformed ideas? There were some early
conversions to the evangelical cause. John Sturgeon, a prominent Liveryman and
later Chamberlain of the City from 1550 to 1563, was among those indicted under
the Act of Six Articles (1539) which ushered in the reaction of Henry VIII's later
years. To judge from the frequency with which he was named as an executor or
overseer by those of a reformed persuasion in subsequent years, it would appear
that Sturgeon stood at the centre of the godly nexus within the Company.[28] It may
be a sign of early evangelical commitment that Anthony Marler received the patent
to print the Bible for four years from March 1542.[29] These stray fragments of
information are suggestive, but lack any quantitative dimension. For that we must
look to wills with all their attendant problems.

The wills suggest that the progress of reformed ideas was hesitant and faltering.
No less than nine of the 26 haberdasher wills coming from the last seven years of
Henry VIII's reign (1540–7) adopted a reformed preamble in which the testator
entrusted the fate of his soul to the mediation of Jesus Christ alone, relying on his
faith in his resurrected saviour. Another five adopted the neutral form of bequeathing
the soul to God alone. However the conclusion that at least one third of the Company's members had been persuaded by the preaching of the reformed should be
resisted. The interpretation of such testamentary evidence is rendered difficult by
the influence brought to bear in the composition of the preamble by the clergy, who
often attended the drawing up of the will. It is possible that we are learning more
about the attitudes of the local clergy than about the theological persuasion of the
testator. Such a conclusion is rendered the more persuasive by the fact that the
testator's instructions about the disposal of his wealth are sometimes at odds with
the theology of the reformers.[30] Thus Robert Baxter, drawing up his will in 1543,
after expressing his confidence in his salvation through the merits of Jesus Christ
alone, went on to request a priest to say mass three times a week and the placebo
and dirige twice a week on Wednesdays and Fridays for three years after his

death. Whereas the clause which disposed his soul implicitly denied the existence of Purgatory, his instructions for masses nevertheless affirmed his belief in its existence. Likewise Thomas Huntlowe combined a similar preamble with the requirement that his wife provide an annual obit out of the revenues of his property in West Wickham, Hayes, and St Giles Cripplegate. Even Rauffe Johnson, adopting a reformed pre-amble and leaving money for six collations or sermons nevertheless confused the issue by also requesting torches and tapers.[31] This evidence of a syncretic theology does not allow us to express great confidence in the notion of the rapid spread of protestantism within the Company. However to the extent that even those of a basically conservative persuasion were becoming more reluctant to demonstrate their faith through the provision of intercessory masses, it is clear that the traditional religion was being undermined. Leading haberdashers like John Hasilfoot, Thomas Lewys, and William Bayly, although adopting the conservative form in the preambles to their wills, nevertheless failed to provide for masses to ease their progress through the pains of Purgatory.[32] Moreover the use of wills may well understate the progress of reformed ideas which spread more rapidly among the young. The catholic consen-sus was undoubtedly seriously weakened in the reign of Henry VIII.

The number of haberdasher wills surviving from the reigns of Edward VI and Mary, which witnessed very different forms of official religion as the realm veered from radical protestantism to restored catholicism, is too slight to permit of very firm conclusions about religious attitudes. Of the five Edwardian wills none adopted the conservative form, four were reformed and one neutral. But lest this be taken as a sign of protestant fervour within the Company, we should note that the ten wills from Mary's reign suggest that many were merely paying lip-service to the new ideas: six adopted the conservative formula, two were neutral, and only two had the confidence to assert the reformed position. Many Londoners followed prudential considerations by falling in line with the prevailing orthodoxy of the day. It would be easy to criticise them for a lack of faith, but it is well to remember that they faced peculiarly complex and difficult choices in these mid-Tudor years. When in October 1549 the City was approached by conservative Privy Councillors for aid against the wayward Protector Somerset, it was a haberdasher, George Tadlowe, who reminded the Common Council of the penalty paid by London for making the wrong choices at earlier points in its history: for supporting the barons against Henry III 'the liberties of the City were taken away and strangers appointed to be our heads and governors'.[33] Little wonder then that many followed the line of least resistance in falling in with the forms prescribed by the authorities, especially as they were often genuinely confused.

It was only in Elizabeth's reign that protestant values became deeply embedded within the Company. The godly form of the preamble became near-universal, and some testators chose to express their faith in lengthy discourses of some originality. Thus Clement Kelke, drawing up his will in 1593, expounded his faith in a fashion which betrays the influence of Calvinist theology:

Ffirst ffor that it becometh every Christian to professe his faithe I testifye and declare that I beleve all and every article of the Christian faithe, And also the same and wholle contentes of the holye scriptures, utterly abhorring all kinds of heresye And reposing my wholle trust and confidence in that most sure rocke my Redemer Jesus Christ whoe with the olbacion of his owne bodye purchased the Redempcion of all our sins and transgressions. I also stedfastly beleve that at the last daye when all fleshe shall arise againe and appeare, my sinnes and iniquities shall not be laide to my Charge, And althoughe by nature I am the Childe of Wrathe and subiecte to everlasting damnacion yet by Jesus Christ I stedfastly believe, passing the first deathe whiche is the rewerde of sinne, And all fleshe of necessitye must taste thereof, to live after in glorye prepared for the sainctes of god from the beginning of the worlde, And in stedfast hope and assurance there of I committ and submitt my selfe under the mighty hande of god whome I desyre from the bottome of my harte to directe my doinges according to his good will and pleasure to deliver me from a sodayne and unprovided deathe.

Kelke was one of the key members of the London godly, an active Common Councillor and one of the more energetic Governors of Bridewell Hospital who had conducted a determined campaign against vice in the 1570s.[34] Likewise, the will of Thomas Bates (1585), one of the Bridgemasters of the City, bears that characteristic stamp of godly values, anti-popery:

I doe thus signifie unto all men that may have the sight hereof, my whole trust is in Jhesus Christ onely to be saved by faith in him accordinge to the epistles of Sainte Paule learninge me and all others the same my duety untoe god onely to beleve, and wholy to have remission of our synnes alone in him Jhesus Christ our onely saviour and redemer, and as I have the moste parte of my lyfe denounced the Pope, and all popery whatsover, my truste is in the Allmightie god so to ende my lyfe through his power in me geven of his mercy.[35]

The practical implications of such sentiments are more apparent in the will of Richard Gourney, an Alderman and one of the Company's benefactors (1596), who specified that none of the money he wished to have distributed in the London prisons should go to those imprisoned for 'hereticall or superstitious Religion'.[36] Some of the London godly developed particularly strong ties with members of the Haberdashers' Company. William Charke, the disciple of the presbyterian, Thomas Cartwright, was brother-in-law to Alderman William Romeney (whose will speaks of men on earth as 'pilgrims and strangers, looking for a city whose builder is God eternal in the heavens'), apprenticed his son, Benjamin, to a member of the Company, and enjoyed a close friendship with Sir Thomas Smith (his 'dear landlord'), the sympathiser of the earl of Essex and dedicatee of puritan writings. In the early 17th century, as a later chapter will show, the Company seems to have deliberately patronised those of advanced religious leanings.[37]

It is true that only a few of the wills of Elizabethan haberdashers show material signs of protestant commitment by comparison with the outpouring of pious bequests that had characterised their conservative forbears. Neither Kelke nor Bates backed up their protestant sentiments with bequests to further the godly cause through support of the preaching ministry. Richard Gourney left £16 13s. 4d. to provide 52 sermons to be preached by a bachelor or doctor of divinity in the church where he was buried but, of 35 Elizabethan haberdasher wills proved in the Prerogative Court of Canterbury in the sample years of 1570–3 and 1594–7, only five provided for a series of sermons, although another three asked for a sermon to be preached at their funerals.[38] Just six left money for the support of education, whether in the form of the endowed scholarships provided by Nicholas Culverwell, Robert Offley, and Richard Gourney, or smaller cash bequests to the universities and schools. However slender the basis of giving to education, their generosity to the poor suggests that they should not be written off as miserly and tight-fisted. 80 per cent of the wealthier haberdashers whose wills were proved in the Prerogative Court of Canterbury made some kind of bequest to the poor, and 47 per cent of the less prosperous members of the Company whose wills were proved in lesser jurisdictions gave such support. We should not forget that the relief of the poor was itself regarded by the preachers as a badge of protestant piety.

Moreover progress was being made in the provision of a preaching ministry. The encouragement of learning at the universities by the Livery Companies was a development of the 16th century. In April 1551 the Twelve Great Companies were approached by the Lord Mayor with the proposal that they support one scholar each. First to respond were the Haberdashers. Alderman William Garrard reported on 28 April that his Company was willing to provide £5 per annum towards the support of a scholar studying divinity on condition that the other Companies did the same and that they were able to nominate the recipient.[39] The scheme appears to have collapsed during the Marian reaction, but it was revived in the early years of Elizabeth. At Eastertide in 1564 the Great Twelve were exhorted to support one scholar each by the preachers of the Spittle sermons with the encouragement of Edmund Grindal, then Bishop of London. By October the Haberdashers had agreed to support Thomas Best at Jesus College, Cambridge on the unusually generous stipend of £10 per annum.[40] Over the ensuing decades the number of scholars supported out of Company stock increased to two, and they were joined by those supported by charities endowed specifically for that purpose.[41] Nicholas Culverwell left £200 to the Haberdashers' Company in 1569 to provide two scholarships of £5 each for the study of divinity, one of which was to be held at Christ's College, Cambridge, and the other at Magdalen College, Oxford. Under the terms of the will the recipients were to be named by his widow during her lifetime and thereafter by the Bishop of London. By 1600 there were six endowed Haberdasher scholarships, and 15 by 1640 supported by incomes of £30 per annum and £84 per annum respectively.[42] The scholarships were topped up by *ad hoc* grants from Company funds for specific purposes such as the provision of books or the financing of the costly B.A. commencement. In granting these scholarships the Company seems to have exercised preference towards the sons of its members, although it also took into account the recommendations of leading clergymen and Oxbridge colleges.[43] The sons of Company officers were particularly favoured. Two sons of the late Elizabethan Clerk, Lambert Osbolston, William and Lambert junior, received scholarships from the Company at Christ Church, Oxford. In addition to his scholarship William received £10 towards his M.A. commencement in 1604 and a loan of £100 towards the repair of his parsonage house on his presentation in 1614 to a living in Essex by the Governors of St Thomas' Hospital (to which his father had also been clerk).[44] Company scholars were sometimes invited to preach the sermons at the Publication ceremony on St Katherine's day, a symbolic affirmation of the Company's role in furthering the Gospel. Thus William Osbolston journeyed down from Oxford to

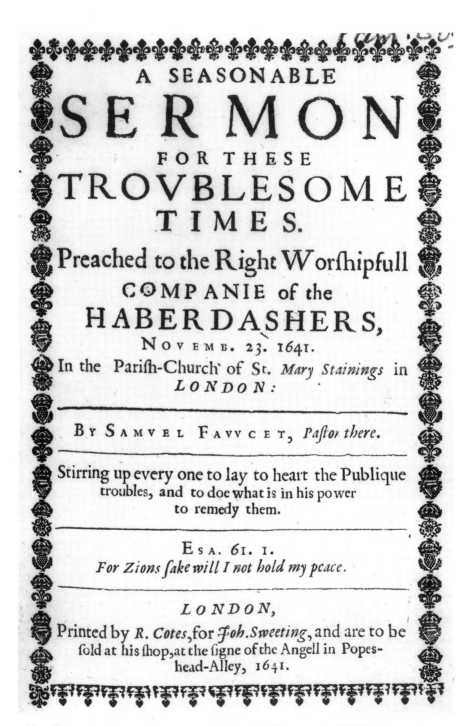

A SEASONABLE

SERMON

FOR THESE

TROVBLESOME

TIMES.

Preached to the Right Worshipfull

COMPANIE of the

HABERDASHERS,

NOVEMB. 23. 1641.

In the Parish-Church of St. *Mary Stainings* in
LONDON:

BY SAMVEL FAVVCET, *Pastor there.*

Stirring up every one to lay to heart the Publique
troubles, and to doe what is in his power
to remedy them.

ESA. 61. 1.
For Zions sake will I not hold my peace.

LONDON,

Printed by *R. Cotes,* for *Joh. Sweeting,* and are to be
sold at his shop, at the signe of the Angell in Popes-
head-Alley, 1641.

11. Title page from a sermon preached to the Company in 1641 by the puritan,
Samuel Fawcet, later Lecturer at Newland and Monmouth.

preach to the Livery in November 1607.[45] It was not only towards the universities that the energies of godly haberdashers were directed. A later chapter will show how they were responsible for the foundation of the Company's schools.[46]

The task of creating a godly commonwealth was not neglected even in the precincts of the Company's Hall. It was provided with chained copies of the Bible and Foxe's Book of Martyrs by Thomas Bramley, a member of the Court of Assistants, with the intention that members should peruse their contents while waiting for admission to the Court Room.[47] Moreover the Company joined in the huge catechising effort which marked the early 17th century. From 1627 the accounts of the Wardens of the Yeomanry regularly record the purchase of catechisms to be given to each apprentice at the start of his term, a recognition of the spiritually unprovided state in which many apprentices reached the city, having been brought up in the darker corners of the land.[48]

The Reformation therefore ushered in major changes in the religious culture of the Company. However the extent of the discontinuity should not be exaggerated; there were some important continuities with the medieval past. Although the patronal imagery was much less prominent after the Reformation, the Company's rulers continued to enjoy a spiritual sanction. The Livery still processed solemnly to the church of St Mary Staining Lane to hear a sermon and offer a penny each before the dinner on St Katherine's Day at which the new Master and Wardens were presented to the assembled company by the delivery of garlands (the 'Publication' ceremony as it is described for the first time in the ordinances of 1629).[49] Liverymen also attended sermons at St Paul's at All Saints, Christmas, Twelfth Day, and Candlemas.[50] At Eastertide the Livery attended the cycle of civic sermons which began on Good Friday at Paul's Cross, continued on Easter Monday, Tuesday and Wednesday at the churchyard of the former priory of St Mary Spital without Bishopsgate, and was completed by a sermon at Paul's Cross commenting on the earlier ones.[51] There also developed a distinctively protestant religious calendar in which the Company played its part. Liverymen gathered at Paul's Cross for sermons celebrating the monarch's accession and the delivery of King and Parliament from gunpowder treason on 5 November. Thus the first year of surviving Wardens' accounts for 1633–4 record expenditure on the hire of forms at Paul's Cross on 27 March (the accession day of Charles I), and on a dinner provided for the Aldermen, Assistants and Livery after the sermon on 5 November costing the handsome sum of £24 7s. 0d.[52]

The obligation on members of the Livery to attend the funerals of their deceased brethren continued to be included in the Company ordinances of 1567 and 1629. Indeed the later ordinances extended the obligation to cover the funerals of all members of the Livery whereas in the early 16th century it had been prescribed only for the ex-Wardens. By the ordinances of 1629 the wives of Liverymen could also be accompanied to their graves by the Livery provided that their husbands gave either a piece of plate worth five marks or five marks in money.[53] Eight of the 35 wealthier Elizabethan haberdashers included in the Prerogative Court of Canterbury will sample left money to provide a dinner for the Livery after their funerals. Nicholas Spackman (d. 1560), reflecting the residual conservatism of this

12.   Sermon at St Paul's Cross, attended by King James I, the Lord Mayor
and Aldermen, and the Liverymen of the London Companies.

era, left £5 for a repast among the Livery after his burial together with 20s. for wine
and sugar 'for that I loved hit well all my lyef and doe therfore pray them all to
saye god have mercy on my sowle Amen. And so I trust they will doe'.[54] But the
'recreations', as they were called, were maintained by those of impeccably godly
credentials, like Richard Gourney. Typically these dinners cost between £10 and

£13 6s. 8d., and involved such fare as capons roasted and boiled, brawn and mustard, roast goose, roast larks, mince pies and apple tarts.[55] Thomas Blanke the elder (d. 1563) left £10 for a dinner for Liverymen at the hall on the day of his burial, but did not neglect his obligations to the poor, specifying that 'the pore people dwellinge up the staires by the same hall shall have some of the fragmentes which shall be lefte when all the lyverie have dined'.[56] Some arranged for the distribution of cakes and buns or spiced bread after their funerals. Few were so specific as William Johnson (d. c.1575) who graduated the provision of food according to the Company hierarchy: Aldermen members of the fellowship were to receive three cakes and three buns, ex-Wardens two each, and Liverymen one each.[57] Company inventories in the early 17th century continue to record the hearse cloth which was available to members on payment of a fee to the clerk and beadle.[58]

The changes in the religious culture of the Company in the 16th and 17th centuries had important implications for its future course of development. It was the godly who provided much of the impetus for the foundation of the charitable trusts which was to change the character of the Company from an organisation concerned with the regulation of a trade to one involved in the management of charities. These themes will be developed in subsequent chapters of this book.[59]

Chapter Four

The Organisation of the Company, 1500–1650

By the early 17th century the right to elect the Master and Wardens was confined to the Wardens and ex-Wardens who comprised the Court of Assistants. The electing body had been wider in the early 16th century, for the relevant ordinance of 1505 specified that the Master and Wardens should be elected by those who had already served as Master and Wardens as well as by 'other honest persons of the clothing', although even that phrasing suggests considerable discretion on the part of the ruling group to exclude members of the Livery, so that the pattern evident in the ordinances of 1567 and 1629 may well represent merely the formalisation of existing practices rather than a radically new departure in the direction of greater exclusivity. The conventions were that the Assistants should choose as Master someone who had served the senior Wardenships, that the senior Wardens should be men who had served the lower Wardenships, and that the junior Wardens should be recruited from among the senior Liverymen not already on the Court.[1] These procedures could be modified by the accelerated promotion within the Company that election to high civic office entailed. Thus election to the offices of Sheriff or Alderman could lead to immediate service as Master, even if the junior offices had not been served. Thus Nicholas Rainton served as Master in 1622–3, just after his service as Sheriff, in spite of his not having served any of the more junior Company offices, and the practice was repeated in 1642–3 on John Fowke's election as Alderman.[2]

Service as Warden was usually a precondition for admission to the Court of Assistants, but if the Court was getting thin it was possible to reinforce it by direct recruitment from the Livery. Thus in October 1627, noting the small number of Assistants, it was agreed that the Court should be afforced with 14 recruits, on condition that they take their turn as younger Wardens in due course. There seems to have been some doubt about the wisdom of this practice, because in 1633 it was ordered that no-one should become an Assistant until he had served for one year as Warden, perhaps because of the perceived impropriety of allowing onto the Court men who had not already shown their competence by service to the Company in the junior Wardenships.[3]

The *cursus honorum* of the Company rulers can be reconstructed from the freedom records, lists of Livery admissions, and dates of service as Wardens.[4] Those serving on the Court of Assistants in 1641 had been admitted to the Livery about 15 (14.9) years after gaining the freedom of the Company. They served one of the junior Wardenships about 14 years after that (13.8), and the first of the senior Wardenships after another four years. The second of the senior Wardenships usually followed within a year or two, although payments (usually of £25) might be made for overleaping one of the senior Wardenships. Service as Master of the Company usually came three years after the second senior Wardenship, or 38 years after achieving the freedom. This pattern of service, assuming that men became free at the age of 24, meant that men were normally recruited to the Assistants in their early fifties and that they achieved the pinnacle of honour in their early sixties. The average age of the members of the Court of Assistants in 1641 can be estimated at 63. Wealth was not the sole determinant of status within the Company: the discretion deriving from age and experience was a crucial qualification for office.

The holding of office entailed enhanced social capital, and was frequently recorded by men in establishing their credibility in court cases, but it brought little in the way of direct material reward. There is little sign, for example, that the Company used its property holdings to reward members of the Court. Some, like Randolph Crew, the first lessee of the manor of Hatcham Barnes, held leases from the Company, but they do not appear to have held the property on particularly favourable terms.[5] On the contrary, office usually involved heavy outlay both in terms of time and money on the part of those who held it. The round of Company feasting was heavily subsidised by the Wardens. It was the responsibility of the four Wardens to bear the full costs of the quarter dinners, and the Master and Wardens paid the costs of the election feast over and above the allowance from the Company stock (in the 1630s, £50) and the capitation fee (in the 1630s, 5s. a head) on those dining. In the absence of full dinner accounts it is difficult to determine the precise level of outlay, but the fines for avoiding office of £20 for the Mastership and £30 for a Wardenship in the 1630s suggest a minimum level of expenditure.[6]

Courts of Assistants met about eight times a year in the later 1630s, admittedly rather less frequently than in the 1580s when there were ten meetings a year. Greater inroads were made on the time of the Master and Wardens by the requirement that they keep courts among themselves, 'monethly or oftner . . . for ye hearing, deciding and determyning of all Controversies and debates of for or concerning the said art trade or mystery and for the making free, binding and presenting of Apprentices'. Although full records of such meetings do not survive before the 18th century, there are traces that they took place in the earliest surviving minutes of the Court of Assistants. The practice of other Companies suggests that the arbitration of disputes between members and between masters and apprentices was a major component of the business at such meetings. The business of handling the Company's cash was also time consuming to the Wardens.[7] It is true that not all Assistants were equally conscientious. Of the 42 members of the Court in 1641, 13 attended none of the seven meetings held that year, two only one, and ten only two. Just 13 attended five or more meetings. The core of assiduous Assistants tended to be drawn from those at the centre of the *cursus honorum*, while those who were less active included many who had given sterling service in the past and in many cases were now retired in the country.[8]

Some provision was made for the division of responsibility among the Wardens. The upper Wardens took responsibility for the plate, deeds, evidences and the key of the treasury where they were kept, while the youngest Warden took charge of the specialties (meaning bonds in which obligations were recorded), pewter, linen, carpets and the furniture of the hall, and the key of the counting house where they were kept.[9] The junior Wardenships usually involved more work: the youngest

Warden, sometimes called the Renter Warden, was responsible for the collection of the Company's rents, and until 1632 he was also heavily involved in the management of the Company's corn stock. In that year, after an unexplained loss from the corn account, the Court of Assistants agreed to transfer the management of the account to the Third Warden whose duties of accompanying young men to the Guildhall to their freedom ceremonies were hitherto not onerous compared with those of the youngest Warden. The Fourth Warden also retained a responsibility for the management of the Company's loan stocks.[10]

Given the burdens of office, it is not surprising that some men sought to avoid it. Successive sets of Company ordinances recognised the possibility that men should turn down the honour. In 1505 and 1567 the fine for refusing the offices of Master and Warden was fixed at £5, but in fact fines higher than this are recorded in the later 16th century. In November 1583, for example, Anselm Becket was dispensed from the office of Upper Warden for a fine of £20. The ordinances were brought into line with practice in 1629 when the fines were fixed at £20 and £30 for the refusal of the Mastership and Wardenship respectively.[11] Sometimes men sought dispensation in advance of the election, knowing that they were next in line; sometimes they waited until they had been chosen. Sometimes they sought a release for one year only; sometimes they sought an absolute discharge from the specific office to which they had been elected, or indeed, from all Company office. The commonest reasons alleged for turning down office were residence outside the capital and sickness. Thus in 1630 Thomas Underhill turned down the Upper Wardenship 'in regard of his weaknes and ynabilitie of bodie not being well able to goe from his house to the hall'; in 1634 William Cranmore pointed out that he was living in Canterbury and would not be able to perform the services required; Henry Haselfoot turned down the Mastership in 1636 because of his age, physical weakness and continual residence in the country.[12] The incidence of fining for office was undoubtedly more common in the early 17th century than earlier, but whether it should be seen as an index of the weakness of the ethic of service and the Company's inability to command the loyalty of its senior members is much more questionable. Indeed one can only be impressed by the ability of the Company to assert its will over men living in Cheshire, Nottingham, Canterbury, and Rutland as it did in the 1620s and 1630s.[13] Thirty-five individuals fined for offices on 44 occasions in the period 1630–44, in 11 cases seeking dispensation before election, and in 33 cases after actually being elected. However, 19 of these 35 men served the Company in other offices, showing that they had no principled opposition to service, and indeed they were often among the most assiduous attenders of Court meetings. The strength of the service ethic is underscored by the consideration that it was not only in the sphere of their Company that these men were expected to undertake office, but they also were the group from whom the onerous and also unpaid positions of Common Councillors and Governors of Hospitals were recruited.

An attempt has been made to assemble as much information as possible from Company and other sources in order to create a profile of the men serving as Assistants in 1641. The data from the apprenticeship and freedom records can be used to establish family background and the identity of their masters; the records

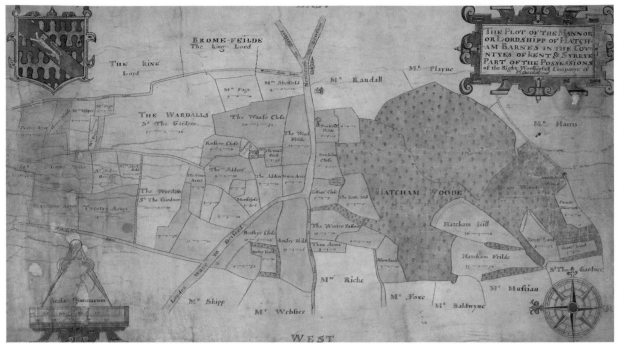

VII.   Map of the Hatcham estate in 1619, soon after its purchase to support William Jones' charity.

VIII.   The almshouses at Newland, part of William Jones' foundation.

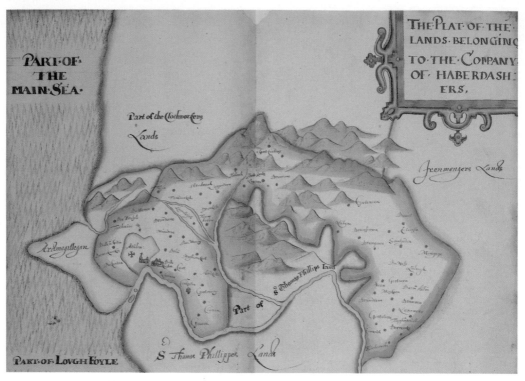

IX.   Map by Thomas Raven of the Haberdashers' estates in Londonderry, 1622.

X.   Plan by Thomas Raven showing layout of the settlements at Ballycastle and Artikelly, Londonderry, 1622.

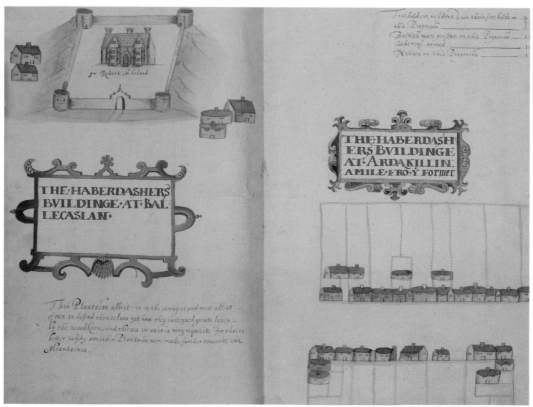

Sir George
Whitmore
L.ᵈ Mayor
Of London

XI. Sir George Whitmore (Master in 1621–2 and 1631–2, Lord Mayor in 1631–2), a leading royalist.

XII.   The list of subscribers to the rebuilding of the Hall after the Great Fire of London.

of trading companies and the port books reveal something about the business interests of those who were involved in overseas trade; tax records as well as providing information concerning their wealth provide information about where they lived; wills furnish an insight into their families and friendships. All this information is very patchy. There is a gap in the apprenticeship registers from 1596 to 1602, and the freedom register is incomplete, having been copied from other sources by the Clerk, Basill Nicholl, in 1608. Participation in overseas trade by Company members can be documented with comparative ease, but it is much more difficult to identify other areas of economic activity, and this may well distort one's sense of how individuals made their money as well as leaving the historian woefully ignorant about some members altogether. The pitfalls of tax records as a guide to wealth are well known, because contemporary assessments of an individual's wealth were highly relative rather than being based on declarations of income or formal appraisal of wealth. Testators were not consistent about the range of acquaintance they named: the readiness with which friends and kin were named depended as much on the number of surviving children to be provided for as it did on relative levels of sociability. Nevertheless, enough material is available for a few outline remarks.

The family background of the Haberdasher Assistants gives a limited endorsement to the picture of an apprenticeship in London as a social escalator that might be derived from the rags to riches story of Dick Whittington which enjoyed a particular vogue at this time. The occupational designation of the fathers of 18 of the 44 Assistants of 1641 are known from the apprenticeship registers. Seven were from artisan or commercial backgrounds, the occupations of their fathers ranging from a shoemaker through a wealthy clothier to a merchant of London; the remainder from rural society. The lowest reaches of the labouring poor were not represented, but three came from the ranks of husbandmen (humbler farmers), and one (Simon Willimott) was the son of an Aldenham schoolmaster. The upper echelons of rural society were the most common recruiting ground for the prosperous Londoners who came to dominate the Company's affairs; no less than six were the sons of yeomen and two were from gentry families.[14] Other sources are perhaps more biased in terms of the range of their coverage. Thus it can be shown that another six of the Assistants had become free of the Company by patrimony, and that their fathers were thus free of the Company themselves. These men included Martin Bond, George Whitmore and Robert Fenn, the sons of former Assistants and thus very influential within the Company. Another, Henry Haselfoot, came from a family with Haberdasher connections stretching through several generations. This was a rare phenomenon at this time when lines died out quickly and second generation City men sought the respectability of landed wealth. Both Henry's father and grandfather were haberdashers. His grandfather, John, had married the daughter of Sir Stephen Peacock, Haberdasher Lord Mayor in 1532–3.[15]

Thus it would be true to say that the Assistants tended to be recruited from the middling ranks of society upwards. Although apprenticeship to a merchant was not a necessary condition for a successful career in the Company, it was a help, and there were financial barriers to such apprenticeship which ensured that the Company was not an open society. In addition to the premiums which accompanied apprentice-

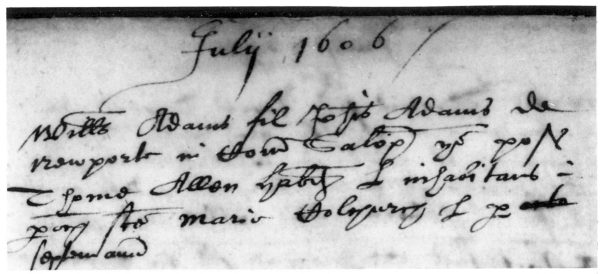

13.   Extract from the Company's register of apprentice bindings, showing apprenticeship of William Adams, founder of Adams' Grammar School, Newport, to Thomas Allen.

ship to a merchant, the prospective apprentice was required to post bonds that he would not defraud his master, and such bonds required sureties who commanded the necessary social and commercial credit. Thus Edmund Berkeley, a Shrewsbury clothier, had to stand surety for his son, William in the sum of £300 at the latter's apprenticeship to Edward Skeggs in 1604.[16] Another indication of the limits of the openness of Haberdasher society is the fact that the masters of 17 of the 41 Assistants of 1641 whose masters are known were themselves Assistants: clearly the connections provided by an apprenticeship with the right person were a launching pad for a successful career within the Company.[17]

What lines of business did the Haberdasher Assistants pursue? An earlier chapter has shown how the Company was penetrated by mercantile wealth in the 16th century and how this provided the key to the Company's growing stature within City government. Merchants remained a prominent component of the ruling body in the mid–17th century, although they now represented a wider range of trading groups with potentially divergent interests. Twenty of the 44 Assistants in 1641 can be shown to have engaged in overseas trade at some point in their careers, although the precise contribution of that activity to their income is often obscure.[18] Men like George Whitmore and Paul Pindar were heavily involved in the customs and money-lending in the later stages of their careers; for Randolph Crew his office in the naval administration may well have proved more lucrative than the trade in which he engaged; and for Nicholas Rainton the domestic wholesaling side of his trade in silk may have been the key to his fortune.[19] The traditional trading interests of the Merchant Adventurers were represented by men like William Cranmore, Governor of the Company at Rotterdam, Anthony Biddulph, Humfrey Berrington, and Robert Fenn. But the newer and highly lucrative East India and Levant trades accounted for a growing number of the more powerful members of the Company, including

Simon Edmondes and John Trott. Others still were prominent in the American and West Indian trades. Thomas Stone, an interloper in the area of the Merchant Adventurers' privileges in the second decade of the 17th century, turned to tobacco planting from the later 1620s, and he soon became one of the leading importers of Bermuda tobacco. William Berkeley began his mercantile career conventionally enough in trade with France, but during the war with France in the later 1620s turned to projects in Canada. William Thompson was closely associated with Maurice Thompson's American trading group, as well as being involved with rivals to the East India Company monopoly. Some individuals spread their interests widely, combining a great variety of commercial ventures. Thus Humphrey Slaney was involved not only in the Merchant Adventurers' Company and in the Levant trades, but also in trade to Guinea and Newfoundland.[20]

Men with Slaney's breadth of interests were rare and the tendency was for specialisation in particular branches of trade. Its diversity of trading interests made the Court of Assistants potentially more prone to division than in the later 16th century because of the different attitudes they struck over the royal prerogative and foreign policy. Whereas those involved in the American trades tended to be motivated by an anti-Spanish sentiment often deriving its force from strongly felt religious principles which brought them into conflict with the Crown's religious and foreign policies, the overlapping Levant and East Indian trading groups tended towards conservatism and a position of support for detente with Spain. The support of men like Thompson, Stone, and Berkeley for Parliament was a natural outgrowth of their trading interests. George Whitmore's combination of East Indies trade with money-lending and involvement in the customs, made him a natural 'sufferer for his Majesty's government'. However, the sphere of an individual's trading interest was not the only determinant of civil war allegiance. Some Levant and East India Company men turned out to be among the most prominent supporters of Parliament. Simon Edmunds, a close associate of the presbyterian reformation of Edmund Calamy in St Mary Aldermanbury, was drawn by his religious inclinations to support Parliament in spite of his Levant trading interests. John Fowke, although a leading East India Company merchant, was a long-standing opponent of the unrestrained prerogative, having refused to pay unparliamentary tonnage and poundage in 1627, and he became so thoroughly alienated from the establishment of the Company by its pursuit of a debt for which he had stood security that he embroiled himself in nearly 30 years of litigation with his former associates. He increasingly detached himself from involvement in the Levant and East India trades and became a leading participant in the Parliamentary customs farms.[21]

It is much more difficult to profile the interests of those lacking mercantile investments. Presumably large numbers were involved in domestic wholesaling and retailing, selling cloth and supplying chapmen. A list of Londoners occupying silks from 1562 includes ten haberdashers, some of them very prominent in the Company.[22] The records of the equity courts show that the supply of chapmen was a standard business interest of leading Company members.[23] What is more tantalising, however, is the question of the degree to which humbler members of the Company were represented among the Assistants. There are certainly one or two signs that they made it this far on occasion. John Stourton is named as a haberdasher of hats, Nicholas Dickens as a hatmaker, and John Broome as a hosier on the prime retail site of London Bridge.[24] Clearly the interests of the trade were represented on the Court, although one is left with the powerful impression that they lacked a strong voice.

Nor did all the Assistants enjoy an equal weight in the Company's affairs. It is quite clear that within the Court of Assistants greater weight was given to some voices than others. This is hardly surprising, given the long experience of some Court members and their influence at Guildhall and in central government as Aldermen. The sway that such men wielded over the Court shows in their successful sponsorship of suits. Thus Sir Thomas Lowe promoted requests for reversions to the humble offices of the Company's Porter and Keeper of Corn, as well as seeking leases of Company property for his clients. His servant, William Heitley, received a lease of a tenement in Maiden Lane in 1609, and was promised a favourable hearing in his suit for the Porter's job ten years later, on both occasions at his master's request. The children of such men also received favourable treatment through such marks of favour as accelerated admission to the Livery and dispensation from office. Lowe's son was admitted to the Livery in 1610 within a year of becoming free, and in 1622 was dispensed from all office in the Company.[25] The weight enjoyed by key individuals in the Company's affairs is shown by the reluctance with which discussion on sensitive matters proceeded in their absence; thus the reading of the proposed new ordinances was deferred in November 1624 because of the absence of the Aldermen members of the Court.[26]

Power was undoubtedly concentrated in the hands of men whose business interests and social life were somewhat remote from the rank-and-file. Nevertheless the analysis of the distribution of power within the Company would be incomplete without considering those areas in which a more consensual approach to government prevailed. It is true that the Assistants were largely autonomous in the key policy areas, but on some issues the practicalities were such that a wider basis of consent was thought appropriate. Thus, when assessments were made on the membership, a committee of Assistants would act in conjunction with key members of the Livery, and in conducting the search an effort would be made to involve members of the trade with expertise in the relevant areas.[27]

Power was also devolved downwards, albeit to a limited extent, through the involvement of the Wardens of the Yeomanry in the government of the Company. There were six Wardens of the Yeomanry until 1634, when the number was reduced to four. The Wardens were chosen every August by the Court of Assistants from a panel of 12 names presented by the outgoing Wardens of the Yeomanry. Not only did the Court of Assistants exercise firm control over the Yeomanry Wardens, but their competence was strictly limited. There are few signs of their active involvement in the promotion of suits for the benefit of the handitrade that characterised Companies such as the Clothworkers. They did have the power to bind and make free apprentices and arbitrate disputes in the absence of the Wardens of the Livery, and they were coopted into the search. But otherwise their role was confined to the collection of quarterage and involvement in the collection of assessments on the membership. Another key, although irregular, activity was the organisation of the triumph for Haberdasher Lord Mayors, when the Yeomanry Wardens were responsible for choosing the bachelors to serve in foins or budge and for making the necessary assessment on the membership. Not surprisingly an element in the decision to reduce the number of Yeomanry Wardens to four in 1634 was the limited scope of their duties.[28]

Moreover, because the office required a certain amount of wealth the Yeomanry Wardens were only representative of the membership to a limited extent. The financing of the Yeomanry feast, although an increasingly irregular occurrence in the later 16th and early 17th centuries, entailed an expenditure of probably £10 by each of the Wardens.[29] Further hints of the costs of office are provided by the £10 penalty for refusal and by the differential fees paid by those admitted to the Livery. In the early 17th century those who had not served as Yeomanry Wardens paid £25 on their admission to the Livery compared to the 40s. paid by those who had held the office.[30] Although not vital to promotion within the Company, service at the middle tier of the hierarchy was a stepping-stone to the Livery. In 1625 we learn that 'the yeomanry wardens . . . come by force upon the clothing'.[31] Because most of those serving as Yeomanry Wardens were subsequently admitted to the Livery, the artisans tended not to enjoy the lasting advocacy of men whose loyalties lay with them. To the extent that promotion was linked to the effective discharge of one's duties as Yeomanry Warden, the Yeomanry rulers would strive to dampen down disputes with the Assistants for the sake of a quiet year.

This account of the organisation of the Company's affairs would be incomplete without a consideration of the role played by its permanent staff, that is to say the Company's Porter, the Beadle of the Yeomanry, the Beadle of the Livery, and the Company Clerk. The Porter was responsible for keeping the Hall in good order. He was regularly paid for mops, brooms, and baskets, and for washing the Hall, strewing its floor with herbs and scouring andirons.[32] The Beadles were essential to maintaining the flow of information between the Hall and the membership. They were responsible for summoning members to Courts and informing them of the Court's decisions. For example, in 1636 John Elsworth, Beadle of the Yeomanry, received a total of £4 6s. 0d. for his trouble and expenses in journeys about the country to inform distant members of their election to Company offices.[33] Although they might be paid extra monies in respect of such extraordinary services, the basic salaries were modest. In the 1630s the Porter was paid a fee of £6 per annum, the Beadle of the Yeomanry £6 13s. 4d. per annum from the main account and £6 13s. 4d. from the Yeomanry stock, and the Beadle of the Livery £20 per annum from the main account and £1 from the Yeomanry account. The salary of the latter was supplemented by a share of fees on freedom and Livery admissions of 12d. and 20d. respectively.[34] All those serving the Company might benefit from special grants from the Assistants in recognition of particularly hard work or in response to particularly severe economic difficulties. Thus in the accounting year 1635–6 the Beadle of the Livery and the Beadle of the Yeomanry received £3 each and the Porter £2 'in regard of the hardness of the time'.[35] Among these lesser officers there was a career structure in the sense that individuals were promoted from one to the other. William

Squire served successively as Porter (1615–17), Beadle of the Yeomanry (1617–25), and Beadle of the Livery (1627–34).[36]

Much more important to the smooth transaction of Company business was the Clerk. His duties included the recording of all bindings of apprentices, the making of indentures, the registration of admissions to the freedom, attendance at all Courts, and the handling of the Company's correspondence. He was also involved in the management of the Company's property, collecting rents, giving the Court notification of necessary repairs, and enjoying the power of re-entry in the event of non-payment of rent or non-compliance with repair orders.[37] Beyond these basic tasks, however, the Clerk would be included on policy-making committees and involved in executive action. Basil Nicholl, Clerk from 1602 to 1646, played a crucial role in the establishment of the charities at Monmouth and Newland, spending several successive summers there, looking for suitable sites for buildings and overseeing the work of construction. Much of his time was also taken up with legal business in the early years of the Jones charity, following bills in the 1614 Parliament relating to it, securing licences of mortmain, and drawing up the conveyances of the property purchased to support the charity. It was to Nicholl that the Company entrusted the choice of the first inhabitants of Jones' almshouses at Newland, and he was included on the early visitations.[38] Nicholl was one of those exceptional men like Robert Smith, City Solicitor, and Richard Langley, Clerk to the Merchant Tailors' Company, who shared the enthusiasm for better record keeping evident in several quarters of the City at the turn of the century, and interpreted their responsibilities more widely. Almost immediately after his appointment he embarked on improving the Company's information resources. He produced the indexed register of freedom admissions since 1525, and separate registers of leases, of property owned by the Company with the relevant deeds and conveyances, and of covenants, obligations and bonds under the common seal.[39]

The Clerk's basic stipend of £40 per annum was fairly modest in the 1630s, although it had increased markedly in real terms since 1583 when it had stood at just £5 per annum. Nicholl's basic fee was supplemented at this time by a further payment of £20 per annum for his extraordinary pains, the kind of discretionary payment that the Company made for good service without committing itself to the payment to a successor. The Clerk also received £6 13s. 4d. per annum from the Yeomanry stock and 20s. for drawing and engrossing their account, as well as payments from various charity accounts for his work in administering them, 8s. from the Buckland charity, 15s. 3d. from Bramley's charity, 20s. from the Aldersey charity, and £5 from the Weld charity. Fees were also paid to the Clerk for the various services he performed for Company members: 4d. for the registration of apprentices, 20d. for making the indentures of apprenticeship, 12d. for the registration of freedom admissions, and 6s. 8d. on the admission of any member to the Livery. In the first 40 years of the 17th century annual earnings from the performance of these services can be estimated at £4 15s. 0d., £24 0s. 0d., £6 5s. 0d., and £3 13s. 4d. respectively, a total of £38 13s. 4d. Other perks included the second Livery gown or 20s. from every Liveryman at death (probably £10 per annum if enforced). Thus the total emoluments of the Clerkship can be estimated at a minimum of £123 9s. 8d. during the 1630s, a figure which excludes the fees taken for drawing up arbitrations or bonds involving Company members.[40] Exceptional industry might be rewarded with yet further discretionary payments. In 1615, for example, Nicholl had been paid £100 for his labours in setting up the Jones charities.[41]

The work of the Clerk on the Company's behalf was also recognised in indirect ways. In 1607 in recognition of his superogatory labours Nicholl was granted a lease in reversion (to take effect in 1622) of the *Horseshoe Inn* in the parish of St Sepulchre without Newgate for a period of 31 years, extended to 51 years in 1609. After he had enjoyed this lease for a period of seven years, a new lease was granted for a period of another 31 years from the expiration of his existing lease at the same rent (£11 13s. 4d. per annum), making a total of 75 years, a far longer term than was customarily allowed. Nicholl also enjoyed a lease of two tenements in Maiden Lane granted for an extended term of 40 years from 1624.[42]

The Clerkship of the Company was not necessarily a full-time job. Nicholl's predecessor, Lambert Osbolston, had also been Under-Renter and Clerk of St Thomas' Hospital from 1577, and in 1592 he had secured the collection of wheelage on London Bridge, one of the City's tolls, the reversion to which he had been granted in 1580 at the request of Lord Chancellor Bromley.[43] In spite of his pluralism Osbolston ended his life in prison for debt, discharged from both his Clerkships, having clearly over-extended himself.[44] Perhaps for this reason the Clerkship under Nicholl became more professionalised. In 1607 it was noted that 'he bestoweth almost his whole tyme in the affaires and busynesses of this Company, and the profittes of his Clarkship scarcely sufficient to defray his houshold expences'.[45]

This chapter has outlined the structures of the Company's government in a basically static way. It has revealed little of the dynamics of government, of the ways in which these structures negotiated the conflicting pressures to which the Assistants were subjected, whether they be the conflicts between wholesalers and retailers in the regulation of the trade, or those between local and metropolitan interests in the management of the Company's charities. The two chapters which follow are intended to address these questions.

Chapter Five

Merchants and Artisans, 1500–1650

Previous chapters have shown how in the course of the 16th century the Court of Assistants came to be dominated by merchants and large-scale retailers. They had relatively little in common with the artisans, mostly cappers and, later in the century, feltmakers, who remained confined to a subordinate status within the Yeomanry organisation. This did not necessarily mean that the Company became an instrument of economic exploitation, because the ideal of the community of the Company meant that the wealthier and poorer members were bound by reciprocal obligations: the Assistants were expected to have regard to the interests of the poorer members. It is true that on some issues, such as the desire on the part of artisans that goods should not be sent out of the capital in an unfinished state, the interests of the wholesalers and artisans clashed directly. But on others, such as the need for restrictions on alien competitors, there was a greater level of consensus. The attitudes of the artisans towards the ruling group were therefore likely to be ambiguous rather than characterised by outright and continuing resentment. Nevertheless the potential for trouble was great. It is therefore necessary to probe the performance of the Company as an instrument for promoting the grievances of its artisan members. This chapter begins by looking at the Company's response to the decay of the capping industry, and then turns to the suits promoted by the feltmakers in the later 16th century.

It is clear that the 16th century saw major problems in the capping industry. From every corner of the realm arose the chorus of complaint. John Leland, writing in 1538, remarked of Coventry, that 'the towne rose by makynge of clothe and capps, that now decayenge, the glory of the city decayethe'. In 1523 the cappers of Chester vented their wrath against the mercers who, they alleged, were impoverishing their trade by bringing goods up from London. Likewise, in 1543 the cappers of Bristol complained that Londoners resorting to their fair with head-gear were undermining the local producers, and the carders, spinners, and knitters dependent upon them were being impoverished. Of Gloucester it was said in 1583 that 'before Sir Thomas Bell and one Mr Falkoner kept great numbers of people at work spinning and knitting of caps . . . [but] now there are very few set to work in that trade'.[1]

The causes of this decay were several. Some of the complaints cited above suggest that the decline of provincial industries was a result of the greater penetration by London interests, and this may well be another reflection of that greater prosperity among London haberdashers at this date that was noted in the second chapter. But penetration by London interests reflected the greater awareness of changing metropolitan fashions in the provinces. Sir Thomas Smith remarked that

Nowe the porest yonge man in a countrey can not be contented either with a lether girdle, or lether pointes, gloves, knyves, or daggers made nighe home. And specially no gentleman can be content to have eyther cappe, coate, dublet, hose or shirt made in his countrey, but they must have theire geare from London; and yet manye thinges thearof are not theare made, but beyonde the sea; whearby the artificers of oure townes are Idle

The major change in fashions in head-gear was that from knitted woollen caps to felted hats. Edmund Howes, the early 17th-century continuator of John Stow's chronicle, explained that the manufacture of Spanish felts by Spaniards and Dutchmen was started in the early years of the reign of Henry VIII; that formerly the English had worn 'winter and sommer knit caps, cloth hoods and . . . silk thromd hats'. He may well have been exaggerating the extent of the change, because felt hats had certainly been available in England for some time prior to 1500, although the scale of domestic manufacture as opposed to imports is unclear. It is also likely that the taste of the upper classes for felt hats was spreading down the social scale in the 16th century: certainly this was the thrust of the complaints of contemporary moralists about the meaner sort imitating their betters.[2] This meant that the London producers of traditional head-gear were themselves in trouble, as the promotion of protective legislation by London interests indicates. The process of adaptation was a painful one, particularly as the new skills spread slowly, and the immediate beneficiaries appeared to be the aliens settled in London, which produced further tension. Moreover, it is clear that native producers of the new fashions were unable to satisfy all the demand with the result that imports of hats surged forwards. In 1559–60 imports of hats were valued at £7,915.[3]

The industry's response to these pressures therefore was not surprisingly the promotion of protectionist legislation. In 1512 Parliament banned the import of foreign-made head-gear, the interests of consumers being safeguarded by provisions limiting the prices of goods manufactured in England. Among Cardinal Wolsey's schemes to revive domestic manufactures in 1527 was the proposal that no freeman buy French bonnets of any persons on pain of imprisonment. These measures were probably too draconian, because Parliament relaxed the 1512 legislation in 1529 by allowing imports of head-gear provided that maximum prices were observed. However, this statute was widely evaded. In 1531 the London cappers complained that foreigners were concealing the origins of the hats they imported by altering them with laces, brooches, and buttons, and then selling them 'in ample manner and at such prices as in the past'. The Common Council therefore put its weight behind the parliamentary legislation by banning the sale of imported hats garnished in this way.[4]

But complaints about the weakness of the act and its lack of enforcement remained common. By the mid-Tudor decades more draconian legislation was again being promoted. Sir Thomas Smith refers in his *Discourse of the Commonweal* (1549) to a recent bill to ban the import of caps, probably the bill for hats and caps read in 1549. It failed apparently because it was felt that it would upset treaty obligations and invite retaliatory measures. There were other unsuccessful bills in 1553, the contents of which are unknown, one in Edward's last Parliament 'for selling divers foreign haberdashery wares', and another in Mary's first Parliament 'for hats and

14.   Flemish street scene, *c.*1460, showing transition in head-gear between
the old-fashioned *chaperons* worn by the tradesmen, and the hats worn by
the more fashionable élite figures.

caps to be brought from overseas'. But the following year a statute was secured
tightening the provisions of the 1529 act. Importers of hats and caps were instructed
to deliver their goods to the customs officials who, in association with the town
officials, were to sell the goods at the prices appointed, delivering the money they
received to the owner. A further restriction on the trade, striking at domestic wholesalers, was that no-one should bargain for more than 12 foreign-made hats or caps
at any one time. We know little of how this act worked in practice, but the provisions

were hardly likely to be greeted with enthusiasm either by domestic wholesalers or by hard-pressed customs officials. The chances are that it remained a dead letter.[5]

Further legislation promoted in the early Elizabethan period took a different tack. A statute of 1567, the preamble to which alleged that subjects making woollen hats had been decayed by the excessive use of felts, attempted to tackle the problem by restricting the expansion of feltmaking in England, and vesting the Haberdashers' Company with rights of search over the industry in the metropolitan area. No-one was to manufacture felts without having served a seven-year apprenticeship in the trade, and no hatmaker was to take on more than two apprentices at any one time. The Master and Wardens of the Haberdashers' Company, accompanied by one capper and one hatmaker, were to enjoy rights of search over all hatmakers within a three-mile radius of London. Another prong in the protectionist attack was the bill first promoted in this same Parliament, and made law in 1571, which compelled people to wear caps and not hats on Sundays and holidays. Making exception for peers, gentlemen worth £13 6s. 8d. per annum from land, and those who had borne high office in towns, the act enforced the wearing of knitted woollen caps on all others, under penalty of a fine of 3s. 4d. per day. This measure, which remained on the statute book until 1598, therefore performed the dual function of protecting capmakers and sustaining those distinctions of dress which Elizabethan Englishmen felt to be so essential to maintaining the social order.[6] The sumptuary regulations imposed on apprentices in 1582 likewise forbade them to wear hats, allowing them only woollen caps 'without any silk in or about the same'. Such knitted caps became known as statute caps, and were a source of jokes for the dramatists, proverbially associated with a dull-witted citizenry. Thus Rosaline's remark of the courtiers in *Love's Labour's Lost* that 'better wits have worn plain statute-caps', is deeply sarcastic.[7]

Because of the loss of the Company's own archive before 1582, and because of the variety of provincial interests also concerned in the fate of capmaking, it is difficult to be sure about the precise role of the Haberdashers' Company in securing this legislation. Clearly, the Company must have been behind the statute of 1567 because of the powers of search it received, but the measures limiting imports and for the wearing of caps may have been more widely promoted: the statute of 1571 identified 26 towns by name that would benefit from the statute. The possibility that London and provincial interests co-operated in securing the legislation is a strong one. Certainly, both London and provincial interests were actively involved in its enforcement. In February 1574 the Aldermen of London received a petition from the Haberdashers being cappers that the statute for the wearing of caps be put in execution, and they instructed their Townclerk to proceed against offenders in the Mayor's Court forthwith. The Haberdashers also supported the suit of Thomas Walker and Edward Aberet before the Privy Council for powers to enforce the statute in 1595. The licence they sought was presumably similar in form to that obtained in January 1576 by two cappers of Lichfield, John Baylye and Robert Blunt, which empowered them to compound with offenders against the statute, applying the monies they received to the relief of decayed towns, and accounting annually for the money they received before auditors appointed by the Mayors of Coventry, Hereford, Lichfield, Shrewsbury, and Stafford.[8]

15.   Felt hat from Southwark, *c.*1560.

One of the striking features of the legislation to protect the capping industry, particularly in the early 16th century, is the way it conflicted with the interests of the wholesaling groups who were so dominant in the running of the Company. Wholesalers probably cared little whether the hats and caps they sold to country chapmen were imported or not. Such was the thrust of the early 16th-century complaints against the haberdashers for draining the realm of treasure and contributing to balance of payments problems. Unfortunately the sources do not afford us any insight on the tensions that this legislation produced within the Company. We are, however, much better informed about the clashes of interest that developed in the later 16th century between the feltmakers, themselves now an increasing component of the Company's Yeomanry, and the ruling group.[9] The concerns of the artisans may be summarised as follows. Their basic aim was to maximise the employment available to them. This meant restricting the competition from strangers and foreigners, and from feltmakers who were free of other companies. They had to restrict the recruitment of apprentices by these groups, and they had to ensure that standards of production were maintained lest rivals undercut them by producing shoddy goods. These aims were not especially controversial within the Company. But the maximisation of employment opportunities might also bring the artisans into direct conflict with the rulers, as over the demands that goods should be properly finished in London before being delivered to rural chapmen. Such tensions might be further exacerbated by the dependence of the artisans on wholesalers for raw material supplies, and for an outlet for their product.

The feltmakers' basic problem was that the Haberdashers' Company did not provide an adequate framework for the regulation of the trade, because the new skills were never confined to the Company's members. Initially they were particularly associated with foreign immigrants. Thus the names of the Wardens of the Hatmakers' fraternity of St James in the early 16th century betray their foreign origins: Andrew Morter, James Lees, Bartholomew Brynke, and Henry Graver in 1505, and Gerard Rowse, Anthony de Wyne, Anthony Levyson, and James Lees in 1511. The 1505 ordinances of this fraternity were translated into Dutch and were preoccupied with the conditions under which strangers might work in the craft. No stranger was to be received by any member of the fraternity to work unless he had been training under a master overseas for at least two years. In 1511 it was agreed that every stranger should pay at his admission a fee of 26s. 8d., double that for Englishmen, which was to be divided between the fraternity of St James and the Haberdashers' Company. But hostility towards the strangers was muted by an appreciation of the skills they had to offer: the very fact that they were so prominent in running this fraternity is an indication of the degree of integration they had achieved. When the City's Common Council passed legislation against the employment of foreigners by freemen in 1555, an exception was made for feltmakers and cap-thickers. The aliens were also encouraged by Elizabeth's government, anxious to substitute domestic products for foreign imports. Her chief minister, Sir William Cecil, encouraged the widespread denizations among which hatmakers were prominent in 1561.[10]

The alien element in the craft remained prominent in the later 16th century. In 1571 there were at least 78 stranger householders engaged in the hat- and cap-making trades in the metropolitan area. They were particularly concentrated in the parish of St Olave Southwark and the precinct of St Katharine-by-the-Tower. There were no less than 30 in St Katharine's. Some were working for Englishmen like John Dewsbury, the prominent hatmaker and vestryman of St Olave's. Others themselves employed large numbers of Englishmen. Thus, Robert Bonfoire, born at Falaise in Normandy but resident in England for 35 years by 1593, was then employing ten English journeymen and two English apprentices.[11] But in spite of these cases of integration apparently successfully achieved, there is evidence that the aliens were much more widely resented in this later period. Among the provisions of a bill promoted by the Haberdashers in 1581 was a ban on working by aliens in hat-making. In 1584 the Company refused to promise protection from the anti-alien statutes to strangers who had set up hatmaking near the city in spite of the support enjoyed by the newcomers from Lord Chancellor Hatton and Secretary of State Walsingham. A statute of 1604 laid down that no-one was to retain or set on work any alien.[12] The greater level of friction reflects the fact that the skills the aliens enjoyed were now much more widespread. The result was that they were perceived as a threat to the employment of Englishmen rather than as a means to training the English to produce goods which might substitute imports.

But the threat came not only from the aliens. By the custom of London, once a man had achieved the freedom, he was entitled to engage in any trade and not just the one to which he had been apprenticed. Originally this may have been intended to apply only to those engaged in wholesaling rather than in production and retailing, but by the 16th century it was being cited in the crafts to justify the pursuit of trades other than that from which the Company took its name. Thus the new skills of feltmaking did not diffuse through the Haberdashers' Company alone, but feltmakers are to be found in the Merchant Tailors', Curriers', and Clothworkers' Companies. With all these Companies the Haberdashers came into conflict as they sought to regulate the trade on behalf of the feltmakers in their own Company. The custom of London made it much more difficult to enforce the ordinances. How were standards to be maintained, the labour supply regulated, the employment of foreigners and strangers restrained, among freemen feltmakers outside the Haberdashers' Company? In May 1557 the Haberdashers clashed with the Merchant Tailors over their claims to search merchant tailors who were involved in the making and trimming of hats and caps. Their attempted search ran contrary to the exclusive rights of search over their members obtained by the Merchant Tailors in their charter of 1504. A compromise was negotiated by the Aldermen under which the Merchant Tailor hatmakers were free to continue their own trades, and the Haberdashers were not to search without associating two members of the Merchant Tailors' Company with them.[13] Thereafter we hear little of friction between the Haberdashers and the other Companies until the mid–1570s when, apparently in response to vigorous agitation from their artisan members, the Haberdashers found themselves embroiled on several fronts. Most controversial was the ordinance passed in 1574 that no member of the Company put out hats or caps to be dressed save by fellow-members. In passing the ordinance the Haberdashers stressed their obligations to the poor of their Company:

> those of the sayde Companie whome povertie hathe greveously oppressed of whome there are a greate nomber in the sayde Companie that partlie for lack of work as by other Accions are sore opressed with povertie that many of them are dryven to be relyved by thalmes and Charittie of the saide Companie.

They further argued for the public utility of their ordinances, tending

> to the utilitie and holsome provision of manye and to the preiudice of none ffor reasone willeth that every Socyetie and Companie sholde provide thinges necessary of themselves although not to the preiudice of others

But the ordinance was vigorously resisted by the Merchant Tailors' Company who complained to the Aldermen. Learned counsel having been heard on both sides, the Lord Mayor ruled in April 1576 that the ordinance was against the franchises of

the City.[14] Nevertheless the Haberdashers were undeterred and continued to pressurise the feltmakers in other Companies by every means possible. In 1578 they were
seeking payments in quarterage from members of other Companies and demanding
that they enjoy the power to admit journeymen and householders. The result was
friction with both the Clothworkers' and Curriers' Companies.[15]

The strangers and the non-Haberdasher feltmakers do not exhaust the threats to
the Company's position. A third, and increasingly pressing, challenge was represented by the English non-free, or 'foreigners' as they were called. Those Englishmen who served the aliens and learned their new skills doubtless included many
who did not enjoy the freedom of the City. It was also alleged that many freemen
took on apprentices as a source of cheap labour and discharged them before their
terms were completed. Although they never became free of the City they had learned
enough to set up the trade for themselves, sometimes in rural areas, sometimes in
the suburbs of London. Feltmaking tended to be concentrated in the suburbs because
of the need for large quantities of water and access to fields for drying wools. Thus
no less than 16 per cent of the householders in the parish of St Olave Southwark in
the 1620s were feltmakers. The suburban location of the industry made regulation
still more difficult, and further encouraged the penetration by foreigners of the
trade.[16]

The statute of 1567 which had required that all feltmakers should have served an
apprenticeship for seven years should have provided the Company with a suitable
weapon against the foreigners. Unfortunately the statute had serious defects, in
particular because of its failure to allot a portion of the forfeitures to the informers
who were responsible for its enforcement. The Haberdashers' Company therefore
pushed for amendments to the statute in Parliament. Bills were unsuccessfully
promoted in the Parliaments of 1571, 1576, 1581, 1584–5, and 1601.[17] As an alternative to this quest for a solution through Parliament the Company also sought a
prerogative solution, in other words by exploiting the licensing powers of the Crown
to obtain a grant of the forfeitures for a period of 21 years. It is probable that the
feltmakers were seeking a deputation from a courtier, for the negotiations reveal that
a patentee was to enjoy half the forfeitures and the Haberdashers' Company the
other half. This dubious enterprise to link the Company's interests with that of a
courtier on the make, so typical of the murky world of the projectors of the later
Elizabethan years, was unsuccessful on both occasions it was tried, in 1583 and
1591.[18] However, in 1594 the Company was successful in securing from the Privy
Council a warrant to apprehend persons disobedient to the Company ordinances in
the London area, and to discipline apprentices and journeymen who had left their
masters' service to set up hatmaking in the countryside. And the campaign in
Parliament eventually triumphed with a revised statute in 1604, granting the long-
sought powers of enforcement.[19]

The challenges to the Haberdashers' Company's control over hatmaking were
therefore manifold. The message that it might be an inappropriate mechanism for
regulating the trade was not lost on some of the artisans who appear to have begun
in the last quarter of the century to develop a sense of a trade solidarity which
transcended the divisions between free and foreigner. Many foreigners about the

capital, who after all lived and worked in the same areas as the free feltmakers, shared the desire of the Haberdasher feltmakers for greater regulation to eliminate unfair rural competitors evading apprenticeship regulations and producing shoddy goods. One must be very careful lest one ascribes the perceptions of a vocal minority to the whole trade; it is probable that opinions among the feltmakers were highly divided; and it is unlikely that proposals to legitimise the position of the foreigners would be welcome to all freemen. Certainly, the Wardens of the Haberdashers' Company claimed that their critics enjoyed by no means unanimous support. Nevertheless, as early as 1577 the feltmakers described themselves as a company 'although having no government of themselves as other companies have'; and they petitioned that they be incorporated by letters patent. The petition was referred to the Lord Treasurer and the Lord Chief Justices who ruled in 1578 that the feltmakers should remain under the control of the Haberdashers' Company.[20] There are other instances of alleged co-operation between free and foreigner. For example, in 1594 the feltmaker members of the Curriers' Company claimed that they were being harassed by 'the Wardens of the Company of Haberdashers and other foreigners associate with them', demanding to license craftsmen, levying arbitrary fines, and seeking control over their apprentices.[21]

There were other areas on which free and foreign feltmakers shared grievances. During the later 1570s the feltmakers sought to ensure that the imported Spanish and estridge wools that they used in manufacturing felt were properly washed and sorted before being delivered to them. To this end it was proposed that a courtier, Edward Schetz, should receive a grant from the Crown of an office for the sorting, washing, and weighing of wools, for which fees would be levied. The feltmakers were to act as the deputies of the patentee. The office was necessary, it was alleged, because poor quality wools were mixed with the good by the wholesalers. On this occasion the interests of the feltmakers clashed directly with those of the rulers of the Haberdashers' Company. As the leaders of the feltmakers, Thomas Bradford and Thomas Cawnton, pointed out, the 'cheifest and moste parte of the merchantes that bringeth in and the ingrosers of wools are haberdasshers'. As the Assistants pointed out, the Company's recent ordinances already made provision for the search of wools and, they further claimed, representatives of the feltmakers were involved in the search. Opponents of the grant could point to the high fees required by the patentee for his services which would push up prices. But they also lost no opportunity to blacken the name of the agitators. Bradford and Cawnton were described as men of very slender credit and of the worst sort of feltmakers, haunters of taverns where they conspire, not to do any good to the commonwealth, but to keep up their idle life-style with other men's goods. Moreover, they did not truly represent the craftsmen:

> And to that end heretofore they went about to sue to make themselves a corporation and . . . gathered contributions of poor men to maintain their busy labouring therein . . . Likewise at this tyme they have made like collections to set themselves on worke in suit and have gathered names and associate themselves with a few of the worst of that trade and (as it is thought) some names are marked and subscribed without the parties assent . . . and so they make clamorous show of

a multitude of 3,000 which is wholly untrue . . . The best and honestest sort of feltmakers who live by their true labour and skill make no such request.

The last we hear of the suit is a letter written by the Haberdasher Lord Mayor, Nicholas Woodrofe, to Lord Treasurer Burghley in March 1580, requesting that the Company's rights should not be impeached during his Mastership of the Company.[22]

Another area where the interests of the wholesalers clashed with those of the artisans was over the pressure exerted by the latter to ensure that haberdashery wares were finished in London before delivery to the chapmen for distribution to the provinces. In June 1585, for example, the workmen of the Company presented the Assistants with a petition complaining of members of the Company who 'sell greate quantities of wares unto them [chapmen] alltogether untrymmed, whereby they saie a multitude might be sett on worke and relieved, yf the same might be done here as heretofore'. On this occasion the artisans were fobbed off with a promise that if they put their grievances in writing they would be better considered, and nothing further is heard of the matter. The issue raised in 1585 recurred at the end of the century. In November 1599 the Assistants promised to refer the petition of the artisans to the Court of Aldermen in the hope of securing their support for legislation from Common Council. But no action was taken by either the Aldermen or the Common Council and one strongly suspects that the wholesalers were too influential in City politics for the proposals to have any chance of success.[23]

Some qualifications to this picture of artisans confronting the ruling wholesaling interests should be made clear. It would be mistaken to draw the battle lines within the Company too starkly, and wise to stress the ambiguity of the attitude of the artisans towards their rulers. The artisans appreciated that, however frustrating the Assistants might be on some issues, they nevertheless derived advantages from their membership in other areas. The rhetoric with which the Assistants framed the ordinance of 1574 on the trimming of hats by Company members shows that they took seriously their obligations to the poorer brethren, that membership of the community of the Company created a framework of obligations which aggrieved groups might hope to manipulate to achieve their objectives. The enforcement of restrictions on apprentice recruitment, and the prosecution of aliens and rural producers were areas on which a broad degree of consensus prevailed. Moreover, it would not be correct to see the business activities of all the Assistants as diametrically opposed to the interest of the artisans. Contrary to the impression one might gain from the polemics of the conflict over the search of wools in the later 1570s, the importers of wools included several merchants not free of the Haberdashers' Company at all, and those merchants who did deal in wools represented only a fraction of the ruling body of the Company.[24] Arguably the artisans could hope to achieve more within the framework of the Company and the powerful connections the Assistants brought with them than if they enjoyed their own company. Nor were the artisans a cohesive interest group. Bradford and Cawnton admitted that the richer feltmakers did not see eye to eye with them because they were in a position to resell faulty wools to the poorer feltmakers and were therefore not as seriously affected by the practices of the merchants.[25]

16. A 16th-century hatter at work, from Jost Amman's *Panoplia Omnium Artium*, 1568.

There are signs that the framework of the Company was adaptable to the problems faced by the artisans. The Wardens of the Yeomanry acted as a conduit for their grievances and were probably the mainstay of the enforcement of Company ordinances on apprenticeship recruitment which were so vital to the small masters and journeymen. It is true that the degree to which they could effectively represent the artisans was limited because the Yeomanry Wardenship was often held not by artisans but by young merchants as the first rung of the *cursus honorum*. But in response to this problem, we find that the Company was making efforts to associate the artisans directly in the regulation of the trade in the closing years of the 16th century. In 1591, for example, it was agreed that five feltmakers should assist the Master and Wardens in the enforcement of the ordinances, and that two of them should normally be free of Companies other than the Haberdashers. The latter provision was clearly a means of securing more effective control over feltmakers in other Companies by making the search appear less partial. The five artisans were probably the 'sitters for the hatmakers causes', referred to in 1596, who were active in prosecuting foreigners and in enforcing the making of satisfactory masterpieces as a precondition for setting up the trade by those in other Companies. To judge from the complaints of the Curriers' Company cited above, they probably also included representatives of the non-free feltmakers.[26]

Nevertheless it remains difficult to escape the powerful impression that the relationship of the artisans with the Company was a particularly fraught one. The support of the Assistants for the suits of the feltmakers was grudging. When in July 1591 the feltmakers asked for their assistance in the suit to the Privy Council for a grant of the penalties arising from the 1567 statute, the Assistants only promised to take advice of their learned counsel, 'so as it be at the charge of the said hatmakers'. In the following year the Assistants merely agreed that the artisans should enjoy the quarterage and fines taken of foreigners when their support for the campaign against the non-free element in the trade was invoked. The last straw was the threat in 1601 that the artisans be sued for about £10 owing to the Company for monies loaned for the suit in Parliament in 1601. The Assistants were extraordinarily reluctant to release Company funds for the suits of the artisans. Rather the craftsmen were expected to find the money themselves. The contrast with the Clothworkers' Company, whose rulers were confronted by a similarly articulate and discontented artisan group, and which poured huge quantities of Company revenue into suits for the benefit of the handitrade, could not have been more marked.[27] Many feltmakers doubtless came to feel that a brighter future could be secured outside the framework of the Haberdashers' Company.

There was, of course, one major advantage which the Company brought, and that was its control over access to the freedom of the City and the privileges that went with it. It was on the loyalties that the freedom generated that the rulers of the Haberdashers drew in their response to the incorporation of the Feltmakers as a separate Company in 1604. On 4 August 1604 James I granted a charter incorporating the feltmakers within London and a four-mile radius with powers of search over all workmanship and wools deceitfully packed. The Feltmakers' Company's rights of search were not to be prejudicial to the rights of the Haberdashers' Company, and two haberdashers were to join in the search if they wished.[28] In spite of these provisos the Assistants of the Haberdashers' Company were hostile to the new Company from the start. They claimed that the feltmakers were tied to them by their charter, the Act of Parliament of 1567, and the Star Chamber decree of 1578 and, as a Court order of 18 August 1604 explained, they doubted 'what inconveniences the same may growe to this Companie by reason thereof'.[29]

It is difficult to tell whether the feltmakers free of the Haberdashers' Company greeted the new Company with the same hostility as their rulers. As we have seen there were some issues, such as the search of wools and the restrictions on wholesalers, on which the free and foreign feltmakers could unite. It is striking that after 1604 it was the Feltmakers' Company which was most vigorous in the promotion of suits for the benefit of the handitrade. The statute of 1604 which closed some of the loopholes in the 1567 legislation was apparently promoted by the advocates of the new incorporation, working through the courtier, William Typper who, in a rather dubious transaction, was paid £100 in order to secure the passage of the act. In 1606 the Feltmakers were busily enforcing their ordinances, suing artisans who kept journeymen for terms of less than a year, who denied the search, and who set up shop without serving three years as journeymen. The fierce resistance they encountered led to further litigation in Star Chamber. In 1612–13 the Haberdashers had to spend over £200 in defending themselves from suits over the buying and selling of foreign wools.[30] This was action of a kind for which the feltmakers in the Haberdashers' Company had long been pressing. However, most of the supporters of the new Company did not enjoy the freedom of the City, and therefore the Assistants were able to play on hostility towards the non-free as a means of splitting the feltmakers. A long battle followed over the next half century in which the Aldermen and Common Council, strongly pushed by the Haberdashers, refused to support the new corporation.

The members of the new corporation sought to persuade the City authorities to admit them, or at least their rulers, to the freedom. But the City was generally hostile. As early as 1605 the Chamberlain of the City was instructed to shut up the shop windows of all foreign feltmakers. It is true that occasionally the City wavered. In March 1607, for example, the Court of Common Council, reporting itself favourable to the admission of leading feltmakers to the freedom by redemption, appointed a committee to consider the matter. In January 1612 a committee of the Court of Aldermen, acting at the instigation of Lord Harrington who had intervened on behalf of the Feltmakers, reported that they were favourable to their admission to the freedom on certain conditions, in particular that they should not involve themselves in haberdashery nor any other trade but feltmaking, that they should maintain their own poor, and that they should pay the sum of £1,500 to the City. But the attitude of the City became increasingly hard-line after the recommendations of the aldermanic committee were rejected by Common Council at a meeting on 28 February 1612. The Feltmakers now turned to the King for support, and their petition was referred back to the Aldermen in September. Again the Haberdashers stonewalled, bringing up some unspecified 'points questionable in law'. So the petition was referred to the Chief Justices of Common Pleas and King's Bench. The outcome was again inconclusive. Meanwhile, the Haberdashers put their energies into the promotion of suits against the foreigners. In November 1614, for example, the Assistants agreed to pay 30s. to Clement Mosse, the City Solicitor, and 20s. to Thomas Barrow, a professional informer, for their pains in litigation in the Mayor's Court against the foreign feltmakers for using their trades in the City contrary to an Act of Common Council. The Feltmakers, however, retained powerful backing, because the King wrote to the Aldermen in June 1618 to secure a stay of the informations against them.[31]

Another push for recognition was made in 1622. Again James wrote in support of the Feltmakers who were now asking that 400 of their members should be admitted to the freedom. Confronted by a specific royal request which had to be repeated when the City appeared to hesitate, Common Council appointed a committee to draw up a detailed exposition of the City's reasons for rejecting it. The City's petition was cleverly framed to appeal to the King's prejudices about the metropolitan environment. It pointed to the unsavoury nature of the feltmakers' trade, the fire risks from their furnaces, the threat that immigration of provincial feltmakers would be encouraged, and the increase in new buildings and the escalating costs of poor relief that would then ensue. Perhaps more crucial to the City were the arguments which were relegated to the close of the petition. The Common Council stressed that there were no precedents for even 'the tenth part of this number to be made free at one time in any age', and that even individual grants of the freedom were widely resented among the citizenry. And, reflecting the specific interests of the Haberdashers' Company, it was claimed that the government of the feltmakers rested by charter and Act of Parliament in the Haberdashers' Company in spite of the fact that the charter to the Feltmakers' Company expressed the King's will in a contrary manner.[32]

The Common Council thus stood firm against the King. In the years which followed the two Companies competing for control over the feltmakers continued to skirmish. In September 1632 the Haberdashers expressed themselves willing to take in some of the foreigners into their own Company probably in an effort to detach leading figures from the Feltmakers' Company. There was more trouble in 1640 when one Peter Robinson, a feltmaker free of the Haberdashers' Company, was imprisoned when he refused to appear at the Feltmakers' Hall with his masterpiece. Once again the Privy Council upheld the Feltmakers' position in the face of opposition from the Haberdashers.[33]

In the event it was not until the more liberal Interregnum regime was installed at the Guildhall that the Feltmakers' Company was able to secure a favourable hearing for its case. On this occasion the arguments of the feltmakers were skilfully contrived. They stressed how essential regulation by a Company was to the maintenance of standards, and pointed out that the Haberdashers' Company was an inappropriate mechanism of control because it now comprised only 40 master feltmakers, and because its wholesalers were themselves responsible for deceiving the consumer, for example in supplying shoddy goods as part of precontracted bargains, and were therefore unlikely to enforce ordinances. It would also be prejudicial to the City if the feltmakers were forced to leave, which they might be, if they did not get their way. The Haberdashers' arguments in reply strike one as visceral conservatism, an unwillingness to confront the new realities. The complaint that shortly there would be no hatmakers free of their Company, and that in this way there would be two companies 'called by one and the same name of trade' is not convincing when one considers that the Feltmakers' Company already included most of the hatmakers in the City: recognition of their right to trade in the City probably would not materially affect the position of the Haberdashers' Company. In the end the best the Haberdashers could come up with was that the Aldermen should consider 'the Antiquitye of ye Corporacion, the reputacion they have borne, the charge they have been at and yet are, the services they have donne and doe'. A committee of the Court of Aldermen duly reported in July 1650 that the feltmakers should be admitted to the freedom subject to certain conditions to protect the interests of the Haberdashers' Company. First, the Haberdashers were to retain control over all members of the Feltmakers' Company who were free of their Company, and these men were to be free to bind their apprentices with whichever Company they wished. Secondly, the Feltmakers were not to make any claim to the property of the Haberdashers' Company. Thirdly, the Haberdashers were to enjoy all their rights of search as before. With these provisos the Aldermen adopted the recommendation of the report and instructed the Chamberlain to enroll all apprentices bound to any freeman of the corporation of Feltmakers and make them free of the Company.[34]

The connections of the Haberdashers' Company with the regulation of the trade were therefore becoming increasingly attenuated in the early 17th century. The search does not appear to have been widely enforced, probably only activated when it became important to the Company to make a public demonstration of its powers, usually because there was the threat that they would otherwise be exercised by someone else. Thus there is evidence for the enforcement of the search in 1611, 1624, and 1650, all occasions coinciding with, or following upon, vigorous action by the Feltmakers.[35]

The story of the relations of the feltmakers with the Haberdashers' Company is not one of the happier episodes in its history. Conflicts of interest appear to have been sharper than in other Companies. Perhaps the sense of obligation of the Assistants towards the feltmakers was weakened because the Company's ability to enforce its will over the whole trade was undermined by the unusually large numbers of feltmakers who were either free of Companies other than the Haberdashers or not free of the City at all. Whether because of direct exploitation or, more likely, because of neglect, the feltmakers came increasingly to regard their future outside the Haberdashers as brighter than that within it.

Chapter Six

The Establishment of the Charities, 1550–1680

The century-and-a-half following the Reformation witnessed a huge expansion in the scope of the charitable activities of the Haberdashers' Company, as leading members vested it with the management of endowments for purposes as varied as the provision of grammar schools and university scholarships, the augmentation of the stipends of the parish clergy, the support of parish Lecturers, and the relief of the poor, both in London and in distant corners of the realm, by means as varied as almshouses, weekly pensions in outdoor relief, annual gifts of clothing, and stocks to provide materials for the poor to work upon and to subsidise apprenticeships for their children. Thus by 1680 the Company was running Schools at Bunbury, Monmouth, Newport, all on the Welsh border, and at Bunhill in the capital.[1] Nineteen exhibitions of between £5 and £6 13s.4d. per annum each were available to students at the universities as a result of the endowments. Lecturers were being supported at Newland in the Forest of Dean, Monmouth, and Bunbury, all on stipends of 100 marks (£66 13s. 4d.), supplemented by free accommodation. In London there were lectures paid for by the Company in the central parish of St Bartholomew Exchange, much frequented by the City's commercial elite, and in the suburban parish of St Giles Cripplegate, teeming with poor. Under the terms of the benefaction of Lady Mary Weld, the Company had purchased the impropriated tithes of Leiston in Suffolk, Wigston Magna, Bitteswell, and Diseworth in Leicestershire, and Albrighton in Shropshire. A bequest from Edmund Hammond had added the rectory of Awre in Gloucestershire to the Company's ecclesiastical patronage. Rather than passing into the hands of a lay impropriator paying the minister a pittance, the tithes now went to provide further financial support for the local ministers, essential if the services of well qualified men were to be secured. The Haberdashers were running almshouses at Newland, Monmouth, and Newport in the provinces, and at Snow Hill in the capital. Together these accommodated 46 people rent-free and provided pensions of between £5 and £10 per annum. The inhabitants of the almshouses of William Jones at Monmouth and Newland also received annual gifts of clothing. Other charities provided small sums to provincial parishes for distribution to the poor by the churchwardens. Lady Burghley, the wife of Elizabeth's Lord Treasurer, for example, arranged for the regular distribution of food to poor householders attending morning prayers at her local parish church of Cheshunt in Hertfordshire, as well as providing £3 each year to purchase wool and flax to set the poor of the parish to work. Company members were the beneficiaries of endowments directed specifically at the needs of the Company's own poor. In 1680 the annual yield of these endowments was £553, nearly a quarter of the total endowed charity administered by the Company. This charity was provided in a variety of ways. Prior to the destruction of the almshouses at the Company Hall in the Great Fire, some of it was directed at the ten almsmen the Company supported as a voluntary charity. Thereafter these benefactions joined a growing volume of pensions in outdoor relief, such as the nine pensioners supported at £8 per annum each by the Jones estate, or the 25 supported at 26s. per annum each by the bequest of Sir Nicholas Rainton. Other bequests, like those of Anne Whitmore and Florence Caldwall, provided clothing for poor members.

This achievement is the more remarkable when we compare the charity administered by the Company in 1680 with that available in 1560 (see Table 6.1). Whereas at Elizabeth's accession the charities administered by the Company yielded just £27 6s. 0d. per annum, by 1680 they were providing nearly one hundred times this amount, £2,394 per annum, representing a capital value of £47,880. As the vast majority of this derived from members of the Company, it might be taken as a tribute to the generosity of the mercantile elite who dominated the Company's affairs. However, lest we get carried away on a tide of superlatives, it would be salutary to insert a few qualifications. In fact the bulk of the endowments derived from a small group of men. The bequests of William Jones (d. 1615), who endowed the complex of charities at Monmouth and Newland as well as the London Lectureship and pensions to Company members, amounted to a staggering 27 per cent of the total. Another six benefactors accounted for a further 42 per cent of the expenditure. Having purchased the rectory and advowson of Bunbury from the Queen, in 1594 Thomas Aldersey endowed the Lectureship and School at Bunbury in Cheshire, providing for stipends of 100 marks to the preacher, £20 to the assistant curate, and £30 for the staff of the school, as well as requiring the distribution of £10 per annum to the poor of Bunbury and £7 per annum to the poor of the Company. Lady Mary Weld (d. 1623), as we have seen, left £2,000 to buy impropriated rectories. Edmund Hammond (d. 1642) provided £400 for the purchase of land for what were to be the Snow Hill almshouses, and vested the Company with a rent charge of £80 per annum from his property in Tower Street and Mincing Lane, to support the inmates of the almshouses and to finance annual distributions to the Company poor on the occasion of the St Katherine's feast. He left a further £1,000 for the purchase of impropriated rectories. Sir Nicholas Rainton (d. 1646) left £2,000 to support not only the Company poor but also the poor in St Bartholomew's Hospital and a variety of provincial parishes. In 1656, five years before his death, William Adams established the School at Newport in Shropshire as well as other charities for the benefit of the town, charging his Knighton estate with £175 per annum to provide the funding. £4,000 was given to the Company by Throckmorton Trotman (d. 1666), to support poor relief in St Giles Cripplegate in London and the parish of Cam in Gloucestershire, and to fund the School at Bunhill and the Lecturers at St Giles and Dursley in Gloucestershire. Thus these seven individuals accounted for well over two-thirds of the charity administered by the Company in the closing years of the reign of Charles II.

These men had directed a much higher proportion of their wealth than was customary towards charitable purposes. Few 17th-century Englishmen could match the generosity of William Jones, whose charitable bequests, including some not vested in the Haberdashers' Company, amounted to £19,440, a staggering 48 per

Key

○ Lectureships
● Advowsons
□ Schools
■ Distributions to poor
▲ Almshouses
△ University Town
X Manors

17.   Map to show the location of the Company's charitable interests in the 17th century.

cent of his total inventoried wealth of £40,065.[2] Much more characteristic were two haberdashers who died in the 1590s, the Alderman, Richard Gourney, with a net estate of £16,757, and the Common Councillor, Thomas Bowcher, with a net estate of £9,860, who both left the Company loan stocks, and whose total charitable giving amounted to just 3.2 per cent and 2.5 per cent respectively of their inventoried wealth. A general survey of philanthropy among the London elite undertaken by the author shows that those with estates of between £3,000 and £10,000 gave an average of 2.23 per cent of their wealth, and those worth over £10,000, 4.43 per cent. Jones was clearly a remarkable exception.[3]

Part of the explanation for Jones' generosity lies in the very simple fact that he died childless. Indeed there is no evidence that he ever married. The primary responsibility of patriarchs in this society was to provide for their families, and only once these responsibilities were discharged would men think of turning to large-scale charitable projects. Jones himself was very careful to provide for his kin, leaving nearly £15,000 among his various nephews and nieces. So seriously did he take his responsibilities that he did not omit to remember the daughter of the illegitimate child of his father, who received £100. But the absence of a wife and children, relationships in which people, then as now, invested most of their emotional energies, meant that his obligations towards his family were unusually limited, and he therefore could afford large-scale charitable works. What is equally striking is that the same is true of other of the major benefactors to the Company. Neither Aldersey, nor Rainton, nor Hammond, nor Adams left any children behind them.[4]

It is difficult to disentangle the complex mesh of motives which underpinned the action of these benefactors. It is perhaps overly cynical to point to the vanity of donors, but charitable endowments answered a persistent craving for the respect of posterity. Each gift was separately accounted for, and each year's Wardens thus reminded of the munificence of their forbears. Every recipient would be made aware of the individual whose generosity lay behind the gift by the practice of describing each charity after the name of its donor. The message could be driven home still more forcefully. By an order of the Court of Assistants issued in 1618, and repeated 40 years later, the recipients of William Jones' pensions in London were required to attend the weekly lectures at St Bartholomew Exchange both 'for theire better instruction in the Christian religion and to shew theire thanckfulnes to almightie god for so worthie and bountifull a benefactor'. The same message was projected visually. In 1596, shortly after the establishment of the Aldersey charity, it was agreed that the Hall should be hung with the portraits of ten of the Company's leading benefactors. In 1652 the Assistants ordered that the Company's charities should be 'methodized', and written up on tables to hang about the Hall 'whereby the memory of their worthy deeds may bee preferred and made knowne in honor to themselves and encouragement to and example of others whose hartes God shall stirr upp and incline to workes of this nature'. It was a message taken down into the provinces also. In 1657 the Visitors of Monmouth School recommended that a brass recording Jones' charity should be set up over the gateway, and that his portrait should be hung in the School. Thus donors could be assured a continually respectful audience.[5]

Prudential considerations also lay behind this outpouring of charity. The rapid demographic growth of the 16th and 17th centuries combined with sluggish economic expansion fuelled a growing polarisation of society, and the numbers of the poor mushroomed. There was undoubtedly a heightened perception of the problem of poverty. Thus when in 1634, 12 years before his death, Sir Nicholas Rainton began the annual distribution of £26 to 20 poor of the Company, it was explained that he acted in this way because he saw 'and much [pitied] the povertie and neede of the poore of this Company and the great nomber of them which yeerely appeare at St Katherines Day by their lamentable suite to this Company for releefe'. Elites had reason to be fearful of the threat posed by the poor, and sought to avert disorder by demonstrating their concern through the exercise of charity. A concern with social cohesion emerges in the way in which charity was distributed. It is striking how many donors arranged for the distribution of their bequests to the Company's poor at the St Katherine feast at which the election of the new Master and Wardens was published before the Livery. Florence Caldwall arranged that six gowns should be provided for poor members of the Company about the time of the Lord Mayor's swearing in at the end of October, so that the recipients would be ready to wait upon the Master and Wardens when they progressed to church on the day of the election feast. Thus at the moment when the leadership of the Company was renewed, the power of the elite was legitimated through the exercise of charity. Moreover, the bonds of patronage and deference which cemented this society were reinforced by the practice whereby Assistants nominated the individuals who were to receive the gifts. Thus it was customary for the Aldermen, Wardens and the most ancient Assistants to nominate the recipients of the gifts of Sir Nicholas Rainton, Thomas Aldersey, Edmund Hammond, and Robert Offley on the Saturday before the election day, and the gifts were handed over by the Assistants in person in the order of their precedence in the Company. In this way the hierarchy was articulated in a dual sense, both among the Assistants, and between the Assistants and the poor.[6]

But one of the most powerful impulses to charity lay in godly protestantism, and the motives with which the major themes of Calvinist religious discourse invested its adherents. It was not mere vanity, nor a fear that the world might be turned upside down, which alone pushed the London elite into charity. For all the downplaying by protestants of good works in achieving salvation, the exercise of charity remained essential as a mark of God's election, and this must play a major role in explaining the surge in philanthropic activity which provided the Haberdashers' Company with the bulk of its endowments. A closer look at the religious orientation of the Company's leading benefactors will illustrate the truth of this judgement.

Thomas Aldersey's puritan credentials are impeccable. He was among the 119 prominent citizens, who in 1584 put their names to a petition in support of the puritan lecturer of St Mary Bow, recently suspended as part of Archbishop Whitgift's campaign to enforce subscription to the Thirty-nine Articles and the Prayer Book. In the previous decade as a Governor of Bridewell Hospital he had been associated with the highly controversial campaign by the London godly to impose a stricter moral discipline in the capital by a crackdown on City prostitution, involving the punishment of well-connected clients. Bridewell was remembered in his will with a bequest of £50. He had a long-standing interest in charitable works, serving as one of the City's collectors for donations to poor scholars at the universities in the 1570s, and as treasurer of the Nantwich fire disaster relief fund in 1584. His nomineee to the Preacher's place at Bunbury was Christopher Harvey of Brasenose College, Oxford, described by one of his puritan successors as 'that learned and godly Master Harvey'. In his will, Aldersey promised to forgive Harvey a debt of £27 17s. 8d. for books he had supplied, provided that he remained at Bunbury for another seven years, 'God sparing him life further to plant the true knowledge of God there which is graciously begonne by his ministery'. The will also breathes that stern moralising spirit so characteristic of the godly. His generous bequests to the children of his nephew, John Aldersey of Berden, were accompanied by a warning that 'they maye not by my liberality be puft up in pryde as I knowe some can to muche be disposed'.[7]

We know rather less about William Jones because much of his working life was spent abroad, a resident of the Merchant Adventurers' colonies at Stoade, where he lived for 20 years, and later at Hamburg. But again his will provides crucial evidence of his religious attitudes. The mere fact of his having established three Lectureships is a significant indication of the priority he gave to the spreading of the gospel, a litmus test of godly commitment. In addition he left £1,000 to be distributed among the poor preachers in England at the discretion of Richard Gore, Stephen Egerton, and Richard Sedgwick. Egerton was a supporter of the Elizabethan presbyterian movement who, between three suspensions for nonconformity, served as Lecturer at St Anne Blackfriars in London. Richard Sedgwick, the preacher to the Merchant Adventurers at Hamburg, was a close friend of Jones, nominated as one of the overseers of his will and appointed to receive a personal bequest of £150. The English churches abroad were notorious hotbeds of radical protestantism, and were shortly to incur the wrath of Archbishop Laud for the deviant practices they sanctioned. Sedgwick himself, whose early career in England had seen him frequently in trouble with the church authorities, was credited with having introduced 'a purer church discipline' to the church at Hamburg, 'and the Lord abundantly blessed his labours'. In May 1615, the Haberdashers' Company, probably out of respect to Jones, appointed Sedgwick to the Lectureship at Monmouth.[8]

There are suggestive indications as to the religious attitudes of other of the Company's main donors. Lady Mary Weld's support for the learned ministry, which was so much a feature of the godly impulse, is evident in her bequest of the revolving fund to buy impropriations 'for ever, if it shall please Almighty God . . . unto the world's end for the increase of learned preachers', and in the £300 she left to the parish of St Olave Jewry for the support of a lecture to be preached 'by some godly, zealous and learned preacher'. Her rhetoric was decidedly godly:

> And I most hartily praye and intreate the said Company that shall have the said twoe thouszand poundes and their successors even as they love or tender the service of Almightie God, or the propagacion of Christian Religion or the increase of Christs Church or the benefitt and advancement of faythfull ministers and Preachers of God's word That they wilbe Carefull diligent and inclineable by all the best meanes they can . . . to putt in use the whole substance and effect of this my Will and devise within soe short tyme as may be after they shall have received the first some of twoe thousand poundes of myne executers.[9]

Another well-known puritan sympathiser was Nicholas Rainton. The preamble to his will was a lengthy personal testimony of his faith, expressing his confidence in his election among the saints in spite of his 'many abhominable sins'. In 1632 he had been elected by the City Feoffees for Impropriations as chairman of their meetings to give a casting vote, and Thomas Foxley, their clerk and Rainton's 'loving friend', was the beneficiary of a bequest of £5 in his will. Other godly legatees included three City ministers, Richard Culverwell, Fellow of Trinity College, Cambridge, and Rector of St Margaret Moses, Ephraim Pagett, minister at St Edmund the King, and Nathaniel Hardy, the presbyterian minister at St Dionis Backchurch, who had just announced his conversion to Anglicanism, but remarkably managed to retain his City preferments.[10] William Adams, the founder of Newport School, should also be numbered among the godly. His 'loving friends' included the presbyterian Dr Thomas Horton, Vice-Chancellor of Cambridge University during the Interregnum, and preacher of Adams' funeral sermon.[11] Yet another example of the prevalence of the godly among the donors was Throckmorton Trotman, founder of Bunhill School, who left his dwelling house and ten other properties to nine trustees composed of leading Congregationalist ministers 'for the education of poor ministers that they may prove Instrumentall in the convertion of soules'. Drawing up his will in 1663, dark days for nonconformists, his bequests testify to a keenly felt religious commitment.[12]

This is, of course, not to say that every donor was a puritan. Some haberdashers were rather more ambiguous in their religious outlook. Edmund Hammond left bequests to ministers as diverse as John Downham, the populariser of puritan doctrine, who served as Jones' London Lecturer at St Bartholomew Exchange from 1615 to 1650, and Laudians like Dr Christopher Potter, Provost of Queen's College, Oxford, and chaplain to Charles I. Conservative clerics were numbered among his relatives. His uncle was the Dr Henry Hammond, an Arminian and member of the Great Tew circle, and his cousin, Dr Charles Sonnibanke, was a canon of Windsor. Hammond left £500 to that most favoured of Laudian projects, the rebuilding of St Paul's Cathedral.[13]

But it is unquestionable that the godly impulse towards works of charity was a powerful one. Godly preachers drove home repeatedly the message that the wealth with which London's merchant elite had been vested was held in stewardship, that it could only be justified by the uses to which it was put. The puritan divine, William Perkins, stressed that the fact of wealth and the necessity of almsgiving were inseparable, for charity 'is the best kinde of thrift or husbandry . . . it is not giving, but lending, and that to the Lord, who in his good time will return the gift with increase'. Thomas Lever excoriated those merchants who used their wealth for the purposes of self-aggrandisement, for being not content with 'the prosperous welth of that vocacion to satisfye themselves and to helpe other, but their riches must abrode in the contrey to bie farmes out of the handes of worshypfull gentlemen, honeste yeomen, and poore laboringe husbandes'. It is true that these themes had a conventional ring by the later 16th century as part of the common humanist heritage, but they had added force for the godly, because of the 'salvation anxiety' in which the stark doctrine of predestination left many of the faithful. Uncertain of their salvation

18.   Monument to the puritan City magnate, Sir Nicholas Rainton (Master and Lord Mayor in 1632–3), at St Andrew's church, Enfield.

there was no way puritans could achieve assurance of their election among the saints save by going forth to do good works, showing what Richard Sibbes called 'a holy violence' in the world, and thus legitimating their godly status. Indeed the exercise of charity became part of the anti-catholic polemic of the period, protestant controversialists attempting to demonstrate their superiority over the Roman foe by the argument that 'the Gospell in the space of 60 yeeres hath brought forth more fruit, than twice so many of the late times of popery can shew'. Moreover, for the puritan, the connections between poverty, ignorance, and the triumph of the Anti-Christian forces of papistry, were more clearly apparent: papistry fed on ignorance, ignorance fed on poverty. Hence if the Gospel was to triumph, efforts must be made both to eliminate poverty, and to preach the Word of God more widely. Hence the emphasis on the funding of scholarships at the universities, the foundation of schools and lectureships, and the buying up of impropriated tithes so that ministers might be more adequately remunerated.[14]

It is striking that so much of the evangelical effort supported by the Haberdashers' Company was directed at those darker corners of the land where poverty, ignorance and popery together flourished. As Sir Benjamin Rudyerd put it in the House of Commons in 1628, 'there were some places in England which were scarce in Christendom, where God was little better known than amongst the Indians . . . where the prayers of the common people are more like spells and charms than devotions'. He was rehearsing a familiar theme among members of the establishment. Chief Justice Lewknor spoke in 1601 of 'great backsliding in religion . . . especially in the confines of the shires between England and Wales, as Monmouth, Hereford and Shropshire, and the skirts of Wales bordering upon them'. The area he described included Bunbury, Newport, Monmouth, and Newland, the locations for key Haberdasher charities. Bunbury was the Cheshire parish which harboured the largest number of recusants in the county in 1640. In 1603 Monmouthshire led the country with 117 convicted recusants per 1,000 of population. Protected by the earls of Worcester as the dominant local landowners, the Jesuits enjoyed a major centre of missionary activity in the College of St Francis Xavier in The Cwm. Richard Baxter described the Shropshire of his youth as a pastoral desert:

> These were the Schoolmasters of my Youth . . . who read Common Prayer on Sundays and Holy-Days and taught School and tipled on Week-days, and whipt the Boys when they were drunk, so that we changed them very oft. Within a few miles about us were near a dozen more Ministers that were near Eighty years old apiece, and never preached; poor ignorant Readers, and most of them of Scandalous Lives.

The Haberdasher Lecturers and Schoolmasters faced a decidedly uphill struggle.[15]

Many of those who enjoyed the patronage of the Haberdashers' Company in the early years of the operation of these charities were puritan in sympathies. Popular puritan preachers were often used by the Company in their assessment of the credentials of applicants to their posts. Thus Robert Brabourne, successor to the radical Richard Sedgwick at the Monmouth Lectureship, was appointed after consultation with the City preachers, John Downham, Thomas Gataker and one Mr Squire. Downham, the Company's Lecturer at St Bartholomew Exchange, was a constant consultant in the early 17th-century appointments to Company posts. It is true that Brabourne proved a disappointment, one of the easy-going, alehouse-gadding clerics so often denounced by the puritans, eventually ejected from Monmouth during the civil war by the committee for plundered ministers for his scandalous and malignant behaviour.[16] Newland furnishes a clearer case of constant puritan influence. It was served for the 12 years after 1615 by Lawrence Potts, a real hot protestant and recently preacher to the Merchant Adventurers at Middelburg. Potts was a divisive influence in the parish, from which there was a petition to the Company for his removal in 1620. It was ignored by the Assistants because the parishioners did not show 'good and sufficient cause for the displacing of the said mr Potts'.[17] He was succeeded by another puritan, Peter Symonds, whose support for Parliament in the civil war caused him to flee Newland, situated as it was in a predominantly royalist area, until ordered to return by the Company on the cessation of hostilities in 1646.[18]

The clearest instance of the use of the Haberdashers' charities as bastions of godliness against the hordes of Midian is the parish of Bunbury. When Aldersey's appointee, Christopher Harvey, died in 1601, the Company chose William Hinde, a disciple of Dr John Reynolds, a representative of the puritans at the Hampton Court conference, to fill the preacher's place. Hinde soon became a central figure among the Cheshire godly, a close friend of John Bruen, whose household was described as 'the common Inne, or constant harbour of the Church, and of God's children'. Frequently in trouble with the diocesan authorities for his refusal to follow all the Prayer Book ceremonies, he was nevertheless consistently supported by the Company, who interceded with the Bishop of Chester on his behalf in 1606 and 1618, the two occasions when he was suspended for nonconformity.[19] Hinde was succeeded in 1629 by Samuel Torshell, then curate at St Bartholomew Exchange, where Downham preached the Jones lecture.[20] Meanwhile at the school, Edward Burghall was appointed Usher (the assistant teacher responsible for the lower forms), and from 1633 enjoyed the Schoolmastership. Burghall's diary, packed full of the providences in which puritans sought God's hand revealed in the world, shows him to have been an exceptionally godly man. He delighted in the nasty fates which awaited those who dishonoured God by their drunkenness, adultery, usury, resort to unlawful games, and so on. Typical is the following entry:

> There was a remarkable judgement fell upon a wicked, debauched fellow in Bunbury, one Robinson a bearward, who followed that unlawful calling, whereby God is much dishonoured (especially at those popish festivals called wakes), was cruelly rent in pieces by a bear, and so died fearfully. That worthy man Mr Hind, who then preached at Bunbury, had, not without cause, much inveighed against those disorders which were usually at Bunbury wakes, and had threatened God's judgements against the same, but could not prevail utterly to remove them, tho' he endeavoured it to the uttermost: but in due time God makes good his word in the mouth of his ministers to the confusion of the wicked. Oh! that men would learn at last to be wise before the wrath of God falls upon them.[21]

It was not surprising then that Bunbury attracted the hostile attentions of the Laudian regime. In 1634 Archbishop Neile complained to the king that Bunbury

19.   The Chantry House at Bunbury given to the Company by Thomas Aldersey as a residence for the master of his school.

was a 'gross example of the evil of lectureships . . . a good nursery of Novelists'. Both Torshell and his curate, John Swan, were suspended until they had promised to perform the whole Prayer Book service.[22]

This brief exposition of the religious position favoured by those appointed by the Haberdashers has touched on just some of the practical problems encountered by the Company in the management of its charities. In the opposition of the parishioners of Newland to Lawrence Potts we can see the tensions between local interests and the Company rulers. In the difficulties faced by the Bunbury preachers we can see the suspicions harboured by the local ecclesiastical hierarchy towards the Company. The remainder of this chapter attempts to elaborate on these and other problems the charities brought to the Company, for many of these problems will be recurrent themes in the rest of this history.

The arrangements made by donors to finance their charities varied. Some supported relatively small payments to the poor or university exhibitions out of the interest received on loan stocks. For example, in 1603 Ralph Benskyn left the company £50 to be loaned for periods of four years successively to a merchant adventurer free of the Company who was to pay 20s. interest to the poor of St Martin Orgars parish in London. Donors could in this way support two charitable objects, both the relief of the poor and the supplying of credit at rates of interest far below those prevailing in the money market. Other donors arranged for the payment to the Company of rent-charges out of properties which would remain in private ownership. Thus the annuity of £80 per annum to support Hammond's almshouses came from properties in Tower Street, which were vested in his cousins and their descendants. Others still made cash bequests out of which the Company was expected to purchase lands. William Jones, for example, left the Company £17,040 to implement his charities. This was supplemented by his house in St Sithes Lane rented at £70 per annum, illustrating another option, the straightforward transference to the Company of property. Thomas Aldersey vested the Company with the rectory of Bunbury in 1594, but tied its hands by the lease he had made in October 1593 to his cousin, John Aldersey, for a period of 500 years at a rent of £122 per annum. The Aldersey family as lessees were responsible for the payments to the charity and repairs to the buildings subject to supervision by the Haberdashers' Company. Likewise, the payments under William Adams' foundation at Newport were initially made by the lessee of the manor of Knighton, the donor's nephew, Luke Justice.[23]

These arrangements all brought the Company their own distinctive problems. With the loan stocks the difficulty was that without extremely vigilant management by the Company, the funds supporting the charities might be lost if the creditors went bankrupt. Hence the insistence that all loans were backed by two sureties, friends of the creditor who would guarantee to repay the loan if the creditor failed. In 1607 the Assistants ordered that once a year the names of those having loans were to be read together with the names and addresses of their sureties so that it could be determined whether the sureties were sufficient, or indeed, even alive. If they were not, then they were to be replaced, or the money called in. The problem with such a procedure was that it required an intimate knowledge of the circumstances of sureties which, because they were usually men free of other Companies, the Haberdasher Assistants were unlikely to have. Not surprisingly the Company had sometimes to resort to litigation to recover loan monies. Moreover, it was tempting to the Company in periods of financial difficulty to raid the loan stocks as a financial reserve. This appears to have been the explanation for the disappearance of so many loan stocks in the 1670s as a result of the Company's financial embarrassment through the rebuilding after the Great Fire. In most cases the Company appears to have continued the charitable payments out of general Company stock. There may have been a short-term financial gain, but the Company was eroding its long-term financial base.[24]

The purchase of property from cash bequests to support charities was a complex business. The Company had to find estates free from encumbrances and possible legal challenges, and the Assistants had to negotiate licences from the Crown to enable the Company to hold property in mortmain. Thus the Assistants negotiated first with Sir William Throckmorton, a landowner in Gloucestershire, before purchasing the Hatcham Barnes estate in two stages (in November 1613 and April 1614) from Sir John Brooke for £7,280. Their legal adviser, Thomas Coventry, explained that 'he feared they wold hardlie fynd any purchase so cleere for the title and tenure as this is'. But there remained hiccups over securing the exemption of the estate from the mortmain legislation. Brooke promised that he would procure a private Act of Parliament to this effect covering the whole estate, but although the act passed both houses, the sudden dissolution of the Addled Parliament in 1614 meant that it failed to secure the royal assent. Nevertheless Brooke, who had agreed to secure the licence at his own expense should the parliamentary demarche fail, duly delivered it to the Court of Assistants on 27 November of that year.[25] The purchase of estates to fund the Newland charities was further delayed by the parish's contesting of the Company's right to manage the charity. Even after these disputes were resolved in 1618, the finding of an estate proved difficult. It took a search of four years, involving the viewing of estates in Buckinghamshire, Warwickshire, and at Rampton in Cambridgeshire, before the Company agreed with Sir Oliver Luke for the purchase of the manors of Caldecott and Puttocks in the parish of Eynesbury near St Neot's, Huntingdonshire.[26] The extraordinary burden on the time of Company officers in establishing charities is shown by the agreement of the Court of Assistants to pay their Clerk, Basill Nicholl, £100 for his great pains in supervising the buildings at Monmouth, in procuring two licences of mortmain, in following bills in Parliament, and in drawing up the conveyance.[27]

Other problems confronted the Company when the amounts left by the donor were insufficient to cover the full costs of establishing the charity. For all of Jones' generosity, the funds he left the Company did not cover the full costs of purchasing the lands and building the School and almshouses. The total expenditure on the establishment of the Monmouth charity, including the £3,400 spent on buildings, was £10,680, exceeding by £1,680 the money received from Jones for this part of his charitable scheme. £1,000 of the deficit presumably came from a bequest of that amount by Jones for the company's pains in managing the charity, but the residue would have come out of general stock.[28] Possibly the relatively healthy financial situation of the Company in the early 17th century meant that this was not a painful blow, but the later financial embarrassments caused by civil war taxation and the financing of post-fire rebuilding made this kind of problem a more acute one. The £400 left by Edmund Hammond for the purchase of the houses in which his almsmen were to live proved too little.[29] Likewise the £400 left by Throckmorton Trotman was inadequate for the purchase of a site for his School in St Giles Cripplegate. Relations between the Company and the parishioners were strained because the Company initially refused to underwrite the extra costs. In the end the Company agreed to use a year's income from the money intended for the payment of the Schoolmaster's salary to subsidise the building costs, although obviously such a solution delayed the opening of the School, and the parishioners were required to contribute part of the costs by subscription.[30]

Another problem faced by the Company in managing charities the income for which derived from land was that of taxation. This became a serious problem for the first time during the high tax regimes of the civil wars and Interregnum. As there was no surplus from the Jones estates to defray the taxes, the Company responded by cutting the salaries of its Lecturers and Schoolmasters and the pensions paid to the almsmen. In an effort to counter the problem, the Company ordered in October 1657 that every effort be made to secure the remission of the taxes on the Huntingdonshire estate which supported the Newland charity, but their best endeavours availed little, because the preacher there was petitioning (again unsuccessfully) in 1668 that his salary be paid without deduction for taxes.[31] In 1651 the Company threatened litigation against Mrs Bower, who enjoyed the tenements in Tower Street out of which Hammond had ordered his annuity to the Company to be paid, when she refused to pay it without a deduction for taxes, with which course they were eventually forced to comply.[32] It was doubtless because of these problems that William Adams secured the inclusion in the statute of 1660 confirming the letters patent establishing the Newport School of a clause freeing the manor of Knighton from all taxes imposed by authority of Parliament, a concession which no other Haberdasher charity enjoyed.[33]

Those charities which were paid by a local lessee, namely the Aldersey and Adams benefactions, produced problems of yet another type. First, there was the problem of securing proper accounting from the lessees of their expenditures. This became a problem at Bunbury during the civil war, when the payments lapsed. Even after the Restoration the Usher, John Swan, continued to dispute whether Aldersey had paid adequate compensation to his father, Nathaniel, then the assistant preacher, for covering for Torshell after the preacher's flight in 1643.[34] These disputes were exacerbated by disagreements as to what precisely were the responsibilities of the Aldersey family. In particular, the Company had to apply a considerable amount of pressure to induce them to repair the houses of the Schoolmaster and Usher as their lease required. He was reminded of this obligation in a visitation by the Company in 1657, but the warning had still not been heeded nearly four years later.[35] There was also the question of what influence the family should exert over appointments. In 1633 the Company had ignored Samuel Aldersey's recommendation of George Burges for the vacant post of Schoolmaster, picking the godly Usher, Edward Burghall, instead. It is true that his candidate, John Orpe, then succeeded Burghall to the Usher's place, but Orpe had other referees too, including Torshell, whose support may have weighed more heavily with the Company. The family nominee for the Schoolmaster's place was again rejected by the Company in 1655, although it does not appear that Thomas Aldersey harboured a grudge, because the successful candidate, Annias Vaughan, soon won his respect, and in later years he cooperated with the preacher, Francis Moseley, in making recommendations to fill vacancies.[36]

This discussion of appointments brings us to one of the central problems of charity management, that of balancing the pressures for a share in decision-making from locals, sometimes themselves divided into factions, and the demands of professional competence and the assertion of the Company's control on which its 'honour' and 'worship' depended. These tensions were present from the outset. As early as 1617 the parishioners of Newland challenged the Company's right to nominate the inmates of the almshouses and its control over the lands to support the charity, although they did not pursue the struggle into the courts as the Company expected. But their efforts to get rid of Lawrence Potts, the Lecturer, show that they remained unsatisfied on the basic point.[37] At Monmouth there was a dispute between the Company and the townspeople in 1649 when the town installed an almsman before getting the

20.   The old schoolhouse at Monmouth.

Company's formal approval. The Company was determined to uphold the point of principle and forced the town council to write with a formal acknowledgement of the Haberdashers' power to appoint the almspeople. In future the town council was to nominate three candidates from whom the Company would choose one to fill vacancies.[38]

The Company appears to have made an effort to accommodate the wishes of the locals within the constraints of the School statutes. There were tensions at Monmouth over their insistence that the Schoolmasters should not hold any other ecclesiastical preferments because the townspeople took a more flexible line, arguing that this was a sufficient price to pay for the services of an able man. Both Robert Frampton and Charles Hoole, Schoolmasters of Monmouth between 1658 and 1663 and 1663 and 1664 respectively, were supported by the town against a critical Court of Assistants in spite of the cures of souls they enjoyed elsewhere.[39] But the Company was willing to listen to the town's advice in making appointments. Thus William Morrice, Schoolmaster from 1664 to 1672, was elected after the Company received 'several letters from the Towne of Monmouth and some eminent gentlemen of the county on his behalfe', although the Assistants took the precaution of checking out his credentials with a couple of London clergymen and Mr Goad, the Schoolmaster of the Merchant Tailors' School in the capital. In choosing Morrice, the Company actually passed over Mr Rawlins, their assistant curate at Awre, and Thomas Pollington, a son of one of their Assistants. The potential for tension between the town and the Company is clearly revealed in the petulant tone the Assistants took when replying to complaints against Morrice from the town in 1671. They deeply resented the complaints coming to them because, as they asserted, they had nothing to do with his election beyond their inclination to give the town and the gentlemen of the county what they wanted. They added that in future, they would act on their own in making appointments 'without any interposicion or remendacion in regard this Court is likely to provide better for them herein then they can for themselves'. When they elected his successor in the following year their sensitivity over appointments emerges in the order that the Clerk register the certificates produced on behalf of the successful candidate 'to ye end the same may be preserved and this Court ye better justified in that their eleccion'.[40]

This tussle was but the prelude to a far more bitter controversy at Monmouth over the appointment of a successor to Charles Goodwin as Lecturer in 1676. There were six applicants, and after trial sermons in London from a short-list of four, the Court chose John Wickins. But the decision was contested by the town who supported Herbert Pye, the local Vicar and a member of a local family, and prevented Wickins from securing the necessary preaching licence from the Bishop of Hereford. The local authorities enjoyed the powerful support of the leading local magnate, the Marquess of Worcester, whom the Court of Assistants frantically tried to contact to disabuse him of the misinformations with which the townspeople had won him over. When, at length the licence was obtained, Pye was induced by the local Recorder and Townclerk, apparently on the promise of an increase to his stipend, to deny Wickins the use of his pulpit, so that Wickins was forced to preach at a church nearby Monmouth. The town alleged, on what authority it is not clear, that it had been the founder's original intention that the local Vicar should enjoy the Lectureship as the Vicarage was only worth £22 per annum. Together with the Lecturer's salary of 100 marks the united cures would provide an adequate living. In fact Wickins' predecessor had held both posts, establishing a precedent, but the Company denied that Jones had intended this to be a general rule, pointing out that those who held both posts had only been presented to the Vicarage after their election by the Haberdashers, and the Assistants asserted their complete autonomy in matters of appointments.[41]

Another flash-point at this time was provided by the Company's treatment of the Usher at Monmouth school, Edmund Evans, appointed in October 1677. The School appears to have been in a parlous condition for much of the post-Restoration period, with the number of scholars declining sharply. Evans was instructed to report on the state of the School, and in particular to investigate the complaints that had reached the Court against Thomas Basset, the Headmaster. In suggesting that Evans spy on his boss the Company were inviting trouble. Sure enough, in July 1678 the Usher delivered a paper with 'articles and informations' against Basset, and relating to differences between the two men over their rights to fees from the admission of scholars. The Court responded by appointing the preachers at Newland and Monmouth to investigate the charges. Basset apparently managed to clear himself, and it was concluded that there was 'noe better way to preserve and recover the sayd Schoole then by parting the sayd Master and Usher'. Evans, who had been appointed only during good behaviour, was therefore dismissed in September 1678. This was an astonishing outcome, and it is difficult to resist the conclusion that the Usher had been shabbily treated. After all he had been encouraged to stir things up on the grounds that all was not well with the running of the School before his arrival. The conclusion that things would settle down on his removal was therefore naive in the extreme. Basset was clearly a Schoolmaster of dubious credentials. In November 1678 he was charged with a catalogue of offences which make one still more sympathetic to the Usher. He had taken fees from children who should have been freely taught; he was over-severe in punishing the boys; he was characterised by a 'morose and ill humor and carriage' and an 'indulged Sloth and negligence'; he was inclined to quarrel with his ushers; he kept the boarders in poor quality accommodation; and he refused to sit with the boys in church. Not surprisingly the town took Evans' side alleging, with probable exaggeration given the short time he was actually at the School, that 'by his industry, good behaviour, learning and method in teaching he had lately raised the schoole from its late low and despised condition to a good degree of reputacion'. The Corporation supported Evans in his refusal to hand over the Usher's house to his successor.[42]

These disputes reached the Court of Chancery in 1679, and focused criticism of the Company's whole management. The townspeople demanded that other persons, presumably themselves, be appointed to receive the charity and make the appointments. They cast doubt on whether the Company had in fact applied all of Jones' money to the charity, and complained that the dimensions of the buildings appointed for the schoolhouse, almshouses, and the accommodation for the Lecturer, Schoolmaster and Usher suggested skimping by the Company. In reply, the Company stressed the costs of the licences from the Crown and the frequent journeys between Monmouth and London. The decree which emerged from Chancery in 1681 upheld the status quo. The Company's rights to appoint the teachers and Lecturers were enshrined in the statutes for the charity, so that the law stood with the Company. Although initially the Monmouth Corporation refused to cooperate in making nominations to vacant almshouses as a sign of their frustration with this outcome, it appears to have been reconciled by a mission from one of the Wardens, Robert Chaplin, a man with good local connections, in the following year.[43]

This account of the disputes at Monmouth has touched on some of the recurrent problems encountered by the Haberdashers in the management of other of their charities. First, the tendency to blame the decay of Monmouth School on the masters rather than on the inappropriateness of a classical curriculum already felt in some quarters is paralleled by the criticisms of Annias Vaughan at Bunbury in 1661 for his 'negligence and indiscreet correction of the scholars'.[44] Secondly, the conflict between Basset and Evans is mirrored by the disputes between Francis Potts, Schoolmaster of Newport School from 1663, and the Usher already in office. Although Potts was required to leave in October 1666, it was difficult to fill the vacant post because of Millington's reputation for quarrelsomeness. The Company was probably relieved when Millington became ineligible to continue as Usher because of his promotion to the post of minister of Newport. The next two Schoolmasters at Newport were allowed to choose their own Ushers. Such conflicts were probably inevitable given the close proximity in which the Schoolmasters and Ushers had to live, their rival claims to fees, and the jealousy likely to be felt by any usher confronted by a master who had frustrated his own prospects of promotion.[45] A third area in which the Monmouth disputes were typical of those elsewhere lies in the town's proposal to unite the Vicarage and Lectureship. This reflects an already dawning perception that the salaries provided by the founders were inadequate to attract well qualified candidates. The frequency with which the Lecturers and Schoolmasters sought to hold on to additional preferments, with the result that they neglected their responsibilities to the Haberdasher charities, reflects their need to boost their incomes.[46] Nowhere were the pressures more acutely felt than at Bunbury where the teachers' salaries were much lower than those provided at the other Haberdasher schools. Whereas the Schoolmaster at Monmouth received £60 per annum, his equivalent at Bunbury received just £20 per annum. In 1658 there had been an abortive proposal to unite the stipends of the Schoolmaster and Usher, and seven years later the parishioners promised to increase the Schoolmaster's stipend by £10 if the Company allowed their nominee. But he was rejected because not possessed of the relevant university qualifications.[47] These problems were to become the more acute as the financial pressures on the Company tightened in the decades after the Great Fire.

Table 6.1: Annual Yield of Endowments for Charitable Purposes (£ per annum)

Date	1560	1600	1640	1680
Company Poor	24. 1.4	51. 5.10	214.10.2	553. 0.2
Poor of London	0.17.4	8.12.8	27.13.0	47.13.0
Poor in Provinces	NIL	22. 1.4	325. 0.2	435. 8.2
Poor in Prisons	0.12.0	5. 0.0	6. 0.0	6. 0.0
Poor in Hospitals	NIL	9. 6.8	45. 9.1	57. 9.1
University Exhibitions	NIL	30. 0.0	84. 0.0	104. 0.0
Schools	NIL	30. 0.0	125. 0.0	272. 0.0
Preachers	NIL	89. 6.8	462. 0.0	864.13.4
Company Officers	1.15.4	15. 7.4	36.13.11	51.17.3
Total	27. 6.0	261. 0.6	1326. 6.4	2394. 1.0

Note: The figures for 1680 are notional because of the effect of the Great Fire on rental income: they represent what the Company would otherwise have been receiving.

Chapter Seven

The Company in Difficulties, 1650–1800

Surveying a parlous financial situation in 1753, the Company's Grand Committee identified the root causes of its problems as lying in the loans made to Parliament between 1640 and 1643, and in its losses in the Great Fire of London of 1666.[1] The weak financial base of the Company proved the most acute of the problems confronting the Assistants, but it was not the only factor in the difficult century and a half which followed the Civil War. Financial problems were compounded by the Company's weakening hold over the loyalties of its members, demonstrated most vividly in a growing reluctance to take up the Livery and to serve high Company office. The truth was that the high costs of membership were not matched by commensurate benefits, as the freedom was no longer essential to the pursuit of trade in a capital which had burst its medieval bounds. This chapter will examine the nature of the Company's difficulties in this period and its responses to them, while the chapter which follows looks at the implications of these problems for the management of the charities.

Between October 1640 and August 1643 the Haberdashers were required to lend a total of £15,400 to the government. Although Charles I's request for a loan of £4,500 had been turned down in August 1640, just two months later the Company responded with alacrity to his request for the loan of £3,850, now backed by the bonds of ten of his leading aristocratic opponents who had just induced the King to call a Parliament. In June 1642, as Civil War became more likely, Parliament approached the City for the loan of £100,000, of which the Haberdashers' share was £7,700. A further loan of £3,850 was made in August 1643 as royalist forces closed in on the City. The loans of October 1640 and August 1643 were supposedly to be repaid within six months, and that of June 1642 within a year.[2] But repayment was never made. Sales of plate to ease the burden of debt in April 1643 had realised £727 9s. 2d.[3] The only way Parliament's financial demands could be satisfied was by borrowing from Company members on the common seal, and paying interest at the rate of eight per cent per annum: thus the Company incurred interest payments of over £1,200 each year from late 1643.[4] So weak was the Company's financial position, and so heavy the taxation imposed by Parliament that it was often necessary to borrow still more to make the interest payments. By 1650 the Haberdashers owed £18,000 and were paying interest of £1,500 per annum. Joining with the other Livery Companies, the Haberdashers repeatedly petitioned Parliament for repayment without which, they noted in August 1649, 'this Company must inevitably sincke under ye burthen'. But it was to no avail: Parliament's debt remained unpaid at the Restoration.[5]

In responding to the challenge represented by its huge debt, the Company resorted to devices which were to become very familiar in ensuing years. The Assistants were

89

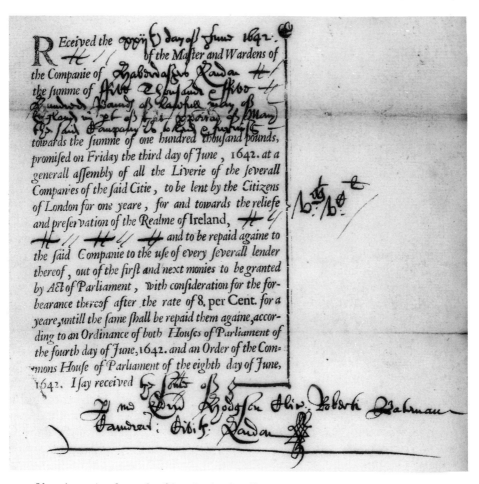

21. A receipt from the Chamberlain's office for £5,500 as contribution to loan to Parliament, June 1642.

averse to the sale of property, but in 1650 a committee was appointed to look into the possibility of granting properties on long leases to raise windfalls through heavy entry fines. In September 1658 an entry fine of £700 on a property at Aldgate was directed towards the repayment of the Company's debts.[6] The fines taken from members on admission to the Livery were also used in the same way. In November 1661 it was suggested that the Livery should be expanded up to a maximum of 200 with the explicit purpose of reducing the Company's debts.[7] Another development was the practice of admitting men to the Court of Assistants on payment of a fine without serving the usual offices. Thus in 1663 it was agreed that 20 men should be admitted as Assistants, paying fines of £40 apiece.[8] In order to economise, new Company projects were financed by subscriptions rather than raiding stock. The building of a new barge and barge house in 1656–8 was financed through subscriptions from the Livery.[9]

The modest gains that were made as a result of these measures were consumed by that 'most horrid malicious bloody flame' which destroyed much of the City between 2 and 6 September 1666. Assembling on 2 October at Cooks' Hall in Aldersgate Street, the Assistants contemplated the wrath of God. They declared themselves

> very sensible of the great Displeasure of Almighty God which hath beene lately manifested against this City in the late dreadfull and lamentable fire, and how deeply with the rest of the City this Company and members of it doe suffer thereby (their Hall and most of their houses in London being consumed).

Their desire, they continued, was 'to implore the mercies of the Divine Majestie for sanctifying this heavy hand and averting the further effects of his just wrath against us'. They also recognised the need for urgent action to protect the charitable trusts for which they were responsible and to pay the great debts they had recently incurred in trying to fulfil them.[10] A committee was appointed to look into the finances of the Company and to 'do all transactions in connection with company business'. Because of the immense amount of work involved and because of the somewhat unwieldy nature of the Court of Assistants, over the next few years a succession of committees tackled the problems of rebuilding the Hall, negotiating with tenants over rebuilding, and raising the money to repay the Company's debts. Sometimes all Court members were authorised to participate; sometimes a more select group consisting of the Master and Wardens and named Assistants, but in all cases the quorum for meetings was small (between three and seven), so that business might be transacted with greater expedition. In organising the rebuilding the Company took the first steps in the direction of the establishment of standing committees.[11]

The Haberdashers proceeded with the rebuilding of their Hall with great speed. In October 1667 the Assistants were considering plans from Edward Jerman, one of the three Surveyors appointed by the City Corporation to assist Sir Christopher Wren and others in controlling the rebuilding of the City, and they were able to hold their first meeting on the new premises within seven months (6 May 1668).[12] The building nevertheless remained incomplete, as subsequent minutes make clear. The staircase between the Hall and the parlour was inserted in the winter months of 1670–1, and the Hall roofed in early 1671. The decoration of the interior was a still more protracted affair. Arrangements were made for ceiling, plastering, and flooring the hall, and senior Court members invited to pay for the glazing of windows incorporating their arms, in 1672. Wainscot was obtained from Essex House in 1675 at a cost of £26 and used in the great and little parlours, but the wainscotting of the Hall proper was deferred until 1681 when the Livery were invited to subscribe for the project. It was at this late date also that the paving of the Hall courtyard and the completion of the lantern were undertaken.[13]

The rebuilding of the Company's other properties in London was financed by the

HABERDASHERS' HALL.

22.   Exterior of the post-Fire Hall, designed by Edward Jerman.

tenants, to whom the Company granted of necessity very favourable terms. Mr
Fletcher, a tenant in the Poultry, was granted a 99-year lease and had his rent
reduced by £4 to £10 per annum. By order of the Fire Court established by Parliament to adjudicate the disputes between landlords and tenants, the rents of the
properties in Lombard Street which supported Sir Nicholas Rainton's charity were
reduced from £100 per annum to £65 per annum, and the tenements leased for 61
years. Such arrangements had the effect not only of undermining the Company's
long-term financial base, but also of making it impossible for the Company to fulfil
its charitable trusts. As a result of the decree relating to the Lombard Street properties, the Haberdashers cut the charitable expenditure on the Rainton estate from
£87 1s. 4d. per annum to £56 14s. 0d. per annum, and found their surplus after
payment of the charities cut from £12 18s. 8d. per annum to £8 6s. 0d. per annum.[14]
     The erosion of the value of the Company's London properties was not immediately

made up by the rural landholdings. This was because the later 17th century was a period of agricultural depression and low rents as a result of a stagnating population. When it came to renewing the lease of the manor of Puttocks Hardwick in 1672, the Company took cognizance of 'the Generall fall and decay of Rents in all Counties', and granted favourable terms. Tenants found themselves in difficulties. Richard Spooner, tenant at Hatcham, was so heavily in arrears by 1683 that the Company took steps to dispossess him. And when it came to leasing his farm in 1687 the bids which came in to the Company were lower than the existing rent.[15]

Such a situation made the clearing of the Company's accumulated debts, which stood at approximately £10,000 in 1671, a particularly difficult operation. Four basic strategies were employed.[16] First, Company members were invited to participate in subscription schemes. Secondly, the Livery and the Court of Assistants were expanded, the fines of £25 and £40 respectively being earmarked for debt repayment. Thirdly, where possible, property was sold off. Finally, although this expedient can hardly be described as a strategy, charity funds were raided. Each of these methods will be discussed in turn.

A variety of subscription schemes was under consideration from 1669. In December 1671 an annuity scheme was projected whereby members would subscribe monies for two lives at six per cent, but the scheme seems to have required greater authority than was available under the ordinances, and was replaced by straight-forward donations.[17] The scheme was underway by the early months of 1672, a committee meeting daily in early February to induce Court members to participate. Its activities soon broadened to include Liverymen. Enthusiasm was however lacking. The complaint made on 17 October 1672 that many Liverymen had not subscribed was to be echoed many times in the ensuing years. In April 1674 it was noted that, if effective action was not taken to carry on the subscription scheme, it would 'fall to the ground and come to nothing'. There was much foot-dragging even on the Court, and eventually sanctions were applied to the refusers in the form of the withdrawal of the right to participate in the distribution of the Company's charity. The high hopes expressed in 1674 that the scheme might raise £600 per annum were not realised, but the Company did receive a total of £1,698 from the Livery towards the rebuilding of the Hall.[18]

Recruitment to the Livery and the Court of Assistants was increasingly the method of raising cash quickly. In 1671 it was reckoned that £3,000 could be raised at once by these means. Certainly in October 1673 it was recorded that £1,200 had been received from admissions to the Court of Assistants alone, and a further 25 were admitted early in 1675, raising another £1,000.[19] But the most persistently used device was recruitment to the Livery which became increasingly diluted. In October 1673 a committee was appointed for taking into the Livery as many as it thought fit; in early 1675, 25 were admitted. Sixty-eight names were put forward for the Livery in June 1676. In December 1677 the Court looked favourably on a proposal for 12 men a year to be admitted to the Livery in order to pay charities for which there was no settled revenue. The following summer, in the largest clothing ever seen by the Company, they allowed the Livery to be offered to 136 men with the explicit purpose of raising the money to pay the Company's debts.[20]

The third option, that of sales of property, was actively pursued in the mid–1670s. In April 1674 several members of the Court expressed an interest in purchasing the reversions to several of the Company's London properties, and offers were accepted from Mr Hams, Peter Daniell and Henry Cornish. A general review of property was ordered, and a committee report swiftly produced by October. At the heart of the proposals was a scheme for reordering the finances of the Jones charities. It was proposed to sell the Huntingdonshire farms of Caldecott and Puttocks Hardwick, for which it was hoped to receive £5,000. This sale would finance the buying out of the remaining 22 years of the lessees at Hatcham Barnes for a probable £3,000 which would enable the Company to cash in on the improved rent, estimated at £300 per annum above the £320 per annum then paid. This would be sufficient to discharge both the Monmouth and Newland charities, and the Company would have £2,000 in hand to repay its ever-pressing creditors. Other sales about London would realise £3,670 making a total gain to the Company of £5,670.[21] The scheme was implemented over the following year. Caldecott was sold in January 1675 for £2,221 17s. 8d., Puttocks Hardwick for £2,394 in April. Thomas Pepys was bought out at Hatcham for £2,047 10s. 0d., and Oliver Bowles for £920, leaving the Company with a rather less than anticipated gain to its stock of £1,648 7s. 8d.[22] Further sales of property mainly in London realised £2,875 between February 1675 and June 1678. Care was taken in these sales to ensure that the Company's charities were not compromised. Those to whom the properties were sold were made responsible for the payment of the annuities due for charitable purposes. Thus Nicholas Burt was sold a house in Holborn for £1,000 in satisfaction of debts owing to him, on the condition that he continue to pay 21s.8d. to the Company for the charities of the donor, Alderman Garrard.[23]

In spite of a rhetoric which stressed the primary importance of maintaining the charities, some of the Company's actions served to undermine charitable trusts. It is striking how many of the loan stocks intended for young freemen disappeared into the Company's general funds at the Great Fire. This expedient was a rather foolish measure because it eroded the capital intended for the maintenance of scholarships and some annual gifts to the poor, which the Company continued to pay.[24] Also swallowed up in the rebuilding fund was the £4,000 bequeathed by Throckmorton Trotman in 1663 for charities in Gloucestershire and St Giles Cripplegate, London. The Haberdashers did not follow Trotman's instructions to buy lands to support the charity, putting the money into the Company stock, and arranging to settle tenements in Maiden Lane, St Swithin's Lane, Sherborne Lane, and Holborn from the Company's existing estate to support the charities. This was a reasonable enough course of action in the circumstances but it further eroded the Haberdashers' long-term capital base. Moreover, although the charities continued to be paid, the Court noted with alarm that the order for the appropriating of tenements to the Trotman charity had still not been implemented in 1702.[25] Yet another fund to be swallowed up in the years after the Fire was that supporting Lady Weld's benefaction for the purchase of impropriated tithes. The Company failed to account with the Governors of Christ's Hospital after 1679. In 1702 the Company was required to answer to the Commissioners for Charitable Uses at the suit of Christ's Hospital for its management of the fund. The Haberdashers explained that the great sums exacted from them by previous governments and the costs of rebuilding meant that they in fact had not a penny of the £1,323 for which they had accounted as being due to the charity in 1679.[26]

The measures just described certainly contributed to an easing of the Company's financial problems over the course of the 1670s. In November 1678 the Assistants recorded that the debt had been reduced from £10,000 to £2,500 since 1670, and that the Company had paid out on building £4,500 over and above the money received in subscriptions.[27] However, there was a price to be paid in terms of the weakening of the Company's capital base, which meant that finances remained precarious well into the 18th century. Hence the oft-expressed anxieties about the number of charities paid by the Company without a settled fund; hence the retrenchments or cuts made to the outgoings of various charities in 1693. Fines remained essential to the financial well-being of the Company. In 1740 the Master and Wardens pointed to the deteriorating situation over the previous decade which had turned a credit balance of £718 1s. 11½ in November 1729 into a debt of £1,146 14s. 6.d. in November 1739. It was reckoned that without fines the Company's outgoings would exceed receipts to the tune of £600, and that it was unreasonable to expect that so high an income from fines could be sustained for long. The only course of action, they concluded, was an economy drive.[29] But the recommended economies never materialised. The Court authorised the sale of a few annuities; it took a firm line with a defaulting tenant at Pitley; it attempted to control expenditure more tightly by requiring that no repairs costing more than 40s. be made without their authority; and it insisted on accounts being available at all meetings so that the financial position would be clear. But no economies were implemented.[30]

It was only in 1753 that the Company showed itself prepared to take the bit between the teeth. The Grand Committee had been instructed to examine the state of the Company's finances on 20 October 1752, and reported almost exactly a year later (16 October 1753). The report made very gloomy reading. Anxiety centred once again on the unappropriated charities, which amounted to £466 19s. 2d. per annum (including the Trotman charity accounting for £173 5s. 0d. per annum) after deduction of land tax at 3s. in the pound on those prpoerties liable. The Company's unappropriated estates yielded just £157 10s. 2¾d., including £133 per annum from the tenements set aside for the Trotman charity. The Company's corporate income (excluding for this purpose the various appropriated funds) amounted to £1,013 8s.1¼d. to cover outgoings of £993 5s. 6¼d., which left it highly vulnerable, given that so much of its income was constituted by casualties such as fines and fees for apprentice bindings and freedom admissions. The prospects for increasing this income substantially were dim, chiefly because the potential for raising fines was exhausted: 'it is generally apprehended that the Yeomanry is pretty well drained, and that there are not many to be found capable of taking on them the Clothing of this Company'. The Company also owed the Aske charity £2,128 1s. 10d. Worse still, the Assistants faced heavy outgoings in ensuing years. £2,000 was due to be laid out on impropriations from the Weld fund in 1757. If raised from investments in public funds, income would be reduced by approximately £60 per annum.

So what was to be done? The Assistants were reluctant to invoke the ordinances to make an assessment on the membership probably because of the likelihood that they would encounter a storm of opposition. The memory of the post-Fire subscriptions was not an entirely happy one. In a rather candid note to the report the committee pointed out that the Company had not reached its present plight by mismanagement *'other than* their spending more Money annually than was suitable to their Circumstances' (my italics). The solution was obvious. The committee recommended swingeing cuts in corporate expenditures. Dinners should be ended. £70 10s. 0d. could be saved by ending the feasting and use of the barge on Lord Mayor's day. £63 9s. 0d. could be saved from the corporate allowances by ending the dinners on the Master's day and at the Publication ceremony. Still more could be raised if the Master and Wardens could be induced to hand over the money they would have spent on those junketings, about £15 each for the Wardens and £25 for the Master. Further economies of about £34 could be made in the dinners provided at bindings and freedom ceremonies and at committee meetings. With bankruptcy looming and the Company confronting the prospect of being unable to discharge its charitable trusts, things were sufficiently bad to concentrate the minds of the Assistants. They accepted the recommendations in full, although slightly reducing the amounts payable by the Master and Wardens in lieu of dinners to £20 and £12 10s. 0d. each respectively. On 26 October 1753 the report was read to the Livery who expressed themselves satisfied, and thanked the Master and Wardens 'for their prudent and timely care'.[31]

Other devices followed in the years which followed. In 1754 the Land Tax Commissioners were persuaded to reduce the valuation of the Hall from £230 to £200. A serious effort was made to improve the collection of quarterage. The barge was sold to the Tallow Chandlers' Company in 1755 for £262 10s. 0d. Advertisements were placed in the press for the letting of the Hall. In September 1754 the Castle Concert hired the Hall and binding room for 30 subscription concerts between October and May for 40 guineas. This arrangement was renewed annually. From 1759 the patrons of the Castle Concert were joined by the City Assembly who hired the Hall, binding room, great parlour, and dancing room for weekly meetings between October and May paying £84. Publicity was given to the Company's efforts to retrench its finances by arranging for the printing of 500 copies of the *Brief Statement* for distribution to members. This was in the hope of tapping their benevolence to provide contributions to a fund started by a bequest from William Seabrooke for supplying the unappropriated charities.[32]

But in so far as the economy drive resulted in the loss of entertainments it contributed to the weakening sense of identity of members with the Company, which in turn made it more difficult to escape from financial trouble by subscription schemes as the goodwill was no longer there. The economies were therefore an aggravating factor in a deep-seated malaise among members. The fact of the matter was that the benefits of membership of the London Livery Companies were increasingly unclear. By the later 17th century the custom of London had made serious inroads into the occupational homogeneity of the Haberdashers' Company. A sample of 30 members of the middle station from the Company recently surveyed by Dr

Peter Earle shows 11 haberdashers, three merchants, two leathersellers, two lacemen, a cloth-presser, an oilman, a woollen-draper, a silk-hatbandmaker, an innkeeper, a timber merchant, a hatter, a gold and silver wire-drawer, a tailor, a moneylender, a cloth factor and a rentier. An analysis of the occupations of those taking apprentices in the mid–18th century reveals that 43.8 per cent of masters were engaged in some form of manufacturing, 35.3 per cent in the distributive trades, 13.1 per cent in building, 2.27 per cent in agriculture, 1.76 per cent in domestic service, 1.76 per cent in transport, and 0.76 per cent in the professions (1.25 per cent not stating an occupation). Of the 397 men in the sample, 24 described themselves as haberdashers, nine as haberdashers of hats, five as feltmakers, and one as a hatmaker, making a total of just 9.8 per cent pursuing trades originally associated with the Company. Almost as popular as haberdashery as a trade among Company members was carpentry (21), cabinet making (19), and coopering (17). Such an association of people of varied trades had less rationale than the more homogeneous membership of the 16th century.[33] Nor was the civic freedom so essential to the making of money in the capital as it had once been. This was because the growth in London's population had breached the boundaries of the medieval City, spilling into the suburbs, where the freedom was not necessary to the pursuit of retail trade and where the Companies' rights of search were much more difficult to exercise. Whereas the population of the City proper increased from 80,000 to 105,000 between 1560 and 1680, that of the suburbs expanded eleven-fold from 30,000 to 330,000 over the same period.[34] Moreover the Haberdashers' Company had abandoned its rights of search: the last recorded search was in 1650.[35] It is true that the Company joined in the rather half-hearted rear-guard action fought by the Livery Companies against growing liberalisation. In 1677 they expressed their willingness to campaign against a bill to allow protestant refugees from France and the Netherlands to trade in London and its environs, but waited on Common Council to take the initiative. In 1706 the Assistants gave their blessing to a petition to Parliament for the repeal of an act licensing hawkers and pedlars, but insisted that the petitioners should withdraw the proposal for compensation to be paid to the government in lieu of the licensing fees. Otherwise the Haberdashers took no action against the forces of economic liberalisation which were undermining their rationale.[36]

Not only was the relevance of the Company to the pursuit of business much less obvious, but its role in the social life of citizens was also being diluted. This was a reflection of the proliferation of alternative contexts for popular sociability. Clubs developed for all sorts and conditions of men, from the box clubs or friendly societies among the lower orders to the more prestigious literary and philosophical clubs. Defoe drew attention in the 1720s to 'that new fashion'd way of conversing by assemblies', at which the subscribers joined in dancing, cards, and conversation. The uses to which the Haberdashers' Hall itself was put reflects the growing range of alternatives to the rather artificial sociability of the Livery Company. The Castle Concert and the City Assembly were typical of the organisations within which polite society socialised in the 18th century. The complaints from the Hall's neighbours about the sedan chairs cluttering the streets reflects the appeal of such entertainments.[37]

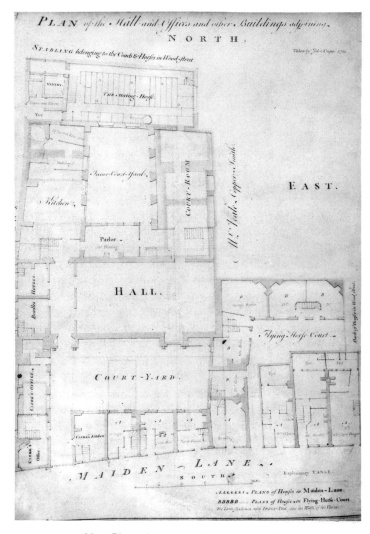

23.   Plan of the post-Fire Hall in 1761.

It was already becoming harder to provide a rationale for the Livery Companies. Campbell's *London Tradesman* was decidedly double-edged on the benefits of membership:

> Now a Youth having taken up his Freedom, if he is a popular Man, he may in two or three Years have the Honour to be appointed Renter Warden, or Steward, which entitles him to the Privilege of treating the Fraternity unto an elegant and expensive Entertainment on Lord Mayor's Day.[38]

In one respect, the availability of the Company's charitable rsources, membership certainly remained attractive, but this brought its own problems. A recurrent anxiety among the Assistants was that some men sought the freedom merely for the purpose of availing themselves of these resources. In 1687 they responded with palpable distaste to the freedom secured by Robert Kent 'with intention to be a burthen and charge to this Company', expelling him from the place in the Snow Hill almshouses to which they had recently admitted him.[39] In discussing the desirability of lowering the fees for redemptioners with the intention of attracting more men into the Company in 1707, the possibility that this might encourage men like Kent was seriously considered, although the consideration eventually discounted because the Company was under no obligation to relieve them.[40]

Discussions about the desirability of attracting redemptioners are an indication of the Company's failure to recruit new members. The less obvious advantages of membership resulted in a reduced level of freedom admissions. Whereas an average of 119.5 freemen were being admitted each year between 1605 and 1614, by the first decade of the 18th century the figure was 87.6, and during the decade 1737–47 50.4 per annum.[41] Fees for redemptioners were lowered from £20 to 40s. in 1699 and to 26s.8d. the following year to bring the Company into line with the practice of the Twelve Great Companies.[42] It was also intended to stave off the haemorrhaging of members caused by the acts of Common Council which required members in some crafts to bind their apprentices at the Halls of the lesser Companies so that they might become free of the craft with jurisdiction over their trade rather than of the Haberdashers. Recurrent anxieties over this practice was another manifestation of the shrinkage of the Company's membership, and hence of the pool of talent for office, and of the pool of wealth to be tapped for Company projects.[43]

The Company's lack of appeal to its membership is demonstrated by the high levels of default on quarterage payment which characterised the later 17th and 18th centuries. This had always been a problem, but its scale made it the subject of increasing concern to the Assistants. Beadles were offered the incentive of a portion of the arrears that they collected, 2s. in the pound in 1674, and 2s. 6d. in the pound in 1693 and 1739.[44] Part of the problem was the sheer difficulty of keeping track of members. Efforts were being made to improve the Company's information gathering in this regard, the Clerk having recorded members' addresses in the freedom register since 1708, and in 1724 the Beadle was instructed to record this information in his quarterage book, as well as adding the details of moves as they became known to him. Nor was it easy to find out when members had died. The 1724 orders also instructed the Clerk and Beadle to make a note of deaths when freemen's widows applied for charity, but this represented a rather haphazard solution.[45] It is clear that some Beadles found the trouble of chasing up recalcitrant members not worth the financial rewards, and they were reprimanded for their lack of attention to the business of collecting dues. But at the root of the problem lay the diminishing sense of identity with the Company: some refused to pay until they came to bind an apprentice at the Hall, this act probably representing their only point of contact with the Company.[46] In 1754 the arrears of the Assistants on quarterage stood at £32 8s. 0d. (324 man years at 2s. per annum), of the Livery at £99 1s. 6d. (991 man years), and of the Yeomanry at £2,782 0s. 0d. (27,820 man years). Some members owed for over 40 years.[47]

At the upper echelons of the Company a lack of enthusiasm is evident in the growing recalcitrance of members over the payment of their fines to enter the Livery, and a reluctance to accept the burdens of Company office. It is hardly surprising that the huge expansion in the numbers of Liverymen in the later 17th century should have proved controversial. Some refused their call to the Livery; fines from those who had accepted were slow to come in; and some refused to pay the fines altogether. It was necessary to summon some offenders before the Lord Mayor and Aldermen; others were prosecuted for their fines.[48] One of the consequences of the expansion of the Livery was that it was offered to those who would not normally be eligible for it. The Assistants recognised that they were advancing men more rapidly than was customarily the case, for at the call in 1694 it was ordered that no-one should be compelled to accept the Livery who had not been free for at least seven years.[49] The lower than usual levels of wealth of Liverymen were reflected in an order of 1697 from the Aldermen that no-one should receive the Livery in the Great Twelve unless possessed of an estate of £1,000, because many recipients had been impoverished by the honour and had subsequently become a burden on their Companies. This order had the effect of making recruitment stll more hazardous because at the next call in 1699 it was cited by those who wished to turn down the Livery, probably in some cases for other reasons.[50] This was not a problem which receded, given the readiness with which a call to the Livery was resorted to as a money-raising device. In May 1733, for example, the Master reported that several people summoned before the committee for Livery admissions 'disregarded their summons and even bid defiance to their power'.[51] The Company was also increasingly cautious about the prosecution of the recalcitrant. In 1730 litigation against Mr Cutts for his Livery fine was abandoned after consultations with Serjeant Cheshire, and Reeves and Fazakerly, leading lawyers.[52]

It was also increasingly difficult to persuade Liverymen to accept the burdens of higher Company office. In the period 1671–84, 38 men refused to serve the offices to which they had been elected and paid fines, 13 for the Mastership and 25 for the Wardenships. By the reign of Queen Anne the practice was still more widespread. Between 1701 and 1714, 35 refused the Mastership and 27 the Wardenships. These figures exclude those who pleaded illness and were discharged for a year or so without fine. More worrying still was the tendency for men to fine for all offices rather than the specific one to which they had been elected: no less than 10 men took this course of action in 1671–84. It should also be emphasised that the figures exclude those who were recruited directly onto the Court of Assistants paying the fees of £40 and discharging themselves of the three Wardenships they were supposed to serve. Such practices broke the conventional association of service to one's fellows with status in the Company.[53] Moreover, the growing number of refusals meant that in some years offices remained unfilled for most of the year. Take, for example, the Company year 1702–3. Twelve men in that year alone refused the office of Master, bringing in fines of £20 apiece. Another two requested discharges for that year only. The result was that the Mastership still remained unfilled in September 1703 when

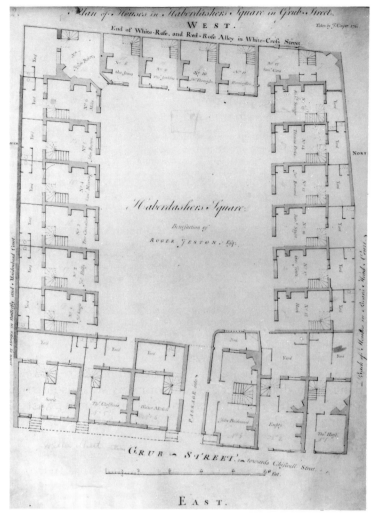

24.   Plan of Haberdashers' Square, 1761.

the Assistants bowed to the inevitable and accepted that the Immediate Past Master, Thomas Allen, who had been filling in for most of the year anyway, should carry on until the next election due in less than two months, and that the Company stock should pay the full cost of the Master's dinner and one-fifth the cost of the Publication dinner. Not only could senior members not be induced to serve, but in many cases they also resisted the payment of fines. To take 1702 again. Richard Sylls pleaded his physical infirmities as a reason for declining the Mastership and alleged that his financial circumstances were such that he could not afford the fine of £20. Considering him to be reasonably well-off, the Company ordered him before the Lord Mayor and Aldermen to explain himself, and the order was repeated no less than three times that year. Robert Chaplin, another refuser, repeatedly failed to give the Court a satisfactory answer about the payment of his fine, and remained recalcitrant even after the arrival of the Barbados fleet, at which time he had earlier promised payment. Yet another member, Farrington, had to be threatened with prosecution before paying his fine.[54] This was admittedly a particularly difficult year, but there were lengthy quests for someone to fill the Master's chair in 1705–6 and 1711–12, and few years passed without some difficulty being encountered over the payment of fines.[55] The frustrations of the Court over this matter are reflected in an order taken in April 1703 that those refusing office and failing to pay their fines should be deprived of a share in the disposal of Company gifts.[56]

The prevalence of fining was related to the expense of office. One of the by-products of the expansion of the Livery was that office-holding became more expensive because of the larger numbers to be catered for at Company functions, the support of which, it will be recalled, was the responsibility of the Wardens. Those eligible for the Mastership calculated that it would be cheaper to fine for the office than to serve. John Banks, Second Warden in 1706, warned the Court that the expenses of the Wardens 'were really become so very burthensome that there would very great inconveniences arise to the Company as great damage unless speedily remedied and the Wardens assisted'. He noted that the Wardens had lost the fees of redemptioners to which they were traditionally entitled in 1689, and that the grant of a Livery fine in lieu had not proved adequate compensation. The Court accepted the logic of his argument and agreed that a further grant of £25 be made to the Wardens to assist in the payment of their expenses. Other measures to make office more attractive included increasing the fines for the Mastership from £20 to £30 which occurred in 1764.[57]

The reluctance to serve in Company office is but one manifestation of the unwillingness to put in the necessary time to Company affairs that was essential to sound management. So poor was attendance at Courts of Assistants that meetings often lacked a quorum. This was true also of meetings of the Grand Committee which prepared business for the Assistants: for this reason the quorum of the committee was reduced from five to three in 1755.[58] In an effort to improve attentiveness to Company business, it was agreed in 1723 that members would not be eligible to participate in the distribution of gifts unless they had attended two Courts in addition to the Courts at which gifts were distributed, these latter being always the most popular for reasons of the social prestige which attached to them. Such a sanction proved unpopular: the order was suspended the following year, reinstated in 1750, repealed after a year, and then reinstated once again at a meeting in February 1752 at which members were left hanging around waiting for a quorum to be achieved.[59] Assistants also adopted the irritating practice of leaving meetings as soon as the most interesting items of business were concluded, leaving the Court without a quorum. Typically they would attend the election of officers to the charities, because this gave them the opportunity to exercise patronage. In order to stamp out this practice it was agreed in 1760 that elections should be the last item on the agenda.[60] Low levels of attendance left key individuals in a state of some ignorance about Company affairs. This was recognised in 1752 when the composition of the Grand Committee was altered to include those in line for the Mastership.[61]

This chapter will have made pretty gloomy reading. It would perhaps be unfair not to stress some of the more positive aspects of the Company's management of its affairs in this period. Innovations were made to streamline the transaction of business. The most important development was the emergence of the standing committee. We observed earlier how the committee appointed to direct the rebuilding of the Hall was used as a general purposes committee and annually renewed. Likewise, after the Glorious Revolution the committee set up to establish the Hoxton charity found itself transacting a wider range of business. In 1709 this committee stood at 25 people; in 1713 it was increased to thirty. From 1729 it was constituted by the current Master and Wardens, the immediately preceding Master and Wardens, all those who had passed the chair, and eight Court members serving by rotation according to their seniority. In 1752 those next in line for the chair were included to give these men familiarity with the minutiae of current Company business. Finally in 1758 recognising that the committee was too unwieldy its membership was streamlined to comprise the Master and Wardens, those above the chair, the four men immediately below the chair, and any three more.[62] The information available to the Assistants was improved, as the Clerk began to record the addresses of members from 1708, and lists of the Yeomanry were published at roughly decadal intervals from 1730.[63] From 1702 the Clerk was instructed to table the Company's accounts at each meeting of the Court of Assistants so that the current situation could be seen readily.[64] Efforts were made to professionalise the management of the Company's estates: the employment of surveyors became standard practice, and from 1708 annual views of the London properties were ordered.[65]

Finally it is worth underlining how central the effective discharge of its charitable trusts remained to the Company. The call for economies in 1753 was couched very much in terms of the threatened loss of honour should the Company fail in this duty. Talking of their management of the charities in 1753 the Assistants noted that 'the Honour and Justice of this Court are very much concerned in it, and the future Welfare and Subsistance of the Company intirely depend on it'.[66] It is arguable that they could have got the charities on an even keel more quickly had they been prepared to contemplate economies at an earlier stage. But we should not ignore the dilemmas of their position. They were operating in a context in which the Livery Company seemed increasingly irrelevant to its members. Take away the sociability, and it would appear even less relevant, and members become less willing to make the commitment which the management of the charities entailed.

Chapter Eight

The Management of the Charities, 1680–1800

In the closing years of the 17th and through the 18th centuries the Company continued to accumulate charitable benefactions albeit from fewer donors than in the later 16th and early 17th centuries. In the 70 years after 1680 the Company was entrusted with 11 endowments, and in the 60 years thereafter with another two. The London Livery Companies were becoming less popular trustees for charities with the proliferation of alternative mechanisms for the channelling of philanthropy in the 18th century. It is true that the capital value of the endowments made in the period 1680–1750 was at least £41,619, not far below the £47,880 accumulated by 1680. However, it was also the case that a disproportionate amount of the endowments was accounted for by key individuals. No less than £39,829 (96 per cent) of the endowments made in the period 1680–1750 were accounted for by the charities of Robert Aske (d. 1689) and John Banks (d. 1722). Robert Aske entrusted the Company with the establishment of a Hospital within a mile of London for 20 old men free of the Company, and further provided that the sons of Company freemen should be maintained and educated in the hospital as far as the funds would permit. The £20 per person per annum which he envisaged the charity providing was among the more generous charitable outlays of the period. John Banks left the Company his leasehold estate of 72 houses in St James Westminster on condition that it pay annuities to his family and discharge the estate of £10,000 of his debts. In return for their pains he instructed that the trustees should be allowed £12 per annum for dinners, and made allowances to the Company's officers. Once the debt was discharged, the Company was to increase the annuities to his descendants and start paying a further £562 per annum for charitable purposes. The objects of Banks' charity included poor freemen and widows of the Company (to whom £250 per annum was to be paid) and the poor of St Benet Paul's Wharf, Battersea, and Southwark. Not only had the number of donors shrunk since the earlier period, but also the range of charitable activity had narrowed. Apart from Banks' bequests to the parishes noted above, all the new charity of the years after 1680 was destined for the Company's own poor. Gone were the days when the London Companies were seen as appropriate trustees for charities in the distant corners of the land. The reasons for this development will become plain as the story of the Haberdashers' troubled relations with their provincial charities over the course of the 18th century unfolds through this chapter.[1]

However, the exploration of the Company's management of its charities through these difficult years will begin by looking at the problems encountered in the running of the Company's most important new undertaking of the period, Aske's Hospital at Hoxton. After considering alternative sites at Islington and Mile End, the Company decided on the purchase of a 20 acre site at Hoxton in the parish of Shoreditch for

25.   John Banks (Master in 1717).

26.   A statue of Robert Aske at Haberdashers' Aske's Hatcham Boys' School.

which £2,000 was paid in June 1690. The scientist and surveyor, Robert Hooke, acted as architect, and the Hospital building began to go up towards the end of 1691. The first 20 pensioners entered the Hospital in 1695, and the first 20 boys in November 1697. Although the Hoxton estate provided a rent of £81 per annum, the bulk of the Hospital finances derived from an estate situated in the parishes of Great Chart, Kingsnorth, Bethersden, Shadoxhurst, Woodchurch, Marsham, Wearhorne, Shingleton, and Ashford in Kent. In total 1,600 acres of freehold land were purchased for £11,146, and a further 450 acres of leasehold land for £2,268 8s. 0d. A rent roll of 1697 indicates that gross receipts of £841 18s. 4d. per annum were expected from this estate. At first sight this would appear adequate to the financing of the charity. Twenty men and twenty boys could be supported at the level envisaged by the founder for £800 per annum. However, the charity finances were in such a parlous state by 1714 that the Company decided that no more boys were to be elected. Not until 1739 were they readmitted.[2]

This situation reflects the extravagance of the Hospital building and the problems

27.   Aske's Hospital at Hoxton, designed by Robert Hooke, as it was in 1754.

of estate management. In *A New View of London*, published in 1708, the Hospital was described in terms which make its favourable impact upon contemporaries plain: 'The new Hospital here is a sumptuous Edifice built of Brick and Stone, with a Piazza in the Front, where is an Ambulatory 340 feet in length, constituted by the Elevation of that part on Stone Columns of the Tuscan Order, but the middle part is adorned with Columns, Entablatures and Pediment of the Ionick Order; under the Pediment is a Nich wherein stands the Figure of the Founder carved in full proportion'.[3] Unfortunately such elegance did not come cheap. The building and furnishing of the Hospital cost no less than £11,787 6s. 7d., a figure which occasioned disputes with the builders. By December 1693, after consulting other builders on the value of the work done, the Haberdashers felt that they had been overcharged to the tune of at least £600 by the bricklayers and carpenters, and refused to pay the bill. The difficulties with the builders also appear to have brought the Company into conflict with their architect, Robert Hooke, who in turn complained that the Company had altered his original design and not involved him in the negotiations with the contractors. The escalating cost of the Hospital led the Assistants into economies. In 1694 Hooke's plan for a cupola, that acme of architectural fashion, was abandoned, and the north end of the Hospital remained incomplete at its opening.[4] As late as 1707 a lease of the north end was granted for 51 years at a rent of 4d. per annum for 30 years and £10 per annum thereafter on condition that the necessary building work was completed. In 1729 the lessee, William Seabright, a member of the Court, claimed that he had spent no less than £800 on the property, although it had been reckoned at the time of his lease that only £300 would be necessary to complete the building. The accusation that the original design had been too extravagant is regularly encountered in the 18th century. In his *History of London* of 1775 Entick summed up the prevailing view: 'But a moiety of this sum [Aske's benefaction] being shamefully squandered in erecting an Edifice fitter for a Palace than an Almshouse to the great reproach of those concerned, the Company were obliged to turn off the Boys for several years'.[5]

These problems were compounded by a lower than anticipated income from the rents. The rental of the Kent estate stood at £841 18s. 4d. in 1697. This sum was realised in the early years. But what was less expected was the haemorrhaging caused by allowances for taxes and repairs by tenants, which reduced the net income by an average of £280 per annum between 1697 and 1707. The charity suffered from Parliament's determination to finance the wars against Louis XIV as far as possible by land taxes rather than by the excise which was felt to enlarge the scope for monarchical independence. The situation further deteriorated in later years. Net annual income from the Kent estate stood at £573 per annum beween 1704 and 1706, £501 per annum between 1713 and 1715, and £407 per annum between 1722 and 1724. Because the accounts only record net receipts after 1707 it is difficult to determine the reasons for this deteriorating position.[6] Taxation on land dropped sharply after the Peace of Utrecht (1713) which settled the war against Louis XIV, and the decline in income probably reflected the diligence of the individual stewards to whom the management of the estate was delegated. J.R. Meredith has drawn attention to the way in which the enthusiasm of new stewards, who tightened the screws and achieved a modest recovery in income, soon waned allowing the erosion of the income to continue. It was probably for this reason that in 1723 the Company chose to abandon the management of 34 separate tenants in favour of a lease to a single individual. This strategy, however, produced no improvement in the situation. The lessee, John Johnson, was repeatedly warned about his arrears in the ensuing years, and the threat of legal action was necessary before he was brought to heel in 1730, and the lease was surrendered. In the meantime the estate had been subject to an exhaustive series of visitations costing £180 14s. 11d. between 1728 and 1730. In February of the latter year the committee charged with the supervision of the Hospital's affairs took 'into consideration Mr Seabrooke's accounts for his Trouble, Horse hire and expences for several journeys which he had taken into Kent, by the Company's directions, to look after the workmen employed in repairing the Estate, And Mr Seabrooke having made it appear that he had spent two hundred days and odd therein' was granted £100. The attention that was given to the estate at this time and the energy of the new steward, Darcy Stone, secured a dramatic improvement in the state of the Hospital's finances as the net receipts from the Kent estate averaged £742 per annum between 1731 and 1733.[7] Perhaps the reluctance of the Company to make the necessary commitment to the visitations in the preceding years points to the lack of direct intervention by the Assistants in the management of the estate as another factor in its low yield. Whatever the case, the recovery of the revenues of the Kent estate made possible the readmission of the boys in 1739.[8]

The failure of estate income to match expenditure is depressingly repeated in other of the Company's charities. Between 1677 and 1700 the receipts from the Hatcham estate of £14,177 2s. 5d. (about £616 per annum) were insufficient to match the outgoings on the Jones charities which amounted to £16,122 17s. 10d. (about £701 per annum) in the same period. This deficit was the result of heavy arrears of rent, the costs of litigation to recover them, the growing burden of taxation particularly in the 1690s, and the cost of the repairs to charity buildings.[9] As was noted in the previous chapter the agricultural depression and the difficulties of finding suitable tenants in the post-Restoration period gave tenants greater leverage against their landlords. The change in the balance of power between landlord and tenant is evident in the Company's willingness to fund the cost of additions to capital stock on the estate. Thus help was given with repairs to farm buildings: Pitcher was allowed £50 towards the cost of building a farmhouse and barn in 1691–2. Drainage costs were regularly reimbursed, allowances for the cost of repairs to Earl's Sluice assessed on the tenants by the Commissioners of Sewers appearing on most years' accounts.[10] The Company was also willing to support the pleas of tenants for help in difficult years: £40 of arrears from Goodman Streeke was written off in 1699 'in respect of many losses by wet years'. Tenants faced with lower prices for their produce stood a greater chance of withholding rent with impunity for want of others to take on the farm.[11] The difficulty of finding tenants is dramatically revealed by the Company's unusual recourse to direct farming in 1697 on Widow Wolford's farm of 55 acres at Hatcham while another tenant was found.[12] Not surprisingly the arrears mounted, reaching £1,224 4s. 0d. in 1691. In 1696 the Company took the bit between its teeth and sued its tenant Pitcher for arrears. Although arrears of £325 4s. 0d. (the equivalent of nearly three years of his rent of £116 per annum) were secured, the cost of this litigation to the charity was £118 14s. 0d.[13] Allowances to tenants for taxes further eroded the charity's income: in 1693–4 £13 8s. 2d. was paid, in 1695–6 £27 14s. 10d., and in 1697–8 £38 12s. 4d.[14] Nor was the cost of repairs to the charity buildings a trifling sum. Between 1677 and 1700 these amounted to just over £15 per annum. The lion's share of £189 14s. 5d. went on the School buildings at Monmouth; another £97 0s. 10d. was spent on the almshouses at Monmouth and Newland, and £68 15s. 11d. on the buildings occupied by the Lecturers and schoolteachers in spite of the fact that according to the statutes of the charity these latter were the responsibility of the incumbents.[15]

The last chapter drew attention to the way in which the Great Fire resulted in a lower rental income because of the favourable terms that were necessary in building leases. Rents from the Rainton estate were so far reduced that the payments in charity were cut to two-thirds of what the donor had intended.[16] A similar fate lay in store for the Jeston charity in 1689 when the buildings in Grub Street fell into disrepair, and the building leases cut the income from the estate by a half. The donor had in fact foreseen this situation and instructed that in such circumstances the payments should be reduced. Other charities disappeared altogether. The remaining years of the leasehold property in St Bartholomew Exchange held from the Clothworkers' Company were surrendered because the Haberdashers lacked funds for rebuilding, and the payments from the property to the Hospitals and Company poor ceased.[17] Several loan stocks vanished into the Company's general fund. The erosion of the financial base of the Company resulted in a programme of retrenchment. In 1693, after surveying the numerous charities which lacked settled funds for their payment, the Company embarked on a programme of retrenchment 'as farr as may be consistent with the equity of affaires and to obviate suites of Law and Chancery'. It was proposed to cut charitable expenditure by £52 per annum, by ending the payment of several university exhibitions (established by Lady Romeney, Martha Barrett, Nicholas Culverwell, and Frances Clarke) and a number of payments to the Company poor (those of Mary Paradine and Robert Offley). Further cuts in the payments on the Jones charity amounting to a saving of £71 6s. 8d. per annum were discussed, but quickly abandoned in the face of local opposition.[18]

The heavy taxation of the years after the Glorious Revolution and the Company's lack of funds made it inevitable that the Haberdashers should reduce their charity payments accordingly. This policy encountered much hostility from the recipients. By 1701 the Company was several years in arrears with its payments under the Trotman benefaction to the parish of Cam in Gloucestershire because the parishioners had refused to make allowances for taxes. The parishioners brought the matter to the attention of the Court of Chancery which was sufficient to bring the parties to a hasty arbitration, in which the parish accepted the deduction of taxes for the period in which the payments were in arrears, but only allowed a portion of the taxes during the period when the charity had been paid.[19] More controversially, it appears that the Company was making deductions for taxes from charities for which no land was appropriated. The Assistants were wise to curtail the practice in a series of orders in 1706.[20]

Structural problems in the Company's finances were compounded by the duplicity of individuals. The Haselfoot charity was emasculated in the mid–18th century by the underhand dealing of James Thomason, tenant of Pitley farm in Essex from 1735. He had promised to clear the arrears of the preceding lessee, a relative of his, but not only did he fail to do so, but he also refused to pay rent himself, setting up his own title to the property. The Company brought a suit of ejectment against him, recovered the property in 1744, and in 1756 took possession of a copyhold farm at Matching which had been acquired by an execution against their wayward tenant. Nevertheless the arrears from the estate (rented prior to 1745 at £70 per annum) amounted to the staggering sum of £749 19s. 3d. in 1755, and £772 12s. 0d. was owing to the beneficiaries of Haselfoot's charity, bringing the Governors of the London Hospitals clamouring at the Company's gate in Staining Lane. Only with the acquisition of Matching could the payment of the arrears commence. In the meantime relations with the hospitals had deteriorated to the extent that there was an acrimonious dispute with St Bartholomew's about whether allowances should be made for taxes on the arrears.[21]

The problems with Thomason at Pitley probably owed something to the weakening hold of the Company over its estates. There was something of a vicious circle about the Company's financial malaise in this period. The weakening of its financial base made it impossible to conduct regular surveys of the estates with the result that abuses flourished, and income remained stagnant or falling. The visitations in Kent in 1728–30 were admittedly exceptionally expensive; more typical was the £50 2s. 0d.

spent on that estate in 1739. But the trend was unquestionably upwards: a visitation of the same estate in 1700 had cost £25 0s. 9d. It was therefore only when the Company's finances were restored to a healthier state as a result of the economy drive commenced in 1753 that the use of surveyors and regular visitations became a reality.[22] At the survey of Pitley in 1760 the Company's Surveyor, Sloane, alleged that there had been no survey since 1652. He was exaggerating (there had been a survey in 1686 on which £12 18s. 10d. had been spent), but it was unquestionable that by the accession of George III the estate was suffering from neglect. Sloane found that no courts had been held since 1701, and no payments received for the admission and surrender of subtenants since 1714. A survey of 1765 revealed that some subtenants were paying quitrents to another manor and that land within the manor was lapsing to freehold for want of proper administration and the Company's regular assertion of its rights.[23] The casual arrangements that were made by the Court to inform itself of developments on the estates such as the use of two friends of an Assistant to make a report on the woods at Knighton in 1702 was a poor substitute for inspection by Court members themselves. But there may have been more than a lack of money behind the failure to visit the properties more regularly.[24] In 1708 in one of those flurries of enthusiasm for reform which were all too often not sustained, the Assistants instructed the Master and Wardens to make annual visitations of the London properties. In 1760 it was alleged that there had been no survey since 1715 (again this was slightly misleading in that there had been one in 1728).[25] One cannot help but feel that a limited commitment to the Company's affairs among its rulers as well as financial constraints played a part in the loosening grip of the Company over its estates.

Indeed it is clear that not all of the Company's difficulties in the course of the later 17th and 18th centuries can be ascribed to the difficult circumstances it confronted. The failure to impose stricter terms on the Justice family in renewing their lcasc of the Knighton estate is a case in point. In 1667 Luke Justice was granted a lease of 70 years of the manor of Knighton and the recently purchased addition to the estate of Woodseaves in Drayton for the rent of £175 per annum. William Adams, the donor, clearly intended favour towards the Justice family, specifying that the lease should be made 'for so long afterwards as Luke Justice might reasonably desire'. Whether Adams intended his favour to extend down the generations is less clear. Nevertheless in September 1714 in consideration of the surrender of the 1667 lease the properties were redemised to William Justice for another 70 years still at the rent of £175 per annum. They were probably already worth considerably more. Certainly by the time this long lease fell in in 1784 the rents of the estate were £476 14s. 0d. per annum. The Company's behaviour is probably to be explained by the fact that the payments specified in Adams' will amounted to £175 per annum and these were paid by the Justice family directly in the locality. But in acting in this way the Haberdashers were depriving themselves of the opportunity to make regular visitations of the estate, and keep a check on the woodland, the value of which was increasing because of the growing demand for timber for the iron forges nearby. As shall be shown shortly, the visitations of the 1760s revealed a parlous situation on the Knighton estate. At the very least the Assistants of the early 18th century were guilty of a lack of vision.[26]

It will already be clear from the foregoing that the expedients into which the Company was forced as a result of its financial weakness brought it into frequent collision with those whom its revenues were supposed to support. The clashes over allowances for taxes and the frequently protracted negotiations for the settlement of arrears are obvious examples. But the charity which suffered from the greatest level of conflict was that of William Jones, formerly the jewel in the Company's crown. The root of the problem here was the decision in 1675 to sell the manors of Caldecott and Puttocks Hardwick to buy out the lessees at Hatcham and maximise the income from the latter estate. As has been shown, the receipts from the Hatcham estate were not sufficient to defray the full costs of the charity, and in circumstances where the Company's stock was drained the process of subsidy from Company stock was not one which found much favour among the Assistants. Economies in the charity became inevitable. However, as far as the inhabitants of Newland were concerned, the sale of the Huntingdonshire manors was a grave error, because it now seemed that there were no properties appropriated to the support of the charities there. By 1698 their patience had snapped, and the parishioners began a costly suit with the Company in Chancery in which they sought to force the Haberdashers into appropriating lands for the payment of their charity. At the root of the litigation lay a disagreement over whether the properties at Hatcham Barnes and in Huntingdon-shire belonged to the Company, in which case additional revenues could be applied as the Assistants saw fit, or whether the properties belonged to the charities alone, in which case all increments should be applied to Monmouth and Newland, and the Company's pocketing of the money received from the sale of the Huntingdonshire manors was against equity. The Lord Keeper's ruling of 13 December 1701 was harsh. The Company was instructed to pay the arrears of £200 per annum due since the filing of the information together with the plaintiffs' costs, and required to purchase lands to the value of £200 per annum, or assign lands from their existing properties not encumbered with other charities to support the Newland charity. The Haberdashers remained unbowed and appealed to the House of Lords. Although the appeal was dismissed in January 1703, the Company refused to comply with the order. The parishioners of Newland tightened the screws by securing a sequestration order on the Company Hall and on the Hatcham estate, the full proceeds of which were to be paid to them. This action, of course, endangered the Monmouth charities with the result that in 1704 yet another suit against the Company was launched, this time by the Corporation of Monmouth as the payments to them stopped.[27]

The mess was eventually disentangled by a further Chancery decree of 1708 which discharged the sequestration against Hatcham Barnes and ordered that all the rents and profits should be applied to the Monmouth charity alone. The estate was to be under the management of a receiver appointed by the Court of Chancery and leases were to be granted under the authority of Chancery. As for Newland, the Haberdashers were instructed to purchase lands to the value of £200 per annum. This the low state of their funds did not allow them to do, and the Newland charity had to be paid out of Company stock. The parishioners of Newland in fact emerged

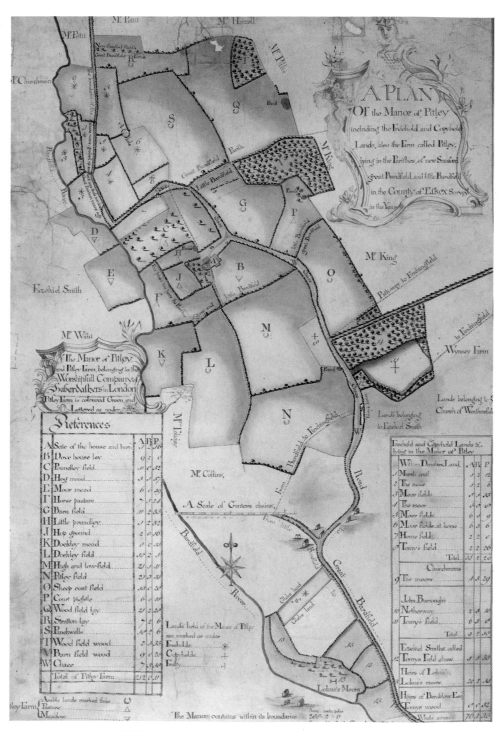

XIII. Map of the Pitley estate in Essex, *c*.1761.

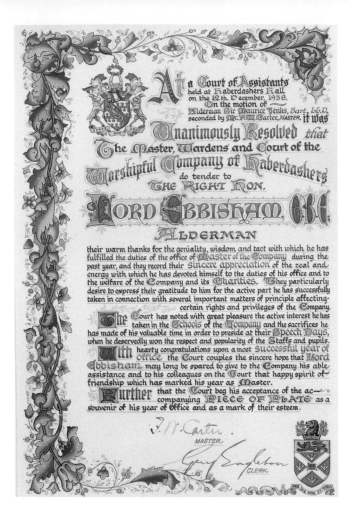

At a Court of Assistants
held at Haberdashers Hall
on the 12th December, 1938.
On the motion of
Alderman Sir Maurice Jenks, Bart., LL.D.
seconded by Mr. F.W. Carter, MASTER, it was

Unanimously Resolved that
The Master, Wardens and Court of the
Worshipful Company of Haberdashers
do tender to
THE RIGHT HON.

LORD EBBISHAM, G.B.E,
ALDERMAN

their warm thanks for the geniality, wisdom and tact with which he has fulfilled the duties of the office of Master of the Company during the past year, and they record their sincere appreciation of the zeal and energy with which he has devoted himself to the duties of his office and to the welfare of the Company and its Charities. They particularly desire to express their gratitude to him for the active part he has successfully taken in connection with several important matters of principle affecting certain rights and privileges of the Company.

The Court has noted with great pleasure the active interest he has taken in the Schools of the Company and the sacrifices he has made of his valuable time in order to preside at their Speech Days, when he deservedly won the respect and popularity of the Staffs and pupils.

With hearty congratulations upon a most successful year of office the Court couples the sincere hope that Lord Ebbisham may long be spared to give to the Company his able assistance and to his colleagues on the Court that happy spirit of friendship which has marked his year as Master.

Further that the Court beg his acceptance of the accompanying PIECE OF PLATE as a souvenir of his year of Office and as a mark of their esteem.

F.W. Carter
MASTER

Geo. Eagleton
CLERK

XIV. Vote of thanks from the Court of Assistants to Alderman the Lord Ebbisham on his leaving office in 1938.

XV. The Master's badge, *c.*1875; gold and enamelwork set with emeralds, rubies, sapphires and diamonds.

XVI. Adams' Grammar School, Newport.

XVII. Haberdashers' Monmouth School for Girls.

XVIII. The almshouses at Monmouth.

XIX. The modern Livery Hall set for the Publication Dinner.

XX. The modern Luncheon Room, with portrayal of St Katherine by Timothy Whidbourne, the gift of Sir Guy Bracewell Smith, Bt.

in a worse position than when they had embarked on litigation. Because the corporate funds were so low, the Company could not afford to support the charity at the level envisaged by Jones. Severe cut-backs followed. In 1714 it was agreed between the Company and the parish that the Lecturer should receive a salary of £33 6s. 8d. instead of the £66 13s. 4d. he had been paid in 1624, and the almspeople 1s. per week instead of 2s.6d. per week. The parishioners expressed the hope that the Company would restore the charity in due course 'and Establish with it your own Glory that the Generations to Come may praise you as well as the founder'.[28] In 1729 the payments to the Lecturer and almspeople were increased to £40 per annum (£50 per annum in 1731) and 1s. 6d. per week respectively.[29] But neither can the outcome for the Company be considered a happy one. Although they retained responsibility for making appointments to the Jones charities, control over the finances was now exercised at one remove through a receiver. Moreover the litigation had brought them much unwelcome publicity and cost them £627 2s. 9d. over the period 1700–8, equivalent to more than one year's receipts from the Hatcham estate.[30] Ironically the real beneficiaries of the lawsuit were the people of Monmouth. Now that the entire income of the Hatcham estate could be applied to their charities, the sums they were paid increased handsomely. From 1714 the Lecturer received £100 per annum instead of £66 13s. 4d., the Schoolmaster £90 per annum instead of £60, the Usher £45 instead of £30, and the almspeople 3s. 6d. per week instead of 2s. 6d.[31]

Most of the discussion thus far has turned around the financial problems confronting the Company in attempting to discharge its charitable trusts. However the parlous state into which many of the charities had fallen by the mid–18th century was not solely the result of financial problems. The Company's minutes are littered with complaints about the decay of the Schools. At one point in the 1740s the School at Monmouth had only three pupils; there were only 28 in 1771.[32] A visitation found just 17 pupils at Newport School in 1782. Decline was not constant. Newport School was described as flourishing in 1703, decaying in 1722, improving in 1755, satisfactory in 1760, decaying again in 1771, and 1782.[33] After the difficulties in the mid–1740s Monmouth School had recovered to provide education for between 50 and 60 boys by 1748, but the complaints about decay resurfaced in 1766.[34] This uneven pattern reflected the impact of changes in school staffing. One key to the problem of the Schools is provided by the fact that masters tended to serve until they died. In spite of the Company's insistence on annual re-election of their staff, it was extremely reluctant to invoke the final sanction of dismissal which would take away a man's livelihood. The result was that the Schools were all too often left in the hands of men whose powers were failing. Such a situation would be likely to intensify conflicts between Schoolmasters and Ushers as the latter found themselves having to take on ever greater responsibilities for which they felt they were inadequately remunerated. The two themes of the decrepitude of Masters and clashes of personality in the claustrophobic conditions of the Schools recur time and again. The Schoolmaster and Usher at Newport were in conflict in 1704; in 1722 the School was said to be in a bad state because of the indisposition of the Schoolmaster, Greenwood; in 1771 its decay was to be explained by 'the advanced age of Mr Lea [the Schoolmaster] and the Inattention of Mr Forrester [the Usher]'.[35] Complaints from the inhabitants of Bunbury about their School in 1739 laid the problem at the feet of John Fletcher, their Schoolmaster, 'worn out by age and infirmities'.[36] In 1766 enquiries into the decay of Monmouth School turned around the history of disputes between the Schoolmaster and Usher, and in 1779 attention centred on the old age and incapacity of the Revd. Crowe, the Schoolmaster there. Crowe indeed provides the most spectacular example of this problem, because he had gone mad. The visitation report of 1779 makes gloomy reading. Locals reported that he was 'naturally of so Morose Tyrannic Disposition and in fact so much the School Master It was Impossible an Usher of any Ability or eveness of Temper would ever agree to Conduct the School amicably with him'. He had converted the area at the back of the School which had been used by the boys as a playground into pasture for a horse and so 'deprived the Boys of their favorite Divirsion of Fives'. He had made unsatisfactory repairs to the Usher's house which was described as 'absolutely money thrown away'. Books had gone missing from the library because of his lack of proper supervision.[37]

To the extent that until the end of the 18th century the Company's analysis of the causes of the problems of the Schools was limited to issues of personalities, it was guilty of rather simplistic thinking in that it failed to recognise the deep-seated problems caused by the inappropriateness of the classical curriculum to which the Schools were committed by the terms of their statutes. The issue had been raised at Newport in 1771 where the Visitors were told that the decline of the School reflected the fact that the inhabitants preferred to apprentice their children to trades rather than give them a liberal education. The Company ignored this, falling back on the problem of Lea's infirmities.[38] However in 1788 the Assistants at last acknowledged that those of lower and middle rank found writing and arithmetic more useful than languages, while the upper echelons of society desired a more polite education for their sons than could be provided in a free grammar school where they rubbed shoulders with the lower orders. By that date some progress towards reform had already been made at Newport, where a Writing Master had been appointed in 1784 as the Knighton leases were renewed on terms more favourable to the charity. The problem was confronted at Monmouth in 1793 when the new Usher was instructed to provide instruction in writing and arithmetic as well as Latin.[39]

It is difficult to criticise the Company for failing to take firmer action to deal with the problems of the curriculum. The Assistants were wise to adhere to the statutes, for as they explained in 1692 when confronted by the request that the Usher at Monmouth should be allowed to hold another living concurrently with his post at the School, they were bound 'to maintaine all the good and wholsome Statutes of theire government to the utmost of theire powre And further that there were persons behind the Curtaine that watch all opertunityes to see the Company make a breach in theire owne Constitutions thereby to wrest the government of that benefaction out of the Companyes hands'.[40] Nevertheless there are signs that the Company complicated matters for itself by inconsistency over the statute they were referring to here, which banned the holders of positions in the Jones charities from holding other livings. In 1708 Charles Herbert, Lecturer at Monmouth was presented to the

Vicarage of Ringwood by King's College, Cambridge, but the Company allowed him to retain his post in the Jones charity after a petition from the Common Council of Monmouth, stressing that 'by his pious and painfull labours in the discharge of his Ministry and promotion of the Gosple was and always had been of great adavantage to the town and parish'.[41] John Thomas, appointed Usher at Monmouth in 1738, was allowed to retain the living of Langhany give him by Lord Leicester, while the Schoolmaster, Baynam Barnes continued to hold the Vicarage of Dixton.[42] On the other hand in 1751 the Assistants were adamant that Roynon Jones, Lecturer at Monmouth, should not accept other preferments without their permission, and underlined the duties of residence.[43]

Another of the statutes which caused major headaches was that which made the Lecturer, Schoolmaster, and Usher responsible for the repairs of their houses. Although the Company did pay for the cost of at least some of the repairs in the later 17th century, it continued to insist on the statute when confronted by requests for help with repairs.[44] The problem was that the Company did not visit the charities sufficiently often to keep an eye on the buildings so that their condition deteriorated so far that it was impossible for the incumbents to finance the necessary repairs. The Haberdashers got into serious difficulties when the Lecturers failed to fulfil their obligations. In these circumstances the Lecturers would be drawn into disputes with the widows of their predecessors over the responsibility for the repairs. This occurred successively between Roynon Jones (Lecturer, 1749–73) and the widow of Andrew Cuthbert (Lecturer, 1723–49), and between George Smyth (Lecturer, 1773–93) and Jones' widow. In the meantime the condition of the house deteriorated dramatically. In 1775 Smyth was forced to go into lodgings, having 'lukely' escaped the danger of the house falling in on him. Smyth sent in an estimate for repairs amounting to £400. Lacking the necessary funds and being without sufficient authority to act in the matter, the Company referred the whole question of the repairs to Chancery. In 1778 Chancery ordered the house to be rebuilt at a cost of £500, although in the event the estimates were exceeded by £66 14s. 9d. This was financed partly from the balance in the hands of the receiver and partly by one-quarter abatements in the salaries of the Lecturer, Schoolmaster, Usher and receiver. As the new house neared completion, a deputation from the Company arrived in Monmouth. It was dismayed by what it found. The house with its huge garden complete with gazebo and ha-ha was thought to be more appropriate to a man of large fortune, it was seen as an expensive encumbrance, and it was alleged that the old house could have been patched up for £150–200. This same visitation also revealed the major repairs necessary to the schoolroom and the houses of the Schoolmaster and Usher, for which the estimates were £926. The expense of the Lecturer's house had whittled away the balance in the hands of the receiver, and an attempt to raise the necessary money by a mortgage on the charity estate was unsuccessful. In 1782 the Company undertook to advance the money out of its corporate stock at five per cent, repayment being made out of the abatements in salaries to the officials which were continued by Chancery decree. Indeed in 1784 a further abatement was found necessary reducing the salaries by one third. It was not until March 1791 that the salaries were restored, the debt having been paid off.[45]

Problems over the quality of incumbents and the repair of charity buildings would have been dealt with more satisfactorily had the machinery of visitation been functioning properly. It was intended that visitations should be made every seven years but this remained a pious hope. In 1692 the first visitation of the charities for 19 years occurred ; there was then another interval until 1705 before the Company embarked on another. Newport remained without visitation between 1730 and 1762. Visitations were time-consuming and expensive. That of 1692 which visited Bunbury, Newport and Monmouth cost £52 6s. 0d. The comprehensive visitation of Newport and the estates supporting the Adams charity in 1762 lasted a fortnight and the visitors were 'busy morning to night'.[46] The more normal practice in the later 17th and early 18th centuries was for communication with the charities to be *ad hoc*. It was usually officials of the Company (at Monmouth, for example, usually the Lecturer) who brought abuses to the attention of the Court of Assistants. In 1689 the brother of the Lecturer at Newland brought information regarding repairs that were needed to the almshouses. Occasionally a Court member would happen to be in the area and make a report to the Company. Thus in October 1701 Thomas Carpenter reported that on a recent visit to Monmouth he had been told that the almspeople frequently entertained inmates. In 1706 Warden Ives promised to get in touch with a friend who lived near to Bunbury to find out about the progress of repairs to the schoolhouse.[47] At Bunbury and Newport the Company relied much on the Aldersey and Justice families who were responsible for the payments from a lease of tithes and the Knighton estate respectively. But the Alderseys were frequently remiss in seeing to the repairs to charity buildings, while charity management by remote control ran the risk of making the Company the catspaw of local faction. In December 1697 the Company received a complaint from Mr Justice concerning the Usher at Newport who was charged with 'severe and Rigoreous Correction of the Children under his Care'. But the following month there appeared 'divers Gentlemen of very great Reputation in his behalf, some of which were parliament men who had heretofore been his scholars' who attested his integrity. The Assistants, 'perceiveing the ground of the severall Complaints against him were the effect of some private and personall pique and Animosity rather then any just cause', dismissed the case against him.[48] The Justices' domination of the neighbourhood allowed many abuses in the management of the estates to go unchecked, and in the 1760s the Company toyed with the idea of an action of trespass against their lessee to prevent future trespasses on the woods.[49] A further consequence of the lack of visitation was that the loyalty felt by locals to the Company was highly attenuated as the view took root that the Londoners cared little for the charities with which they were entrusted. The people of Monmouth were evidently pleasantly surprised in 1766 by the vigour with which the visitors inquired into the causes of the School's decline, remarking 'that they had often heard it sayd the Company would never trouble themselves about it nor would act in the Trust'.[50]

To the extent that financial problems lay at the root of many of the problems with the charities the situation did begin to improve in the later 18th century. The key developments were the falling in of the post-Fire building leases, the programme of drastic economies on which the Company embarked in 1753, and the ending of the more-than-century-long association of the Justice family with the Knighton estate in 1784. The first of the post-Fire leases came to an end in 1730, and almost immediately proposals were laid before the Court of Assistants for the restoration of the charities. In November of that year increases were ordered to the payments out of the charities of William Bond, Thomas Barnes, and Sir Nicholas Rainton. Outgoings from these charities rose from £75 10s. 0d. to £131 18s. 0d. per annum. The Rainton charity, for example, was restored almost to the level of payments envisaged by the founder. Another round of restorations to charities occurred in 1757 when the Company noted that its recent economy drive meant that £200 15s. 10d. per annum was available for this purpose. Such revisions occurred regularly through the later 18th century. In 1811, reviewing the progress since 1757, the Company engaged in one of its bouts of self-congratulation, in this case probably deserved: 'We cannot sufficiently admire the Prudence, Fortitude, and Vigour which were then displayed to relieve the Company from the Complicated Scene of Distress which nearly overwhelmed this Corporation. By a rigid Economy persevered in for nearly half a century the situation of the Company was greatly altered and Improved; its private Funds were increased; many Charities that had been partially paid were Improved; Many that had been totally omitted were partially discharged; And a Fund for accumulation had begun'.[51]

The new 21½ year leases on the Knighton estate in 1784 realised £476 14s. 0d. per annum, a substantial improvement on the £175 per annum paid by the Justice family in their successive leases. This meant that repairs to the School could be carried out, the salaries paid to the School staff increased, and a Writing Master taken on. The salaries of the Schoolmaster and Usher were increased by £10 and £5 respectively, with the promise of further increases if the number of boys in the school expanded. The Writing Master on an initial salary of £15 per annum was a new appointment designed to increase the attractiveness of the School to the parents of prospective pupils.[52] Nevertheless the Country Visitors did not regard these increases as adequate and there followed a protracted Chancery suit lasting from 1788 to 1797 over whether the surpluses on the Knighton estate would be best applied by being put into a fund for rebuilding the School as the Company desired or into further increases in salaries as the Country Visitors argued. The argument was won by the Country Visitors, and under the scheme of 1797 the payments to all the beneficiaries of the Adams charity increased: the Schoolmaster and Usher were to be paid £100 and £50 respectively instead of the £40 and £20 envisaged by the founder.[53]

The charity of Monmouth had benefited from the Chancery decree of 1708 which appropriated the entire Hatcham Barnes estate to support it, and the payments had been increased accordingly in 1714. Although the charity at Newland had suffered particularly badly in the early 18th century, the payments were restored to something close to their original level in 1739.[54] But further improvements to the Jones charities were rendered impossible by the leasing policy of the Court of Chancery which was something less than entrepreneurial. The rents were static through the early 18th century, realising £543 per annum in 1714 and £555 per annum in 1763. It is true that there was an increase thereafter because of new leases granted under the

28. William Adams' Newport Grammar School in the early 19th century.

authority of the Court of Chancery that year, but these leases were on extraordinarily favourable terms which reduced considerably the potential for future increases in estate income. Four units of property at Hatcham Barnes covering over one third of the total estate were let for a period of 150 years. The result was that as late as 1830 the estate was still only realising about £780 per annum, and that was after some more advantageous leasing of other parts of the estate in the early 19th century. The rents therefore advanced more slowly than they should have done in this period of rising metropolitan property values. The parlous state of the charity's finances is revealed by the expedients to which the charity was forced in financing the repair programme of the 1780s. Nevertheless the modest gains in rent income around 1763 did enable the Company to repay the officers of the charity the sums by which their salaries had been cut in 1779.[55] The accumulation of a fund for repairs became the Company's main priority thereafter, and it was not until 1808, and after the grant of a new lease on part of the Hatcham estate, that a sufficient fund (of £2,640 3s. 1d. invested in 3 per cent consols) had been built up to enable an application to be made to Chancery for further increases in the salaries of the officers and pensions to the almspeople.[56]

But the corner had probably been turned around 1760. It is at about that date that the Company's management of its estates became more professionalised with the more frequent use of surveyors and the visitations to the charities more regular, developments which coincided with the economy drive and efforts to put the charities on a more secure footing. The improvement in administration can be examined in microcosm by considering the management of the Knighton estate. The reports of Surveyor Sloane make initially depressing reading as he uncovered many depredations by the tenants in the Company's woodlands. It was difficult to secure reliable agents in the locality: the woodreeve, George was vulnerable to threats from the farmers; his successor, Richard Whitworth exploited the position for his own gain, cutting down trees without authority, and ignored Sloane's proposals for a nursery of trees. To the suggestion that the underwood might be improved Whitworth responded: 'Gentlemen that live at so great Distance from their Estates Seldom have much Underwood'. Fences were improperly maintained and tenants asserted unlawful rights of way through the woods.[57] But firm action by the Company undoubtedly yielded dividends. New fences were constructed, advertisements placed with the promise of rewards for information about trespasses, and a gamekeeper appointed in 1768. By 1766 Sloane could already report that the 'Determin'd Resolution' of the Company had wrought great benefits as the underwood was flourishing. The successful prosecution of Heaford at the Staffordshire assizes in 1769 for trespass provided a clear demonstration of the Company's resolve: Parton who claimed a right of way through the woods was warned that 'he had as much a Right to the same as Heaford had to the Grange Wood and would have the same success if he contested it with the Company'. Sure enough Parton was brought to heel in 1772 through another suit. And the firm line that the Company was taking brought much valuable information about local conditions which ensured a more favourable settlement for the Company when the Justice leases fell in in 1784.[59]

Thus by the end of the 18th century there were signs of recovery: the first steps had been taken in curriculum reform; the Company was reasserting its control over its estates; and charitable expenditures, cut in the post-Fire decades, were being restored. And yet the recovery was patchy and faltering. The Court of Chancery's leases of the Hatcham estate had severely curtailed the scope for improvement at Monmouth; the priority of the repair of charity buildings restricted the scope for improving the salaries of staff; and the curriculum changes were as yet insufficient to capture the support of middle-class parents.

Chapter Nine

The Company in the Life of its Members, 1500–1800

The rule of the Assistants was shaped by a rhetoric which stressed the brotherhood of the Company, the responsibility of the rich for the poor, and the importance of avoiding contention. Thus, in November 1659 when imposing a penalty of 10s. on members who 'by any abusive and uncivill words or gestures shall affront or iniure any other member', they framed their order in terms of their desire for 'the continuance of all Amicable and brotherly respect and for the prevention of all discord and Animosities betweene the members and brethren of this Court and Company'.[1]

The social ideal was recreated on Lord Mayor's day when the Lord Mayor was a member of the Company. On the festival of Saints Simon and Jude (29 October) the new Lord Mayor, accompanied by a flotilla of barges carrying the Liveries of the different Companies, proceeded by water to Westminster Hall where he took his oath before the Barons of the Exchequer. Returning to the City, and disembarking at Baynard's Castle, he put himself at the rear of a procession headed by the Companies to which his Sheriffs and the previous Lord Mayor belonged, followed by his own Company. Whereas in the other Companies only the Livery processed, in the Lord Mayor's own the social organism was more properly articulated. At the front of the Haberdashers' procession were up to 140 poor men carrying javelins in one hand and in the other targets (small shields) bearing the coats of arms of the new Lord Mayor and of earlier incumbents of the office who had enjoyed membership of the Company. Behind them came between 90 and 100 bachelors. These were members of the Yeomanry organisation selected to perform a variety of ritual roles, usually waiting upon the Lord Mayor, through his year of office. They were differentiated by wealth, being divided into the bachelors in foins or rich bachelors and the bachelors in budge. Behind them came the Livery (probably about another 100 men at the beginning of the 17th century, but rising to 168 in 1664), the Assistants, and the Master and Wardens of the Company. The hierarchy of age was recognised as the younger members of the Livery came first, and the ancients of the Company brought up the rear. The Liverymen were followed by the officers of the Mayor's and Sheriffs' households and by key City officials such as the Chamberlain, Common Serjeant, Common Crier, and the Swordbearer. The Mayor followed accompanied by his predecessor, and followed by the Aldermen, all on horseback.

Each of the key social boundaries was marked out by music, banners, and the presence of whifflers (otherwise called gentlemen ushers) or household officials. Thus before the poor marched two standards bearing the arms of the City and Company respectively, and two drummers and a fife; behind them marched another two banners with the coats of arms of the monarch and Lord Mayor, some more fifes, between ten and twelve whifflers, and ten trumpeters. Between the bachelors and the Livery there were more whifflers, twelve trumpeters, a drum and fife, and the

The dischardge of the said accompt
by payemente made by the said Accomptante

Inprimis paid for xxij broad clothes
for pore mens gownes and cotes and for ⎫ 134 . 14 . 0
dressing the same clothes ⎭

Item paid for p peces of crimson Mockadoes o 010 . 00 . 0

Item paid for xij dozen and a half of red tape ⎫ 013 . 15 . 0
with bandes at xxij d o ⎭

Item paid for making lxxxix gownes ⎫ 007 . 04 . 0
and xlv cotes at vj d ⎭

Item paid for making the mockado sleeues o 000 . 16 . 0

Item paid for making xj ferkins and vj ⎫ 000 . 13 . 0
hose for those that raued the wamds o streands ⎭

Item paid for ix dosen statute lace for the ⎫ 000 . 09 . 0
ferkins and hose o ⎭

Item paid for a peece of white feane fustian ⎫ 001 . 07 . 6
and Canvas and Buttons o ⎭

Item paid to xxxiij pore men for their Dynners 003 . 12 . 0

Item paid to John Erskin for the Pageant ⎫ 046 . 00 . 0
lion, mermaides, Chariott o other thinge ⎭

Item geven to his men for their paines o 000 . 02 . 6

Item paid to the Churchwardens of Chrischurch ⎫ 001 . 00 . 0
for rome to make the pageant o other worke in ⎭

Item paid for taking downe o setting vp y Cailo stall 000 . 03 . 4

Item paid to Antony Munday for his paines o 002 . 00 . 0

Item paid to Beniamyn Johnson for his devise ⎫ 012 . 00 . 0
and speech for the Children o ⎭

Item paid for printing the booke of the devise o 001 . 10 . 0

Item paid to Thomas Kendall for furnishing ⎫
the Children wth apparrell and other 022 . 00 . 0
thinge needfull for the showe ⎭

Item paid for hire of the iiij or Corse horse wth ⎫ 001 . 00 . 0
the furniture to drawe the Chariott o ⎭

Item paid to iiij or men to ride the horses in ⎫ 000 . 11 . 0
armor and for their Dynner o ⎭

Item paid to Thomas Spener for x6 yards ⎫ 05 . 07 . 0
of tinsell for the apparison and the baskes ⎭

Item paid to Kendall for making o repairing o for charge by ⎫ 002 . 07 . 0
burkbram o other thinge in xij whereof ⎭
is allowed back xxd for the stuffe being spoiled
so paid to Kendall

29. Extract from the accounts of the Company's expenses in the Lord Mayor's show on the occasion of the mayoralty of Sir Thomas Lowe (1604), showing payment to Benjamin Jonson 'for his device and the speech to the children'.

City waits (municipal musicians). The Assistants were separated from the Lord Mayor and the Aldermen by the City officials. Each section of the procession was also differentiated by its dress for which tight regulations were laid down. The poor wore blue gowns with red sleeves and caps, all provided by subscription among the Yeomanry at a cost in 1604, for example, of £168 19s. 2d. The whifflers wore velvet coats with chains of gold, and carried white staves. The rich bachelors wore satin coats guarded with velvet and faced with foins; the other bachelors wore coats of damask faced with budge; all bore crimson satin hoods. The Liverymen wore their Livery gowns and hoods; their gowns were faced with foins if they were Assistants and with budge if they were not. The procession on Lord Mayor's day therefore provided an idealised vision of the social order within the Company: each section was in its place, the poor acknowledging their dependence on the wealthier members by the shields they carried, and the wealthy admitting their responsibilities for the poor by the gowns they had provided.[2]

But was it more than an ideal? Could the Company ever really provide the framework of brotherly love and a stable social order which the rulers' rhetoric articulated and the Mayor's procession visually represented? Exhortations to brotherly love such as that of 1659 were necessary precisely because of the name-calling in which members indulged. In 1653, for example, William Barriffe's admission to the Livery was held up because in his recent service as Yeomanry Warden he had 'scandaliously defamed Mr Alderman Fowke in publique manner'.[3] And the timing of the order of 1659 is significant. The republican experiment was disintegrating, and the threat that the deep divisions in English society would flare up in renewed civil war was a real one. The Haberdashers were desperately seeking to avoid the public expression of those tensions which might endanger the rough and ready consensus essential to the transaction of Company business and the avoidance of outside interference. The ideal of reciprocity in relations between rich and poor was endangered by the underlying resentments between artisans and wholesalers explored in an earlier chapter. Behind the ideal represented in the Mayor's procession there are signs of a lack of enthusiasm for the whole business among at least some Companymen. The triumph accounts for 1604 include payments to Dod and Farmer, officers of the Lord Mayor's household, for their 'paines about such as refused to pay their Cesementes', and to the Mayor's clerk for three warrants. Each time that a triumph was held there were difficulties in inducing men to serve as bachelors and pay the assessments which financed the costly celebrations (£750 8s. 6d. in 1620 and £1,330 16s. 5d. in 1664), and often defaulters had to be brought before the Mayor before their compliance was secured. Nor is it exactly true to say that the whole Company was represented in the triumphs, for apprentices were excluded from any role save as spectators. And they seized the opportunities the occasion presented for misrule. The Venetian ambassador, describing proceedings in 1615, was shocked by the insolence of the apprentices, jumping on the tail-boards of coaches, pelting the coachmen with mud, and picking fights.[4] The social reality was a good deal less comfortable than the Assistants cared to think. This chapter will scrutinise the ways in which the Company sought to realise the ideal of brotherhood, to determine what measure of success attended their efforts. It begins by considering that all too often invisible group constituted by the apprentices.

Invisible, that is to historians, but certainly not to contemporaries. With an average of no less than 311 apprentice bindings each year between 1605 and 1614, there were probably between 1,500 and 1,750 young men apprenticed to freemen of the Haberdashers' Company in the capital in 1615. Apprentices probably nearly equalled and possibly exceeded the number of freemen in the Company.[5] It is therefore hardly surprising that contemporary anxieties about the social order centred on this group thought to embody all the headstrong qualities that characterised youth and affrighted their elders. The ideal was that the system of apprenticeship would not only enable a young man to learn a trade but also to acquire the habits of sobriety, piety, and hard work essential to the maintenance of the social order. Indentures of apprenticeship regulated the behaviour of the apprentice strictly. He was not to engage in fornication or marry during his term. He was not to play at 'cards, dice, tables, or any other unlawful games'. Nor could he haunt taverns and playhouses. His primary loyalty was to his master whose 'lawful commandments' he must obey, and whose service he must not neglect day or night. Religion was also a key element in the socialising process. Apprentices were expected to accompany their masters to church, and from at least 1627 the Company presented them with a copy of the church catechism (later *The Whole Duty of Man*) at the commencement of their terms. Among other things the catechism taught that through obedience lay salvation. It was, however, a reciprocal relationship. Indentures also specified the responsibilities of the master. He was to instruct the apprentice in his trade and to find him 'meat, drink, apparel, lodgings, and all other necessaries, according to the custom of the City of London'. Thus apprenticeship ensured the acquisition of skills in a secure environment and the internalisation of the values which supported the social order.[6]

Relations between many apprentices and their masters conformed to this pattern. Apprentices were often remembered in the wills of their masters. Wealthier masters would leave bequests of £10 to £20; the humbler ones 6s. 8d. to 40s. The more faithful servants would be singled out by larger bequests than went to the others. Other ways of rewarding an apprentice would be remission of a portion of the term of service. Thus William Paige (d. 1501) gave £10 to Stephen Stone, his apprentice, and released him of three years of his term. Others would leave their tools: Edmund Love (d.?1548) left to his apprentice, Philip 'a paire of sheeres, a paire of burlynge yernes, and all my pynnes with their tasselles'. Others gave clothes and household goods in addition to tools: Henry Hunt (d. 1518) left his apprentice a gown of marble colour, two doublets, a jacket, a flock bed, coverlet, bolster, and a pair of sheets, together with 'all my sherys, pynnys, and tasyllys'. But the basically unequal nature of the relationship between masters and apprentices would often be underscored by the way in which such bequests were made conditional on continuing good service to the widow. Rauffe Johnson (d. 1543) left £5 to his apprentice, 'being good and diligent to my wife in helping her to the best of his powre in good and true utteryng and ordereyng of my wares yf he so contynewe with her'.[7]

It is clear, however, that apprenticeship was often a highly fraught relationship.

Unfortunately the lack of minutes of the Courts of Wardens, where disputes were most frequently arbitrated, means that we cannot observe these frictions in the detail which is possible in other Companies. We do know that only about 40 per cent of apprentices completed their terms, and only a small proportion of this wastage can be explained by mortality. Perhaps some apprentices acquired a smattering of the trade and returned home to practise in an environment less hedged about with restrictions than London.[8] But many others were probably genuine drop-outs, the kind of men who appeared with monotonous regularity before the Governors of Bridewell, the London house of correction with jurisdiction over the petty delinquencies of the poor. Between May 1559 and April 1560 the Governors of Bridewell were confronted with several delinquent haberdasher apprentices: William Hanley and Oliver Morley were both guilty of petty theft and 'despoiling' their masters' maids; Richard Brooke had attempted to defile his master's daughter; William Cassell was whipped for stubbornness and disobedience to his master; John Hamlyn was brought in by the Alderman's Deputy for withstanding his master; Roger Wood, apprentice with Alexander Best, took his master's keys when the rest of the household was asleep, went next door to play cards, and set upon his master when discovered.[9] But the record of this court also reveals a key reason why the household could not serve as a fully effective agency of socialisation in the way the social commentators of the time envisaged. The truth was that many masters were also guilty of moral shortcomings. Among the freemen haberdashers prosecuted in that same year were Robert Parradice for sex with the daughter of an attorney of the Guildhall, John Lyny for keeping a harlot, John Austyn for breaking the Lenten regulations and for allowing his wife to keep the company of another man, Thomas Spackman, the son of a highly respected Assistant, for haunting prostitutes. An offence which caused the Governors such scandal that the offenders were carted occurred the following year and involved two haberdasher families. Agnes Browne, wife of Thomas Browne, haberdasher, had been caught having sex with a vintner's apprentice in the house of John Mosse, also a haberdasher. Agnes Browne, Anne and John Mosse were carted as a notorious harlot, a bawd, and 'a cuckhold and wythold' respectively. Households as clearly out of joint as these could hardly fulfil the socialising roles the rulers expected of them.[10]

The Wardens recognised the shortcomings of the household as an agency of socialisation by providing within the Court of Wardens a framework within which the disputes between masters and apprentices could be arbitrated. The early minutes of the Court of Assistants include a few records of meetings of the Court of Wardens and enable an assessment of the nature of their arbitrations to be made. Their justice did not work entirely to the master's favour. Two cases considered in July 1584 will illustrate this point. Nicholas and Margaret Hill of Hoggesdon brought a complaint against Robert Pavie for putting in suit the bond by which Margaret had stood surety for the true dealing of Richard Nicholas, apprenticed to Pavie. The details of Pavie's disagreement with his apprentice are not given, but the Wardens were evidently unimpressed, for they instructed that all litigation should cease, that Pavie should receive the apprentice back, and that Hill should provide him with new apparel and 10s. In another case William Frost was fined £7 for refusing to submit his quarrels with Martin Smith, his former apprentice, to the arbitration either of his neighbours or the Company. Frost was a difficult master for another of his apprentices was complaining of misusage in Novemeber 1585. To the extent that their rulings cannot be reduced to simple notions of 'class justice', the Wardens ensured that apprentices did not feel the institutions of the Company completely alien to them.[11] However, lest we fall prey to the delusion that the Wardens acted with sympathy to the underdog, we should recognise that usually in cases where rulings favourable to the apprentice were secured, it was because more powerful interests had interceded on his behalf. Thus the intervention of the Hills was crucial to the ruling in favour of Richard Nicholas, while in 1585 it was the intercession of his 'friends' which helped one Pedley in his efforts to persuade his master, Florence Caldwell, a leading Assistant, to take him back with 'a supply of yeres for the tyme myspent'. The realities of differential social power should not be neglected.[12] However numerous the cases of trusting relations between masters and apprentices, it cannot be denied that the Company's success in integrating its apprentices was at best partial. The high drop-out rate, though no worse than that of other Companies, is clear testimony to the frustrations and disappointments of many apprentices.

What of that minority who did take up the freedom? How important was the Company to their business and social life? How successful was the Company in achieving a sense of identity among its membership? In the first place, it is essential to bear in mind that membership of a Livery Company brought key political and economic privileges. Freemen enjoyed the right to vote at wardmotes for ward officials including Aldermen, and only freemen could engage in retail trade within the boundaries of the City. They enjoyed the privilege of only being sued in City courts, and they were subject to civic customs like that of orphans which protected the interests of their wives and minors after their death. The practice of describing oneself by reference to membership of a Livery Company was widespread. In their wills members regularly adopted the title of 'citizen and haberdasher'.[13] The freedom of the City clearly mattered, but whether the freedom of the Haberdashers' Company, as opposed to any other, really mattered, is more doubtful because of the erosion of the Company's economic functions over the course of the later 16th and 17th centuries. An earlier chapter showed how the Company's control over hat making broke down in the 17th century with the establishment of the rival Feltmakers. The custom of London by which a freeman could pursue any trade and not just that to which he had been apprenticed, eroded the occupational homogeneity of the guild so that members had less in common with each other. Little effort seems to have been made in the 17th century to enforce the ordinance limiting the number of apprentices a man might keep: this was one of the ordinances which had traditionally been supported by small producers and journeymen anxious to limit the competition of more powerfully placed interests. Moreover, the Company's rights of search lapsed after 1650.[14] But the regulation of the trade and conditions of employment was not the only rationale for the Company. It also served a variety of social functions for its members. Through a round of feasting it provided opportunities for convivial exchange, the nurturing of friendships and business connections. By arranging for the arbitration of disputes it sought to defuse tensions between members without recourse to the law. The obligation of Liverymen to turn up at the funerals of their deceased brethren helped to mark out the status of Companymen in the eyes of the world. And the large volume of welfare administered through the Companies gave the poor good reason for cultivating good relations with the rulers. It is to a discussion of the Company's fulfilment of these various integrating roles that the rest of this chapter is dedicated.

Under the terms of the Company ordinances of 1629, which encapsulated current practice, the Company was to assemble at quarterly intervals within one month of the feasts of Michaelmas, Christmas, Our Lady, and Midsummer to hear the ordinances read. Separate gatherings were to be held for the Livery and Yeomanry, presided over by the Master and Wardens of the Livery and the Wardens of the Yeomanry respectively. The occasion was to be rounded off by a dinner. Liverymen also gathered at the Hall for a dinner after the celebrations attending the Lord Mayor's oath-taking at which the Liveries lined the streets. But the highlight of the Company's cycle of feasting was the dinner for the Livery held on the Tuesday after the feast of St Katherine's at which the election held on the previous Saturday was published to the Company by the crowning ceremony of garlands. References in the Court minutes make it clear that, in addition to the Publication dinner, there were other dinners, probably just for the Assistants, on the occasion of the election itself, which was paid for entirely by the Master, and on the delivery of the plate, evidences, and specialties on the Wednesday after the election.[15] The development of a protestant ritual calendar added other occasions to the round of Company-sponsored conviviality. In November 1607 the Assistants noted that after attending the sermons at Paul's Cross on 24 March and 5 November, the anniversaries of the King's accession and the saving of King and Parliament from gunpowder treason respectively, the Liveries of most Companies attended feasts at their Company Halls, and not to be outdone the Haberdashers took up the practice.[16] The arrangements for dinners were subject to frequent ammendment, and there are several orders over the course of the 17th century altering the Company's practice, usually in the direction of streamlining by assimilating the additional celebrations to the quarter dinners in order to reduce the cost to the Wardens. In December 1658, for example, it was ordered that the quarter dinners should be held on the second Tuesday in February, Lord Mayor's day (29 October), 5 November, and at the election of the Master and Wardens, although it should be noted that the feast at the Publication ceremony following the election was also to be continued. One obvious consequence of the order of 1658 was that the Company's feasting became concentrated in the last days of October and the first three weeks of November.[17]

From a comparatively early date this expenditure on feasting came under attack for the waste of resources it represented. Thomas Barnabe, writing to the young Secretary of State William Cecil in 1552, alleged that

> there be so many . . . rich halls of lands. Some may spend viii hondred pound, some vi hondred, some less and some more . . . and nothing don withal but make great feasts every month or six weeks at their halls and cause vittayls to be dere.[18]

The criticism was unfair as far as the Haberdashers were concerned because the contribution from corporate funds to the dinners was relatively slight. Dinners were financed predominantly by the Master and Wardens and by contributions from the diners. According to the ordinances the charges of the St Katherine Feast besides the customary allowances were to be borne by the outgoing Master and Wardens. During the 1630s, when the accounts begin, the customary allowance was £50 of Company stock, and this was supplemented by payments in dinner money (a handsome 5s. a head in the 1630s) from those members attending the feast. The election dinner was normally paid for by the Master, although in the mid–17th century it was briefly scheduled as one of the quarter dinners. The quarter dinners were to be paid for entirely by the Wardens. When the Company began holding dinners on the occasion of the anniversary of the King's accession and Gunpowder Day it was ordered that Liverymen attending these dinners should pay 2s. each and that the residue of the monies spent should come from house stock.[19] It is true that in 1634 it was noted that many Liverymen were unwilling to pay their contributions to the dinner on 5 November, and that the gathering of the money after the dinner was 'both inconvenient and disgracefull', so it was ordered that the full costs should be borne by Company stock, but the Assistants insisted that the cost should not exceed £25. When this dinner was rescheduled as a quarter feast in 1658 its provision became the responsibility of the Wardens.[20] A rough idea of the costs to the Wardens of providing these dinners can be obtained from the money paid in lieu of feasts in the later 1620s and 1630s in response to measures taken in times of dearth. In 1625 and 1626 the Wardens paid £16 and £20 respectively in lieu of their July quarter dinner. In 1630 the Wardens were instructed to pay £6 13s. 4d. each and the Master £10 for not keeping the election feast. These figures suggest an expenditure on feasting of the order of £100 by the Master and Wardens each year. It can be shown from the Wardens' accounts of the 1630s that the contribution of Company stock to feasting (including the dinners for the Assistants on the occasion of the auditing of accounts and the view of the Company's lands about London) amounted to about £88 per annum, which does not seem an excessive amount given what members contributed in the way of apprenticeship and freedom fees, quarterage payments, Livery fines and so on.[21]

The Companies were, however, vulnerable to attack because their dinners were unquestionably lavish. Unfortunately there are no accounts of expenditure at Haberdasher dinners before the 18th century, but a surviving set of feast accounts from the Drapers' Company for the Elizabethan period may be taken as representing the then practice of the Great Twelve Companies, for feasting was one of those areas subject to escalation induced by competition between Companies for the prestige which lavish provision represented. It was usual practice in this period for the food to be served on several large dishes from which guests helped themselves. Each of these dishes or 'messes' usually served for four people. At the Drapers' feast of 1564 each of the messes in the first course consisted of three 'rands' (long slices) and a shield of boar (this latter was a cylinder made from skin from the flank of the animal filled with meat), two boiled capons, two roast capons, a venison pasty, a large pike, and a custard (which was then an open meat pie covered with broth or milk thickened with eggs and seasoned with spices). For the second course each mess entailed six quails, a sturgeon, and a marchpane (marzipan), accompanied by wafers and hippocras (wine flavoured with spices). Typical fare for a quarter dinner was fourteen capons, five geese, a turkey cock, six dozen larks, a sirloin of beef, three lambs, five dozen loaves, fifty eggs, twelve pies, six custards, five gallons of claret, two gallons of white wine, a gallon of sack, and a quart of muscadine. The celebrations attending the Drapers' feasts in 1564 cost a total of £82 9s. 4d., paid for largely by the Wardens, and each of the quarter dinners about £7.[22]

The presence of 'royal' foods such as venison, swans, and sturgeon is particularly to be noted. The acquisition of venison was a matter for much competition among the Wardens who mobilised their gentry connections to secure the largest amount possible. Thus at the Drapers' feast of 1564 no less than 25¼ bucks were delivered to the Hall, and baked into 162 pasties. This prodigious quantity gave the Company an opportunity to demonstrate its status before the wider world, for pasties were delivered out to civic and local parochial officials, and 15 were distributed to 'the neighbours afore our gate'. Thirty were given to the Wardens to distribute among their household servants, neighbours and friends as a mark of their status. Such ostentation gave offence to an ever snobbish Queen Elizabeth I. In 1573 it was learnt in the City that 'the nobilitie and gentlemen about the Court were much offended at the great number of bucks' consumed at City feasts and, in the context of dearth, the Lord Mayor intervened at Burghley's request to curb the extravagance, imposing a ban (which proved temporary) on election feasts but allowing quarter dinners and dinners on Lord Mayor's day provided that no venison was consumed.[23]

Feasting served a variety of functions within the Company. Most obviously they brought members together and fostered the spirit of brotherhood the rulers regarded as essential to effective government as well as providing the Company with a tangible means of self-identification. They also emphasised the reciprocity of relations within the Company. The right to participate in decision-making on the Court of Assistants was earned by providing services for one's fellow Liverymen in the form of sumptuous dinners. Feasting also articulated the hierarchy within the Company. Careful attention was paid to seating, guests and Assistants taking the places at the high table, and the Livery occupying the side tables. Until 1628 the Livery customarily accompanied the Wardens home after the feast. It was also normal practice for four of the Yeomanry Wardens to carry the cups before the Wardens at the Publication feast (the Master's cup was borne by the Clerk), and 18 or 20 of the Yeomanry 'of good quality and personage' were appointed for each feast 'in decent and comely manner to carrie in the meate to the tables'. In this way the subordinate position of the Yeomanry was ceremonially underlined. Service earned its reward, because the dutiful performance of the Yeomanry Wardens was reciprocated by their later elevation to the Livery.[24] Feasting also provided an opportunity to celebrate the wealth and worship of the Company. Although guest lists are not extant for the Haberdashers' Company, it is unlikely that they diverged from the practice of other Companies who would invite Aldermen, Privy Councillors, nobles, customs officials, and royal bureaucrats. There was a chance to cultivate valuable contacts in central government, to bring the Company's problems to the attention of ministers, as well as furthering the 'honour and worship' of the Company by putting on a good show.[25]

However, the ideals behind the feasting were not always realised. In the early years of the 17th century there are regular complaints that the Wardens were failing to turn up to the Publication feast causing 'great disparagement to the reputation of the company and a great blemish unto their feast'. In 1612 it was ordered that Wardens who absented themselves should pay fines of 20s., but the following year this was found not to 'produce that good effect as was expected by reason it is so small', and the fine was increased to £3ˢ6s. 8d. Although less is heard of the problem after the 1620s this probably represented an admission of defeat by the Assistants, for it will be recalled that it was more frequently the case that, because of refusals of office, the Wardens had not even been decided upon by the time of the St Katherine's feast.[26] Another complaint which surfaced in the mid 17th century suggests that the ordered hierarchy the Assistants strived for was not easily accomplished. For Liverymen were in the habit of coming to Company dinners accompanied by children and servants, apparently to wait on their parents and masters, but crowding out the hall, damaging property, and behaving in a generally rude manner. Liverymen apparently even passed food from the table to their servants. The repetition of orders against such unseemly practices in 1632, 1658, and 1677 suggests that they were deep-rooted.[27]

There was also inevitably a limit on the degree to which the feasts could promote brotherhood because attendance at the vast majority of Company dinners was restricted to the Livery. It is true that the Yeomanry had developed their own cycle of convivial gatherings. The election proceedings of the Yeomanry aped those of the Livery, for they enjoyed their own dinner on the second Tuesday in August. That the Yeomanry feast included a crowning ceremony is shown by the Yeomanry's inventories which record

> vj garlands of purple velvet the gift of George Tadlowe with viij scutcheons of silver, viz. ij of Saint George, ij of Saint Katherine, and iiij of the letters G.T. for Mr Tadlowe's name.

We are fortunate in possessing a set of Yeomanry accounts for the early 17th century which makes it clear how the dinners were financed. An allowance of £13 6s. 8d. was made from Yeomanry stock, supplemented by contributions from the diners, and 6d. on every apprentice presentment. In 1601 the contributions from those dining amounted to £31 4s. 4d., and the allowances on apprentice presentments to £3 16s. 6d. Together with the customary allowance from the stock that came to £48 7s. 6d. But the total cost of the dinner was £105 7s. 1d., the difference being provided by the six Yeomanry Wardens out of their own pockets, no mean sum of about £9 9s. 2d. each. In addition to providing the feast, the Wardens of the Yeomanry were expected to supervise the Yeomanry on quarter days. They were allowed 26s. 8d. for their expenses on these occasions, which if the practice of other Companies was followed, would have gone towards the provision of bread, cheese, and beer for the company.[28]

Yeomanry feasts could only have brought a minority of the Company together. This was simply because the sheer size of the Company, which can be estimated at 1,546 in 1595, precluded the attendance of all members at the Hall. But the numbers of Yeomen who could attend the dinner were further reduced by the presence of Liverymen at the Yeomanry feasts. So much is clear from the payments in dinner money at the 1601 feast: £7 13s. 4d. from the Livery who dined, £1 13s. 4d. from the Livery who did not dine, £16 16s. 0d. from the Yeomanry who dined, and £5 1s. 0d. from the Yeomanry who did not dine.[29] Another consideration limiting the degree to which the Yeomanry feasts could promote incorporation within the Company was the growing infrequency with which they were held. This was because of reluctance on the part of the Yeomanry Wardens to pay for them, and because of the increasingly pressing claims of the poor on Company resources. There was no Yeomanry feast between 1586 and 1595. In the first 40 years of the 17th century feasts only took place on 12 occasions. The civil war caused the Yeomanry feasts to lapse, and the abandonment of the Yeomanry Wardens after the Restoration entailed the disappearance of the feasts altogether. As the feasts were probably for many members one of the few Company functions they were able to attend, their suppression was unpopular: in the words of the Assistants on reviving the feast in 1595 its suppression 'hath growen to a greate dislike of the generalitie of this Company'. It is true that the feasts for the Livery were also periodically curtailed, but the Yeomanry had very much less to cut back on, and the distancing of many members from the Company is to be accounted for by the drive for economy in feasting.[30]

Feasting among the Livery, as has been shown, came under particularly close scrutiny in times of plague and dearth when the sufferings of the poor made feasting seem inappropriate. Better that the monies spent on feasts should be redirected to poor relief, and that members should turn to prayer and fasting to avert the wrath of God which they perhaps deserved for their lives of luxury. Thus in July 1596 Companies were ordered by the Lord Mayor to cease feasting and hand over the monies saved to a treasurer appointed by the Aldermen for distribution to the poor.[31] Sympathy for the international protestant cause led to the abandonment of all the quarter dinners in 1620–1, the Wardens paying £100 to the Palatinate defence fund set up at the order of James I.[32] The plague of 1625 and the years of war which followed saw severe curtailments to the Company's feasting. In 1625 the Wardens distributed £16 to the Company poor instead of providing the Midsummer quarter dinner, and in 1626 and 1627 the Publication feast was reduced to a small private dinner for the Aldermen, Assistants, and Livery only. In response to another plague in 1636 the Yeomanry Wardens handed over £20 to the Lord Mayor for the relief of plague victims, while the Master and Wardens distributed a total of £80 to the Company's poor in lieu of the Midsummer quarter dinner and Publication feast.[33]

Over the course of the later 17th century the pressures on Company feasting became still more acute. In November 1649 it was noted that 'the sadnes of ye times for some yeeres past hath caused ye omission of some things which were formerly observed'. The quarter dinners had apparently lapsed altogether during the civil wars. They were revived, although as has been seen efforts were made to economise by rescheduling other dinners as quarter dinners.[34] The Great Fire brought further disruptions. In spite of an order of November 1669 that the quarter dinners should be revived, four years later the Assistants were complaining that the dinners had not been kept as in the past 'to the great prejudice of the Company by the discontent

30. The Sheriff's Feast, actually at Fishmongers' Hall, but capturing the character of civic feasting in the mid-18th century; from William Hogarth's *Industry and Idleness* (1747).

therein given to ye Livery and also to the ill example of Succeeding Wardens'. The recent Wardens were to be fined for not keeping the dinners and, in order to provide an incentive for the better keeping of the feasts, the Wardens were granted the benefit of the fees of the first ten men made free by redemption each year.[35] Although in 1690 the Assistants ordered that the Company should continue to observe the anniversary of the Restoration (29 May) as a quarter day, they were complaining in 1699 that this festival had been completely neglected for several years.[36] In the face of the growing reluctance to accept Company office in the later 17th and early 18th centuries it became necessary to grant incentives to Wardens in the form of the fees for redemptioners in 1673, later replaced by Livery fines of £25 apiece (one in 1689, and two in 1706).[37]

The 18th-century feast accounts show that the entertainments were a shadow of their former selves. In the 1730s dinners were still being provided on Lord Mayor's day, Gunpowder day, and at the election and Publication feasts. But the total cost of these entertainments was just £196 8s. 1d. in 1731, and the bill for the St Katherine's feast (allotting half the wine bill for the year to that feast) £69 6s. 11d.

The early 17th-century Yeomanry feasts alone had cost upwards of £100, and a staggering £173 10s. 3d. in 1640. The fare was not much changed from the mid 16th-century, but the quantities were less overwhelming, and the continued absence of vegetables rather worrying. In 1731 the St Katherine's feast involved the preparation for the first course of one fish dish, twelve dishes of oysters with herbs, four venison pasties, nine turkeys, eight marrow puddings, eight dishes of tongue with udders, eight of mince pies, ten of boar, and nine of custards for the whole company. For the second course one dish of wildfowl, eleven dishes of ducks and larks, and nine of apple pies were provided. This was washed down with red and white oporto wine and sack.[38]

The Haberdashers suspended their dinners altogether for 30 years between 1754 and 1784 as part of their heroic economy drive to rescue the Company from looming bankruptcy. The Master was to be excused providing the dinner on the Master's day and one-fifth the cost of the Publication dinner paying £20 to the Company, and the Wardens were relieved of the obligation of providing a dinner on Lord Mayor's day and at the Publication ceremony, paying £15 each to the stock. There is no reference to the quarter dinners which appear to have ceased at about the time of the accession of the Hanoverians. A modest dinner continued to be provided by subscription for the Publication ceremony through the 1760s and 1770s, but if the number of subscribers (usually 30) is anything to go by, only a fraction of the Assistants, let alone the Livery attended. When the Publication feasts revived, they were on a grander scale once more (the Publication dinner in 1795 cost £174 4s. 11d.), and the full cost now borne by Company stock, but they were the only entertainment provided for the Company.[39]

This discussion of feasting has revealed that it was often perceived as being in conflict with the Company's responsibilities to its poor. Indeed one might claim that the early modern period witnessed a transition from a society in which the social bond was expressed through shared activities like feasting to one where the bonds were more hierarchically articulated, the poor acknowledging their dependence on the rich through the quest for relief. Poor relief was certainly growing in importance as an aspect of Company activity through the early modern period. The loss of the early accounts makes it impossible to determine with any exactitude the scale of the Company's involvement in poor relief. The pattern of other Companies suggests that until the mid–16th century almsmen would have accounted for the bulk of the charity directed at members, but that thereafter, and in line with the growing intervention of the municipal authorities in provision for the poor with the establishment of the hospitals and the poor rate, the contribution from house stock and from endowments would have grown.[40] Certainly the earliest Hall incorporated provision for rooms where almsmen were resident, and we know that the volume of endowments directed at the Company poor grew precipitously from a yield of £24 1s. 4d. per annum in 1560 to £553 0s. 2d. per annum in 1680.[41] Grants from house stock were made more regularly for purposes as varied as apprenticing a child, helping members who had suffered losses through fire, redeeming members from imprisonment for debt, ransoming members from the captivity of Barbary pirates, or paying a contribution towards the journey a Company member proposed to make to York with the condition that he never more burden the Company.[42] By the early 17th century the Company was making so many grants from house stock (as opposed to endowments) that its long-term financial position was felt to be endangered. In 1611 it was ordered that pensioners paid from Company stock should not be replaced as they died 'untill the Company shalbe better able to geve the same'.[43] It is not clear at what date a poor box emerged, but there are references to distributions from it of sums of about £13 each year in the 1760s: as poor boxes were a long-standing feature of many companies, it is probable that the infrequency of references to it earlier merely reflects the fact that it was already taken for granted by the time that the Company's records become fulsome in the later 16th century.[44]

The order of 1611 curtailing pensions from house stock is one of several signs of strains on the Company's resources. Inevitably there were more claimants for relief than the Company was able to cater for. It is this which explains the practice of granting reversions to pensions and places in almshouses which nevertheless caused the Assistants much anxiety because of the mortgaging of future resources that it represented. Petitioners for relief were so insistent that the Assistants had to order in 1611 that no petitions should be heard except at the court held for that purpose on St Katherine's Day.[45] Pressure on resources also explains the Company's inability to supply its almsmen with the alternative accommodation long thought to be desirable. The residence of the almsmen in the rooms over the kitchen, an order of 1639 explains, had been

found to bee very inconvenyent in tyme of Infection and very offensive to the Company by spilling of water in those roomes thereby decaying and breaking downe the seeling and rotting the Tymber, besides the great danger of fire, the Chimneys of those roomes having noe other foundacion than the Boards of the floore.

However, the Wardens had been instructed to find an alternative site as early as 1617, and in 1621 it had been ordered that no more poor were to be admitted to live over the kitchens, but the Assistants were still being exercised by the problem on the eve of the civil war. The problem was money, for an extensive programme of alterations at the Hall in 1621–2 had left the Company in debt and unable to contemplate the purchase of a new site for almshouses. The rooms over the kitchen had been made vacant by 1649.[46] Although the Company never built its new alms-houses, the vacuum in charitable provision was partially alleviated by the acquisition of the site at Snow Hill in 1651 to provide accommodation for six almsmen free of the Company supported by pensions of £10 per annum each under the terms of the will of Edmund Hammond. Robert Aske's Hospital at Hoxton later provided accommodation for 20 decayed freemen with generous allowances for their clothing and support.[47]

In considering the contribution that the Haberdashers' Company made to the relief of its poor it is important to put its efforts in perspective by considering them by comparison with parochial poor relief. One striking fact is that much of the Haberdashers' relief was on a grander scale than that available in the parishes. Whereas a typical pension from the parishes in the 17th century was 1s. per week

(£2 12s. 0d. per annum) the Company offered nine pensions of £8 per annum under the Jones benefaction and two pensions of £6 per annum provided by Lady Romeney, in addition to the generous allowances to the almsmen in the Hammond almshouses and Aske's Hospital at Hoxton.[48] The Livery Companies catered not merely for the absolutely destitute, but also for those who had formerly enjoyed prosperity, but now fallen on hard times. This group was quite large in pre-modern London because of the vulnerability of business fortunes in an economy so dangerously dependent on credit. Charity was often granted to decayed Liverymen and, increasingly in the later 17th and early 18th centuries, to men who had served as Assistants, some of whom even found their way into Hoxton Hospital. In making grants to these men their former service to the Company was often emphasised as a means of justifying the larger than normal pensions. Sometimes they were the recipients of extraordinary grants from Company stock. In 1731 on the recommendation of Sir Harcourt Master the Assistants considered the case of Robert Castle who had fined for the Mastership, but now lay in 'very necessitous circumstances', making it difficult for him to support his wife and four children. Taking into account his former services to the Company, he was granted £5 for his immediate needs and promised a pension of £20 per annum.[49]

The charity granted to Company members, however, was no exception to the rule that conformity to the norms of the Company's rulers was insisted upon. The lives of the Company's poor, particularly those in the Company's almshouses, were closely regulated. In 1605 the occupants of the almshouses were warned against the taking of inmates, a contemporary obsession because of the prospect of additional burdens on the poor rates, but one which had been focused for the Assistants by the fact that their own almsmen had recently harboured other persons 'sometimes such as have ben there delyvered of childe'. This warning was followed up the next year by a more comprehensive order which stated that no almsman's place should be granted to anyone young enough to have children, nor to anyone having children with them, and that almsmen must seek the permission of the Master and Wardens before marrying.[50] The Company was willing to suspend pensioners whose behaviour gave grounds for concern: Hugh Thornley was deprived of his Jones pension for nine months in December 1676 because of his 'evill and vitious conversacion', and it was only restored when the Court was satisfied that he had amended his behaviour. The most explicit order relating to the control dimension to poor relief came at the height of the Tory reaction in 1684, when it was declared that it was important for the 'publick good' that no-one be admitted to a pension 'but such as are of sober and reguler lives and conformable to the Government in Church and State'. For this reason no-one was to receive a pension without a certificate of their good behaviour and conformity from the minister and churchwardens of their parish. The implications of this order were that poor relief was only to go to practising members of the Church of England.[51] Once Aske's Hospital was opened the committee appointed to manage it was regularly confronted by the problem of disorderly inmates. In 1696, for example, shortly after the opening, they had to discipline Christopher Banister whose 'nastinesse and loathsomest' (*sic*) had threatened the hospital with fire as he had burned wood on his open hearth in spite of the provision of coals in the chimney, and Christopher Coppleston whose 'quarrelsome temper' was reflected in his conflict with another pensioner and in his 'contumelious speeches and scandalous reports about ye said Hospitall'. The Governors were doubtless relieved when Banister died shortly after this episode, and they were able to bring Coppleston into line by suspending him from his pension.[52] It would, however, be unwise to suggest that all recipients of Haberdasher charity received their pensions in a spirit of sullen conformity, browbeaten into dependence by the threat that what the Wardens gave they might take away once more. The respectable poor were not an elite fiction, but a reality in those many members who sweated out their lives, feared God, and gave heartfelt thanks to those members of the elite who sponsored their petitions for relief.

How then does the balance sheet concerning the identification of the members with the Company stand? One should be wary of arguing merely from silence. The poor are much less visible in our records. Just because they did not leave money in their wills to the Company in the way that elite members often did does not mean that the Company meant nothing to them: rather it is simply an index of their humbler circumstances. Nor should we argue that merely because the Yeomanry only had bread, cheese, and beer at their quarter days, they felt less keen about the Company than Liverymen who were tucking into their juicy venison pasties at the same time. For the truth is that Yeomen and Liverymen probably had different expectations. However, it is inescapably the case that the number of occasions of social intercourse among the Yeomanry were always fewer than those for the Livery: apart from the fact of their limited number of dinners, there is no sign that Yeomen members were expected to attend the funerals of their deceased brethren. Moreover the sheer numbers of Yeomen increasingly precluded any sense of identity among them. This was further sapped by the growing occupational heterogeneity of the Company, the withdrawal of the Company from the regulation of the trade beyond the administration of the apprenticeship system, the abandonment of the Yeomanry Wardens after the Restoration, and the consequent collapse of entertainments for Yeomen members. For those Yeomen who did not achieve the Livery (and it should be admitted that an increasing proportion did in the years after the Great Fire) the Company meant little beyond the institution through which apprentices were registered and from which poor relief might be expected in the event of a change for the worse in family circumstances.

As for the Livery, the picture is more favourable. There were numerous occasions at which they gathered at the Hall for social engagements. In addition to the dinners already noted, their additional political rights brought them together at meetings of Common Hall to vote for the Lord Mayor, Sheriffs, and Members of Parliament. There were also a number of civic sermons attended by Liverymen: in the 16th century these were held at St Paul's at the festivals of All Saints, Christmas, Twelfth Day, and Candlemas, and even in the later 18th century the Company accounts record payments to the vergers of St Paul's for giving the Company access on six occasions each year. The ordinances also laid down that Liverymen were to attend the funerals of their brethren on pain of a fine of 3s. 4d. The Company provided a forum within which many friendships were forged. Nineteen of the 41 Haberdasher Assistants whose wills were proved in the Prerogative Court of Canterbury between

1470 and 1558 were sufficiently confident of fellow-members to appoint them as their executors or overseers. Fifteen appointed other haberdashers as overseers, and six as executors (in two cases both executors and overseers were Company members). These statistics are the more impressive when we appreciate that seven failed to appoint overseers at all.[53]

However, the loyalty of the Livery towards the Company was unquestionably deteriorating in the later 16th and 17th centuries. In this period there were constant complaints about the failure of the Livery to appear on quarter days. The problem was so great, the Assistants alleged in 1607, 'that it is conceyved to growe rather of contempt then onlie of negligence'. The problem was 'verie likelie to be the ruine and overthrowe of this most auncient and heretofore well governed and obedient Societie'.[54] Nor was their attendance at funerals as diligent as it might have been. Complaints about this neglect are less strident after 1620, but this probably represented the Assistants' acknowledgement of realities. Certainly, as the century advanced identity would have eroded with the expansion in the size of the Livery, the quest for privacy which made people less inclined to favour large gatherings at funerals, and the growing reluctance to take up Company office.

Chapter Ten

The Company in the Life of City and Nation

The previous chapter used the celebrations on Lord Mayor's day as a way into a discussion of the degree to which the Company embodied an ideal of community. The present chapter takes the same point of departure in order to explore the nature of the relationship between the Company and the government of the City and nation. For the celebrations on Lord Mayor's day were an expression of the intertwining of the governments of Companies, City, and nation. The organisation of the procession and pageants by the new Lord Mayor's Company demonstrated the way in which the City elite drew part of its power from its roots in the Livery Companies. A similar message was embodied in the payments of £33 6s. 8d. and £133 6s. 8d. respectively to Sheriffs and Lord Mayors who were members of the Company for the trimming of their houses.[1] The river procession from London to Westminster for the Lord Mayor's oath taking expressed the close relationship between City and Crown, while the procession through the streets of the capital marked out the main centres of power in the City: the Company Hall, the Guildhall, the sacred power represented by St Paul's Cathedral, and the world of business in Cheapside. The procession initially assembled at the Company Hall and proceeded to the Mayor's house, whence he was accompanied to Three Crane's Wharf, where the river procession to Westminster started. Returning to the City at Baynard's Castle, the procession then mounted Paul's Wharf Hill, skirted the churchyard of St Paul's, passed into the City's main commercial thoroughfare, Cheapside, and thence moved on to the Guildhall for the feast which brought together representatives of the Companies and members of the national elite. After the feast the Company processed to a sermon at St Paul's. The processional route was punctuated by various pageants which celebrated the honour and worship of the Mayor's Company, emphasised through compliments to the monarch the close relationship between City and Crown, and offered a commentary on the virtues felt to be appropriate to the exercise of the magisterial office.[2] The rich heraldry of the occasion underlined the interconnections between the various sources of power, private, Company, civic, and national: banners were carried of the arms of the new Lord Mayor, his Company, the City of London, and the monarch.[3] It is worth underlining that involvement in these processions was not confined simply to the occasions on which the Mayor came from the Haberdashers' Company. The Livery were always involved in the river procession and lined the streets on Lord Mayor's day; the difference that a Haberdasher Lord Mayor made was in the degree of the elaboration of the procession.

The celebration of Lord Mayor's day was only one of several occasions which expressed the interconnections between the Livery Companies, the City Corporation, and the Crown. At more irregular intervals there were various royal entries, particularly those associated with coronations. Coronation rituals took place over four days.

On the first day the monarch was escorted by a procession of barges of the London Livery Companies to the Tower; the next was given over to court rituals; on the third there took place the procession from the Tower to Westminster through the City streets lined by the Liverymen in order of their Companies' precedence; and the final day saw the actual coronation and the great banquet at Westminster Hall at which one representative from each of the Great Twelve waited on the Lord Chief Butler of England, and the Mayor and Aldermen and senior commoners of the City dined.[4] Considerable effort went into the provision of a sumptuous display. For the procession of Mary Tudor through the City streets in 1553 the Companies were ordered to stand 'in good and decent order in the open stretes of the Cytie in theire beste lyveryes' and to provide 'verye comly and clenly banners or flaggs of theire patrones and armes of theire said companies holden at the wardens backes', and also 'as many fyne and Riche clothes of sylk and Aras as they can conveynyentleye gette hanged owte at the wyndowes or stalles at theire backes wheare they shall stonde'. For the river procession in the same year Liverymen were instructed to appear 'in comely and good Apparell and in barges or botes well garnysshed and trymmed with flages, banners and mynstralcye or suche other ornamentes as they shall think mete'.[5] For Charles I's long delayed entry into his capital in November 1641 the Haberdashers spent £82 2s. 0d. They kitted out 35 footmen in jackets and drawers, decked them with ribbons, and arranged for their leader, wearing a striking white and blue silk scarf and with a large feather in his hat, to carry a 'coronet'.[6]

Civic ceremonial frequently brought the Liveries of the Companies to express visually the organic unity of the civic community, with each part in its place and working for the good of the whole commonwealth. For example, Liverymen attended sermons at St Paul's on the festivals of All Saints, Christmas, Twelfth Day, and Candlemas. Over the course of the 17th century this cycle of civic sermons was extended with the preaching of sermons at St Paul's Cross on the anniversary of the monarch's accession and gunpowder treason. The Wardens' accounts regularly record payments for the hire of forms at Paul's Cross on these occasions.[7] It is also likely that the Company processed collectively, as other Companies did, to the gatherings of Common Hall at which civic elections were held: certainly in June 1678 the Assistants ordered that henceforth the Livery were to process to the Guildhall on Midsummer Day for the elections of the Sheriffs, Chamberlain and Bridgemasters.[8]

Such civic occasions as well as expressing the bonds between the different levels of government also provided an opportunity for the display of the 'honour and worship' of the Company. Companies tried to outbid each other in the sumptuousness of their display, and kept a jealous eye on the practice of the others. Thus when ordering a new barge in 1638 the Haberdashers followed the dimensions of that recently provided for the Fishmongers' Company lest they be outdone.[9] The costs of the Lord Mayor's show rose to dizzying heights as a result of this competition. Whereas the Haberdashers spent £545 12s. 5d. on the pageants for Sir Thomas Lowe in 1604, on the next occasion of a Haberdasher Lord Mayor (Sir Francis Jones in 1620) the cost was £750 8s. 6d., and reached a peak of £1,330 16s. 5d. in the pageants for Sir John Lawrence in 1664. Thereafter this inflation of pomp ceased as

31.   Charles I's entry into the City of London, 25 November 1641.

the shows became less fashionable among the gentry for whose benefit they were partly provided, and the Companies less able to bear the enormous cost: the pageants for Sir Richard Levett in 1699 cost a more reasonable £714 19s. 8d.[10]

The Haberdashers' choice of themes for their pageants shows a desire to emphasise their own identity. There were, for example, numerous references to the Company's heraldry. In one of the earliest references to the Company's pageants on Lord Mayor's day in 1601 it was ordered that 'an Ounce [a leopard] & a lyon' should be provided with clear reference to the leopard passant included on the Company's arms of 1502 as a sign of royal patronage. The pageants for Sir John Lawrence in 1664 incorporated a lion, two goats (being the supporters of the arms), and a sprig of laurel (being the crest of the arms).[11] There were also often references to the Company's patroness, St Katherine, who features in the extant pageant texts for 1620, 1631, 1632, 1637, 1664, 1699. Of the various colourful roles in which the saint appears one example must suffice. The pageant in Cheapside in 1664 presented a scene 'in manner of an Imperial Crown', under which was a living figure representing St Katherine her hair light brown dishelv'd, her Temples circled with a Coronet of Gold adorned with pretious Stones, her Robe of Crimson Sarsenet, a loose Skye-coloured Scarf about her Shoulder with Gold and Silver fringe; on one side of her a Broken Wheel and an Axe, on which she lays one hand, and in the other she bears the Banner of St George.

Waiting upon her were figures representing Patience, Constancy, Chastity, and Fidelity, and at her feet lay Scientia, alluding to her knowledge of the arts. The whole scene was flanked by two goats and two boys, each holding a banner and shield with the arms of the City and company. As Lawrence approached St Katherine addressed the Mayor:

'Taught by the Example of this pious Guide
Uphold that Faith for which she boldly dy'd,
Gainst Faction and Prophaneness; By the one
She is Defac'd, by th'other Overthrown.
Root out those spreading and pernitious Weeds
Which Clemency instead of Killing breeds:
If you defend this, this will you defend,
And make your Name live when your life shall end'

The whole scene was presented as 'a Hieroglyphic of Integrity': St Katherine's constancy in the face of religious persecution made her the obvious medium for homilies on the importance of faith.[12]

It was customary also to allude to the craft from which the Company took its name. St Paul's churchyard was the setting in 1664 for another scene,

the Angles of one part whereof is adorned with small Shelters in the manner of Arbours, under which are discovered some persons knitting Caps, others spinning, others making Brushes, and such like part of the Haberdashers-Trade. In one part of the Stage is a Table, and thereat several persons making Hats, and other dependences thereon.

The whole scene was presided over by an overseer, 'seeming to smile on their labour and Industry'. The workers before him were engaged in 'continual Action, working and singing at their Work, and sometimes wantonly tumbling'. The four trees which marked out the stage were hung with the Company's motto, 'Serve and Obey', which provided the theme for the overseer's address to the Mayor:

' . . . the Ingenious Motto that they give
Teacheth Men how to labour and to live
SERVE and OBEY; By the one Men come to know,
And by th'other they wise Rulers grow . . .
. . . The Root of Honour Prudent Men conclude
To be Humility and Gratitude'.

In 1699 the message of a similar tableau, 'the Factory of Commerce', this time interspersing tobacco cutting with haberdashery in allusion to the origin of Sir Richard Levett's fortune, was more explicitly that through industry came prosperity: 'from Trade's Rich Crop . . . whole Nations shine'.[13]

There were usually two or three other pageants which continued the programme of moral instruction for the new Mayor. In addition to the pageants of Integrity and Humility, Lawrence was treated to pageants of Honour and Magnanimity. The theme of the pageant of Honour was that honour would come to Lawrence through the office of Lord Mayor, and the presence of the figures of Reason, Judgement, Resolution, Fortitude, and Munificence attending the figure of Honour in her bower adorned with flowers and fruit suggested the qualities of character that would bring honour. Magnanimity was mounted on a lion bearing the banner of St George in one hand and a sword in the other. Before the lion grazed lambs, goats and beavers; while on the other side of the hill on which these figures stood were 'Beasts of prey in a snarling posture, envying the happiness of the Lambs under the Protection of the Lyon'. Magnanimity is presented as a quality of good government and in the speech accompanying the pageant as the key to honour.[14]

It is tempting to dwell on the pomp and circumstance of civic celebration for its colour and drama. In a culture in which messages were still transmitted and learned through symbols and ritual rather than the written word the pageants were unquestionably important in their representation of the overlapping nature of the authorities, company, civic, and national, by which the capital was ruled. But it is also important to probe the reality of these relationships. Pageantry often presents an image of society as those in authority wish it to be ordered rather than society as it is. Behind the outward front of harmony between the different layers of authority there lurked tensions. The remainder of this chapter is dedicated to the exploration of the political relationships between the Haberdashers and the authorities of City and nation.

Because the freedom of the City was a qualification for the holding of office there was inevitably a degree of overlap between the civic and Company elites. The Haberdashers came to prominence within the elite at a relatively late date: the first Haberdasher Mayor did not serve until 1483–4, and only three haberdashers served on the Court of Aldermen in the 15th century. But thereafter their ascent was rapid: 27 were elected to serve as Aldermen and nine served as Lord Mayor in the 16th century. No less than four of the 26 Aldermen in 1597 were haberdashers. In the 17th century 12 haberdashers served as Lord Mayor, but the glory of the Company had passed by the civil war, before which no less than eight of these served. Indeed, if the Company seeks a golden age, then the Elizabethan and early Stuart years supply it.[15] The prominence of haberdashers is replicated at other levels of this civic elite. Professor Mark Benbow's survey of Londoners active in civic government, mainly as Common Councillors, over the Elizabethan period lists 1,669 men whose Company affilations are known; 153, no less than 9.2 per cent, of them were freemen of the Haberdashers' Company.[16] Haberdashers sometimes served in the highly influential posts in the civic bureaucracy, as Chamberlain (for example, John Sturgeon, 1550–63), or Bridgemasters (for example, Thomas Bates, 1568–86 and John Randall, 1569–74).[17] They were also active as Hospital Governors: in 1597 six haberdashers served as Governors of Bridewell, four as Governors of St Thomas', two as Governors of St Bartholomew's, and one as Governor of Christ's; Henry

Billingsley held the senior post of President of St Thomas' from 1594 until his death in 1606.[18]

The corollary of the overlapping of elites was the use of the Companies by the Court of Aldermen as instruments of government. The Companies served as conduits for Aldermanic policies. Thus in 1551 the Wardens of the Companies were instructed to take copies of a recent Act of Common Council on the City's orphanage practices and see that it was read at quarterly gatherings of Companymen 'to the intent that no person may herafter allege ignoraunce therof if they offende'. They were used to mobilise support for new policy initiatives: thus at the time of the foundation of the Hospitals in the mid 16th century Company Wardens were instructed to join in devising 'good orders' for poor relief and to stir up their members to give generously to charity. In times of crisis Wardens would be instructed to communicate to householders the necessity of keeping their servants and apprentices indoors, and sometimes, as when the Duke of Northumberland's regime was threatened by conspiracy in 1551, they would be required to supervise the civic watch.[19]

But the most important areas in which the Companies could be of use to the Corporation was through the levy of City taxation. Taxation could be raised through the wards by the levy of fifteenths, but this was a rather inflexible tax, the quotas for each ward having been fixed in the 14th century, and the customary methods of assessment tended to hit the poor with disproportionate severity. Levy of taxation through the Livery Companies offered greater flexibility because it could be left to the discretion of each Company how the money was raised. Moreover, the availability of corporate reserves meant that often part of the levy could be raised without assessment on the membership, although obviously the reserves of the Companies were not huge and any prolonged period of levies would soon undermine the Companies' ability to follow this policy. The greater vagueness of the precedents relating to levy of taxation through the Companies also meant that it could be raised without the approval of Common Council, although this proved extremely controversial, and became increasingly less common over time. The Corporation used the Companies most often as bodies through which to raise troops and to make the assessments which financed the buffer stocks of grain designed to tide the Corporation over periods of shortage.

When a demand came through from the Crown for troops to be levied, the Aldermen, increasingly acting with the assent of Common Council, would apportion the City's quota among the Livery Companies according to their perceived size and wealth. The Companies then became responsible for pressing the troops concerned, equipping them according to the Crown's specifications, and paying their wages until their embarkation, which was often delayed by the dictates of royal foreign policy. Thus in July 1562, when Elizabeth decided to aid the Huguenots in an effort to recover Calais, she wrote to the City demanding that they raise 600 troops, of whom 420 should wear corslets and carry pikes and bills, 90 should be archers, and 90 arquebusiers. The Haberdashers' quota was fixed by the Aldermen at 29 (21 men in corslets and eight archers and arquebusiers mixed). Although we lack the accounts to determine the cost of this levy to the Company, the experience of other

Londini Speculum : or,
Londons Mirror, Expreſt in ſundry *Triumphs*,
Pageants, and *Showes*, at the Initiation of the right
Honorable *Richard Fenn*, into the Mairolty of the Fa-
mous and farre renowned City *L O N D O N*.

All the Charge and Expence of theſe laborious projects both
by Water and Land, being the ſole undertaking of the Right
Worſhipful Company of the *Habberdaſhers*.

Writtenby Tho. Heywood.

Imprinted at *London* by *I. Okes* dwelling in little St.
Bartholmews. 1 6 3 7.

32.   Title page from the book of pageants by Thomas Heywood inaugurating the
mayoralty of Richard Fenn (1637).

33. Table of coats of arms of Haberdashers who served as Lord Mayor,
the gift of George Lewen in 1726, flanked by the Company's sword and
mace rests; from the Hall destroyed in 1940.

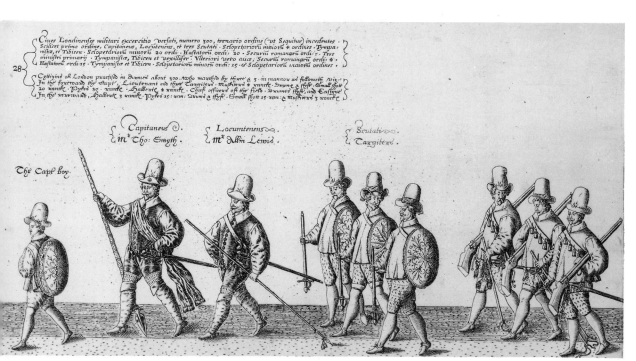

34. A portion of the funeral roll of Sir Philip Sidney, engraved by Theodor de Bry in 1587, showing men of the London trained bands, led by Thomas Smythe, Haberdasher, later Sheriff of London and suspected of complicity in Essex's attempted putsch of 1601.

Companies enables an estimate to be made. The equipment for a pikeman at this time cost 32s., that for an arquebusier 25s.3d., and for an archer 19s.6d. In addition the coats provided for the soldiers cost about 13s.6d. each. The soldiers were pressed on 26 July at a cost of 1s. per man, and their wages at 8d. per day per man paid until until 20 August, when they were ordered to stand down, only to be mobilised once again on 16 September, their wages now being paid until their dispatch to Le Havre on 19 September. When they were handed over to Captain Vaughan at Moorfields 4s. was granted for each man by way of conduct money. This would make the Haberdashers' total bill on this occasion £42 11s. 0d. for equipment, £19 11s. 6d. for coats, and £36 5s. 0d. for press money, wages, and conduct money, that is £98 17s. 6d. in all. If the Company stock was insufficient the Assistants would have resorted to assessment on the membership to raise this money.[20]

It was also through the Livery Companies that London organised for defence against invaders. It was one sign of a shift towards a more defensive posture in foreign relations that Elizabeth I should have concentrated national resources on the training of the militia. Before the eventual outbreak of war with Spain the training of forces for local defence took place in London in 1559, 1572, 1578, and 1585, and on each occasion the forces were raised through the Livery Companies.

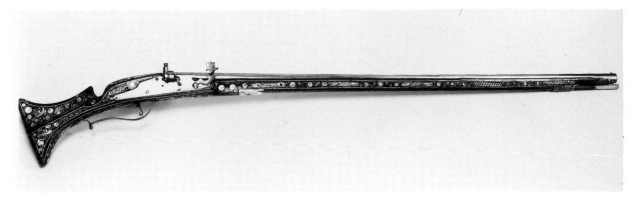

35.   A musket engraved with the Company's arms; from the Museum of London.

In 1585, for example, the Haberdashers were instructed to train 395 men (197 calivermen, 159 pikemen, and 39 halberdiers) as their quota of the 4,000 the Queen had commanded. It was customary practice for the Companies to bear much of the cost of the shot, sometimes recouping their expenditure through assessment, and making it the responsibility of wealthier members to provide the corslets. There survives among the papers of Lord Treasurer Burghley an estimate of the cost of training to the Haberdashers' Company in 1585: the figure given is £350 3s. 10d. By this date Companies had built up sizeable stocks of armour for use in such musters, reducing the cost to individual members.[21]

The 1585 muster, however, was one of the last occasions on which soldiers were raised directly through the Companies. During the war with Spain from 1585 onwards troops were raised through the wards and the charges borne by means of general assessments on the inhabitants of the City authorised by Common Council. This change probably occurred for a combination of administrative convenience and pressure from the freemen. Levy through Companies multiplied the number of bodies with which the Aldermen had to deal and made standardisation difficult to achieve. Moreover, levy through the Companies meant that the burdens of taxation fell most heavily, indeed usually almost wholly, on freemen. Companies were increasingly responding to the Crown's demands by pointing out the foreign population in their midst which was escaping taxation. By means of levies through the wards the burden could be spread more fairly through the population.[22]

But this did not mean the end of the Companies' special role in wartime. Although not directly involved in the recruitment and equipment of troops, they were still drawn upon to provide finance for levies. In 1596 the Companies loaned £10,259 to help pay for the City's 12 ships and two pinnaces accompanying the earl of Essex on his raid on Cadiz: the Haberdashers' contribution on this occasion was £771 12s. 0d., which was never repaid because the expedition failed to realise the hopes of its projectors.[23] In September 1642 Parliament requested the City to loan 10,000 arms to the war effort. 'Unwilling to be behind', the Haberdashers agreed to lend 100 arms from their stores, buying new if necessary, and the following year they purchased 150 swords and belts, and 100 muskets and bandoliers at a cost of £178.[24] Echoing Elizabethan practice, in 1665 Charles II requested a contribution of £10,000 from the City for building a ship, the *Loyall London*, for use against the Dutch: the Haberdashers quota was £770, paid rather more slowly than the King had intended.[25] The last occasion on which money was raised in this way from the Companies for a specifically defined military objective was in 1690 when the Company agreed to raise the money to pay for two light horse by subscription from the Livery and Assistants. But in general the Haberdashers' contribution to war in the 17th century was to pay its share of the taxes paid for by all.[26]

Another way in which the Corporation made frequent use of the services of the Companies in the 16th and 17th centuries was in the financing of its corn policy. Although there were 15th-century precedents, the practice by which the Aldermen organised the import of grain in years of harvest failure to be sold to the poor at prices slightly below those prevailing in the markets, became regular from the 1520s, probably under prodding from Cardinal Wolsey. The Livery Companies were used to provide loans on a year-by-year basis to pay for the purchases. For example, in July 1560 the Haberdashers were required to provide £250 towards a loan of £3,733 6s. 8d. from the Livery Companies for grain imported from the Baltic. These levies often proved unpopular within the Companies as they necessitated assessments on the membership, and feelings were particularly embittered in 1575 when £2,032 19s. 9d. of the Companies' monies was lost as the markets fell unexpectedly. The result was an overhaul of the method by which the grain supplies were financed. In 1578 the Corporation gave up direct dealing in corn, and instructed the Companies to maintain a specified quota in the Bridgehouse municipal granaries. They were not always conscientious in maintaining supplies and, in spite of pressure from Charles I, the practice declined in the 17th century. In 1659, when ordered by the Lord Mayor to supply the markets, the Haberdashers replied that they were without grain and that their granary was rented to a corn merchant.[27]

The Companies therefore performed a variety of roles within the framework of City government. But their relationship with the Aldermen was reciprocal, for there were a variety of ways in which the authority of the Aldermen might be helpful in the running of the Company. The services of the Aldermen might be invoked by the Company in dealing with particularly intractable members. In 1515 the Aldermen arbitrated a dispute between the rulers of the Company and the Yeomen over issues which remain frustratingly unknown. But the terms of their award were disputed by John Atkinson and Robert Herde who 'obstanately and presumptuously and frowardly contrary to the solemn award made by the Mayor and Aldermen under their seal', demanded compensation from their Wardens for imprisoning them in the course of the recent disorders. In September 1516 Common Council ordered that Atkinson should be disfranchised and his shop shut up by the Chamberlain for his refractory behaviour as a man who

36. Monument in the church of St Helen Bishopsgate, London, to Martin
Bond (d.1643) captain of the trained bands shown in the camp at Tilbury
at the time of the Spanish Armada.

does dayly vexe and sue diverse of his sayd Company members by false and forged accions to the grete displesure of almightye god, the grete inquietyng of all the felysshippes aforeseyd and to the perylous example of other well disposyd persones.

Apparently Atkinson had been summoned to appear by the Mayor, but the wayward haberdasher went off into the fields about the city with his bow and arrows, 'and sent him word that he myght not come to him at that tyme'. The ultimate sanction of disfranchisement seems to have made Atkinson more contrite, for he sought the mediation of Cardinal Wolsey, who asked the Lord Mayor to be a 'good lord' to him. He was called to Haberdashers' Hall on 18 July 1517, and there in the presence of four Aldermen, the Wardens of the Company, and 'other worshipfull and honest persones of the haberdasshers', acknowledged his faults. In another similar case in 1583 the Aldermen disfranchised William Cleybrooke, recently a Warden of the Yeomanry, who had refused to make his account. Like Atkinson, he was readmitted to the freedom on his submission a few months later.[28]

The Aldermen also undertook the arbitration of disputes between Companies such as the conflicts betwen the Haberdashers', Merchant Tailors', Curriers', and Clothworkers' Companies at various points in Elizabeth's reign over the search of hats, or the conflicts between the Haberdashers and Feltmakers in the early 17th century, or the clashes persisting into the 18th century with lesser Companies over efforts to secure the translation of freemen of the Haberdashers using their trades.[29] Related to this function was the Court of Aldermen's practice of requiring that the legislation which the Companies sought to promote in Parliament should first be approved by them: the Repertories of the Court show committees examining the projected legislation of the Haberdashers in 1542, 1563, and 1576.[30] Likewise the Aldermen maintained a watchful eye over the content of Company charters and ordinances: it was at their insistence that the pretentious and divisive title of Merchant Haberdashers granted by Henry VII's charter of 1502 was dropped in 1510. In general the Companies supported the power of the Aldermen as a means of maintaining harmony between potentially competing forces. When the City's power over the Companies was threatened by the statute of 1504 requiring that Company ordinances be approved by the law officers, the Haberdashers were among the majority of Companies which supported the efforts of the Aldermen to repeal a measure which had enabled the Merchant Tailors, exploiting the personal favour of Henry VII, to acquire an unhealthily favourable position.[31]

The measure of 1504 is a reminder of the power wielded over the Companies by the Crown, whose support underpinned their charters. The Assistants were uneasily aware that what the Crown had given, it might also take away, and this made them generally cooperative. There were tensions in the relationship between Companies and Crown, but it was broadly constructive, and the Crown's approach to the Livery Companies was not as exploitative as it might have been. The Haberdashers curried favour with courtiers, ministers, and judges by accepting their candidates for freedoms by redemption: thus among the promoters of such freedoms in the Haberdashers' Company in Elizabeth's reign were the Earl of Leicester, the Earl of Bedford,

37. Capital showing Queen Elizabeth I enthroned; from the charter of 1578 which still governs the Company.

Sir Francis Walsingham, Sir Thomas Heneage, Lord Chief Justice Christopher Wray, and Attorney General Gilbert Gerrard.[32] Occasionally honorary freedoms were granted to aristocratic figures: the most socially elevated freeman in the early modern period was George Villiers, second Duke of Buckingham, favourite of James I and Charles I. On 19 September 1620 Buckingham dined at the Hall, and together with Lords Hay and Purbeck, was admitted to the freedom and took the oath, 'which upon theire honors they promised to observe with all love and kyndnes to the company'.[33] Other haberdashers enjoyed close contact with government figures: Sir Thomas Smythe, Sheriff of the City in 1600–1, was a client of Elizabeth's favourite, the second Earl of Essex; the daughter of Sir George Barne, Lord Mayor in 1552–3, was married to Francis Walsingham, Elizabeth's Secretary of State; Sir George Whitmore, Lord Mayor in 1631–2, was a leading creditor of Charles I's hard man, the Earl of Strafford. There were thus a variety of informal routes to favour at court.[34]

The Haberdashers' Company does not seem to have become the victim of predatory patronage seeking court interests in the way that other Companies did. There is little sign of courtiers seeking to lean on the Company to grant leases or offices to their dependants. Sir Ralph Winwood, Secretary of State to James I, did petition for a reversion of the office of Company Porter to be granted to Thomas Spire in 1615, but this is a very rare incident.[35] The pressures on patronage were mainly internal to the Company. However, the Company inevitably shared in some of the ill effects of the Crown's shortage of patronage with which to reward courtiers. One of the most notorious of Elizabeth's devices was the grant of patents of concealed lands. Recipients of such grants successfully recovering title to lands which should have passed to the crown at the dissolution of the monasteries and chantries but had been concealed were rewarded with a portion of the profits. The London Livery Companies were particularly losers by this policy because of conflicting interpretations of the statute of 1547 dissolving chantries. What had happened in 1547 was that the Companies had been allowed to retain the lands out of which chantries were supported in return for paying the Crown a sum equivalent to 20 years' expenditure on the 'superstitious uses', but not making any payment in respect of the surpluses of revenues from the properties. In 1582 Theophilus Adams and James Woodshaw, dependants of Sir Christopher Hatton, Vice-Chamberlain of the Household and Elizabeth's latest favourite, obtained a grant of the properties which had supported the chantries of several Companies, among them the Haberdashers. They interpreted the statute rather differently to mean that all the lands should have gone to the Crown, and they had the backing of a section of judicial opinion for this view. The result was five years of costly and inconclusive litigation, to which the Haberdashers seem to have paid £200. At length the patentees withdrew their claims in 1587 in return for a further payment of £100 from the Haberdashers, but without securing the statutory assurance for the security of their property they had initially hoped would be part of the bargain. For that they had to wait until 1606.[36]

Another set of problems attended the Crown's grants of monopolies. In September 1596 Thomas Cornwallis, Groom Porter, received a patent from Elizabeth I enabling him to license gaming houses about the city, as well as to search and seal dice. He was doubtless able to dress up this grant in terms of its benefit to the commonwealth: he would only license respectable premises, and the powers of sealing meant that the Queen's subjects would be safe from cozeners. But Cornwallis' motives were unquestionably pecuniary as the fees for licensing and searching and sealing would provide him with a handsome income. Unfortunately the haberdashers were the main retailers of dice and their Company enjoyed the power to search for false dice by their charter from Henry VII. In October 1598 the Haberdashers informed Cornwallis that 'the Company cannot without greate preiudyce to their owne charter geve any waie unto his graunt'. But under pressure from the Aldermen they retreated from this uncompromising stand, for in January of the following year they agreed that two or three discreet citizens chosen by the Lord Mayor should join with Cornwallis' deputies to search dice and that fees of ½ d. per bale should be taken for sealing.[37]

The financial resources of the Companies were a tempting prospect for a hard pressed Crown. Typical of the policies which had their root in a financially embarrassed Crown in the early 17th century was the Plantation of Londonderry at the expense of the London Livery Companies. The flight of the Earls in 1607 offered the Crown a golden opportunity for the settlement of Ulster, but great difficulties were experienced in finding reliable undertakers. Hence the Crown turned to the City of London, and by 1610 a scheme had been drawn up by which the Companies were allotted territory in Londonderry in return for providing the capital for development. The Haberdashers were allotted 23,100 acres (about 5 per cent of the total area of Londonderry), including settlements at Ballycastle and Artikelly. By the spring of 1611 the Company had raised £1,124 for the venture, but the task of getting members to pay their contributions had been extremely arduous, and the Haberdashers' was the first Company to disengage itself from the whole scheme. In April 1611 the Company relinquished to William Freeman and Adrian Moore, two freemen of the Company, all its interest and the monies already paid into the joint stock on condition that Freeman and Moore take on responsibility for all future payments.[38]

The disputes that occurred with the Crown were, however, contained with relative ease. The quest for solutions to the Company's problems took place within the framework of institutions provided by the monarch, and the efforts of the Haberdashers to secure redress were attended with some degree of success. In the political conflicts of the 16th century the Haberdashers adopted a low profile, and when presented with an opportunity to attach their grievances to aristocratic dissidence as in Essex's attempted putsch in 1601 they conspicuously failed to act: Sheriff Smythe, a leading member of the Company, failed to offer Essex the expected support of the trained bands. Loyalty to Essex could not be conceived outside the framework of loyalty to the Crown.[39]

Things were different 40 years on, however, when haberdashers were prominent among the City opponents of Charles I. John Bradley was among the six delegates chosen to present the petition of Common Hall concerning the election of the City's Sheriffs in 1641, part of the effort to counter royalist influence in the capital. John Fowke presented the City's mass petition in December 1641 calling for the removal of Bishops from the House of Lords, the punishment of delinquents, and the reformation of abuses that 'are crept into the ancient government of the city'. He was joined on the Committee of Public Safety by William Berkeley and Owen Rowe. Fowke and Berkeley also acted together on the parliamentary customs farm, and Simon Edmunds was an excise farmer. Fowke, Berkeley, and Edmunds were successively masters of the Company between 1642 and 1645. Lawrence Brinley was a prominent presbyterian activist who petitioned Parliament for a stricter form of presbyterianism in 1645–6. However, the Haberdashers' Company cannot be said to have been four-square behind the parliamentary war effort, for the Court of Assistants harboured a number of royalist sympathisers. Sir George Whitmore was rumoured in January 1642 to have offered to raise 10,000 men to guard the King. He refused to lend money to Parliament or pay his assessments and was imprisoned and his estates sequestered. Robert Fenn, a Merchant Adventurer, also adopted a conservative political stance.[40]

What divided these men? Some of the divisions are to be explained by differences of economic interest. As has been argued the opponents of the Crown tended to come from the newer trades to the Americas which pressed for a more vigorous anti-Spanish foreign policy, whereas the merchants of the Levant-East India Company connection were of more conservative persuasion.[41] Another line of division was caused by religion. It was this issue, above all others, which separated Charles from his opponents, for it was his Laudian programme which did most to alienate the support of large sections of the political nation from him. Of those listed above Simon Edmunds was a prominent supporter of the presbyterian divine, Edmund Calamy; Owen Rowe was in contact with the puritan Governor of Massachusetts, John Winthrop, through the 1630s; Lawrence Brinley's presbyterian credentials have been noted; and John Fowke was strongly identified with the presbyterian offensive in the City in 1645-7. Religion probably reinforced economic self-interest in many cases in so far as puritans tended to show greater enthusiasm for the American trades as a way of weakening the popish foe. Others were more willing to cooperate with the Laudian regime. Sir Hugh Hamersley, for example, made a bequest to the prominent Laudian, Dr William Fuller, Vicar of St Giles Cripplegate; Richard Venn left money to Jeremiah Leach, the Rector of St Mary Bow, sequestered from his living in the Civil War; and Henry Andrewes ambiguously patronised both the puritan, John Downham, and the Laudian, Dr Thomas Howell, Rector of St Stephen Walbrook.[42]

Support for Parliament's war to protect protestantism did not necessarily entail support for all the actions of Parliament. Even John Fowke, who was prepared to go further than many in supporting the Interregnum regime nevertheless refused to sign the death warrant of Charles I.[43] The inability of the King's former opponents to agree on a stable form of polity, and the regime's failure to repay the loans that the Company had made in 1640-3 while continuing to impose high taxation, probably caused many to greet the monarchy's Restoration in 1660 with relief. Indeed, reading the minutes of the early Restoration years one cannot help but be impressed by the enthusiasm with which the Company cooperated with the Crown. It was determined that, when the King entered London in May 1660, he should 'be received with ye greatest demonstracion and manifestacion of their own and all their fellow Citizens most bounden duties, hearty affections, and joy for his happy Returne'. In receiving the request from the Mayor for a contribution towards the coronation pageants, the Assistants determined on showing 'all possible readinesse and willingnes to further the said Solemnity'.[44]

But neither was support for the Restoration unconditional, and goodwill towards Charles II began to evaporate as his pro-catholic leanings became more manifest. Typical of the evolution of attitudes in the City was Sir Thomas Player, haberdasher and Chamberlain of the City in succession to his father from 1672 until 1683. The Players had been enthusiastic court supporters, knighted by the King in recognition of the senior Player's help in the collection of loans in the City. The son's election to the Common Council in 1672 was greeted with enthusiasm by the court. But in spite of his declaration that he was 'a devout son of the Church of England', Player had dissenting connections. In common with other earlier allies of the court like the former Lord Mayor, Sir John Lawrence, a fellow haberdasher, ran into court disfavour because of his vigorous advocacy of the grievances of the City (includuing the assertion of the supremacy of Common Council) and his petitioning for a new Parliament. By 1677 he was strongly identified with the interests of the Earl of Shaftesbury, and the court had him removed from the Lieutenancy as well as trying to oust him as Chamberlain. Elected to the Exclusion Parliament, he was zealous in the investigation of the Popish Plot and the promotion of citizens' petitions to pressurise the King into support for the exclusion of the Duke of York from the succession to the Crown. He was a man who aroused strong feelings. Nicknamed 'Sir Thomas Cresswell' by the Tories because of his intimacy with Mother Cresswell, keeper of a brothel in Moorfields, in *Absalom and Achitophel* he appears as 'railing Rabshakeh',

> A saint that can both flesh and spirit use,
> Alike haunts conventicles and stews,
> Of whom the question difficult appears,
> If most i' th' preachers or the bawds arrears.

Not surprisingly Player came under intense suspicion in the Tory reaction which followed the Oxford Parliament, being rumoured to be 'for a free state and no other government', and he was unseated at the Common Council elections of December 1683. He was lucky to escape with his life, as John Rous offered to turn King's evidence against him.[45] Less fortunate was another of Shaftesbury's haberdasher associates, Henry Cornish, Master in 1680 and the unsuccessful Whig nominee for the office of Lord Mayor in 1682 after many votes had been struck out as those of 'Quakers, Exclusionists and Dissenters'. He was executed for high treason in 1685 for his involvement in the Rye House Plot.[46]

The entrenchment of the King's critics in City government led to the most tense period in the relations between central government and the Haberdashers' Company. In 1684 an information of Quo Warranto was laid against the Company on the grounds that its privileges had been abused. By 3 November the Company had been forced to surrender its liberties and submit the regulation of its magistracy to the King under threat of judgement being entered against it The revised charter granted by James II in February 1685 put the government of the Company into the hands of 'men of known loyalty and approved integrity', in other words good Church of England men, naming a Master, four Wardens, and 56 Assistants. The new Master was Robert Aske whose moderate anglican inclinations are evident from his choice of executors, Drs. Tillotson and Sharpe, at the time of his death in 1689 Deans of Canterbury and Norwich, but soon Archbishops of Canterbury and York respectively. The Master and Wardens were required to take the Oaths of Allegiance and Supremacy and the Corporation Oath (by the latter men were to take an oath abhorring the right of resistance). Nor were any who had not received the communion according to the rites of the Church of England within the previous six months to be admitted to office in the Company. Clerks of the Company were in future to be presented to the King for approval, and any Assistant might be removed by an Order in Council. By this charter the Company was much more obviously pliable to monarchical wishes.[47]

As is well known, James' policy backfired because many of the anglicans on whom the Crown felt it could rely were not prepared to support the King's moves to tolerate Roman Catholicism. In September 1687 James thus found himself in the absurd position of further purging the Liveries of the Companies, removing loyal Tories (including Robert Aske and two of the four Wardens appointed in 1685). In February 1688 he recalled some of the dissenters, his former opponents in the hope that they would support his moves towards religious toleration, but they were not to be duped. Conscious of the failure of his policy and facing imminent invasion by William of Orange, on 7 October James reversed the trend of policy once more by ordering the restoration of all Liverymen as at the time of the judgment of Quo Warranto. The blatant manipulation of the Livery only came to a stop with the Act of 1690 which annulled the Quo Warranto and cancelled the charters and grants of Charles II and James II. Hence the Company remains governed by the charter of 1578 to this day.[48]

It is difficult to be entirely sure how representative of political opinion in the Haberdashers' Company men like Player and Cornish were, but they certainly carried much weight in its counsels. Some evidence of sympathy for Dissent is provided by the Company's renting of rooms at the back of its Hall to the congregation of the moderate presbyterian divine, Dr Thomas Jacombe, from 1674.[49] In 1682 Haberdashers' Hall was one of two projected venues for a Whig feast for the 'loyal protestant nobility, gentry, clergy, and citizens', which was banned by the King.[50] At the hotly contested Mayoral election of 1682 a clear majority of the votes of the Haberdashers' Liverymen was cast for the Whig candidates: Sir Thomas Gold received 160 votes and Henry Cornish 159, whereas the Tories, Sir William Prichard and Henry Tulse received 133 and 12 respectively. This was one of the clearest Whig majorities of any Company.[51] Early 18th-century poll books confirm the predominantly Whig sympathies of the Liverymen. In the 1710 election for the City's Members of Parliament, actually the highwater mark of Tory campaigning in the capital when the four seats were secured for their candidates, the Haberdashers' Liverymen retained a Whig majority. 55.9 per cent of the Haberdashers' poll in that year went to the Whig candidates, and 43.2 per cent to the Tories. By 1727 as the Robinocracy established itself the Whigs were still more entrenched, taking 60.7 per cent of the poll compared to 38.6 per cent for the Tories. Among the Assistants the Whig majority was even more striking: 66 per cent to 34 per cent.[52] Influential in the Company's counsels were men like Sir Harcourt Master, a money-lender and director of the South Sea Company, whose loyalist activities on the advent of the Hanoverian dynasty landed him several plum government jobs such as the post of Receiver General of the Land Tax for London and Middlesex.[53] This loyalism left its mark on the Company, for it was Master who donated to the Company a portrait

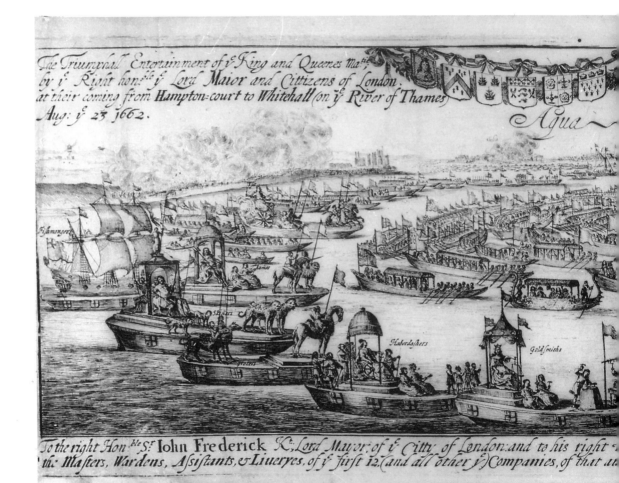

38. The river pageant held on 23 August 1662, when Londoners greeted Charles II and his new Queen, the Portuguese Princess, Catherine of Braganza. The Haberdashers' barge is shown in the left foreground.

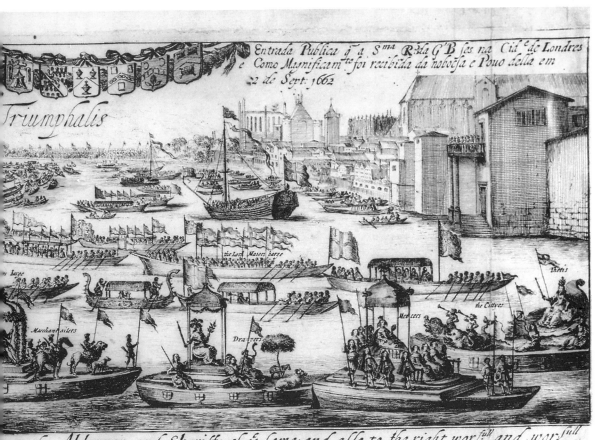

Entrada Publica q̃ a S.ma R.da G.B ses na Cid.e de Londres
e Como Magnificam.te foi recibida da nobeɀa e Pouo della em
22 de Sept: 1662

Triumphalis

the Lord Mayors barge

Thetis

— barge

the Cittes

Merchantailers

Mercers

Drapers

en, the Aldermen, and Sheriffs of y.e same; and also to the right wor.full and wor.full
ble Citty of London. This Plate is most humbly dedicated by theyre most obedient Servant Rod: Stoop

of George I in 1717. Other portraits of the new royal family were donated by Sir George Caswall and Sir John Eyles. They were both of dissenting background and heavily involved in the South Sea Company. Eyles was described by Charles Hornby as one of 'Walpole's Pack-horses . . . void of all Honour and Compassion' for his aid in salvaging the South Sea Company and his involvement in the fraudulent sale of the forfeited estates of English Jacobites.[54]

But as the Company settled into a Whiggish complacency in the early 18th century, its importance in the life of the City shrank. Although the Companies continued to control access to the freedom and the Livery, and the voting rights that went therewith, many of the Companies' roles in the life of the City had withered. No longer were they instruments of civic taxation, and the growing sophistication of local government, combined with the contraction in the proportion of Londoners enjoying the freedom, meant that they ceased to be appopriate instruments for the communication of Aldermanic policies to the citizenry. The state's interest in their affairs had also diminished, as their involvement in economic regulation contracted, and as their financially enervated condition after the Fire, as also the growing sophistication of the money-raising techniques available to the state, meant that the Companies were no longer such obvious milch-cows. The interest of the state was to revive, however, in the 19th century with the expansion in the range of its concerns.

Chapter Eleven

The Company in the Nineteenth Century

The main factors shaping the Company's history in the 19th century were the improvement in its corporate and trust income as a result of the appreciation of property values in the City and the development of the Company's estates; and the growth of government interest in the management of charities and the Companies' internal affairs. The proliferation of business created a pressure for greater professionalisation in the Company's management. The recovery in corporate income meant that the range of social functions the Company could offer was extended, contributing to a growth in its self-confidence. The attentions of reformers resulted in the reshaping of many of the charities to purposes more appropriate to a changed society and an expansion in the horizons of the Assistants to consider other ways in which their corporate income might be used to the benefit of society. The following two chapters elaborate on these basic points.

The running of the Company undoubtedly became more complex over the course of the 19th century. The next chapter will explore the problems encountered in the management of the charities, and the implications of the establishment of the Charity Commissioners and the Endowed Schools Commissioners for the business of the Company. Another aspect of the changing roles of the Company which it is appropriate to discuss here is its involvement in the development of its estates. The development of the Hoxton estate began at the turn of the century; the Hatcham estate had to wait until the mid century because of the long leases granted by Chancery in 1763.

The main device for the development of the estates was the building lease, usually granted for 81 years, by which the lessee was responsible for erecting buildings in accordance with the specifications laid down in the lease to ensure uniformity of development. The Company's role was the approval of the plans prepared by its Surveyor, paying particular attention to matters such as the layout of streets and the provision of drainage; the negotiation of the terms of the leases; and the monitoring of the building activity of the lessees to ensure compliance with the covenants. The story of the early development of the Hoxton estate illustrates some of the difficulties that could be encountered. First, there was the problem of finding the optimum moment in the building cycle for development to occur. The Company's Surveyor, John Baker, had first drawn up plans in 1792, but no action was taken until 1802 because of the wartime slump in the building trade.[1] Secondly, there was disagreement over the nature of the buildings appropriate to the site. Baker's plans for second- and third-rate housing were regarded as unsuitable for a site which was already acquiring its non-respectable character, whatever the Surveyor's ambitions for buildings which reflected the honour of the Company.[2] Thirdly, once leases were approved, there were the difficulties of site management and control of the developers. Theft of materials was a constant worry. On one occasion in 1811 the police and Sheriffs were called out to deal with a mob of 400 residents 'uprooting trees and tearing down buildings'.[3] The failure of the developers to follow the specifications of their leases led to frequent clashes with Baker. In 1811, for example, he complained about one Reeve's proposal to build 'trumpery houses', which would surround the Hospital with 'a second St Giles' where men could not walk safely in the middle of the day for fear of molestation by whores and bullies. The developers did not care who occupied the houses, so long as the ground rent was improved and the property offloaded as soon as possible.[4]

At the time that the Hoxton estate was undergoing this development, the Hatcham estate was still primarily used for agricultural purposes, particularly for market gardening. It also comprised a number of fashionable residences, the Manor House being leased to the Russia merchant and philanthropist, Joseph Hardcastle, for 150 years from 1763.[5] Lying on the main line of communication between London and the south-east ports, the estate received much attention from the projectors of schemes for canals and railways, and portions of the estate were sold. The Grand Surrey Canal connecting the Thames at Rotherhithe with Mitcham met the Croydon Canal at New Cross on the Haberdashers' estate. The first railway development was the Greenwich Railway which opened in 1836, soon to be followed by the London and Croydon Railway (1839) with a station at New Cross. Between 1833 and 1856 the Jones charity raised £17,676 10s. 5d. in 3 per cent consols from purchases by railway companies, and in 1867 there were gains of a further £32,106.[6] The opening of the station encouraged interest in the residential prospects of the site, and the estate map of 1854 shows a number of terraces on the main road close to the new station. However, the site was still relatively underdeveloped because of the length of the leases, some of which were not due to fall in until 1913. But J.A. Hardcastle sold the remainder of his lease to the Company for £4,000 in 1868, and when another interest in the estate was purchased in 1874, a large number of building leases were granted.[7]

All these changes involved the Company in a great deal of work. It set up a special Parliamentary Committee to deal with the negotiations with the railway companies over the sales of land. It was customary to lodge a petition against the bills in Parliament for railway development in order to give the Company the right to watch the proceedings at the committee stage, in the meantime sending their Surveyor out to value the property in question, before negotiating with the railway company's Surveyor over the price. The development of the estate fell to the Estates Committee, which was responsible for laying down the conditions of development to ensure buildings of consistent style, approving the leases, and monitoring compliance.[8]

The growth in the range and complexity of the Company's business, of which the development of its estates provides a good example, created pressures for greater professionalism. This was reflected in efforts to streamline the Company's committee procedure and in the multiplication of staff at the Hall. A major overhaul of Company administration was undertaken in 1826–7, at a time when the Haberdashers were seeking to reform the management of many of their charities, possibly to pre-empt

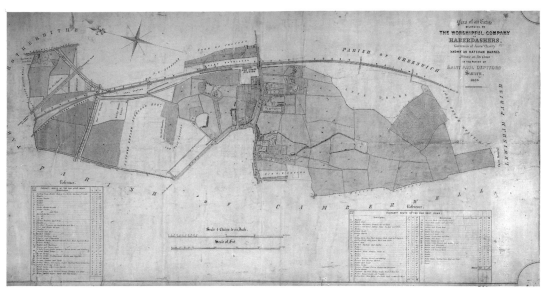

39. Map of the Hatcham estate in 1854, before the major housing developments, but showing impact of railways and canals.

reform by outside agencies. It was recognised that the practice by which so much responsibility devolved upon the Clerk was not healthy and that the lack of familiarity of Assistants with the trusts which they were supposed to be discharging led to ill-informed decision making. To remedy this four key standing committees responsible for Charities, Finance, Estates, and Audit were set up. These were to replace the Grand Committee, standing committees for the separate charities and in some cases their estates (Adams, Jones, Hoxton, Kent estates, and Survey), and *ad hoc* committees set up for particular purposes. In order to ensure that members of the Court of Assistants became more familiar with Company business the Court was to be divided into four groups, each of which would constitute one of the committees. At the end of each year two members of each committee in alphabetical rotation were to stand down and be allocated to another committee. The result would be that each Assistant would progressively serve on each committee in turn.[9] The Charities Committee took over many of the duties of the separate charity committees and was additionally responsible for inquiring into the conduct of the Schools and almshouses. The members of the Estates Committee were required to view the estates regularly, receive estimates, grant leases, conclude contracts, and see that properties were kept in proper repair. The receipt of monies, examination of accounts, discharging of bills, and the quarterly review of the state of the finances fell to the Finance Committee. Finally, the Audit Committee (already in place in 1826) undertook the task of auditing the accounts and entering them in a balance book. The only other committee to emerge unscathed from this reorganisation was the Hoxton Committee which continued to oversee the internal administration of the Hospital.[10] This structure of committees remained largely unchanged through the 19th century, although special committees were appointed for matters such as the rebuilding of the Hall, the holding of balls, and the monitoring of legislation in Parliament.[11] However two major changes occurred subsequently: the merger of the Finance and Audit Committees in 1869, and the establishment of the Endowed Schools Committee in 1870 in the wake of the Endowed Schools Act and the consequent need to draw up new schemes for the running of the schools.[12]

The measures undertaken in 1826 to improve the Company's administration of its business included new regulations designed to ensure the impartial conduct of business. Notice now had to be given at a preceding Court of Assistants of any grant exceeding £10; all offices and benefices in the Company's patronage were to be decided by ballot; all matters of business were to be specified in an agenda to be circulated to members of the Court beforehand; no Assistant was to enjoy a financial interest in the Company; any member of the Court falling into dependence on the charity of the Company was to lose his place on the Court; Assistants failing to appear for more than one committee meeting in any given year would not be eligible to sit on the committees and would lose their rights to present gifts. Also consistent with this drive for a more professional Court of Assistants was the compilation of the *Compendium*, later published in abbreviated form as the *Manual*, being a directory of Company practice with notes on each charity.[13] As a further improvement, in order to secure a Court better representing the talents of the Livery, the methods used to fill the junior Wardenships were changed. Instead of appointing the most senior members of the Livery, six names, selected from those Liverymen of twelve or more years standing, for each vacancy were to be brought forward by the Master and Wardens, and the slate reduced to two by the Court of Assistants, who then held a ballot to select their Junior Wardens. However, because the Court was often depleted, it was agreed that members of the Livery could apply in writing for membership without serving the office of Third or Fourth Warden, on payment of 100 guineas, provided that they could secure the backing of six existing members of the Court.[14]

The Select Committee of 1826 which produced this scheme of reform also looked at the salary, emoluments, and duties of the Clerk, which were all henceforth to be more tightly defined. From 1826 the salary of the Clerk was fixed at £250 from the Company's 'private' income, together with allowances of £316 8s. 4d. from various charities (the bulk coming from the Aske, Banks and Jones trusts). The value of his house free of rent, taxes, and the cost of repairs was estimated at £130, and the value of the allowance of 15 chaldrons of coal and 36 dozen candles at £60. Furthermore, the Clerk remained entitled to a portion of the fees from Company members. He was to get £1 for each binding, 10s. 6d. for each turning over, 15s. for each freedom by service or patrimony, £2 for each freedom by redemption and £1 10s. 0d. for each man admitted to the Livery. The annual income from these fees was estimated at £120. Other fees derived from what might be called the soliciting side of his work, for example the drawing up of leases, and this was estimated at

£225 per annum. His total receipts from the Company in the later 1820s were therefore of the order of £1,100. This was perhaps not quite as impressive as it seemed, for the Clerk had to pay for any assistance that he needed, and both Hambly Knapp (Clerk, 1825–43) and William Beechey (Clerk, 1843–9) employed an Assistant Clerk. On the other hand the Clerk, at this time always an attorney or solicitor practising in the superior courts of law, was able to continue in private practice.[15]

The main changes in the Clerk's office in the 19th century were the multiplication of staff for whom the Company took responsibility and the gradual elimination of fees from the Clerk's emoluments. The first step to increasing the bureaucracy at the Hall was the appointment in 1826 of William Fisk, accountant, as Book-Keeper on a salary of £105. In 1865 the Company took over the responsibility for the payment of the Assistant Clerk's salary of £180 per annum, and there was now also a Junior Clerk on the pay-roll. On Fisk's retirement in 1869 the duties of the Accountant were divided between the Assistant Clerk and the Junior Clerk.[16] When John Curtis resigned as Clerk in 1875 it was decided to separate the soliciting aspect of the Clerk's work with the appointment of a separate Solicitor, probably because of the expansion of this component of the job with the development of the Company's estates.[17] It was another mark of greater professionalisation that the fee component of the Clerk's salary was gradually eliminated. The reforms of 1826 had been insistent on the need to regularise fees, and it was not long before the Company decided to curtail them. In 1843 all fees for bindings, freedoms, and so on were removed from the Clerk, although he could continue to take fees for soliciting.[18] The result was that the Clerk's income declined, compounding the effects of a cut in the allowance from the Aske charity from £200 to £100, and the reduction in legal costs as the Jones and Adams charity estates were removed from Chancery control in 1853. In 1865 Curtis estimated his total earnings from the Company at £686 per annum over the whole period of his service, but in the years 1859–63 he had only received £578 per annum, comprising a salary of £540 and costs and fees of £138, less £100 expenses. His case for a rise was compelling and it was agreed that he should henceforth receive a salary of £750, although this was cut in 1875 with the appointment of a Solicitor (initially to £500, but soon increased to £600).[19] It is also evident that the Clerk was becoming much more clearly a full-time official of the Company, and his opportunities for private practice curtailed. In 1875 his hours were specified for the first time as being from ten o'clock to four o'clock, still gentlemanly, but a sufficient discipline to preclude extensive commitments outside the Company.[20]

Another key member of the Hall staff was the Surveyor. His most important duty was the conducting of an annual survey of the state of the Company's property within the metropolis, including the Hatcham estate. He was also responsible for issuing notices of repair to the Company's tenants. He received a basic salary (£70 in 1809, £102 16s. 0d. in 1844, £202 16s. 0d. by 1880) made up of allowances on the charity accounts, together with various emoluments. In 1809 these included three guineas for superintending the erection of any house by a tenant, one guinea for the insertion of plans on the leases of Company tenants, and 5 per cent of the costs of any building enagaged in by the Company. The earnings of the Surveyor from the Company were therefore inclined to fluctuate: George Colebatch received

£209 5s. 0d. per annum in the mid 1820s, but only an average of £116 per annum over the whole period 1822–44. Nor did the employment of a Surveyor preclude the use of an Architect for separate projects: from 1822 Colebatch acted as Surveyor while J.B. Bunning executed several commissions as Architect.[21] But in the later 19th century the Surveyor generally acted also as Architect: the ubiquitous William Snooke drew up plans for new school buildings at Monmouth, houses on the Hatcham estate, the new schools at Hatcham and the churches of St Catherine's, Hatcham, and St Peter's, Hoxton. In addition to the London Surveyor, two additional Surveyors were employed for the Kent and Knighton estates.[22]

Thus by 1880 the Hall staff comprised the Clerk (salary, £600 per annum), Assistant Clerk (£225 per annum), Junior Clerk (£75 per annum), Solicitor (no salary, paid by assignment), Surveyor/Architect (£202 16s. 0d. per annum), Beadle (£222 7s.8d. per annum), Porter (£93 per annum), and Hall Porter (26s. per week). The range of the professional back-up available to the Assistants had been extended and, combined with the greater involvement of the Assistants in the running of the Company that the standing committees entailed, the transaction of business became more professional.[23] But what was the nature of the institution which these officers served? The next section of this chapter looks at the Company's membership, and the character of its involvement with the Company in the 19th century.

The Company continued to contract in size through the 19th century. Whereas an average of 44.9 persons a year had been admitted to the freedom in the years 1737–47, by the period between 1814 and 1832 the figure had fallen to 31.7 persons a year and, between 1870 and 1879, 18.9 persons a year. In 1880 the Company had 657 members. Even with an association of this size it was difficult to keep track of members: in 1873 the addresses of no less than 24.7 per cent of the members were unknown. A striking difference from the earliest years of the Company's history was the high proportion of Liverymen. The fines for entry to the Livery had become an important component of corporate income in the later 17th century, and the Livery had mushroomed. By 1880 there were 460 Liverymen (including 38 Assistants), comprising no less than 70 per cent of the membership. There was inevitably some dilution in the quality of the Livery: in 1873 18.7 per cent of the Liverymen were accounted 'poor', little different from the 22.4 per cent of the non-Liverymen who were so described. Nevertheless it appears that the Company could draw on a pool of men of talent sufficient to fill the offices, and the signs of a more vigorous social life among the Livery to be discussed shortly suggests that the more streamlined Company was better able to satisfy its members' demand for occasions of social intercourse.[24]

Another change was the increasing proportion of those becoming free by patrimony. In the first decade of the 18th century apprenticeship was the preferred route into the Company taken by 72.6 per cent of those made free, compared to 15.4 per cent by patrimony and 12 per cent by redemption. Patrimony steadily advanced thereafter. In the years 1814–32 60 per cent became free by apprenticeship, 11.8 per cent by redemption, and 28.2 per cent by patrimony; the figures for the years 1870–9 are 44 per cent, 7 per cent, and 49 per cent respectively. Thus by the later nineteenth century nearly half the members were following their fathers into the Company,

40. Apprenticeship certificate from the 19th century.

heightening the dynastic aspects of membership.[25] There are cases of 19th-century Haberdasher dynasties, as a glance at the list of those serving the offices of Master and Warden will readily confirm: the Eagletons, Groves, Hawes, Liddiards, and Tudors were well represented over the generations. Take the case of the Eagleton family. From the 1770s to the 1890s the family carried on a tea-broking business from premises in Newgate Street. Edward Eagleton became free of the Haberdashers by redemption in 1770, and was followed by his two sons, Edward and John Henry, free by patrimony in 1810 and 1812 respectively. The four sons of Edward II Eagleton also became free, John Henry (1831), Edward III (1839), and Augustine,

41. John Eagleton, Clerk to the Company, 1907–30.

all carrying on the tea-dealing business, while Octavius (1845) beacame Clerk to
the Fruiterers' Company from 1860, and Solicitor to the Haberdashers' Company
from 1875. This generation of the family were most prominent in City life, Edward
III serving as Master of the Haberdashers' Company in 1884–5, and as Alderman.
Octavius' sons, Charles (free, 1849), John (free, 1882), and Leonard (free, 1891)
followed their father into the family firm of solicitors, and John gained the post of
Clerk to the Haberdashers in 1907. John's son, Guy, was articled to his uncle
Leonard in 1911, and became free of the Company in 1916, succeeding his father
in the Clerkship in 1930. Guy's brother, Hugh, who worked in banking, was also a
freeman, and the direct line is carried on through his daughter, Margarita, who
became a female freeman. At the time of writing Margarita's son, Michael John
Eagleton-Lytle is apprenticed to Barry Gothard, himself the stepson of Guy Eagleton.[26]

A corollary of the growing numbers of freemen by patrimony was a further diminution of the Company's links with the trade of haberdashery. A comprehensive occupational analysis of the members of the Livery in 1837 has been carried out. Information is available for 337 of the 496 members (68 per cent) of the Livery (excluding the Court of Assistants). Of these 337 only five described themselves as haberdashers, and another nine were hatters. Allied trades were represented by six linen drapers, one woollen draper, and one button seller. In 1880 the Company reported that there were only 15 members of the Company involved in trades connected with some branch of haberdashery (including linen drapers, silk mercers, and hatters). The main shift from the early 18th century was the increased numbers of men engaged in dealing as opposed to manufacturing: 20.7 per cent of Liverymen with known occupations were engaged in manufacturing in 1837 as opposed to 38.6 per cent in the distributive trades. Also advancing were the professions which accounted for 13.1 per cent, a figure which underestimates their prominence because in the conventional categories of occupations used by 19th-century historians stock-broking comes under the heading of dealers, and architects and surveyors under the building trades (there were eight stockbrokers, five architects, and seven surveyors among the Liverymen of 1837). The figures for the other employment sectors are: building, 8.0 per cent; transport, 3.9 per cent; industrial services 0.3 per cent; and agriculture 0.9 per cent. In addition there were 30 Liverymen (8.9 per cent of those with occupations designated) who described themselves as gentlemen, probably rentiers, and 19 (5.6 per cent) who were pensioners, that is in receipt of poor relief. The most commonly occurring occupations apart from those already mentioned were clergymen (16), tallow chandlers (11), wine merchants (nine), undertakers (eight), and chemists (seven).[27]

One of the most important developments for the corporate life enjoyed by the members of the Company was the great improvement in its corporate (i.e. non-trust) income. When the Company's finances were surveyed in 1806 the corporate income was reported as being approximately £2,382 per annum. By the decade 1870–9 this had increased by 247 per cent to £8,272 per annum, over a period which had actually witnessed a fall in prices of 32 per cent. The bulk of this growth was accounted for by increases in the Company's rents and by the improving balances on those charity accounts where the donor had specified that surpluses should be transferred to the corporate account. Thus whereas receipts from fees, fines, and quarterage accounted for £770 per annum in the seven years prior to 1806 and £1,238 per annum in 1870–9, rents increased from £896 per annum to £3,143 per annum, and the balance of the charity accounts from £343 to £2,553 per annum. Thus it was the growing value of commercial properties in London (where most of the Company's 'private' estate was located) which accounts for the transformation in the Company's financial position.[28] Nevertheless it should be appreciated that the Haberdashers, although ranking third in terms of their trust income, had the lowest corporate income of any of the Twelve Great Companies. During the years 1875–9 the Company's corporate income averaged £8,989 per annum compared to the £50,141 and £47,341 (figures for 1879 only) received by the Drapers and Mercers respectively. But the amelioration in the Company's financial position made possible the improvement of the Hall and the expansion in the range and variety of the social life enjoyed by members.[29]

The quality of the corporate life enjoyed by the members of the Company was determined partly by the state of the Hall. It secured a reasonable, but hardly glowing write-up in Brayley's *Londiniana* (1829). It was described as 'a respectable brick building'. The Livery Hall itself was 'a lofty and spacious room, with wainscotting twelve feet high, painted in white and blue. Over the screen at the lower end is a music gallery and several large glass chandeliers'.[30] Brayley was writing in the wake of repairs which had remedied the most glaring deficiencies, but the reports of the Company's Surveyor in the early 19th century suggested that a rebuilding was only a matter of time. Its state was the result a combination of financial stringency and lack of use by the Company. Such improved amenities as the Livery Hall possessed, such as the chandeliers or the new floor, were the result of investments by the City Assembly which continued to hire it regularly: the Company, by contrast, only made use of the Livery Hall once a year for the Publication dinner.[31] At the turn of the century Baker was reporting dry rot on the floor of the Binding Room and, on inspecting the roof timbers, claimed that they were only fit for firewood. Extensive repairs were made to the roof in 1802 when the lead covering was replaced with slates. But, as Baker lamented, no sooner had one place been mended than another was found defective.[32] In 1820 it was reported that the ceilings of the Livery Hall and Court Room were in danger of collapse. The chimney in the kitchen collapsed during efforts to patch it up before the Publication dinner in the same year, and the food had to be prepared at the Goldsmiths' Hall in order to avoid disappointing members. The Aske portrait was mildewed because of defective guttering and an overheated chimney in an adjacent property. Another programme of costly repairs was embarked upon in 1821, but the precarious state of the Company's finances did not allow for the rebuilding which the Surveyors were coming to regard as inevitable. Nor were the efforts to patch things up always successful. Elmes, wrtiting in 1829, bewailed the recent destruction of the Livery Hall ceiling and its replacement with a 'common place piece of vulgar lath and plaster'.[33]

In the event it was not until June 1852 that the Court of Assistants decided upon a rebuilding. Plans were ordered in April 1853, and a committee appointed to negotiate with the contractors and supervise the work on 9 July 1853. Under the new scheme the houses of the Clerk, Beadle, and Porter, the Company's offices, treasury, kitchen, and gallery were all demolished. A new main entrance to the Hall was constructed from Gresham Street, while access to the offices was by means of a side-entrance from Staining Lane. In place of the demolished buildings there were constructed a new suite of offices for the Company's business on the ground floor and offices for the Clerk on the first floor, with his private apartments above. Adjoining the new Company offices were a new chapel, a house for the Beadle, and apartments for the Assistant Clerk. The basement was fitted out with kitchen and scullery, confectionery room, and strong room. In place of the old passageway a grand staircase was constructed leading into a new gallery over the Binding Parlour and looking into the Livery Hall. As the Buildings Committee somewhat complacently reported at the close of its proceedings in January 1856, 'in lieu of old and

42. The Hall shortly after the 1854–6 redevelopment showing Tapling's warehouses, which boosted the corporate income of the Haberdashers.

nearly worn out buildings far behind the times and insufficient for the Company's requirements, we have new and convenient premises'. At the same time as this development was taking place, the Company's other buildings in Gresham Street were demolished, and the land let on a building lease to Thomas Tapling to set up warehouses. The rents from Tapling's new premises and from the the site of the old chapel (also let on a building lease to Messrs Dent, Allcroft & Co.) exceeded the earlier rental by nearly £500 per annum. The gross cost of the new buildings was £10,959 9s. 9d., but £787 19s. 0d. was received from the sale of materials from the old buildings, and £650 from the proceeds of the sale of a portion of Gresham Street to the Corporation for street widening, thus reducing the net cost to £9,521 10s. 9d. This was met by loans from the Victoria Life Assurance Society at 5 per cent, which the Company was confident of repaying by 1866, given the improvements to corporate income that the Gresham Street developments provided.[34]

Another phase of building work commenced in 1862, when it was decided to extend the Livery Hall by removing the partition at the west end and lowering the floor. New windows were to be inserted with stained glass representing the arms of the Queen, Company, City, and leading Company members (the latter at their own expense). The music gallery was to be extended, and the appearance of the ladies'

43.   The Court Room before the Second World War.

gallery enhanced by making the alignment of its arches correspond with the clerestory windows opposite. A new suite of furniture covered in crimson silk damask was acquired for the elegantly redecorated and gilded drawing room. The total cost of these improvements, which were complete by November 1863, was £2,884 14s. 4d.[35] But scarcely were they ready before the Hall was damaged by a fire on 19 September 1864. Fortunately the repairs were covered by the insurance, and the Company was able to take the opportunity to incorporate some further improvements including a retiring room for the Court of Assistants and visitors, the insertion of lights in the coffered ceiling of the Livery Hall to improve illumination, and central heating. It is worth noting that although extensive rebuilding had occurred on the Hall site in the 1850s and 1860s the core of the main function rooms remained as they had been in the earlier late 17th century Hall: the shell of the Parlour, Court Room, and Livery Hall all appear to have survived intact, and the early 20th century accounts record, for example, the particularly fine 17th-century plasterwork in the ceiling of the Court Room enriched with the Company's arms.[36]

The steady improvement in the Company's financial position in the early decades of the 19th century encouraged the Haberdashers to entertain the Livery on a more lavish scale in the annual Publication Feast. At the turn of the century, expenditure on this occasion had been of the order of £250 per annum; by the mid 1820s the bill had risen to over £500 in spite of falling food costs. It also seems that these entertainments were becoming more attractive to the Livery, for in 1826 it was noted that because the numbers attending the dinner were so large, it was no longer possible to accommodate them all in the Hall. The problem was resolved by splitting the Livery dinner, so that the senior Liverymen would dine on a different day from the more junior Liverymen. Thus in 1826 the whole Livery was summoned to witness the Publication on 5 December, and the Assistants dined with the Liverymen of 12 or more years' standing on the following day, and with the Liverymen of less than 12 years' standing on 20 December. Each sitting was 200 strong in this year, although in later years the total number dining seems to have been of the order of 370–380.[37] The arrangements whereby contracts were drawn up each year by the Master and Wardens with outside caterers continued. In 1828 Mr Angell, the cook, provided the two dinners at a cost of £312. Musical entertainment was to be provided by Mr Keen in the form of three violins, a violincello, two French horns, a clarinet and flute, a harp, and a double bass. Professional singers were to be hired at a cost not exceeding nine guineas. These in outline continued to be the form of arrangements for the Publication Feast for the rest of the century. By the later 1830s the practice of providing music from the band of the Coldstream Guards and professional singers, which was customary by the 1880s, had commenced. The Publication Feast was also an opportunity to entertain the Company's officers about the capital: the Accountant, the Surveyor, the Chaplain of Aske's Hospital, the Jones Lecturer, and the Schoolmaster of the Trotman School were present as a matter of course. Other invitations were sent to the Members of Parliament for the City and to the Sheriffs or senior members of the Court of Aldermen.[38]

In the later 19th century the number of occasions of convivial assembly among the Livery was increased. In 1867 it was agreed that three dinners should be given to the Livery each year, and that each Liveryman shold be invited in rotation to two. What in fact happened was that the two December dinners continued, while the Livery were now also to be invited to the summer dinner of the Court of Assistants held out of town. By the 1890s there were two summer dinners for the Livery (presumably to cater for the demand) as well as the two customary winter dinners.[39] Venues for the out-of-town dinners included hotels like the *Castle* or the *Star and Garter*, both in Richmond-upon-Thames, but most often the Livery decamped to Crystal Palace at Sydenham. Here they could take part in those high Victorian distractions, such as the camera obscura, the aquarium, and the conjuring theatre, before retiring to the dining pavilion for the lavish fare. Hors d'oeuvres were followed by a choice of thick or clear soup, and then by a fish course (in 1885 plaice, eels, salmon, trout, and whitebait), an entree (*sic*) of a veal sweetbread or chicken vol-au-vent, a meat course (with lamb, mutton, ham, and duck), sweets, ices, and dessert. The fare at the December Publication Feasts was much the same, with the critical difference that turtle soup was always among the specifications issued to the caterers.[40]

44. Invitations, menu cards, and programmes of music for Livery Dinner, December 1903.

45. Invitations, menu cards, and programmes of music for the summer Livery entertainments at the Crystal Palace.

The Assistants benefited still further from the Company's recovering capacity to provide occasions of convivial assembly. Another of the decisions of 1826, when the Company's internal affairs were being reorganised, was that there should be four Court dinners each year held on the second Monday in the months of February, April, June, and September. On these occasions the Master was to enjoy the privilege of bringing two guests at the Company's expense and the two senior Wardens one each. These occasions also became more elaborate as the century progressed, one of them being designated a ladies' dinner to which each Court member could bring a lady guest.[41] It was a sign of growing confidence that the numbers of guests on these occasions increased. In 1878 it was resolved that each Assistant could invite a guest to each of the Court dinners in June and October; in 1890 all Assistants were allowed an extra guest at the ladies' dinner in May.[42] Official guests were also increasingly invited to the Court dinners. Thus in February 1875 a raft of invitations was sent to educational specialists: the President and Vice-President of the Committee of the Council on Education, members of the London School Board, the Aske's School Managers, and the senior Charity Commissioner. The Company was not insensitive to the possibilities of furthering its business through the extension of its largesse.[43]

Another event directed at the Court rather than the Livery as a whole was the ball, held regularly from 1870. Members of the Court of Assistants and the Clerk enjoyed six or seven invitations each, the Wardens four extra each, and the Master as many as he wished. Tea, coffee, ices, claret, champagne, and moselle cups were served, and a supper (joints of lamb) was available as an optional extra. Official guests included the Aldermen and the Members of Parliament for the City, and total attendances stood at between 280 and 362. The cost of the entertainment on the first occasion it was held in 1870 (£407 16s. 6d.) caused some anxiety, and never again were expenses allowed to run so out of order as then: the average over the next seven years was £310.[44]

The expression of anxiety over the cost of the Company's entertainment reminds us of the charges made against the Companies that they consumed resources in Thackeray's 'monstrous belly-worship'. In the 1870s refreshments at the Livery dinners cost between 18s. and 21s. a head; at the ladies' dinner, 27s. a head; at the ordinary Court dinners, 22s. a head; and at the ball, 11s. 6d. a head. The average annual expenditure on entertainment in the 1870s was £2,232, that is about 27 per cent of the annual corporate income.[45] But it should be remembered that the fees paid for the privileges of membership justified some return and donors of the Company's 'private' property had often made their gifts for the express purpose of sustaining fellowship. Thus, although the fees for binding apprentices and admission to the freedom were a modest £3 10s. 0d. and £5 5s. 0d. respectively, admission to the Livery and service as junior Warden were more expensive at £27 8s. 0d. and £250 respectively.[46] Moreover, a close watch was kept on the cost of entertainment, and they were periodically curtailed in order to provide savings which might help finance capital improvements. Thus at the time of the rebuilding of the Hall in 1853–4 the Livery dinners were suspended. Such moves were, however, always unpopular, and motions to economise did not always meet with a favourable reception. Thus in January 1856 the proposal that Court dinners and attendance money

46.   The Livery Hall before the Second World War.

should be curtailed for one year in order to restore the Company's finances was rejected.[47]

The corollary of the recovery of the Company's cycle of banqueting in the 19th century was the more regular expression of the bonds between the Company and the City Corporation and the Victorian Establishment. Guest lists included worthies from City and national politics as well as the Company's own clients. In 1863 it was resolved that the Master and Senior Warden should have the privilege of inviting to each of the Livery and Court dinners four visitors 'being either the Lord Mayor, Aldermen, Sheriffs, Members of Parliament, distinguished officers of either service, Masters of the Twelve Companies, or other persons of high position either in the Church or in the Arts, Literature, and Commerce'. The lists of toasts at the dinners underlines the close associations between the Company and the Victorian Establishment. They were regularly the Queen; the Prince and Princess of Wales; the Army, Navy, and Reserve Forces; the Houses of Parliament; the Right Honourable the

Lord Mayor and the Corporation of the City of London; the Clergy connected with the Haberdashers' Company; the Livery Companies of the City of London; 'the Worshipful Company of Haberdashers, root and branch, and may it flourish for ever!'; the Master; the Visitors; and the Clerk. Speeches at Company dinners tended to elaborate on the interlocking of the civic and national elites. Thus at the Publication Feast in 1904 First Warden M.S. Pilcher's toast to the Imperial Forces of the Crown was answered by two guests, Admiral Edward Field and Brigadier-General T.D. Pilcher (evidently relatives of the First Warden and the new Master, Arthur Field, and thereby highlighting these interconnections), who elaborated on the need for support for 'Mr Chamberlain in his great fiscal fight', and warned against the danger of neglecting martial traditions. The Master proposed the toast to the Corporation, noting that it was the mother of Corporations and pointing to its good influence throughout the Empire. In his reply the Lord Mayor stressed the pleasure he derived from visiting Company Halls and meeting the Liverymen to whom he owed his election. Past-Master Alderman Sir David Evans proposed the toast to the clergy of the Company, somewhat complacently suggesting that the Haberdashers had seldom, if ever, made a mistake in the bestowal of their patronage. Prebendary Storr, then the current Golden Lecturer, replied thanking the Company for the honour it had done him and stressing the gratitude of fellow clergymen for the augmentation of their livings by the Company. In proposing the toast to the Master, Sheriff Strong underlined the magnificent work of the Company over 600 years for the citizens and for charity and education.[48] Very occasionally a jarring note entered proceedings: Arthur Toovey took the opportunity presented by his reply to the toast to the junior Livery at the 1874 Publication Feast to criticise the lack of consultation of the Livery over the new scheme for Aske's charity.[49] But generally the messages were ones of consensus within the Establishment. The mutual congratulation, the stress on the reciprocity of the City Corporation and the corporation of the Company, the underlining of the close links between the Company and the Church and armed forces: all served to emphasise the interlocking nature of the elites and their mutual dependence.

The messages of the dinners were reinforced by a recovery of the civic pageantry associated with the installation of a Lord Mayor which had withered during the previous century with the disappearance of the pageantic elements. The last water procession took place in 1856, and the following year proceedings were described as 'little more than a string of private carriages . . . and a few armed men'. Educated opinion treated the whole thing with bemused contempt: as *The Weekly Times* commented in 1853,

> the utilitarian spirit must prevail at last; and as this partiality for street pageantry is on the wane throughout the whole of England . . . we think that the Lord Mayor's day may safely be left to itself and to the growing sense of the people of London . . . The whole thing will die a natural death, or be consigned to a desuetude, the natural result of indifference'.[50]

But from the 1870s onwards there are signs of a recovery. Although the celebrations of the later Victorian period were never on anything like the scale of the 17th century, there were signs of greater elaboration. This was in part a result of the period of renewed influence at Mansion House and Guildhall enjoyed by the Haber-dashers in the later 19th century. There was no Haberdasher Lord Mayor between Thomas Skinner in 1795–6 and David Stone in 1874–5. But Stone inaugurated a line of Haberdasher Lord Mayors: Sir W.J.R. Cotton in 1875–6, Sir F.W. Truscott in 1879–80, Sir D. Evans in 1890–1, Sir J.C. Bell in 1907–8, and Sir G.W. Truscott in 1908–9.[51] On each of these occasions it seems that the Master and Wardens and numerous Assistants breakfasted with the Lord Mayor-elect prior to his installation at the Guildhall, and a few days later accompanied him in horse-drawn carriages to the procession to Westminster for the new Lord Mayor's swearing in at the Exchequer (from 1883 at the Law Courts in the Strand). The heraldry of the Company and its associations with the Crown and Corporation were celebrated in the banners carried. In 1874 these included the Royal Standard and the arms of the Duke of Connaught, the Union Jack, and the arms of the City Corporation, and of the Company. Benefactors to the Company were celebrated with the arms of Robert Aske, William Adams, William Jones, John Banks, and Nicholas Rainton, former civic leaders from the Company with those of Thomas Skinner and Jeremiah Pilcher (Sheriff in 1842), and current civic leaders with those of Aldermen Stone and Cotton. It remained true that the Haberdashers, in common with many other Companies, did not participate in the procession unless supplying the Mayor or one of the Sheriffs. But when they did participate, they did so enthusiastically. So popular was attendance in the carriage procession that the Master and Wardens warned in 1907 that a ballot of the Assistants might be necessary to allocate places.[52]

Pageantry, now with explicit and increasingly elaborate educative functions, was restored to the processions in the 1890s. Evans' pageants in 1891 celebrated his Welsh origins: one car bore Welsh girls in ancient and modern costume 'emblematical of Wales'; another represented Welsh industries; and another showed Edward I pres-enting the first Prince of Wales to the Welsh chieftains at Caernarvon Castle. It was at this time also that the processions began to incorporate lifeboats and steam fire engines. The pageants associated with the mayoralties of Bell and Truscott in 1907 and 1908 were both masterminded by Louis N. Parker, who elaborated the educative pageant to a high point of sophistication. In 1907 he laid on a historical pageant representing the seven Edwards (including Edward the Confessor) who had preceded Edward VII as King, and brought to a close by a car representing the 'Harvest of the Peacemaker', in which the King was shown as Peace enthroned over the four quarters of the globe. A literary theme prevailed in the next year with 'A Pageant of the Press, the Poets, and the Musicians from Chaucer to Milton'. The pageants therefore celebrated national virtues: the stability and continuity provided by the monarchy, the blessings of British Imperialism, and the strength of the nation's creative talents and industries. They fitted into the pattern of growing international ceremonial competitiveness and Londoners' efforts to combat the perceived relative shabbiness of their city identified by David Cannadine in the later Victorian period. Pageantic display was part of the programme to make London a fit imperial capital.[53]

Another manifestation of the way the Company was tied in to the structures of national authority was the acquisition of royal patronage. There had been few signs of conspicuous loyalty to the later Hanoverians, but the Haberdashers participated in the growth of popular veneration for the monarchy under Queen Victoria, as the Crown came to represent 'a unifying symbol of permanence and national community' in a rapidly changing society, as well as embodying the Empire. Occasions such as the entry of the Duke and Duchess of Edinburgh to the City on 12 March 1874, when the Hall was illuminated, or the attendance of representatives of the Company at the service of thanksgiving held in St Paul's Cathedral for the recovery of the Prince of Wales from serious illness in February 1872, are illustrations of the elaboration of ceremonial in the later Victorian period which reflected the greater ritualistic projection of the monarchy.[54] But the most important development for the Haberdashers was the freedom and Livery of the Company granted to Arthur Duke of Connaught (1850–1942), the third son of Queen Victoria, in 1873. The opportunities afforded by such royal patronage to add to the Company's lustre were quickly seized upon when the Prince performed the opening ceremony of the new Hoxton shools in 1875.[55] Other signs of the developing associations with the monarchy were the regular passage of formal messages of congratulation and condolence on the occasion of royal weddings and deaths respectively. In April 1884, for example, the Company sent a letter of condolence to the Duchess of Albany on the loss of her husband, hoping that she 'may be sustained and consoled in her bereavement by the supreme Ruler of the Universe'.[56]

The story so far therefore is one of steady progress towards greater efficiency in the transaction of Company business and of the recovery of a vigorous corporate life. But it should be recognised that the London Livery Companies did not go unchallenged by 19th-century reformers. Many regarded them as out-moded and self-regarding institutions. At the base of the objections lay a hostility to the vesting of the City franchise in the Livery of the Companies (often resident outside the capital) rather than in local rate-payers. The Companies often seemed anachronistic institutions, having lost all contact with their trades, which in turn made much of their charitable endeavour appear anomalous, originally directed by the donors to craftsmen, but now spent on decayed gentlemen. Their reticence as to the state of their finances gave rise to exaggerated ideas of their wealth. 'Like the fly in the treacle pot', alleged Sir John Bennett, the Companies 'could not move for wealth'. It was also frequently asserted that the funds were used for different purposes to those intended by the donors. Their expenditure on feasting was regarded as profligate. 'Some Companies', asserted J.F.B. Firth, chief critic of the unreformed Corporation in the later 1870s, 'have dinners of some kind, as often as once a week, and lucky are the committeemen of such Companies, for in addition to their salaries, they sometimes find a bank-note delicately secreted under their plates, and sometimes find huge boxes of bon-bons upon them'. Worse still, the Companies were regarded as part of 'Old Corruption', their rulers dispensing lucrative patronage to their friends and relatives, and leasing property at an absurd under-value to fellow-members. The Royal Commissioners on Municipal Corporations had reported in 1837 that 'the system is liable to very great objections, attaching a pecuniary interest to a place on the Court, which never ought to be attached to the character of a trustee'. What J.S. Mill had described as the 'unearned increment', in other words

47. *The Fatal Effects of Gluttony* (1830), a satirical attack on the over-indulgence thought
by radicals to be characteristic of City social functions. The turtle commonly represented
the unreformed City, turtle soup being a favourite at Livery Company dinners.

the surplus on charity accounts, was regarded as being wastefully spent on private
purposes. Having more money than they knew what to do with, it was alleged that
the Companies paid salaries to their Clerks of ten times the market value of the
work. It would be much better if these monies were directed to technical education.
The whole system was perpetuated by confining power to the Court of Assistants
and keeping the Livery in a state of ignorance: 'the disclosure of the financial
condition of the Company would be regarded as an act of high treason to the City
and the Company'. No less an authority than W.E. Gladstone asserted in Parliament
his conviction that the revenue of the Companies is 'positively and utterly wasted,
and very imperfectly and doubtfully bestowed'.[57]

Enough has been said to show that many of these charges were wide of the mark
as far as the Haberdashers were concerned. Expenditure on dinners, although clearly
an area on which the Company was vulnerable, was not excessive, given the amounts
contributed by members in dues and the purposes for which the Companies had
been founded.[58] Critics struck a nerve concerning the fees paid for the attendance of
the Assistants at Courts and Committees, which were a drain on resources, no less

than £2,076 15s. 10d. per annum (approximately £55 per Assistant) being spent in the 1870s, although as defenders pointed out these were less than the fees paid to the directors of public companies.[59] Certainly the broader charge of jobbery was unjustified. Only two Company members, Thomas Tapling (lessee of commercial premises in Gresham Street) and G.L. Shand (tenant at New Cross) held leases from the Company in 1880.[60] As for the earnings of the Clerk, in 1865 the Assistants confessed that they themselves had overestimated them, so one can well understand how the misconceptions of outsiders developed. We have also seen how, with the removal of fees and cuts in allowances from the Aske charity, the earnings of the Clerk actually declined between 1800 and 1880.[61]

On another of the key areas of attack, its charitable activities, the Haberdashers were on firm ground. In 1880 there were no less than 152 pensioners on whom £2,968 14s. 0d. was spent. It is true that many of them were people of middling status fallen on hard times. But contrary to the claims of Firth and his followers, this had always been true of Company charity, the Assistants granting money in a way which reflected their anxieties about themselves rather than the location of 'real' poverty. An awareness of the importance of the proprieties in the management of the Company's patronage is shown by the Assistants' rejection of an application for a pension from the widow of a Liveryman on the grounds that her former husband was the son of a Court member, and it was 'inconsistent for trustees to use charitable funds for their own immediate connections'.[62] Moreover, during the 1870s the Company had begun to spend more of the unearned increment on charitable causes. An average of £476 per annum was being spent on gratuities and donations in the 1870s. Petitions flowed in to the Company from the proliferating organs of philanthropic endeavour. At a typical meeting in February 1867 the Charities Committee considered petitions from the Society for Promoting Religious Knowledge among the Poor by Books, the Bishop of Winchester's Church Endowment Fund in South London, the Providence Row Night Refuge, the Cambridge Asylum, the Society for Employing Curates in Additional Places, the London Rifle Brigade, St George's in the East Ragged Schools, the Female Refuge, and the Fox Court Ragged Schools, and recommended grants to the Provident Night Refuge, the London Rifle Brigade, and the three last named charities. So popular were the Livery Companies for those seeking money that a meeting of the Charities Committee in 1882 considered no less than 127 of these applications.[63] To this was added in 1872 a batch of grants for educational and professional development directed at the children and grandchildren of Liverymen, on which over £400 per annum was being spent by 1879. This latter scheme was the brainchild of Prebendary Charles Mackenzie, formerly Headmaster of St Olave's Grammar School, and a leading light behind educational innovations such as evening classes for young men.[64] It is true that other Companies did more, and that the Haberdashers were not among the Companies which supported the City and Guilds Institute, established in 1878 to provide technical education. But this reflected the much lower 'private' (as opposed to trust) income of the Haberdashers.[65]

The Companies and the City Corporation were remarkably successful in resisting the pressures for reform in the 19th century. This was in part a tribute to their lobbying skills; and in part the result of their self-reform in advance of outside interference. They opposed the drastic remedies proposed by the radicals, but took enough notice of the criticisms to blunt the force of future agitation.

London experienced only minor buffeting during the whirlwind of Whig reform in the 1830s. A Royal Commission appointed in 1833 investigated the municipal corporations, and its recommendations were largely implemented in an Act of 1835 which introduced regular elections and a rate-paying franchise in 183 corporations, but London was not among them. This was because the radical Chairman of the Commission, Joseph Parkes, had set the antiquarian-minded and cautious Francis Palsgrave to work on London in order to keep him out of the way. By the time that the report on the Corporation of London was ready in 1837, the radical pressures had subsided, and the easy-going Melbourne was reluctant to create the kind of storm that the implementation of the Commisioners' recommendations concerning London would have aroused. Among their proposals was the removal of the Livery franchise, which would have broken the political power of the Companies. The absurdity of the Livery franchise resulting from the political irrelevance of the Companies was summed up with devastating clarity:

> in form the governing bodies are rulers of the commonalty; but this a mere shadow, and the only authority which they really exercise with respect to the commonalty consists in their ministerial duties appertaining to the admission of new members . . . There is no connection between the governors and the governed because there is no matter out of which such a connection can arise, and the responsibility of the governing bodies is not as towards the commonalty of their Companies, which are no longer governed by them, and render to them no obedience, but as towards the law, for the due execution of their trusts

In common with most other City Companies, the Haberdashers had been hostile to the Commissioners. Of the Great Twelve, only the Drapers and Fishmongers answered all the questions put to them. The Haberdashers produced only their charters and a return of the numbers of freemen and Liverymen, and their Clerk, appearing before the Commissioners at Guildhall, fell back on the claim that he had no authority to furnish further information.[66]

It was not until the 1850s that the City and the Companies again faced a sustained onslaught at Westminster. Lord John Russell, himself one of the City's M.P.s, appears to have been responsible for the appointment of another Royal Commission to investigate London's government in June 1853. Pressure had been building up within the City for moves towards a rate-paying franchise, but they had been strongly resisted by the Companies. The Commissioners recommended a £10 rate-payer franchise in preference to the Livery franchise, but went further than the reformers within the Corporation in their proposals that the functions of the Court of Aldermen be transferred to Common Council, that the number of wards be reduced to between twelve and sixteen, and that their population and representation be as equal as was practicable.[67] A bill for the reform of the Corporation, implementing the bulk of the Commissioners' recommendations, was introduced by the Home Secretary, Sir George Grey, on 1 April 1856. It was strenuously opposed by the Haberdashers. On 14 April the Clerk presented a copy of the bill to the Court of Assistants, together with details of the resolutions of recent meetings of representatives of the London

Companies at the Mansion House and of the Common Council. He had a petition prepared against the bill to which it was agreed the Company's common seal should be attached, and the Court agreed to ask John Masterman, one of the City's M.P.s and a member of the Company, to present it. The Haberdashers' petition joined those of 28 other Companies. In the event the government dropped the bill because of the pressure of other business.[68] Grey retreated to fight another day, for a modified version of the bill was introduced in February 1858. Again the Haberdashers petitioned against it, and again the bill was dropped for lack of Parliamentary time. Other bills appeared in 1859 and 1860, but on each occasion were lost amid petitioning from interested parties like the Haberdashers (who petitioned against the 1860 bill) and disagreements about the degree of reform required.[69]

During the 1860s and 1870s the government withdrew from the promotion of Corporation reform. The Liberal government of 1868–74 gave other matters priority, while Disraeli, in office between 1874 and 1880, although not an enthusiastic supporter of the Corporation, felt that its reform was incompatible with his party's principles. The cause was left to backbenchers like James Beal who, attempting to tackle the lack of a central metropolitan authority, proposed a series of municipalities coordinated by a supervisory body, and when this scheme encountered the opposition of the Corporation, a much more centralised metropolitan authority which would subsume the City.[70] The attacks on the City were combined with mounting attacks on the Companies. As Ian Doolittle has made clear, the attack on the Companies was inseparable from the atack on the Corporation. For the radicals, he says:

> . . . it was axiomatic that the Livery vote in Common Hall made the Companies an integral part of the Corporation . . . It was also argued that the Livery 'lobby' sustained the Corporation in its fight for survival. Again, the Companies were vulnerable, an easy first step in the demolition of the civic edifice. Finally, their wealth could be used as a spectacular endowment for the proposed new Council. No taxes, just a spendid windfall

It was in the mid–1870s that J.F.B. Firth's agitation gathered momentum. His book, *Municipal London*, was published in 1876, and he appears to have followed it with the establishment of the City Guilds Reform Association. When W.H. James, M.P. for Gateshead, moved abortively for an address to the Crown asking for a full return of the Companies' income and property in 1876, he very clearly drew upon Firth's book for inspiration.[71]

On the occasion of James' motion, the opposition was led by W.J.R. Cotton, M.P. for the City and a beneficiary of the Conservative landslide in the City in 1874, Lord Mayor, Chairman of the City Guilds Defence Association, and free of the Haberdashers' Company. He deployed the soon-to-be-familiar argument that the Companies were essentially private associations run by men of honour, integrity, and respectability, faithfully discharging the trusts with which they had been charged.[72] An ominous intervention in the debate came from Gladstone who, though doubting the constitutionality of James' motion, nevertheless strongly supported the idea of an investigation into the Companies. It comes as little surprise to learn that when the Liberals returned to power in 1880, Gladstone responded to the pressure from the radicals and appointed a Royal Commission to investigate the Companies. It included both the arch-conservative Cotton and the radicals, James and Firth. Their colleagues tended to greater moderation. Among them were former ministers like the Earl of Derby, Sir Richard Cross, and Viscount Sherbrooke; the noted philanthropist, Alderman Sir Sydney Waterlow; and the banker, Sir Nathan Rothschild. The majority report of the Commissioners rejected the argument (supported by the Lord Chancellor) that the Companies were merely private institutions and recognised the theoretical right of the state to disendow them (provided compensation was paid to members), but made more modest recommendations. They felt that some kind of state control was necessary, particularly to ensure that a portion of the Companies' corporate income was spent on useful purposes, and to reorganize some of the trusts on more rational grounds. These changes could be implemented, they suggested, by a Standing Commission, which would have the power to reapply income from trusts over 50 years old irrespective of the donors' wishes, as well as undertaking the reform of Company constitutions where appropriate.[73]

The Royal Commission of 1880–4 was treated with considerably more respect by the Companies than the Commission on Municipal Corporations of 1833–7. The Haberdashers established a special committee to consider the answers to be made to the Commissioners' enquiries, and to coordinate action with other Companies. They complied in answering all the questions put to them although, in common with other Companies, they followed the recommendations of the Guilds Defence Association in appending a protest over enquiries into their corporate property, and refused to answer oral questions.[74] The Company's position with regard to the Commission was probably similar to that expressed in the minority report presented by Cross, Rothschild, and Cotton. They took the view that the Companies were essentially private fraternities established for mutual support whose involvement with trade had been contingent and temporary. They were not essential parts of the City Corporation, the voting rights enjoyed by their members being the only point of contact with that body. As far as their corporate income was concerned the state had no right to interfere. Alderman Cotton, the Haberdasher among the Commissioners, added his own splenetic protest to the dissenting report.[75]

The Companies remained determined to resist state interference. Bills were introduced in 1885 by Sir Charles Dilke. The first measure, which appeared in the last months of Gladstone's administration, the Corporate Property Security Bill, was designed to prevent the Companies alienating their property and the members pocketing the proceeds. The second, the London Livery Companies Bill, appeared in July under Salisbury's Conservative premiership and stood little chance of becoming law. It proposed that the Companies should be given three years to frame schemes for devoting more of their corporate resources to projects of public utility, redesigning their trust funds, and reforming their constitutions. Their schemes were to be overseen by a Standing Commission. Both measures came under fire from the Haberdashers. Grants of £100 and £265 were made to the Guilds Defence Association and Liberty and Property Defence League respectively, and a petition adopted according to the form recommended by the Defence Association. The donation to the Earl of Wemyss' Liberty and Property Defence League shows the Haberdashers aligning themselves with the coalition of interests worried by the over-legislation and 'empirical socialism' characteristic of the government of the 'People's William'. To the distaste for Gladstone's attitude to the City was added the blame which attached to him for General Gordon's fate. When the Haberdashers were approached for a donation for a National Memorial for Gordon, C.J. Phillips moved (unsuccessfully, as it turned out) that no grant should be made 'so long as the Rt. Hon. W.E. Gladstone was a member of the Committee'.[76]

From 1886 Conservative rule was uninterrupted until 1905 except for Gladstone's fourth administration of 1892–5. Government-sponsored attacks on the Companies were therefore unlikely.[77] That the Livery Companies escaped the fate of so many aspects of the Ancien Regime was in part a result of the way in which they undertook their own reform. As we have seen it was just as the radical agitation was mounting in the 1870s that the Haberdashers began to allocate more of their corporate income to projects of public utility. It was also, as the next chapter will show, a decade during which its charitable trusts were overhauled under the impact of other state intervention in the form of the Endowed Schools Act of 1869. The Companies were, often reluctantly, and in response to pressure from outside, moving into the modern world.

Chapter Twelve

The Charities in the Nineteenth Century

The previous chapter showed how improvements in the Company's finances were a major factor in the recovery of its corporate life in the 19th century. The same is true of the charities. During the early 19th century the income of the major charities registered modest advances. The rents from the Adams estate increased from £175 per annum in the early 18th century to £476 14s. 0d in 1784, £766 17s. 0d. in 1808, and £957 3s. 6d in 1819. The gross income of the estates in Kent and Hoxton belonging to Aske's charity stood at £3,469 7s. 2d. in 1819 compared to £923 8s. 4d. in 1697. On the Hatcham estate the increases were more modest because of the regressive policy of long leases pursued by the Court of Chancery in the mid–18th century: from £543 in 1714, the receipts advanced to just £555 in 1763, and £779 10s. 1d. in 1822. Looking forward to 1862, it was the Jones charities which registered the most remarkable advances, gross receipts having reached £2,799 7s. 4d. The receipts from the Adams estates and the funds associated with the charity had nearly doubled to £1,841 15s. 10d. As for the Aske charity its gross receipts virtually stood still at £3,581 11s. 0d., hardly any improvement on the position in 1819. These differences in performance reflect the different pace of development of the estates. The Hoxton estate was let on long building leases in the early years of the 19th century, whereas the development of the Hatcham estate did not begin until the mid-century. The income from the Aske charity leapt ahead once more as the building leases fell in: by 1873 gross receipts were about £8,000 per annum, and by 1885 about £12,000 per annum.[1]

Viewed over the long term, the charities did remarkably well in financial terms. Viewed from the perspective of 1800, however, things looked rather less rosy. Although improvements in the income of the major charities meant that the Company was better able to fulfil the terms of its trusts in the sense of being able to support the outgoings envisaged by the founders, nevertheless the state of the charities in the early 19th century can only be described as parlous. This was because resources remained inadequate to meet the multiple demands of funds for the repair of buildings and for the increased salaries necessary in an inflationary age if the Company was to employ able Schoolmasters. Moreover, in the case of Newport and Monmouth the statutes of the Schools imposed an excessively rigid classical curriculum which was alien to the requirements of the middling inhabitants of these provincial towns longing for a more commercial education.

At Hoxton the Company was paying the price for its highly ambitious Hospital building which had so consumed the benefaction that there was no provision for a repair fund. For the first two decades of the century the reports of the Surveyor, John Baker, on Aske's Hospital are a litany of dilapidations. The roofs were in such a bad state of repair that every time the tiles were touched they fell off in heaps;

the external woodwork was so rotten that it could no longer hold nails; the fabric was severely damaged by a hurricane in 1800, and seven years later the north wing was ravaged by a fire started through the irresponsibility of the tenant of that section of the complex. Repairs were made to patch things up but, as Baker warned several times, this was only staving off the evil day when the Company would have to engage in a general repair, the cost of which he estimated at £4,000 in 1801.[2] Building costs so escalated during the Napoleonic Wars and the cost of land tax redemption so sapped the charity's funds that a general repair was not feasible, but the modest surpluses from 1806 onwards were invested in 3 per cent consols to provide a fund for repair or rebuilding, which by 1818 stood at £4,500.[3] Likewise, although the Trotman School at Bunhill had been rebuilt in 1769–70 at a cost of £700, by 1810 it was in a state of disrepair, and the charity funds were insufficient to meet the costs of repair.[4] At Bunbury, where the founder had fixed the income of the charity at a mere £130 per annum, repairs were the responsibility of the Aldersey family as lessees of the tithes, but they do not appear to have been aware of their obligations, and the Company had to threaten legal action in 1812 before any action was taken.[5]

At Monmouth and Newport the buildings were not so dilapidated, but their state of repair occasioned concern. Of Newport, Dugleby, the Company's Surveyor, had reported in 1789 that 'in forty years time it will be necessary for the Company to take down the whole of the school, schoolmaster's and usher's houses and the almshouses and rebuild the same, and that it will then require the sum of £5,000 to be laid out in such buildings'. Repairs were carried out in 1802–3 at a cost of £1,100, but they were marred by acrimonious disputes between the contractor and Joseph Scott, the Headmaster, over the latter's attempt to alter the specifications half-way through the project, and they amounted to no more than a holding operation. In 1820 it was noted that although the charity buidings had been erected in 1656, there had been no general rebuilding, and that no material repairs had been carried out since 1802. In that year an estimate for comprehensive repairs costing £3,564 12s. 5d., which probably amounted to a rebuilding, was approved.[6] Likewise in 1816 it was reported that no repairs had been carried out to the School and almshouses at Monmouth for 23 years, but ameliorative action was taken, and £439 13s. 6d. spent in repairs.[7]

The Schools at Monmouth and Newport also faced other problems. The necessity of accumulating funds for building meant that the staff could not immediately benefit from any improvements in charity income. Thus, although a surplus of about £100 per annum was reported on the Adams charity in 1829, the Governors noted that its finances were precarious because of the need for a fund for repairs and therefore the masters could not have another salary increase. Although salaries were increased at Newport in 1797 and 1808 and at Monmouth in 1808, they were not regarded as adequate by the staff who responded by adopting a variety of strategies to maximise their income.[8] Some took extra livings. Thus the Usher of Monmouth School held the curacy of St Mary's Monmouth to which he added livings at Raglan and Llandenny in 1818.[9] Still more controversial was the admission of boarders. John Powell, the Headmaster of Monmouth from 1793 to 1823, was a notoriously sharp operator, who had 64 boarders but only 10 day boys in the School in 1802. In 1810,

68 inhabitants complained to the Haberdashers' Company that Powell was turning away local boys and neglecting them when admitted. These charges were repeated in 1823 in another petition from the inhabitants against Powell's successor, William Jones. Jones had apparently advertised the School as a boarding school with fees of £20 per annum for board and classical tuition, and had turned away 17 inhabitants of the town applying for the benefits of the free school envisaged by the founder.[10] Similarly there were complaints from the townspeople against Edward Meredith, Headmaster of Newport School, in 1827 for the neglect of foundation boys by the taking of boarders, of which there were 27 in that year, and the admission of boys to the Upper School who had not yet attained the necessary standard, for a fee of ten guineas.[11]

The defence put up by the masters underlines the other critical weakness of the schools, their narrowly classical curriculum. At Monmouth the staff pointed out that according to the statutes boys could not be admitted unless they were prepared to take the full classical curriculum. Jones claimed that the 17 to whom he had refused admission in 1823 were ineligible because they had applied to learn reading, writing, and English grammar only. A strong body of local opinion wanted to establish a commercial school where the three Rs would be central to the curriculum. In 1810 the memorialists, to the Company's horror, had established a subscription fund to petition the Lord Chancellor for a full-time writing master. But it is important to appreciate that opinion in the locality was divided. Powell had been supported by a counter-petition from the clergy and gentry of the area who provided the clientele for his system.[12]

Given the division in Monmouth between the tradesmen and 'respectable' gentry society over the fate of the School it is hardly surprising that it became entangled with the bitter disputes over the constitution of Monmouth Corporation and the domination of the Beaufort interest in the 1820s. The officers of the charity were identified with the narrow clique who controlled the town's affairs. Thus Thomas Prosser combined office in the charities, serving successively as Usher of the School in 1779, Headmaster in 1780, and Lecturer in 1793, with secular magistracy, becoming a member of the Common Council of Monmouth in 1802, and serving as its Mayor in 1806, 1813, 1816, and 1818. The leading agitator on the schools issue in the 1820s was 'Honest Tom' Thackwell, one of the opponents of the town oligarchy.[13]

How did the Haberdashers respond to the agitation? Initially their attitude was a compound of snobbery and an understandable legalism. They were impressed by the status of the supporters of Powell in 1810 and alarmed by the fractious tone taken by the petitioners of the 1820s. Benjamin Hawes, a reform-minded member of the Court of Assistants, alleged in 1824 that a 'very influential opinion considers every attempt to reform to be fractious, and every attempt to do one's duty conscientiously to be troublesome'. But this visceral conservatism was reinforced by an understanding of the very real legal constraints under which the Company operated. The will of the founder had to be adhered to, and this was quite clear on the priority of classical education. In 1810 the Assistants adverted to the decision of Lord Chancellor Eldon on the Leeds Grammar School case of 1805 where on appeal he had overturned the decision of the Court of Chancery to allow the use of the School's endowment for the teaching of reading, writing, and modern languages.[14]

But there was a significant change in the nature of the Company's response in the 1820s. In 1823, shocked by the brazen nature of Jones' advertisements for boarders, the Company did express its concern (although still maintaining that there was no proof that the Headmaster had neglected any pupil in his care), and supported the idea of an application to Chancery for the appointment of a Writing Master to defuse the criticisms of the inhabitants.[15] Although the initial application in 1824 for a Writing Master was rejected by Chancery, another bid in 1827–8 proved successful.[16] In 1824 the Haberdashers came round to support the suggestion of the inhabitants that a body of local Visitors should be appointed to report on the progress of the School. Nine Visitors comprising local clergy and magistrates (although significantly not from the town itself) were appointed in 1825 with the duty of visiting the School at least twice a year, examining the scholars, and reporting on the performance of the masters.[17] The much firmer line the Company was taking with the charity was evident in the revised statutes of 1828 which allowed the admission of outsiders only if the numbers in the School fell below 100 and required that the staff had no other cures. Jones resigned as Headmaster, soon to be followed by his Usher, Henry Prosser, whose request to hold another cure had been turned down by the Haberdashers. They told him that a complete reform was underway and that the Governors and Visitors were united in their resolution that the new regulations should be obeyed.[18]

The Company's response to the complaints against Meredith at Newport also testifies to their determination to set the charities in order in the later 1820s. Their response to boarders was less hostile than at Monmouth because the founder's statutes had apparently envisaged that the Headmaster might take them, but they felt that it was essential for the Visitors to examine the school regularly in order to keep the masters up to the mark, and to ensure that the foundation boys were not neglected. They were also very critical of the Headmaster's differential fees for admission: whereas the founder had authorised entrance fees of 2s. 6d., Meredith was taking anything up to ten guineas.[19]

The agitation in Monmouth seems to have brought home to the Company how out of touch it was with the real state of its charities, dependent as it was in all these controversies on the representations of local interests. Benjamin Hawes told a doubtless uneasy Court of Assistants in 1824 that the Company could not adequately discharge its trusts for lack of information, and that some members did not even know by name the charities of which they were trustees, let alone their duties and the state of the disposable funds. As was shown in the previous chapter, it was shortly after these controversies that the Company undertook the reorganisation of its committees to make the Assistants more knowledgeable in the Company's affairs.[20] And there was a markedly greater appreciation of the beneficial effects of deputations from the Company to their more remote charities. After the deputation of 1834 which visited Monmouth, Newland, Newport, Bunbury, and the Company's livings at Awre, Blakeney, Albrighton, Diseworth, Great Wigston, and Bitteswell, it was noted that this was the only effective way to stop prejudice, correct abuses, and promote good public relations.[21] Likewise there were efforts to improve the level of supervision over the London charities. After serious complaints about the conduct of the Chaplain at Aske's Hospital (for neglecting the pensioners and taking advantage of a maid servant) the Clerk was instructed in 1832 to arrange for fortnightly visits to the Hospital by members of the Hoxton Committee in rotation.[22]

The more sympathetic hearing which the Company gave the reformers in the 1820s may be related to the growing interest of central government in charity administration. As Hawes remarked, 'Public Charities are now watched with a jealous eye. It is fit they should'. There was mounting anxiety in the early 19th century that charitable trusts were improperly administered and that the country was littered with obsolescent trusts in need of considerable reorganisation. The machinery provided by an act of 1601 for the issuing of special commissions to inquire into the misapplication of charity funds had fallen into desuetude, leaving the expensive labyrinth of the Court of Chancery as the only recourse for those minded to reform abuses. The first faltering legislative steps were taken with two statutes of 1812: the Charitable Donations Registrations Act which required the central listing of all endowments, and the Charities Procedures Act which was intended to provide a 'summary' remedy. The effectiveness of the latter measure was curtailed by the continued dependence on the use of the 'perennially hopeless' Court of Chancery. But the most significant move was the huge enterprise of fact-finding, the so-called 'Domesday Book' of English charities, launched by Henry Brougham in 1816. Beginning with a Select Committee to investigate the education of the poor in London in 1816, he secured (in the face of considerable opposition from Lord Chancellor Eldon) a Commission to investigate educational endowments over the entire country two years later. The first reports of the Commissioners allayed some of the fears of Brougham's critics and Castlereagh agreed in 1819 to extend the terms of reference to all charities. The monumentally impressive labours of these Commissioners, involving the interviewing of witnesses over the entire country and the scrutiny of wills, legal documents, and such miscellaneous sources as church memorial tablets, were not complete until 1837.[23]

These first signs of state intervention were regarded with some suspicion by the Haberdashers. In common with other Companies they had sought exemption from an earlier bill for the registration of charities in 1809.[24] Nevertheless they cooperated with Brougham's Commissioners, reporting in 1818 on their educational charities (with the exception of the Jones and Adams Schools which were under Chancery control and initially exempt from the terms of the inquiry), and in 1822–3 on their other charities. The Commissioners made recommendations for the revival of lost loan stocks with a capital value of £2,595 10s. 0d. and of annual charities amounting to £149 4s. 8d. per annum. The Company complied at once with the recommendations relating to the annual grants, but was unable to restore more than £500 of the loan stocks in the first instance.[25]

With the Company taking a firmer line with the Schoolmasters at Newport and Monmouth, repairing the charity buildings there, reorganising its committees to increase awareness among the Assistants of the problems of the charities, and undertaking to restore lost charities, the 1820s emerge as a decade when the Haber-

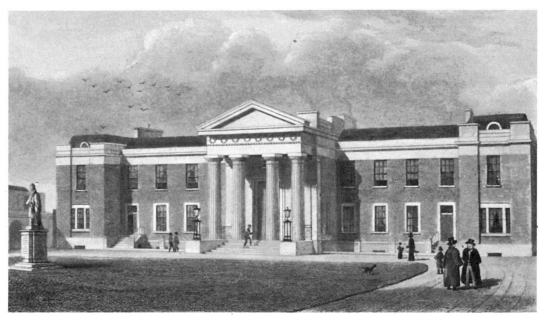

48. Aske's Hospital at Hoxton, after the rebuilding of 1827 to designs of David Riddal Roper.

dashers embarked on serious reform. To some extent their policy was reactive rather than proactive, responding to the agitation of local interests and the threat of state intervention if maladministration remained unchecked. But reform was also rendered more feasible by their growing financial security: it was only the improving rentals on the Adams and Jones estates which enabled the accumulation of repair funds and the payment of more generous salaries.

Another example of the difference that financial health could make, but which also emphasises the dangers of over-ambitious projects, is shown by the rebuilding of Aske's Hospital in 1824–6 to designs by David Riddall Roper. The cost of repairing the existing buildings was estimated at £6,500, while the initial estimates for the new Hospital suggested an outlay of £13,455. A rebuilding would have the advantage of enabling the site of the Hospital to be adjusted to a position more appropriate to the layout of the Hoxton estate then under construction. The contractor undertook the work for £12,295, but the overall costs escalated with the committee's decision to build a new sewer, raise the level of the site to avoid damp, and surround the complex with a new boundary wall. They also instructed that a new statue of the founder (now at Hatcham Boys' School) should be provided to encourage other benefactors. Inclusive of fittings and the architects' fees the total cost was £18,881. This was met by the sale of materials from the old site for £3,185, the sale of consols from the repair fund realising £6,454 14s. 6d., and a loan from the Company's corporate stock of the balance.[26] Confidence in the buoyancy of the charity's income also led the Haberdashers to increase the salaries of the officers and the allowances of its inmates. In 1826 it was agreed that cash allowances of £52 per annum each should replace the communal table for the old men, while the salaries of the Chaplain and Schoolmaster should be raised to £100 and £52 10s. 0d. from £50 and £30 respectively.[27] Confidence, however, rapidly evaporated as an annual deficit of £500 per annum was revealed in the charity in 1830. The allowances to the old men were cut by 20 per cent, and the offices of Chaplain and Schoolmaster amalgamated in 1831, with the incumbent receiving a block grant of £700 per annum to cover both his salary and the cost of maintaining the 20 boys in the School. That the Haberdashers had over-reached themselves in the rebuilding of the Hospital is confirmed by the fact that the bulk of the debt from the Aske charity funds to the Company for the rebuilding still remained unpaid in 1861.[28]

With the formalisation of Visitors' meetings, more regular deputations, and the improved communication between London and the localities, the 30 years after 1830 saw further reforms of the Company's charities. At both Monmouth and Newport there were tentative moves in the direction of loosening the classical strait-jacket. At Newport in 1834 the Governors agreed to make the Writing Master full-time with the intention of broadening the range of subjects on offer, although they resisted the proposals of the Headmaster for the separation of the classical and commercial departments: the new subjects were seen very much as adjuncts to the classics and therefore in line with the founder's intentions. Further pressure for a more commercial education from the inhabitants in 1852 and 1856 led to Latin being confined to the Upper and Middle Schools and Greek to the Upper School.[29] At Monmouth, where a Writing Master had been secured in 1828, a separation of the commercial and classical sides was implemented temporarily in 1831 and permanently in 1854, on the latter occasion with such success that it was held up as an example to Newport in later years.[30] Staff salaries increased at both Schools. At Monmouth, for example, the Headmaster received £120 in 1820, £170 from 1832, £230 from 1842, and £264 from 1865. Moreover, in addition to its Writing Master, Monmouth acquired the so-called Third Master (actually the fourth member of staff) under the scheme of 1854. Another development was the appointment of professional examiners from the universities, at Monmouth from 1851 and at Newport from 1861.[31]

The process of making the decisions which led to these reforms was rendered more complex by the variety of interests the Company had to square. The strongest lobbying for a relaxation of the classical curriculum continued to come from the townspeople, who were also committed to the principle of free education. The Visitors, however, took a rather different line. At Newport in 1833 they dissented from the analysis of the reasons for the School's decay presented by the Headmaster. Against Meredith's argument that the curriculum alienated the parents, they suggested that the problem lay in the disinclination of respectable folk to send their children to schools where they would rub shoulders with the lower orders attracted by the free education. The Visitors were also less enthusiastic about the relaxation of the classical curriculum, pushing for the restoration of elementary Latin to the

49.   The deputation to Monmouth in 1864: W. B. Simpson (Master), B. Edgington
(First Warden), D. Wood (Second Warden), W. H. Mullens (Third Warden),
J. H. Gosling (Fourth Warden), and H. Hooper (Beadle).

Lower School in 1860.[32] Similar differences of opinion emerged at Monmouth over
the question of the advisability of extending the School's area of recruitment and
admitting boarders. It was an objective of the townspeople to secure the benefits of
the School for themselves, and this they achieved through the statutes of 1847, which
limited entry to those whose parents enjoyed two years' residence in the town and
county of Monmouth and banned boarders (thereby effectively limiting recruitment
to the town). The result appears to have been a decay in the quality of the entry
commented upon by both Visitors and examiners. The Visitors were convinced that
this reflected the failure to recruit boys from the country and in 1850 they recommended the extension of the field of recruitment to Gloucestershire and Herefordshire. The boys from the town were of a lower class; they arrived relatively poorly
educated; the counter-culture of the street proved more attractive than learning for
lack of appropriate role models at school; and their parents withdrew them at a

younger age. Thus when the Company embarked on the revision of the statutes in 1852, they were confronted with petitions from both parties, one (signed by the Vicar and 81 inhabitants) requesting the introduction of boarding and fee-paying and the other (signed by the Mayor and 500 inhabitants) that the restrictions of 1847 should remain. By way of compromise the Governors approved the extension of the field of recruitment to Gloucestershire and Herefordshire, but held out against boarders, the memory of the abuses of the 1820s being uppermost in their minds.[33]

Such reforms as were carried out in the early 19th century remained subject to the approval of the Court of Chancery, time-consuming and expensive though it was. Chancery, for example, had to approve the establishment of new teaching posts, changes in the internal organisation of the schools, and all repair works. Some of the issues which had to go before the Court were trifling in nature, such as the extra desks required at Newport in 1826. Sometimes the delays were potentially fatal. For example in 1831 the Company expressed anxiety over whether expenditure on a sewer at Newport necessary to avoid cholera should be authorised lest it be disallowed by the Master in Chancery. Chancery also supervised the Company's management of the estates belonging to the Jones and Adams charities. Chancery approval was necessary for new leases and for exchanges of land. It was, as the Company pointed out to aggrieved Monmouth residents in 1832, Chancery which had granted the disastrously long leases of large sections of the Hatcham estate in 1763.[34]

An interesting exception to the pattern of reform through Chancery is provided by the School at Bunbury. In the early 19th century the Aldersey School was one of the major scandals of the Company's charities. The root of the problem lay in its fixed income which made the stipends of the officers inadequate for the purposes envisaged by the founder. In 1834 the inhabitants complained to the Company against the Headmaster, John Martin, for neglecting his teaching duties and appointing a substitute, who raised his income by charging parents and thereby subverted the principle of a free school. These complaints dragged the Company into the maelstrom of local politics, for Martin's supporters, led by the Company's preacher, John Egerton, claimed that his critics were animated by a violent anticlericalism. After a deputation later that year, the Company ordered Martin to pay his assistant an extra £10 per annum and allow him his house rent free. When Martin sought to dismiss his assistant in 1835, the Company instructed him to attend to the School personally, and as part of a package of reform sponsored by Egerton the principle of the free school was re-established.[35] Nevertheless complaints resurfaced in 1850. Martin was again absent, his duties devolving upon the Usher, who was also Parish Clerk and a local publican, and therefore unable to give the School his undivided attention. So poor was the reputation of the Aldersey School that local farmers were sending their children to another fee-paying school in the parish.[36]

Bunbury was dragged from its torpor by the energetic reform sponsored by the Company's preacher, William Garnet, appointed in 1853. Garnet recommended that a Master bearing a certificate from one of the new metropolitan or diocesan training schools should be appointed and supported by a combination of the endowment income, donations from leading inhabitants, and capitation fees on the pupils, and that an application should be made for a government grant. The Company was initially reluctant to accept the latter measure because it would entail government inspection, but the other proposals were put into effect in 1855. The children of farmers and professional people paid 10s. per quarter, and the children of the labouring classes 2d. per week. Under this scheme the School's popularity soared, numbers rising from 36 to 95 in a matter of months. So successful was the reform, indeed, that the Company overcame its reluctance to accept the grant from the Committee of Council on Education in September 1856. Thus in the year ending 31 December 1856 the School's income comprised £37 4s. 4d. from the endowment, £88 0s. 0d. (higher than in subsequent years as the parish was embarking on the building of the master's house) from donations and individual subscriptions from leading local landowners, £53 9s. 0d. from capitation fees, and £56 15s. 0d. from government grants. Thereafter the School was held up as a model of what could be achieved through the introduction of modest capitation charges. What is remarkable about the project, however, is that it was carried through without reference to the Court of Chancery. Quite why, it is difficult to tell. The School's statutes gave greater flexibility than many, for they did not mention a specific curriculum. Furthermore, David Allsobrook notes that there is no reference to the Aldersey charity in the Charity Commission files, so perhaps it escaped regular monitoring.[37]

Bunbury could not provide a pattern for all Haberdasher charities, because the new scheme, whatever its utility, was of dubious legality, and if unilateral solutions had been attempted in the educationally politicised environments of Monmouth and Newport, litigation would surely have ensued. The long-term solution lay in greater central control of charities. A Parliamentary Select Committee had recommended in 1835 that a central supervisory board of three Commissioners should be established to scrutinise charity accounts and suggest shemes for the amendment of charities and the removal of abuses in their administration.[38] These recommendations were not implemented for nearly 20 years, and the Haberdashers bear some portion of the responsibility for the delay. For, in common with other Livery Companies, they put up considerable opposition to the various efforts to legislate on the matter.

In three successive years (1844–6) during the administration of Sir Robert Peel, Lord Chancellor Lyndhurst introduced proposals for the implementation of the Select Committee's recommendations. In 1845 the Haberdashers, on receiving notification that the Charitable Trusts Bill had been introduced in the House of Lords, appointed a committee to consider the best means of opposing it, and a petition was presented to the House of Lords against the bill. Its eventual postponement to the next session owed something to the mediation of a Liveryman, the M.P. Benjamin Hawes, with a member of the administration. Again in 1846 the Company took measures to oppose Lyndhurst's proposals which were eventually lost as a result of the factional manoeuvring which followed the repeal of the Corn Laws. The Haberdashers argued that as a corporation they were in a position to provide the Governing Body of a kind which had inspired the confidence of the donors in the first place, that the reforms would be expensive, that as regards charities directed at their own members they were in the best position to determine needs, and that abuses were unlikely because of the large body of people interested in their administration and likely to point up any maladministration.[39] Lyndhurst brought the full force of his withering irony to bear on arguments of this kind: of the Mercers' Company, he noted that the expenses for the annual inspection of Northampton's charity at Greenwich amounted to nearly £100 instead of the £5 laid down by the founder. This was the behaviour of a Company, he sarcastically remarked, 'which claims to be exempted from the operation of the Bill on account of the strict and faithful manner in which they have hitherto discharged their duties, and are likely to discharge them again'.[40] In fact the Haberdashers were probably not guilty of the kind of abuses to which the Lord Chancellor here adverted, but they were unquestionably guilty of a certain narrowness of vision in their failure to appreciate the benefits which might flow from a redefinition of the objects of some charities.

The result of the vigorous lobbying of groups such as the Haberdashers was that when the Charitable Trusts Act finally emerged in 1853, it was a rather less sweeping measure than had been envisaged by the Select Committee of 1835. The powers of the new Charity Commission were primarily inquisitorial: the Commissioners were entitled to investigate charities and were to receive annual accounts from trustees, but they could not frame new schemes save through the existing mechanisms of Chancery and Parliament. The scope of their powers was, it is true, gradually extended. By the Charitable Trusts Act of 1860, they were authorised to make orders for establishing schemes and appointing or removing trustees. But these powers only applied to charities with an income of less than £50 per annum; in other cases the Commissioners had to gain the consent of the majority of the trustees. Thus in the case of the larger charities, such as the Adams, Aske, and Jones charities run by the Haberdashers' Company, new schemes could only be framed at the request of the trustees.[41]

Nevertheless these charities were coming under mounting pressure in the 1860s with the launching of a full-scale investigation into secondary education. Responding to pressure from the Social Science Association, Palmerston's government appointed the Schools Inquiry Commission under the chairmanship of Lord Taunton in December 1864. Its most active members were Lord Taunton, a former Whig minister; Lord Lyttleton, Gladstone's brother-in-law; Frederick Temple, then Head-master of Rugby and later Archbishop of Canterbury; Sir Thomas Acland, scholar and agriculturalist; and W.E. Forster, the radical. The Commission compiled reports on nearly 1,000 endowed grammar schools, based on inquiries made by its Assistant Commissioners, and published in 20 volumes between 1867 and 1870.[42] Among the endowments surveyed were the Haberdashers' Schools at Newport and Monmouth. Neither emerged unscathed. Although Assistant Commissioner H.M. Bompas was impressed with the level attained by the pupils at Monmouth, he drew attention to the very large surplus on the charity revenues, which might support expansion, and he was alarmed at the lack of patronage of the School by professional parents, which he attributed to the lack of boarding. Newport was visited by Assistant Commissioner James Bryce, who was critical of the mode of teaching whereby 'the three depart-ments of the school are managed entirely without reference to one another'. In common with his colleague at Monmouth he supported the view that the Head-master's unwillingness to take boarders lowered the tone of the School. He ended his observations waspishly: 'William Adams' foundation already has more money than it knows what to do with; certainly far more than it uses well'.[43]

The recommendations of the Schools Inquiry Commission had serious implications for the Haberdashers' Company. The Commissioners were convinced that the endowed schools must be considered as a whole rather than as isolated units so that schools could be provided appropriate to the needs of each area. To this end they proposed a central Commission with powers to devise new schemes, operating in conjunction with provincial boards which would assess the needs of each area. Schools were to be reclassified into three grades appropriate to the various subdivisions of the middle class. Thus the top-grade schools would offer a strong classical training while those at the third grade would provide an education above the elementary level. Other recommendations related to the constitution of the Governing Bodies of schools. The Commissioners were critical of the usual method of filling vacancies by co-optation, and recommended that in future schemes the Foundation Governors should constitute about one third of the Governing Body: the others would be appointed by the proposed provincial boards and by the local municipal authorities.[44]

Forster's Endowed Schools Act (1869) did not adopt the recommendations in full. A central body, the Endowed Schools Commission, was appointed, but its authority was to run for no more than three years, and the intermediate tier of the provincial boards was scrapped. Wide powers were given to the new Commissioners, who 'by schemes made during the period, and in the manner and subject to the provisions in this Act mentioned, shall have power in such manner as may render any educational endowment most conducive to the advancement of the education of boys and girls or either of them, to alter and add to any existing and to make new trusts, directions and provisions which affect such endowments, and the education promoted thereby, including the consolidation of two or more such endowments, or the division of one endowment into two or more endowments'. It is striking that the Commissioners had the power to abrogate old trusts and create new ones, for example redirecting resources for the poor or apprenticeships to educational purposes.[45]

It will come as little surprise to learn that the Haberdashers opposed this legislation, as another manifestation of the Leviathan's tightening grasp. Indeed, the Haberdashers were responsible for coordinating opposition within the City. When a copy of Forster's bill was presented to a meeting of the Company's Charities Committee on 28 February 1869, it was agreed that the Clerk should call a meeting of the Clerks of the principal Livery Companies as a preliminary to a meeting of the Masters and Clerks to consider the City's response to the bill.[46] Once appointed the Commissioners were to cause a furore within the City. Their scheme for Emmanuel Hospital, Westminster, a foundation very like Aske's Hospital providing accommodation for 20 poor aged persons and education for 60 children, ran into furious opposition from the Court of Aldermen and was a major factor in the City's change of allegiance from the Liberals to the Conservatives in the General Election of 1874. It was one of the first acts of the Conservative government which was then elected to abolish the Endowed Schools Commission and transfer its powers to the Charity Commission. The Charity Commission continued to work under the provisions of the Endowed Schools Act but tended to be more legalistic and cautious in its approach lacking the reforming zeal which the sometimes abrasive Endowed Schools Commissioners had brought to their work.[47]

David Allsobrook has suggested that the Haberdashers had sought to evade reform from without by embarking on their own reform of Monmouth during the 1860s. The William Jones foundation which attracted regular comment as one which was benefiting from a huge increase in revenues as a result of the development of the Hatcham estate and the sales to the railways. No less a figure than W.E. Gladstone had referred to the Company's Hatcham estate when proposing (unsuccessfully, as it turned out) the taxation of charities as Chancellor of the Exchequer in 1863. The same point had been made by Assistant Commissioner Bompas. The implication was that the monies could be used to support a wider range of educational purposes if the dead hand of the past could be removed. The running of the School had already encountered some criticism from Thomas Hare, the indefatigable Inspector of Charities, in 1862. It was as much in response to his observations as out of any machiavellian desire to preempt the School Inquiry Commission that the Haberdashers embarked on reform.[48]

A building programme was set in motion, with the erection in 1864–5 of a chapel and vestry, a new school room, and two classrooms at a cost of £5,294.[49] A new scheme for the School was approved by the Charity Commissioners in 1868 in advance of the Endowed Schools Act. A critical change was the introduction of fees (£6 per annum for boys in the Upper School and £2 per annum for those in the Lower) for all pupils except those enjoying scholarships, of which there were twelve The numbers were no longer limited to 100, and the masters were allowed to take boarders. Entry to the Lower School remained restricted to the counties of Monmouthshire, Gloucestershire, and Herefordshire, but the Upper School could admit boys from all over the country.[50] The Haberdashers had therefore come round to the view long expressed by the Visitors (and now supported by the town council, if not the inhabitants, who still wished the School to be free for all) that the tone of the School would be increased by taking boarders and levying fees.[51] But this scheme did not meet with the full approval of the Endowed Schools Commissioners. Their Assistant Secretary, D.C. Richmond, told the Company in 1870 that the new Commissioners

> are plainly bound by the purport of the Endowed Schools Act to give a general effect to the recommendations of the Schools Inquiry Report. That Report contains many important enunciations of general principles with which the new scheme of the Company, though carefully and in many respects liberally framed, does not in all respects accord.[52]

One respect in which the scheme of 1868 was undoubtedly at odds with the recommendations of the Schools Inquiry Commission was over the composition of the body of Visitors. There were to be 12 Visitors, including the Vicar of Monmouth *ex officio*, but otherwise all nominated by the Haberdashers' Company with the only restriction that two should be residents of the town, and the other nine should come from within a 25-mile radius of it. Another matter of difference between the Company

50. Monmouth School.

and the Endowed Schools Commissioners, and indeed a sticking point in the negotiations between the Company and the Charity Commissioners which lcd to the 1868 scheme, would have been the responsibility for the dismissal of the Headmaster: the scheme of 1868 left this in the hands of the Governors rather than the Visitors. Nevertheless, whatever their doubts about the Monmouth scheme, the Commissioners had other problems on their plate; so the Haberdashers had escaped the attentions of the central authorities with respect to this charity for some time.[53]

The remarkable difference that the schemes of the Endowed Schools Commissioners could make to a charity is shown by the fate of the Aske charity under the scheme of 1873, by which four schools were established. At Hoxton there would be a School for 300 boys and another for 300 girls, and at Hatcham one for 300 boys and another for 200 girls. Fees of between £2 and £4 per annum at Hoxton and £4 and £8 per annum at Hatcham were to be charged. The Schools were to be open to all, but a fund of £400 per annum at Hoxton and £1,200 per annum at Hatcham was to provide exhibitions for the maintenance and education of children, in the case of Hatcham with preference to the children and grandchildren of freemen of the Company. Leaving exhibitions of £600 each for the two pairs of Schools were to be available to those proceeding to the universities or places of professional

51.   The masters at Monmouth School during the 1860s: the Reverend
C. M. Roberts (Headmaster, 1859–91), William Pitt (Second Master,
1857–91), William Roseveare (1858–95), and Robert Earle (1862–91).

training. The Schools were to be run by a Board of Managers of 15 members, nine
of whom were to be appointed by the Company, one by the Lord Mayor and
Aldermen of the City, one by the Common Council of the City, and four by the
London School Board. In this way the scheme met the objectives of the Endowed
Schools Commissioners for the extension of provision for the education of girls, and
for the dilution of the trustees' control. The story of how the scheme emerged
provides an interesting insight into the different priorities of the Company and
charity reformers.[54]

Aske's Hospital had remained in a rather unsatisfactory state in spite of several efforts at reform. The offices of Chaplain and Schoolmaster had been separated once again in 1852, but the lack of a head with overall responsibility resulted in continual clashes and a loss of respect among the boys, who were continually running away. To the utilitarian critics of traditional charities the Hospital was extraordinarily wasteful: many more would benefit from a charity organised on non-residential principles, not least because the Company experienced difficulties in filling all the pensioners' places.[55] By the mid–1860s, the Haberdashers were coming round to the case for reform, particularly in view of the anticipated increases in income as early 19th-century building leases fell in, but their proposals were always less radical than those of outsiders. In 1864 they considered extending the number of boys to be schooled to thirty. Local pressure groups, however, were demanding the expansion of the education provided by the School to all residents of Hoxton rather than being confined to the offspring of Company freemen. The Hoxton Middle Class Education Committee petitioned in 1866 that the School should be made available to local children paying fees. These proposals were rejected by the Company, which in 1868 decided on a gradual extension of the benefits of the School, increasing the number of boarders to 30 and bringing in 50 day boys in the first instance. Only the children of Company members would be eligible to board, but if numbers fell short then the children of the Company's tenants at Hoxton could be admitted as day boys. The preferential treatment to be given to Company members is also evident in the proposed differential in fees: whereas the fees of the Company day boys were to be £2 per annum, the tenants' children were to pay £4 per annum.[56]

But within a few months this scheme had been overtaken by a more ambitious one for the removal of the charity lock, stock, and barrel to Hatcham. The considerations which led to this change of heart are not entirely clear. It seems to have been based on a calculation of the likely increases in charity revenues over the coming years which would support an educational establishment much larger than that envisaged in the 1868 projected scheme, and too large for the cramped Hoxton site. In 1868 the gross income of the Aske charity stood at £4,902 per annum, and there was already a surplus of £1,502 per annum. It was estimated that by 1872–3 the income would be increased by a further £3,066 per annum, and by 1885 by a further £3,728 per annum. Such large-scale increases would provide not only the income to support a larger establishment, but also the security for any borrowing that building projects entailed. Hoxton was not regarded as a fashionable area, none of the boys educated in the school coming from there, and the land available for expansion of the school was restricted. It seemed more profitable to move the charity to the middle-class suburb of Hatcham, well connected by rail with central London, and where the recently built church of All Saints would provide the necessary services for the children and almsfolk. A School could be provided at Hatcham for 40 boarders and 300 day boys for the sons of Company members and of tenants of Hatcham estates. Another School at Hoxton for 100 sons of the Company tenants there could be financed from the sale of the land on which the hospital buildings stood. The proposed fees at Hoxton were between 30s. and £3 per annum, and at Hatcham between £2 and £8 per annum. The sons of Company members alone were to be eligible for the foundation scholarships (with free boarding), and they were also to enjoy priority of admission as day boys and preferential treatment over fees.[57]

Perhaps the Company was trying to pre-empt the possibility of more radical reform in the way it had done at Monmouth, but its negotiations with the Charity Commisioners over this scheme were terminated by the passage of the Endowed Schools Act. The initial comments of the Endowed Schools Commissioners on their proposals in February 1870 were hardly favourable. They thought the scheme too narrow in scope, and were particularly alarmed by the preferential treatment to be given to the sons of Company members as foundation scholars, and by the restriction of the new Schools to the sons of Company tenants. They argued that pecuniary privileges should only be allowed as rewards for merit, and that the Schools should be open to all, so that the catchment area would be determined by 'considerations of convenience and other freely working natural causes'. The other sticking point was, not surprisingly, the composition of the Governing Body of the Schools. To the Haberdashers' proposal that the Schools should have no Visitors but the Company, the Commissioners responded that the Governing Body needed 'a greater variety than one corporation, however eminent, can have'.[58] In the months that followed the Haberdashers began to enlarge the scope of their proposals to incorporate, for example, provision for the education of girls, but the issue of the Governing Body remained a vexed one. Opinion within the Company's Charity Committee was divided, and it was decided that it would be better to leave the Clerk to negotiate with the Assistant Commissioner, Joshua Fitch, whose requests for a meeting with the Governors were put off. This did not go down at all well with the Commission which pointed out that the Company had not responded to the comments on their earlier scheme. So it was agreed in December 1871 that the Committee should meet with the Assistant Commissioner, but that they should confine their discussions to the composition of the Governing Body. The Company wanted to retain absolute control, but Fitch was adamant that a mixed Educational Board should be established, and the Company was forced to surrender on this point in May 1872: the 15 School Managers were to include seven members of the Court of Assistants, and two women nominated by the Company. The Haberdashers nevertheless retained their control over the estates of the charity. Other parts of the Company's scheme were also abandoned under pressure from the Commissioners. In the scheme eventually approved by the Privy Council there was no preference for Company members or tenants in the matter of admissions, and the 40 free boarders had disappeared. In their place were funds for exhibitions to which the children and grandchildren of freemen had preferential access.[59]

At Hoxton the staff of the former Hospital were pensioned off and the almshouses demolished. While the boys were boarded at Margate, the School was enlarged, and opened on 5 June 1875 by by H.R.H. The Duke of Connaught. The Hatcham Schools were opened five months later by Sheriff Knight. The Boys' and Girls' Schools initially shared the Telegraph Hill site, but as numbers expanded to 286 boys and 189 girls by the end of 1879, it was recognised that this site was too cramped, and that a new site for the Girls' School should be found. But, although the School Managers took this decision in 1882, and architects' plans were available

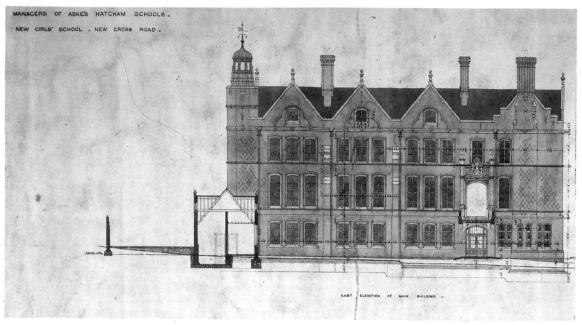

52.   Elevation of Haberdashers' Aske's Hatcham School for Girls, by Henry Stock, Architect, 1887.

soon after, the School at the corner of Jerningham Road and New Cross Road was not completed until 1891, mainly because of delays caused by the financial objections raised by the Charity Commissioners.[60]

The negotiations between the Endowed Schools Commissioners and the Haberdashers' Company over the fate of the Aske endowment have been examined at some length in order to bring out their different priorities. A similar tale could be told of the Adams foundation at Newport, a new scheme for which was promulgated in 1878. This provided for a Boys' School of not less than 100 day boys and 50 boarders and, when funds permitted, for a Girls' School. Fees for the day pupils were fixed at between £6 and £12 per annum (with reduced fees for 80 boys from Newport or Chetwynd End and the vicinity) at the Boys' School and between £4 and £8 at the Girls' School. Foundation scholarships were to be made available to up to 10 per cent of the pupils. In common with the Aske scheme the power of the Haberdashers over the School was diluted. Although they retained control over the estates, the Governing Body of the Schools was to be 13 Managers, consisting of the Master and Senior Warden of the Company *ex officio*, five chosen by the Court of Assistants, two by the local Justices of the Peace, two by the Newport local board, and two by the ratepayers of Newport. The School Managers were empowered to dismiss the Headmaster, as well as determining the curriculum, and matters of

53.   Haberdashers' Aske's School for Girls, Acton.

general policy. This scheme proved extremely controversial in the locality: the fees were resented, the loss of the apprenticeship funds regretted, and the demand for a Girls' School questioned. Indeed a local newspaper editor wrote to the Company complaining that it had been too weak in its opposition. The Haberdashers replied that they had opposed the scheme initially but, finding the Charity Commissioners firm in their resolve, they had complied. In fact their opposition had resulted in some amendments to the initial proposals of the Endowed Schools (and later the Charity) Commissioners. In particular the original suggestion that the management of the estates be vested in Chancery had been defeated and the extent of Haberdasher representation among the School Managers increased.

It was not until 1891 that the Jones charity underwent full-scale reorganisation. By 1889 the gross income of the Monmouth and Newland charities stood at £9,287 6s. 3d. per annum, and some expansion in the scope of the charity was desirable. By the scheme approved by the Charity Commissioners in 1891, it was directed that three new schools should be established: a Girls' School for scholars and boarders and an Elementary School at Monmouth, and a School for day scholars and boarders in West Monmouthshire. Each of the Schools was to receive an annual block grant of an amount fixed by the scheme: £2,800 per annum for Monmouth Boys' School,

£1,000 per annum for Monmouth Girls' School, £250 per annum for the Elementary School, and £1,000 per annum for the West Monmouthshire School. The almshouses, chapel, and Lecturer were to receive £1,500 per annum. The grants from the Haberdashers' Company to the Schools were supplemented by fees, the income from which amounted to £607 6s. 8d. at Monmouth Boys' School in 1893, and £370 0s. 0d. (supplemented by miscellaneous payments for extra tuition in music, science, and wood carving, and for books amounting to a further £298 19s. 1d.) at Monmouth Girls' School in 1898. Other Monmouthshire educational establishments benefited from the redeployment of resources. The scheme of 1891 further specified that £3,000 was to be given to match an equivalent amount in private subscriptions to provide new buildings for the King Henry VII Grammar School at Abergavenny. The Welsh Intermediate Education Act of 1889 added to the Company's responsibilities: £6,000 was to be provided towards the building of a Monmouthshire Agricultural School, and £2,500 for land at the School. Under a later notorious clause of this scheme, against which the Company petitioned in vain, the whole of the residual income of the charity was to be given to Monmouthshire County Council to be applied to educational purposes within the county. The scheme of 1891 also brought the composition of the Governing Bodies of the Schools more into line with those of the other reorganised charities with a diminution in Haberdasher control. There were now to be 17 Governors for the Monmouth schools, five being appointed by the Company (including the Master and Senior Warden *ex officio*, two by Monmouth Borough Council, one by the Monmouth School Board, two by the recently established Monmouthshire County Council, and one each by the Universities of Oxford and Cambridge and the University College of South Wales; the remaining four were co-opted.[62]

The implementation of these schemes was the cause of many headaches to the Company. The quest for suitable sites for both the West Monmouthshire School and the Elementary School at Monmouth was arduous, and there were differences of opinion with the Charity Commissioners over the cost of buildings. There were bids from Newport, Pontypool, and Tredegar to host the new West Monmouthshire School. The Governors favoured Newport initially, but switched to Pontypool, possibly under the influence of the Charity Commissioner, Sir George Young, who felt that the municipality of Newport could themselves fund a school out of the rates.[63] As for the Elementary School at Monmouth, negotiations for a site in Weirhead Street fell through because the price of the property was too high, and it was not until 1897 that a suitable site was found.[64] The location for the Girls' School had been agreed upon in 1892, but the School remained in its temporary accommodation in the initially somewhat insanitary Hardwick House until 1897 while the Company haggled with the Charity Commissioners over the cost of the buildings. Here the Company largely seems to have got its way. Its initial estimates of £20,000-£25,000 were queried by the Commissioners who wanted no more than £10,000 (excluding the architect's commission, fittings, and furniture). Within a few months they had revised this to £15,000, but the Governors remained extremely unhappy, especially as the lowest tender was for £17,643 18s. 6d. After lengthy discussions the Commissioners agreed in 1895 to an expenditure of £16,000 with any excess being repaid out of the foundation income over the next 30 years.[65] The negotiations over the cost of the West Monmouthshire School followed exactly the same pattern, in this case the eventual deal confining the Governors to an expenditure of £23,000 with the same understanding as regards excess expenditure. In the event the costs of the two Schools, both completed in 1897, were £9,650 over the allocated expenditure of £39,000.[66]

Other changes in the Jones charity had extended the scope of the Company's ecclesiastical patronage in the later 19th century. In 1866 the Company sold three houses in Size Lane which constituted the bulk of the income of the London Lecture-ship charity to the Metropolitan Board of Works for the new Queen Victoria Street, and the proceeds of £29,000 were invested in 3 per cent consols. A new scheme for the charity was approved in 1871 by which on the retirement of the present Lecturer the income would be applied to two courses of lectures each year, and provide top-up allowances of between £60 and £80 to clergy about London. This replaced the stipend paid to one cleric for life to give often poorly attended lectures, and spread the benefits of the charity more widely, as well as encouraging attendance at the lectures by varying the individual giving them. More remarkable still was the use of capital from the charity to fund new church building on the Company's rapidly developing estates. In 1870–1, £1,500 was given towards the completion of All Saints' Hatcham, and £4,000 towards the purchase of a site and the building of St Peter's Hoxton. In 1891–2 the Company undertook the building of another church at Hatcham, St Catherine's, at a cost of £18,797, and provided another £6,000 for the endowment of the living. The patronage of St Peter's and St Catherine's was vested in the Company, which also presented to the living of All Saints' for one turn in three.[67]

Many of the minor charities also benefited from reform in the 19th century. The inquiries by Brougham's Commissioners and the later establishment of the Charity Commission encouraged the Company to take steps to ensure the payment of those charities which had been undermined either by loss of properties after the Great Fire or by the loss of the loan monies supporting them. Thus in 1854 the Company invested £166 13s. 4d. in consols to provide the payments to the Company's poor and the parish of Shepperton from the charity established by Richard Buckland. Although the Company was supporting the charity out of its stock in the early 19th century, the houses in Paternoster Row which Buckland had given the Company in 1573 had been sold in 1675, and the designation of a specific piece of capital in 1854 to pay the charity ensured its regular payment. Likewise, in the same year, the Company allocated £666 13s. 4d. 3 per cent consols to provide £20 per annum to support the exhibitions established by Frances Clarke, the original stock having been lost. The involvement of the Charity Commission also enabled a widening of chari-table objects. The scheme of 1876 for William Cleave's charity, for example, allowed the residue of the income to be applied to poor people within the capital generally rather than confining it to the poor of the Company.[68]

Although the Haberdashers had met the growing involvement of the state with considerable hostility, the results were not at the end of the day to the Company's disadvantage. The number and range of schools the Company supported had expanded; the charities were on a surer footing; and the Company's patronage increased. It is true that the reconstitution of the Governing Bodies of its Schools meant that it acted more obviously in partnership with local interests, but the Company still retained the majority say. In the succeeding century, however, as the financial constraints tightened, the pressure from the state became more difficult to resist. That provides a major theme of the next chapter.

Chapter Thirteen

The Company in the Modern World

The major force shaping the Company's history in the 20th century has been the continuing expansion in the role of the state which has led to changes in the character of the Schools as well as having implications for the income and the management of the Company's charities. The effects of two World Wars have left their mark in periods of acute austerity, and the destruction of the Hall and adjacent properties by enemy action in 1940 has continued to cast a shadow (albeit a diminishing one) over the Company's corporate life. The form taken by this final chapter is to consider developments on the corporate side first, looking at membership, the way the Company is governed, and its social life, and then to explore the changing nature of the relationship between the Company and its Schools, and the management of its charities.

Over the course of the 20th century the Company has come to be dominated by the professions and by the industrial services sector. In 1933 these two groups accounted for 31 per cent and 21.4 per cent respectively of the 229 active (i.e. non-retired) Liverymen whose occupations were designated on the list of that year. In 1990 the professions accounted for 36.2 per cent and the industrial services sector for 42.8 per cent. Among the professions the Law has remained prominent throughout the century, with six barristers and 22 solicitors in 1933, and nine barristers and 22 solicitors in 1990. The Church has retreated and Medicine advanced. Whereas 18 clerics wore the Livery in 1933, in 1990 there were four. Six Liverymen practised medicine in 1933 compared to 14 in 1990. In the industrial services sector most notable has been the advance of the chartered accountants and company directors. There were eight chartered accountants enjoying the Livery in 1933, and 18 in 1990; and no less than 41 Liverymen described themselves as company directors in 1990 as compared to 18 in 1933. That still more do not appear within the groups of the professions and the industrial services may reflect the vagaries of the occupational classification system used. The 10.5 per cent of Liverymen in 1990 classified as dealers are largely accounted for by underwriters and stockbrokers, and the 7.4 per cent in the building trades by architects, surveyors, and estate agents. The decline of the manufacturing sector to 12.7 per cent in 1933 and just 1.7 per cent in 1990 is in part a mirage reflecting the onward march of capitalism: the involvement of some Haberdashers in manufacturing is obscured by the opaque occupational designation of company director.[1]

The size of the Company has held up well in the 20th century. In 1990 there were 28 apprentices, 338 freemen, and 306 Liverymen. Admission to the Company is still by the conventional routes of apprenticeship, patrimony, and redemption. In the decade 1981–90 an average of 20 freemen were admitted each year, 23 per cent by apprenticeship, 31 per cent by patrimony, and 46 per cent by redemption. There has thus been a shift from patrimony towards redemption since the later 19th century. This might be thought to have reduced the family element within the Company. But an examination of the realities underlying these modes of entry shows that there remains a strong family tradition, albeit not to the same extent as in some other Companies, and not to the exclusion of the claims of men of talent. Apprentices are taken between the ages of 18 and 21 (rather than as in the 19th and early 20th centuries at 14), and serve a term of between four and seven years such that they will become free at the age of 24 or 25. Apprentices are usually the children of members of the Company born before the parent became a freeman and therefore not eligible for admission by patrimony, or the godchildren or other close connection of the master. Redemptioners comprise three categories: those who missed their opportunities as apprentices; those made free with their 'fines remitted', often being long serving members of the schools' staffs; and those joining from outside, usually sponsored by two or more leading Company members, and bringing some desirable professional expertise.[2]

Redemptioners have aroused ambivalent attitudes within the Company. At the root of the problem lies the fact that applicants for the Livery regularly exceed the number of vacancies. The size of the Livery is limited by ordinance (although not by charter) to 320, regarded as an optimum number in view of the aspiration that members should attend at least one dinner a year and the constraints of the cost of entertainments and the size of the Hall. With so much pressure from those free by apprenticeship and patrimony seeking access to the Livery, redemptioners have sometimes been regarded askance. In 1961 a committee recommended that redemption should only be allowed in exceptional circumstances as long as the Livery exceeded 300 members. Another committee noted in 1969 the dilemmas the Company faced between the claims of redemptioners who might bring talents into the Company and of the children of members who had the right to membership irrespective of merit and to whom the Company felt a strong loyalty. Reports on this issue in the 1970s tended to emphasise that whereas the freedom was a right, the Livery was a privilege for which those free by patrimony must establish their credentials by merit. The ending of the practice whereby men were made free by patrimony and clothed with the Livery on the same day on reaching the age of 21 is a further indication of the force of this distinction.[3]

A major change in the composition of the Company in the later 20th century has been the admission of women freemen in steadily increasing numbers. As an indication of the degree to which thinking has changed on this point it is worth recalling the response to the suggestion in 1944 that an honorary freedom be granted to a representative of the female services. It was rejected as 'a revolutionary measure', Sir Maurice Jenks asserting that 'it would be incongruous'. In the years after the Second World War honorary freedoms were granted to long-serving female members of the schools' staffs such as Miss A.F. McDonald, formerly Headmistress of Monmouth Girls' School, made free in 1960, but a critical departure from customary practice was made in 1964 with the admission of Miss A.R.M. Elliott, daughter of a Past Master, the first woman made free by patrimony since 1806. Two years later the daughter of the Headmaster of Monmouth School was bound apprentice to

54.   Publication Ceremony, 1979: the Clerk (Commander W. R. Miller) places a garland
on the head of the new published Master (H. C. Quitman), watched by the Beadle (F. J.
Oakman), First Warden (W. A. Twiston-Davies – to the left), and the Immediate Past
Master (Major General Sir John Bates).

Commander Prevett, then Clerk, the first female apprentice for 150 years. The
prominence of female members was, of course, immeasurably enhanced by the
acceptance of the freedom by H.R.H. Princess Margaret in 1966. Since then the
numbers of women free by both apprenticeship and patrimony have steadily
increased, so that in 1990 the total number of women members stood at 77, that is
12 per cent of the total Company membership. Women are still not eligible for the
Livery, which means that Company office is denied them. This is an issue on which
opinion among the Assistants is moderately divided. Younger Assistants tend to take
the view that this is anachronistic distinction at a time when women perform jobs
as high powered as those of their male counterparts, while traditionalists assert that
the pressure of demand on the Livery, and the plethora of suitable male candidates
makes the admission of women inappropriate. There is a feeling that sooner or later
women will be admitted, but all agree that the time should be of the Company's
choosing and at a moment when there are plenty of eligible women of talent to avoid
the impression of tokenism.[4]

XXI.   The Queen's Regiment was affiliated to the Company on 7 February 1984. Seated left to right: D. G. C. Inglefield (Third Warden), G. L. Bourne (First Warden), C. I. Bostock (Master), M. W. D. Northcott (Second Warden), P. W. Bedford (Fourth Warden) and I. S. B. Crosse (Immediate Past Master). Brigadier H. C. Millman, O.B.E., Colonel of the Queen's Regiment, stands immediately behind the Master. The Clerk (Captain M. E. Barrow) is shown to the left, and the former Clerk (Commander W. R. Miller) to the right of the picture.

XXII.   Visit of H.R.H. the Princess Margaret to the Adams' Grammar School, Newport on 16 May 1985. She is shown in the laboratories with Mr. D. J. Taylor (Headmaster), Mr. H. A. Wood (chairman of the Governors), G. L. Bourne (Master), and pupils of the school.

XXIII.   H.R.H the Princess Margaret became an Assistant *Honoris Causa* on 29 October 1986. Left to right:
Front: R. E. Liddiard (Past Master), F. S. Bird (Past Master), Vice Admiral J. S. C. Salter (Past Master), the
Reverend A. W. G. Cope (Past Master), B. E. Shawcross (Third Warden), G. R. Fox (First Warden), H.R.H. the
Princess Margaret (Assistant *Honoris Causa*), M. W. D. Northcott (Master), O. M. W. Swingland (Second Warden),
B. C. Gothard (Fourth Warden), Sir Robin Brook (Past Master), P. B. Powell (Past Master), Sir Gilbert Inglefield
(Past Master), G. T. Bentley (Past Master), D. A. H. Sime (Past Master).
Back: K. D. Warren (Honorary Assistant), Commander W. R. Miller (Assistant *Honoris Causa*), F. H. W. Bedford
(Honorary Assistant) standing behind P. W. Bedford, J. E. G. Prevett, A. D. Pilcher, D. E. K. Elliott, M. A. B.
Jenks, H. N. Lund, C. I. Bostock (Past Master), J. G. Carr standing behind, D. G. C. Inglefield, M. D. G. Whelde
Major General Sir John Bates (Past Master), P. J. de C. S. Salter, Sir Maurice Bathurst (Past Master), the
Honourable L. B. Hacking, I. S. B. Crosse (Past Master), G. L. Bourne (Immediate Past Master), A. R. Miller,
M. H. V. Jeans, J. Denza, B. E. Sturgess, G. R. R. Brown (Honorary Assistant), F. J. Oakman (Beadle), Captain
M. E. Barrow (Clerk).

XXIV. The Hamersley Salt.

XXV. A selection of the 17th-century silver: Arnold Flagons (at rear), Company and Wyberd Monteiths (in centre), Willimot Cups (front left) and White Cups (front right).

XXVI.   A selection of 20th-century silver by Omar Ramsden, unless otherwise stated. Left to right and rear to front: the Col. H. L. Florence Basin, the Haberdashers' Company Golf Challenge Cup, the E. B. Florence Cup, the Charles Arnold Cup (by Gilbert Marks), the Eagleton St Katherine figure, the Osborn Salts, the Blundell Mustard and Pepper.

XXVII.   A selection of 20th-century silver by Gerald Benney: Standing Cup and Cover, two Candelabra, pair of claret jugs, Warden's Goblet, Bentley Cup, Vice-Admiral Salter's Cup, the Jenks Cup, Replica of Master's Cup, Clerk's Goblet.

The Company's basic governmental structure still remains that laid down in the charter of 1675. Executive power rests with a Master and four Wardens elected annually in November at the Feast of St Katherine, and policy formation is still the responsibility of the Court of Assistants. Committee structure, however, has been reviewed on several occasions, notably in 1961, 1973, and 1980–1 with a view to avoiding the duplication of authority and to ensure the streamlining of decision making. A particular problem as regards the sale, purchase, and development of property in the post-war cycles of property boom and slump has highlighted the need for swift action which a sometimes cumbersome committee structure precludes. In 1975 after plans for the purchase of a lease in Oxford Street for the Monmouth charity fell through, it was noted that the Company's structure was inadequate for these urgent decisions. Such decisions were increasingly taken by *ad hoc* committees in the later 1970s. A critical overhaul occurred in 1980 on the initiative of Past Master H.C. Quitman, when the Property Committee was established with responsibility for the oversight of the Company's landed investments. The following year the number of standing committees was reduced from three to two as the Aske's and Adams' Charities Committee and the Jones Monmouth Charity Committee were merged into a single Schools Committee, and the Minor Charities Committee was renamed the Charities Committee. The Finance Committee retained its oversight of policy relating to the finances of the Company and its charities, and dealt with the details of Stock Exchange investments until the establishment of the separate Securities (Investment) Committee. The Securities and Property Committees are now kept small in order to ensure swift responses to changing market conditions. The main effect of the changes in the nature of committees has therefore been to render them functional: rather than having a single committee dealing both with finances and educational policy relating to a particular charity, the different aspects of management are divided between specialist committees.[5]

The main criteria for the choice of Assistants have long been 'seniority tempered by selection'. According to the Standing Orders of 1986 the Court of Wardens, in interviewing candidates for admission to the Court of Assistants, should 'consider first those with the greatest seniority'. Every now and again some anxiety has been expressed about this: in 1930, for example, J.H.W. Pilcher moved that the Company should follow the practice of some other Companies in adopting 'selection tempered by seniority'. Nevertheless it cannot be denied that the selection procedure is rigorous. Opinions are invited from members of the Court about the suitability of candidates for Assistantships; they are interviewed and entertained by the Court of Wardens with the assistance of at least two Past Masters and one other Assistant nominated by the Master; and they accompany one of the annual deputations to the Schools; a list of recommendations then appears before the Court of Assistants which makes the final election.[6]

Efforts have been made to ensure that those serving the Company's offices are familiar with its business. As we shall see from the 1980s the Livery were encouraged to involve themselves more in the life of the Company. They attend deputations to the Company's Schools and are sometimes co-opted onto committees where they are felt to have a particular expertise. In 1958 it was decided to elect the Junior Wardens

55.   Deputation to Aldersey Church of England Primary School. The Master (M. A. B. Jenks) is welcomed by the Head Teacher (Mr. R. B. Pearce) and pupils.

only after a period of at least three years' service on the Court so that by the time they came to serve they would know more about how the Company worked. During their first three years they would spend one year on each of the three standing committees instead of the usual three-year term on the committees by rotation for those beneath the chair. At the same time it was resolved that no-one should serve as a School Governor for more than ten years to ensure that others obtained a breadth of experience in this crucial area of Company business. At present the usual *cursus honorum* is for members of the Livery, having been elected to the Court of

Assistants between the ages of 40 and 55, to serve at least three years, gaining experience on the various committees of the Court, before being elected to the office of Fourth Warden, which is usually followed immediately by that of Third Warden. Between four and seven years later, though sometimes after a longer interval depending on individual availability, the two senior Wardenships and Mastership are served, usually in immediately succeeding years.[7]

In recruiting to the Court the Company's major objectives are those of ensuring the presence of men of high calibre representing the full range of professional skills essential to the efficient transaction of its business and of securing Assistants whose careers give them the flexibility in the management of their time to give the Company's business the necessary attention. Periodically the Company has recruited men by redemption with expertise felt to be lacking at the time, with the intention that they receive rapid promotion. A recent example is the tax counsel with a speciality in charitable law, O.M.W. Swingland, made free in 1977, and serving his Wardenships in 1982–3, 1985–6, and 1986–7, and as Master in 1987–8. Another essential criterion in the choice of Assistants is that they should be 'masters of their time'. There have been periodic complaints of the increasing inroads on the time of Assistants that the Wardenships bring, the Company's demands becoming the more difficult to fulfil with the lengthening of hours of work in the City and the professions generally. Anxieties about the burden of the Master's duties in 1958 led to provisions being made for Deputy Chairmen of committees to chair meetings in his absence. Efforts were also made in the 1960s to cut the burden of the social functions attended by the Masters of the Twelve Great Companies. For example, it was agreed that the Masters should attend state functions in groups of two or three by rotation rather than all being expected to attend everything. In 1969 it was suggested that, because several of the recently recruited Assistants found that they could not afford the time for the Company's business, new members of the Court should be appointed for a probationary period of three years before deciding whether they wished to continue. Although the Company has ensured that it has access to a wide range of expertise, it has sometimes in the recent past proved difficult to persuade men to take on the responsibilities of Company office before they are too old to serve the full *cursus honorum*.[8]

There have been points in the 20th century when anxiety has been expressed about the 'top heaviness' of the Court. This became particularly a problem in the 1930s when, because of concern that the Court was growing unwieldy and the fees paid for attendance an expensive drain on resources, it was decided that the size of the Court should not exceed 40 in normal circumstances. In 1931 it was agreed that instead of the Third and Fourth Wardens both being elected directly from the Livery, the Third Warden should be someone already on the Court, an arrangement which should be followed until the Court was reduced to 40 (some members arguing for 35). It was not universally popular among Assistants. When the order was reviewed in 1937 (the Court having been cut in size from 51 to 42) The Revd. F.H. Stock, E.F. Donne, J.W. Carr, and Sir G.W. Wollaston argued unsuccessfully against its continuance on the grounds of the claims of Liverymen for access to the Court. The Court continued to shrink during the Second World War reaching 38 in 1942.

While some Assistants argued for reductions to 36, others protested that they would rather see Past Masters retire from the Court than refuse the injection of fresh blood that recruitment from the Livery would bring. By 1944 these arguments were becoming more persuasive, and it was agreed to take both the Third and Fourth Wardens from the Livery that year. In the years after the Second World War, it became customary to fix limits on the number of Assistants who were not Past Masters. In 1958 it was agreed that there should be 23 Assistants excluding the Past Masters, and six years later the rule was established which prevails today according to which the number of Assistants (excluding the Past Masters and the current Master and Wardens) should not exceed eighteen. This measure has the advantage of ensuring a regular infusion of new blood into the Court. In November 1990 the size of the Court stood at 38 (of whom 16 were Past Masters), supplemented by six Honorary Assistants, and two Assistants Honoris Causa.[9] Honorary Assistants are those who have refused or been passed over for the office of Master: they are eligible to attend meetings but may not vote nor are they eligible for membership of committees unless co-opted. The first Assistant Honoris Causa was Commander W.R. Miller (Clerk, 1966–83), and the second to be so honoured was H.R.H. Princess Margaret. They have basically the same rights as an Honorary Assistant.[10]

As in the 19th century the state of the Company's finances remains the major constraint on the scale of its entertainment. The first half of the 20th century saw some retreat from the lavish banqueting which had characterised the later Victorian era. The restrictions of the Food Controller, heavy war taxation, and the sense that feasting was inappropriate in time of war, made the entertainment of the Livery very limited during the First World War, and the Hall was more regularly used for receptions for wounded soldiers at sandwich teas than for the feasting of the Haberdashers' Livery.[11] In the years immediately after the war Livery gatherings were not as regular as previously, but the revival of dinners remained a high priority for Assistants who deferred increases in Court attendance fees in preference for conviviality among members. The Publication Dinner was revived in 1920, but the summer Livery dinner was not revived until 1923. In the following year the Livery voted in favour of having one-quarter of their number dine in annual rotation at these dinners to be held henceforth at the Hall rather than at a West End hotel (in 1924 itself the dinner was held at the British Empire Exhibition at Wembley), with the added bonus of being able to invite a guest at the Company's expense.[12]

Another era of austerity was ushered in with the Second World War. As soon as hostilities were declared it was decided that there should be no further dinners. Efforts were made to keep members of the Court and Livery in touch by means of luncheons, but together with the Banks luncheon this had to be abandoned in the summer of 1940 during the Battle of Britain; in 1943 it was also decided to abandon the lunch because of the Company's precarious financial position as receipts from rents plummeted. By 1944 Publication was reduced to a luncheon for just 30 Livery-men chosen by ballot. Court lunches lost their sweets at once, and some were reduced to sandwich affairs; sherry consumption was cut; and champagne was replaced by hock.[13] Recovery after the Second World War, when the Company had been bombed out of its Hall and its corporate income had been savagely cut, was

56. A Ladies' Dinner held in the late 1920s: to either side of the Master are seated H.R.H. Prince Arthur of Connaught and H.R.H. Princess Alice, his wife; turning to the camera at the bottom of the centre table is Guy Eagleton, soon to succeed his father as Clerk (1931–50).

slow. Although there was considerable reluctance to cut entertainment further because it was thought to be incompatible with the Company's prestige, and because some felt that the burden of economy should be borne not only by the present generation, nevertheless as late as 1952 the Haberdashers abandoned their Livery dinner, and Court members were required to pay for their guests at the Banks dinner.[14]

One of the most important post-war developments has been the extension in the range of social functions provided at the Hall. This is apparent in two ways: firstly, in terms of the type of function laid on; and secondly, in terms of those who are invited, as apprentices, freemen, and wives have become more involved. The roots of the shift can be seen in the inter-war years. As early as 1921 a Liveryman suggested that, as only one Livery dinner a year was being given, other opportunities for meeting should be developed, for example a conversazione with ladies present at their hosts' expense. After the successful Jubilee dances of 1935 the possibility of continuing them was considered. But there is little sign that such initiatives bore fruit until the sherry reception for 300 Liverymen and their ladies held in 1938 at a cost of £80. Another foretaste of later developments was the invitation extended to some apprentices to the Jubilee dances of 1935.[15] In the post-war years such a widening in the range of participation was increasingly seen as a way of enhancing the identity of members with the Company's work. The Company has realised that if its Assistants are to perform their tasks professionally it must ensure that they have developed an early interest in its affairs. As we shall see, the widening range of social functions is just one of several strategies designed to increase identification.

There was much more discussion about the desirability of admitting women to Company functions in the years after the Second World War, but initially resistance was fierce. In 1948, for example, it was thought to be inappropriate that ladies should attend the United Guilds service. Ladies were invited to the Banks dinners, a rather exclusive gathering of the Court. Motions for the admission of ladies to the Livery dinners were repeatedly lost in the early 1960s, before their eventual acceptance, initially on an experimental basis in 1969. The June Livery dinner was in that year designated as one to which ladies could be invited, while the April and October dinners remained exclusively male. Women were often segregated at Company functions: for example, they watched the Publication ceremony from the gallery until 1975. A further extension in the events available for women came with their invitation to one of the Court lunches in 1978. This move was designed to allow Assistants to invite 'their secretaries and amanuenses' who filled in for them while absent from their usual employment on Company business. Women may also be invited to the Banks Dinner, one of the two Court dinners held each year.[16]

Women have not been the only beneficiaries of the widening of the Company's social net. Apprentices have also found themselves more regularly invited to events at the Hall. Those within two years of completing their terms were invited to the dance held in 1949, and to the coronation ball in 1953. But their involvement was somewhat irregular until the establishment of the annual freemen's and apprentices' reception in July 1986.[17]

The increasing popularity of the Livery dinners led to some discussion in the mid–1960s about whether three a year were enough, but the cost proved prohibitive and attention turned to other ways of generating sociability. A Livery lunch was cancelled for lack of support in 1964, but another attempt in 1971 proved more successful in spite of the modest charge, and thereafter these lunches became regular. Informal receptions for Liverymen became common from 1976. Evening Livery 'gatherings' with wine and a talk on some aspect of the Company's activities (for example the Company's administrative structure, the Schools, other charities, and so on) were instituted in 1985. The later 1980s saw ever more varied social activities for Liverymen: seminars on the development of links between education and industry, musical entertainments provided by the schools, drawing room operas. These initiatives were all part of a broad strategy to increase contact between Liverymen and the Company. Other manifestations are the now regular appearance of Liverymen on deputations to the Schools, and their support of events associated with the affiliated Queen's Regiment and H.M.S. *Brave*.[18]

Thus the social calendar as the Company moves into the 1990s is a varied one. Three Livery dinners are held in March, June, and October, ladies being invited only to the first. In April and November the Livery receptions take place, and in early October the Livery gathering, to which all Liverymen are encouraged to come with their wives. The reception for apprentices and freemen occurs in July. Liverymen are also eligible to attend the Publication dinner, although this is usually oversubscribed, there being 320 members of the Livery and seating for only 150 in the Hall. A services dinner is held in April every two or three years by invitation to those enjoying some connection with the armed forces together with members of the Company's affiliated services. Other innovations include a musical evening in February or March with entertainment provided by the Schools, a wine tasting in April, an opera in May, a bus to the Derby in June, three cricket matches over the summer (against the schools, the Company's professional advisers, and the Queen's Regiment). A lunch is usually provided for those attending the United Guilds service in April, the Golden Lecture in May, and the shrieval election on Midsummer Day.[19]

Company entertainments have their role to play in the furtherance of business. The Company has sought to enhance its prestige, emphasising its associations with the Crown and the Armed Forces, as well as ensuring that it keeps in touch with the policy-makers at Westminster and Whitehall. The net has been cast widely in the 20th century. During the inter-war years it became increasingly common to invite representatives of the Dominions, while special dinners were held for delegates to the World Economic Conference in 1933 and participants in the British Empire Games in 1934.[20] The world of education is regularly represented at Haberdasher functions: the Heads of the Schools, civil servants and politicians from the Department of Education have become frequent visitors to the Hall. The guest list for a Livery dinner in 1951 included the Lord Mayor and Sheriffs, the High Commissioners of Canada, Australia, New Zealand, South Africa, Ceylon, and Southern Rhodesia, the three honorary freemen from the Services (Field Marshal Lord Alexander of Tunis, Marshal of the Royal Air Force Lord Tedder, and Admiral Sir Henry D. Pridham-Whippell), Sir John Maud (Permanent Secretary at the Ministry of Education), Sir A.C. Dawes (Legal Adviser to the Ministry of Education), and the heads of the Company's Schools. Some Masters have attempted to stamp each social event with a particular character. Thus Past Master Powell, reviewing his year on St Katherine's Day 1970, pointed out that he had pursued the themes of education and finance at his April and June Livery dinners respectively. The guests included the Permanent Under Secretary of State for Education and Science, the Secretary for Welsh Education, the Vice-Chancellor of the City University, the Chairman of the Headmasters' Conference, the President of the Headmasters' Association, and the Headmasters of all the Haberdasher Schools on the first occasion; and the Deputy Governor of the Bank of England and the Chairman of the London Commodity Exchange on the second occasion. At the October Livery dinner it is customary to entertain the Lord Mayor, Sheriffs, and officers of the City Corporation.[21]

The connections of the Haberdashers with the Crown have been maintained over the course of the century. From 1919 Arthur William Patrick Albert, Duke of Connaught and Strathearn (1850–1942), the third son of Queen Victoria, was accompanied on the Company's roll of honour by his son, Arthur Frederick Patrick William Albert, Prince of Great Britain and Ireland (1883–1938). Prince Arthur served as Master in 1935–6 (albeit with a deputy) to commemorate the silver jubilee of George V. On their deaths there followed a hiatus in the Company's formal connections with royalty. H.R.H. Princess Margaret was offered the honorary freedom of the Company in 1954, but turned it down: only in 1966 did she accept.[22] Prince Arthur was fairly regular in his attendance at Company functions, and showed himself willing to add the stamp of royal approval to events such as the opening of the new science block at Hampstead School in 1931, or the prize-giving at Monmouth and the opening of the gymnasium and art room block at Hatcham Boys' School in 1936. Princess Margaret has been assiduous in visiting the Company's Schools: in most years since attaining the freedom she has visited at least one of them. In 1986 Her Royal Highness accepted the position of Assistant Honoris Causa. This royal connection brings prestige and valuable publicity for the Company's affairs, but Her Royal Highness also appears to derive real pleasure from her several visits, especially to the Schools and, takes great interest in their activities.[23]

The Haberdashers have joined with the other Great Twelve Companies to make wedding gifts to members of the Royal Family: a mink travelling coat for Princess Mary in 1922, silver for the Duke of York in 1923, six William III chairs for Prince George in 1934, and furniture for Princess Elizabeth in 1948.[24] Royal anniversaries and coronations have always been marked by special arrangements. For the royal jubilee of 1935 two Livery dances were held instead of the summer Livery dinner, and contributions were made to the Silver Jubilee Thankoffering Fund and to the Prince of Wales' Jubilee Fund for the Welfare of the Youth of the Country. For the Silver Jubilee of 1977 the Company joined with the other eleven Great Companies in the river pageant (following the precedent set by the coronation celebrations of 1953) and presented the Queen with a new carpet for the Garter Throne Room at Windsor, as well as making a cash contribution to the Silver Jubilee appeal. The lack of special entertainments on this latter occasion is probably a reflection as much of the Queen's desire that the celebrations should not be too extravagant in the midst of a recession as of the Company's own financial embarrassment.[25] By custom the Masters of the Twelve Great Companies attend coronations in their capacity as Assistant Butlers of England. For the coronation of George VI in 1937 there were two Livery balls, one of which was attended by the Lord Mayor. For the coronation of Elizabeth II both a ball for 400 and a dinner for 380 were provided at a cost of £1,506 and £1,338 respectively. The ball included a buffet supper at 27s. 6d per head, with musical diversion provided by Sydney Lipton's Dance Orchestra. The coronation dinner was graced by an impressive guest list: the First Sea Lord, the Chief of the Imperial General Staff, another senior officer from each of the three services, and, reflecting the Company's interest in its schools, the Minister of Education, and the Heads of the Welsh and Legal Departments at the Ministry of Education.[26]

The Company's service affiliations have developed over the course of the later 20th century. In 1937 the Haberdashers adopted the Queen Victoria's Rifles, and the Master, First Warden, and Clerk were made honorary members of the officers' mess. During the war the wives of Liverymen were encouraged to serve on a committee for arranging 'comforts' for the men. Many serving in the First Battalion were surrounded and captured at Calais in June 1940, and thereafter the Company made regular contributions to the Battalion's Prisoner of War fund.[27] Links were maintained after the war. Replying to the Lord Mayor's suggestion in 1953 that each Livery Company adopt a unit of the Territorial Army, the Haberdashers announced their intention to continue supporting the Queen Victoria's Rifles. In

57. H.R.H. the Princess Margaret visiting Haberdashers' Monmouth School for Girls, 2 November 1950. She is shown carrying the doll 'Katharine Monmouth' with which she had been presented earlier in the day, and leaving the hall with Miss A. F. McDonald (Headmistress); Margaret Anne Massey and Anne Jones Davies (Head and Deputy Head Girls) in the foreground.

58. Visit of H.R.H. the Princess Margaret to Haberdashers' Aske's Schools at Elstree, 15 May 1990. Left to right: Mr. K. Dawson (Headmaster), Her Royal Highness, and Mr. G. L. Bourne (Chairman of the Governors), followed by Mr. D. A. H. Sime (Master).

1957 the Company covenanted to pay them £50 per annum gross for seven years, recommending that it be used for rifle shooting, and hoping that the C.C.F. forces of the Company's Schools would be encouraged to avail themselves of the training facilities. The Queen Victoria's Rifles were amalgamated with the Queen's Westminsters in 1961 to form the Queen's Royal Rifles, and reorganised to form the 4th (Volunteer) Battalion, Royal Green Jackets in 1969, with which the Company maintains its connections. This connection has been supplemented by others. The Frimley and Camberley Cadet Corps, an independent and voluntary youth organisation aiming to develop high standards of christian conduct against a background of military discipline, was adopted in 1977. In 1984 the Company became officially affiliated to the Queen's Regiment, one of the premier Home Counties infantry regiments. The most recent addition to the services connnections has been H.M.S. Brave, a Type 22 frigate, affiliated to the Company in 1986. These links are sustained by mutual visiting, attendance at inspections, sporting competitions, dining, and liaison with the Company's Schools. Officers and men have been entertained at the Hall on an *ad hoc* basis, but in 1988 it was decided to formalise arrangements with a services dinner to be held every two or three years. The military connections are strikingly a more prominent feature of the newsletters of the later 1980s than the 1970s.[28]

Another way in which military connections have been fostered is through grants of honorary freedoms. Immediately after the Second World War it was decided to honour representatives of each of the three services in this fashion. Field Marshal Sir Harold Alexander (Commander-in-Chief of armies in Middle East in 1942–3, North Africa in 1943, and Italy in 1943–4, then Supreme Allied Commander of forces in Mediterranean in 1944–5), Air Chief Marshal Sir Arthur Tedder (Air Commander in North Africa and later Deputy Supreme Allied Commander on Operation 'Overlord'), and Admiral Sir Henry Pridham-Whippell (also active in the Mediterranean theatre) accepted the honour. This practice has continued since, and a proposal from the Wardens to invite an industrialist or educationalist to replace Field Marshal Sir Geoffrey Baker on his death in 1980 was greeted frostily by some members of the Court as a deplorable break with tradition: in the event all parties were satisfied with grants of the honorary Livery to General Sir Peter Hunt (Chief of the General Staff, 1973–6, and Constable of the Tower of London from 1980), Sir Derek Ezra (an Old Monmothian and then Chairman of the National Coal Board), and Sir Alec Merrison (Vice-Chancellor of Bristol University). The present representatives of the services on the Livery are Admiral Sir Guy Grantham (since 1957), Marshal of the Royal Air Force Sir John Grandy (since 1968), and General Sir Edward Burgess (since 1990).[29]

The vigour of the Company's corporate life has unquestionably depended on the state of its finances. Through the mid–20th century decades these were parlous, chiefly because of the legacy of the Second World War, although there has been an improvement of late. The most traumatic event in the Company's history this century was the destruction of the Hall and adjacent properties belonging to the Company by enemy action on the night of 29 December 1940. Incendiary bombs had set fire to property belonging to the Goldsmiths' on the other side of Staining Lane, and

59. H.M.S. *Brave*, a Type 22 frigate commissioned at Devonport on 4 July 1986, was affiliated to the Company on 17 December 1986. Captain W. C. McKnight, L.V.O., R.N., First Commanding Officer, stands to the left of the Master. Seated left to right:. I. S. B. Crosse (Past Master), Vice Admiral J. S. C. Salter (Past Master), M. W. D. Northcott (Immediate Past Master), B. C. Gothard (Third Warden), O. M. W. Swingland (First Warden), G. R. Fox (Master), M. A. B. Jenks (Second Warden), M. D. G. Wheldon (Fourth Warden), Admiral Sir Guy Grantham (Liveryman *Honoris Causa*), D. A. H. Sime (Past Master) and Major General Sir John Bates (Past Master).

the blaze soon spread over the narrow street to the Haberdashers' Hall, carried by the strong westerly wind. Because the water main had been severed, fire-fighting efforts proved futile in spite of the sterling efforts of the staff led by the Acting Beadle.[30] For the rest of the war the Haberdashers were the guests successively of the Grocers and from September 1942 until 1956 of the Vintners. The latter were able to lease office space to the Company so that the administration could be moved back to the capital from Chislehurst whither`it had moved for security on the outbreak of war.[31]

The rebuilding of the Hall was a major priority in the post-war years. But the road to rebuilding was a tortuous one. A Compulsory Purchase Order on the site was threatened in 1947–8, and the Company had hurriedly to prepare its own development scheme. This necessitated the purchase of adjoining properties in Wood Street owned by the Grocers' Company and the Downing Lawrence Trustees. By 1948 the Company had outlined a scheme by which the site would be leased to a body of developers who would undertake to build offices and the new Hall. By 1952 the negotiations with Civic Leases Ltd were well advanced and in January 1953 it was revealed that financial backing would be provided by Legal and General Assurance Ltd, the head lessee of the new office-block. Difficulties were experienced in securing a building licence because of planning controls giving priority to industrial rather than office premises. The licence was not secured until March 1954. Other delicate negotiations were necessary over the Company's War Damages Compensation claim: by opting for replacement rather than value payment, the cost of the new Hall could largely be met by the War Damages Commission, although this had the disadvantage of restricting the new Hall to the dimensions of the old, which has caused the Company some problems in ensuing years. Building work commenced in March 1954 and the new Hall was opened in June 1956 by the Lord Mayor, Alderman Sir Cuthbert Ackroyd, Bt.[32] The redevelopment of the Hall site was one of the more controversial decisions of the post-war era. Some felt that the Company

60.   The Court of Assistants assembled at Vintners' Hall on 15 November 1945 to present the Freedom and Livery (*Honoris Causa*) to Field Marshal Sir Harold Alexander. At the table, left to right: W. B. Franklin (Third Warden), C. E. Fletcher (First Warden), Field Marshal Sir H. Alexander, J. Gibson Harris (Master), F. E. Tudor (Second Warden) and B. G. Donne (Fourth Warden).

61.   The Hall after the German bombing of 29 December 1940.

had sold its birthright to developers, although this is a misrepresentation of the true state of affairs as the Company retains the freehold of Garrard House, and it is difficult to see how otherwise the redevelopment could have been undertaken. Matters were not helped by the rather abrasive personality of E.A. Last-Smith, identified in some quarters as the driving force behind the scheme, and his differences of opinion with Lieutenant-Colonel J. Bamford-Smith, a fellow Past Master, led to the latter's resignation from the Court.[33]

Whatever the arguments for or against early reconstruction, the state of the Company's corporate finances remained precarious. In 1964, 1966–9, and from 1973–5 the corporate account was in deficit. The position has been transformed since then. In 1976 the Company purchased the balance of the long leasehold interest in Fulwood House, High Holborn, of which it was already the freeholder. The subsequent redevelopment of the property brought about substantial improvements in the rental income. Likewise, in 1983–4 the lease on Garrard House was renegotiated such that the Company was assured a guaranteed proportion of the rent passing or a minimum rental, whichever sum was the greater. Other circumstances favouring the Company have been the reduction in Corporation Tax by recent Conservative governments.[34]

Nevertheless the Company's finances remain vulnerable to fluctuations in the state of the property market, particularly because its corporate well-being is so closely tied to a small number of City freeholds. Its ambitions to redevelop the Hall to provide more office space and a larger reception area (taking advantage of a break point in 1990 of the lease of Garrard House to Legal and General who themselves had hoped to redevelop the site), have for the time being (1991) been shelved because of the slump in property values. The Company had hoped that Legal and General would undertake the cost of the Hall redevelopment as part of their scheme for the

62.   Garrard House, the Company's postwar office block, facing onto Gresham Street.

63.   The contributors to the present Hall, built after the destruction
of its predecessor in 1940.

site, but when the sub-leases of Garrard House fell in during September 1990, Legal
and General abandoned their plans and less than 40 per cent of the subleases were
renewed, temporarily halving the Company's receipts from the property. Another
window of opportunity for redevelopment could occur in a few years time. However,
the prospects for redevelopment will turn on such presently unknown variables as
the effect of the Docklands development on demand for office-space in central
London.[35]

The inter-war years were a testing time for the Company's Schools. Financial
strains were acute. The introduction of the Burnham Scale for teachers' salaries in
1921 in response to the wartime inflation added to the wage bills, while the demands

of a more elaborate curriculum necessitated new buildings such as science blocks. One solution was to take more in the way of L.E.A. grants, but the price was felt likely to be increasing interference by politicians and the sacrifice of the distinctive character of the Schools to the demands of local educational uniformity. Alternatively the approval of the Board of Education for increases in fees could have been sought, but such a policy ran the risk of bringing further revision by the Board to the scheme for running the Schools; it fitted uneasily with the Schools' status as charities; and in the educational marketplace it could only be taken so far before parents would vote with their feet in response to fee increases.

To take the example of the Aske's Schools, the Company agonised over these dilemmas in 1918–21. The Chairman of the Governors, The Rev. Prebendary H.P. Prosser was reluctant to seek the help of the London County Council (L.C.C.) because he feared that the Schools would be turned into county secondaries. Could the Schools' problems be solved through increased fees? But the Board of Education were hostile to meeting the cost of increased salaries entirely from the parents and edged the Company in the direction of increased L.C.C. support. Should the Hatcham Schools be sold to the L.C.C. and the endowment applied predominantly to the two Schools at Acton and Hampstead? The problem was that the L.C.C.'s price was likely to be nominal. Could the Governors get away with paying salaries below the Burnham scale? The result would be that the Company's Schools would be left in the words of Prebendary Isaacs with 'the sweepings of the marketplace'. There was no alternative but to seek increased help from the local authority as well as increasing fees. Thus in 1921–2 the foundation income received by the Hatcham Boys' School was only £1,394, compared to grants from the Board of Education and the L.C.C. of £3,825 and £5,407 respectively. A further £2,900 was received in fees for the scholars nominated by the Council as compared to the approximately £4,000 received in private fees. The fees at the School increased to 13 guineas in 1920 and 15 guineas in 1922.[36]

The next crisis faced by the Aske's Schools came in 1927 when the Board of Education revised its rules for grants so that it would no longer provide a grant aid to a school and also recognise for 50 per cent grant the expenditure of a local authority in aiding that school. Schools had therefore to decide between local authority or central government support. The Endowed Schools Committee proposed that the Hatcham Schools be transferred to the L.C.C. and that the entire foundation income should be applied to the Schools at Hampstead and Acton which would cease to receive local authority support thereby enabling them to be 'Haberdasher schools in fact as well as name'. These proposals divided the Court of Assistants: Prosser, still Chairman of the Governors, was anxious about the wholesale transfer of the Hatcham Schools and the likely loss of their identity. Initially a committee of the Court voted 19 to 17 for an amendment that all the Schools should drop their Board of Education grants and continue with L.C.C. support. But the objectors swung round as the scheme began to take shape. In the event it was agreed that Hatcham should receive a fixed annual amount of £4,946 equal to that received in 1926–7. Although the L.C.C. tightened its grip on the Governing Body of the Hatcham Schools, Haberdasher influence was by no means negligible: 12 Governors were nominated by the L.C.C., six by the Haberdashers, one by the Common Council of the City of London, and one by the Senate of the University of London.[37]

In the case of the Monmouth Schools the main bone of contention with the local authority arose out of the provisions relating to the disposal of the so-called residuary income under the scheme of 1910. It had been agreed that the Boys' School at Monmouth should receive £2,800 per annum, the Girls' School, £1,000 per annum, and the School at Pontypool, £1,000 per annum. The residual income from the estates was to be paid to the County Council, who were to pay £2,000 to the Monmouthshire Agricultural College at Usk, and make additional payments to the Schools in an order of priority specified in the scheme (£500 to Monmouth Grammar School, £300 to Monmouth Girls' School, and £500 to Jones' West Monmouthshire School in the first instance, with additions of £920, £480, and £500 respectively if funds permitted). Any further payments were left to the discretion of the County Council who could, of course, alternatively apply the Jones' monies to general educational purposes within the county, thereby reducing the burden on ratepayers. Such arrangements proved highly controversial within the Monmouth Schools. Lionel James, Headmaster of the Monmouth Grammar School, complained at the speech day of 1912 about the 'alienated endowment', and during the inter-war years there were periodic efforts to renegotiate the terms of the settlement with the County Council.[38] In 1928, for example, taking advantage of the strong Conservative government, thought to be favourably inclined, a deputation from the Governors attended on Lord Eustace Percy, President of the Board of Education, to request him to exercise his powers to amend the 1910 scheme and give the Governors a one-quarter share of the residue. The arguments were powerful: the Bruce Committee of 1919 had expressed strong disapproval of the use of school endowments to ease rate burdens; and the inhabitants of Monmouth pointed out that they suffered because the insufficiency of their share made the school fees high, while they also paid heavy rates to support secondary schools elsewhere in the county. In October 1929 following the discussions with Monmouthshire County Council on which Percy had insisted, it was agreed that the residuary income should be split three ways between the Monmouth Schools, the West Monmouthshire School, and general educational purposes within Monmouthshire, but a ceiling of £1,000 was placed on each of the shares of the Monmouth Schools and the West Monmouthshire School. The price to be paid by the Company was its agreement that two of the three co-opted places on the Board of Governors of the Pontypool School should be filled by L.E.A. representatives, and one by a representative of the Company.[39] The Company's next chance for renegotiation came in 1932 when large-scale building improvements at both Monmouth and Pontypool were being contemplated. At a conference held at Pontypool in December 1932 it was agreed that, in return for the Haberdashers as Estates Governors releasing sums of £17,000 and £18,000 for building at Monmouth and Pontypool respectively, the maximum amount of each of the residuary thirds intended for the Jones' Schools should be raised to £1,200 each.[40]

The inadequacy of the endowment for the Adams' Grammar School at Newport began to be apparent in the inter-war years, particularly because of the failure of the income from the predominantly agricultural estate to rise in line with costs. This

School encountered serious problems in raising the money for building improvements. In 1926 it was noted that the School Inspectors had reported adversely on the quality of the classrooms and boarding accommodation, while in the following year the Headmaster reported that prospective parents often declined to send their children to the School because of its dilapidated air. New buildings were erected in 1928–9, but the financing reveals the vulnerability of the charity. The endowment could only afford £3,000, given the need for investment in improvements on the Knighton estate, and a grant of £8,000 had to be applied for from Shropshire County Council. A shortfall was met by means of a loan on the security of the estates up to a maximum of £2,500.[41] By the later 1930s the priorities were a gymnasium, assembly hall, music and art room, as well as extra classrooms. Plans for expansion costing between £10,000 and £12,000 were drawn up, but in June 1937 the Company indicated that the charity was unable to make a contribution. However, another source of funding was available in the newly established Arno charity. Within a year the Company had agreed under pressure from the County Council to make available £2,000 from the Arno funds and (albeit with considerable reluctance) £1,000 from the charity funds. These plans were among the first casualties of the war which broke out in September 1939.[42]

The varying degrees of financial health explain the different responses of the Haberdasher Schools to the 1944 Education Act. For those Schools with sufficient endowment the direct grant option could be followed. This involved fee-paying schools receiving an annual grant direct from the Ministry of Education of £29 per pupil over the age of 11 in return for the allocation of 25 per cent of the annual entry in free places which were to be taken by the L.E.A. or (should the L.E.A. decline) by pupils already in the schools. For the less well provided Schools there were two basic options under which the Schools would form part of the L.E.A. system of free education while the Company could continue to have a say in their running. If the Governors were able and willing to pay for half the cost of improvements and alterations to School buildings then they could apply for voluntary aided status, by which the Governors or Managers would continue to appoint the teachers. But if the endowments would not support 50 per cent of the cost of buildings, then the Governors could apply for voluntary controlled status, by which the L.E.A. took over responsibility for the maintenance of the School and provided two-thirds of the Governors.[43]

It is of interest that when the provisions of the Butler Act were first considered by the Company's Endowed Schools Committee in October 1944, the Haberdashers considered a fourth option for some of its less generously provided Schools. In pursuing its aim of maximising the benefit for its most prestigious Schools, it proposed to pursue the direct grant option for the Aske Schools at Hampstead and Acton and the Jones Schools at Monmouth while transferring to the local authority lock, stock, and barrel, the Hatcham Schools and the West Monmouthshire School on condition that the whole of the income of the respective charities could then be applied to the Company's direct grant Schools. Newport was a different case because there was no other school supported by the charity which could benefit from the terms of such a transfer. This discussion was very revealing about the Company's priorities. A number of Assistants argued strongly in favour of these proposals. F.E. Tudor and Sir G. Wollaston, for example, stressed the need to secure schools as free from outside control as possible because those coming under the government's scheme voluntarily would sooner or later become part of the national system of education and lose their special character: it was better to have four schools on a completely independent basis than eight under partial control.[44]

The result of the Company's deliberations and negotiations with the local authorities concerned was that Acton, Hampstead, and the two Monmouth Schools became direct grant; the Schools at Hatcham became voluntary controlled; and the Schools at Newport and Bunbury voluntary aided. Thus from April 1946 the whole of the foundation income of the Aske charity was applied to the Schools at Hampstead and Acton save for £1,000 per annum which was to be used by the Governors in aiding the further education or training of boys and girls at the Hatcham Schools. The new Board of Governors for the Hatcham Schools, now distinct from that for Acton and Hampstead, consisted of 12 appointees of the L.C.C. and six Foundation Governors appointed by the Haberdashers' Company. It was also provided that at least one third of the Governors should be women.[45] In the case of Newport the Haberdashers contemplated independence and avoided the voluntary aided option, eventually adopted, for as long as possible. In 1947, for example, the Company was considering launching an appeal to raise an endowment which could support the greater independence of the School. But the austerity of the post-war years hardly provided a favourable time for such a project, and voluntary aided status had to be adopted from 1949. Although a *pis aller*, this gave the Haberdashers greater control than at Hatcham. From 1954 the Governing Body at Newport was constituted by the Master of the Haberdashers' Company, seven members appointed by the Company (of whom four were to be resident within ten miles of the school and of whom one was to be nominated by Birmingham University), two appointed by the Old Boys' Association, and five appointed by the L.E.A.[46]

In the case of the Jones Foundation, the Company saw in the 1944 Act the possibility of securing more of the residuary income from the charity for the Monmouth Schools. Everything depended on the status to be adopted by the West Monmouthshire School at Pontypool. The Company was keen to transfer that school to the L.E.A., but on condition that the income, formerly directed to Pontypool together with an increased share of the residue, should now go to the two Monmouth Schools. There was general agreement that the West Monmouthshire School should become a county secondary school. Discussions in March 1949 revealed that although the County Council accepted that the £2,000 per annum paid to the West Monmouthshire School under the 1910 scheme should go to the two Monmouth Schools, in other respects it was determined to hold onto its gains under that scheme. It was reluctant to pay anything for the transfer of the site; it insisted upon the continuance of payments of up to £2,000 per annum to the Usk Agricultural College; it resisted the handing over of the third of the residuary income used for other schools; and it sought to increase its representation on the Governing Body of the two Monmouth Schools. In the course of the negotiations over the next two years the Haberdashers were able to secure modifications to the Council's position, and the scheme eventually adopted in 1955 had already been fleshed out by May 1951. It was agreed that the West Monmouthshire School should be transferred to the County Council and that the £2,000 per annum it had enjoyed from the endowment hitherto should be paid to the two Monmouth Schools. As for the residuary income, two-thirds plus £250 was to be paid to the Monmouth Schools, and the remaining one-third less £250 was to provide a scholarship fund for boarding fees for pupils from the county to be administered by trustees, of whom three were nominated by the L.E.A. and three by the Governors. Thus the Haberdashers had at last recovered the majority of the Jones charity income for the benefit of the two schools at Monmouth.[47]

For Hampstead and Acton the shift to direct grant status in 1946 and the change in the method by which the government's capitation grant was calculated meant that fees had to be increased. More serious were the problems posed by the inadequate buildings and the cramped sites. By 1954 the Company had decided that it was necessary to transfer the site initially of the Boys' School, but later of the Girls' School too. In February 1959 the Aske charity purchased an estate comprising Aldenham House and 31 acres at Elstree from the B.B.C. for the sum of £31,000. The foundation stone of the new boys' school was laid on 29 October 1959 and, the premises at Hampstead having been sold to the L.C.C., the new Boys' School opened in October 1961. It was not until 1974 that the girls followed. The move from Acton was precipitated by the decision of the local authorities in the surrounding area in 1971 to cease underwriting the free places necesssary to qualify the School for direct grant. The site at Acton was sold and the proceeds directed to rebuilding at Elstree on the land acquired in 1959. Hertfordshire County Council undertook to support the free places necessary to qualify for direct grant.[48]

The move from Acton was symptomatic of increasing uncertainty about the status of direct grant schools. The Donnison Report of 1970 had recommended an end to direct grant. Although its proposals did not come into immediate effect because of the election of a Conservative government in 1970, the Labour Party was committed to abolition, and its return to power in 1974 presaged the axe. The Company and the Governors of its Schools at Elstree and Monmouth had therefore to decide whether they should become fully independent fee-paying schools or comprehensive schools within the state system. The former option was chosen, and appeals launched to provide bursaries for children whose parents could not otherwise afford to send them to the schools. By November 1977 the appeal in aid of Monmouth School had reached £204,000, and that in aid of the Elstree schools £334,000. Also helpful in this regard was the St Katherine Foundation set up by the Company in 1970 to provide bursaries for needy pupils both at the Company's Schools and in higher education. By 1985 approximately 80 pupils were being supported from the Foundation in roughly equal numbers at the Company's Schools and others.[49]

The Company's efforts to maintain the distinctive identity of its Schools were continually threatened by the pressures of central educational policy with the drive towards the comprehensive system in the 1960s and 1970s, and the responses to the problem of falling school rolls in closures, amalgamations, and the creation of sixth-form colleges in the 1980s. The Labour administration had announced its intention of adopting a scheme of comprehensive education in 1965, but the Company's

64.   Aerial view of the two Haberdashers' Aske's schools at Elstree.

Schools were not affected until the reassertion of this policy by the Labour government in 1975. The Inner London Education Authority (I.L.E.A.) accordingly
announced that it would cease to maintain any school whose Governors did not
agree to it becoming comprehensive by autumn 1977. More alarming from the
Company's point of view was the local authority's projected merger (prompted by
falling rolls) of the Boys' and Girls' Schools at Hatcham each with another school

which the Company felt would lead to a loss of identity. Such proposed reorganis-
ations also threatened the Schools' status as voluntary controlled and with it the
representation of the Haberdashers on the Board of Governors. The deal which was
eventually negotiated with the I.L.E.A. in 1976 adopted a comprehensive system at
the Hatcham Schools, but preserved their voluntary controlled status, and scotched
the merger proposals. Admissions were to be dealt with by the Heads who were to
endeavour to achieve a balanced intake reflecting the ability range within the feeder
boroughs at the time of the reorganisation. Moreover, the Schools' catchment area
was broader than normal: while recruiting mainly from the Boroughs of Lewisham,
Greenwich, and Southwark, the Schools continued to admit up to 10 children a year
from other boroughs.[50]

Adams' Grammar School at Newport has suffered prolonged periods of uncertainty
reflecting the tergiversations of educational policy and local politics. In the early
1970s protracted negotiations took place with Shropshire County Council for the
absorption of the Girls' High School at Newport by Adams' Grammar School to
create a mixed grammar school. The scheme was approved by Mrs Margaret
Thatcher, then Secretary of State for Education and Science, in 1974, but delay over
approval for the necessary new buildings meant that the scheme was abandoned
with the return of Harold Wilson to Downing Street later that year.[51] The Labour
government's commitment to comprehensive education meant that negotiations
began afresh with the County Council over changing the School from a two-form
entry grammar school into a four-form entry, comprehensive, coeducational school.
The Company's reluctance to swallow this pill was reflected in the commissioning
of a survey by a team of consultants in 1977 to investigate the possibility of the
School becoming independent. Their report indicated that such a course was not
financially viable, and the Company reluctantly conceded the inevitability of comprehensive education. However, the School escaped this fate on account of a further
change of government when the new Conservative Secretary of State refused to
support the Council's proposed scheme in 1980 chiefly on the grounds of cost. A
revised scheme involving the use of the buildings of the Girls' High School about a
mile away was submitted in 1981, but again rejected by the Secretary of State.[52]

However, it was falling school rolls that posed a new and more serious threat to
Adams' Grammar School in the mid–1980s. In 1986 Shropshire County Council's
working party recommended that the Council should cease to maintain the School,
and in 1987 an application to the Secretary of State was made accordingly. It was
rejected in December of that year, but the Company could hardly feel certain about
the future of the School given the kaleidoscopic politics of the County Council and
the possibility of a change in the party in power at Westminster.[53] The Hatcham
Schools had emerged unscathed from the I.L.E.A.'s review in 1980 prompted by
falling rolls, but a new threat emerged in 1987 with the proposed introduction of a
system of tertiary education which seemed set to destroy the sixth forms.[54]

The greater pluralism and competition between schools envisaged by the Education Reform Act of 1988 therefore came as a godsend to the Company. The Act
offered the possibility of opting out of local authority control and funding directly
from central government. This represented an obvious solution to the problems faced

by Adams' Grammar School, enabling it to maintain its distinctive identity for so long under threat, and giving the Governors greater freedom to manage the affairs of the School. In 1989, 91 per cent of the parents voting supported the proposal that the School should seek grant maintained status. The application having been approved by the Secretary of State the new scheme duly went ahead on 1 September 1990. The Governing Body was reconstituted in a form giving the Haberdashers greater scope. There are now five Parent Governors, two Teacher Governors, and 12 Foundation Governors. In addition to the Headmaster and the Master of the Company who sit *ex officio*, the Foundation Governors at present comprise three members of the Court of Assistants, two Liverymen of the Company, and six representatives of the local community (typically local farmers and industrialists, professionals such as accountants and bank managers, and clerics).[55]

The effects of the 1988 Act on the Hatcham schools have been still more dramatic and controversial with their conversion into a City Technology College (C.T.C). The Conservative government's intention in promoting C.T.C.s was to provide children from a wide ability range with a technologically enriched learning environment in schools which are 'beacons of excellence' funded by partnership between the taxpayer and private sponsors. From the Haberdashers' point of view the advantages of the C.T.C. project were seen to lie in the Company's association with the cutting edge of educational innovation, the enhancement of its Schools with the injection of substantial funds from central government, and the recovery of greater control from the local authority. The funding agreement entered into by the Company with the D.E.S. on 21 December 1990 provides that the Haberdashers will hand over the site of the Schools valued in 1990 at £3,445,000 to a specially constituted C.T.C. Trust and provide £1,000,000 towards costs over the first five years of the Schools' operation as C.T.C.s, while the Exchequer will furnish £5,500,000. At the time of writing other offers of private sponsorship are being sought. The new Governing Body of the C.T.C. will consist of three persons appointed by the Haberdashers' Company, one by the Secretary of State, up to seven other nominees of the Company and this group will coopt four parents, the two heads, two teacher representatives, and two representatives of the local community. The College is due to open in September 1991 as a C.T.C. with single-sex education in the Schools up to the age of sixteen.[56]

Needless to say the C.T.C. project was only implemented in the face of tenacious opposition from the I.L.E.A. in its expiring days, and opinion within the Schools and the local community was divided. The main arguments deployed against the Haberdashers' scheme (with varying degrees of emphasis) have centred on doubts about a potentially restricted curriculum, the apparent failure of private sponsorship and the consequent concentration of large sums of taxpayers' money on a limited number of children, the sense that the Schools were already functioning as 'beacons of excellence', hostility to the merging of the Boys' and Girls' Schools (as the government had refused to sanction separate C.T.C.s for the Boys' and Girls' Schools, and a majority of the parents at the Girls' School had initially opposed the scheme), and the problem of assurances to existing staff about the security of their posts.[57] Almost as much controversy has been aroused over the methods used to fight the campaign as over the original proposals themselves. When the proposal first came before the Governing Body in April 1988 the I.L.E.A. instructed the four teacher representatives that they could not vote as they had a pecuniary interest in the outcome, an action which was subsequently upheld in the High Court. The issue was heavily politicised with the eight Labour appointees consistently voting against the scheme, while the other nine Governors (two non-Labour appointees, two parents, and the five Foundation Governors) supported it. The next flashpoint occurred over the consultation process concerning the fate of the Schools, begun in May 1988 and lasting six months. The I.L.E.A. claimed that the period should have been longer, but ultimately lost its case at the High Court and in the Court of Appeal. Meanwhile it sought to ensure that the two non-Labour Governors voted in accordance with the Authority's policy and, when they refused to do so, removed them from office three days before the Governors were due to meet and take a decision on 20 January 1989. This action was contested by the two Governors concerned who took their case to the High Court and were successful in the Court of Appeal and in the House of Lords. The Board of Governors took their decision in favour of the C.T.C. option which was followed by a favourable ballot of parents in May 1989. But in spite of the support given by the Governing Body, parents, and teachers, the I.L.E.A. nevertheless continued its efforts to manipulate the composition of the Governing Body by attempting to remove a Parent Governor whose child was to leave the school in July 1989 although there was a clear understanding that the appointment should be for the whole school year. Again the I.L.E.A. was taken to court, this time settling at the door of the court and agreeing to reinstate the parent and pay her costs. Yet another tactic was the instruction from the I.L.E.A. that the Governing Bodies should split into two in the hope that a vote against the C.T.C. project might be won on the Governing Body of the Girls' School where opposition had always been stronger. The application was turned down by the Secretary of State, and the I.L.E.A. lost further cases in the High Court and Court of Appeal in its efforts to overturn his verdict. Next the I.L.E.A., acting jointly with Lewisham Borough Council, contested the Secretary of State's closure notice, losing yet more legal battles in the High Court and Court of Appeal in February and May 1990. The sorry tale is an indication of the ferocious politicisation of educational issues wrought by the Education Reform Act.[58]

Recent years have witnessed many efforts to give the Haberdasher Schools a greater sense of their belonging to a wider family. Visits of pupils and staff to the Hall are regularly encouraged. The Schools encounter each other more often in sporting and cultural events. In 1973 Past Master Fraser Bird gave a trophy for a seven-a-side rugby competition between the four Boys' Schools, and it was followed in 1976 by a silver quaich presented by Past Master Sime to be competed for at tennis by the three Girls' Schools. Other trophies for netball, lacrosse, and swimming have followed. Past Master Bostock was the moving force behind the Haberdasher Schools Music Festival instituted in 1985.[59]

With approximately 5,500 pupils in its Schools in 1991 it is hardly surprising that so much of the charitable endeavour of the Haberdashers is channelled towards them. Many of the new bequests of the 20th century have been directed towards augmenting the Company's educational charities. Travelling scholarships have been established by Commander W.C. Northcott (1959) and P.B. Powell (1982). Bursaries for specified forms of vocational training for pupils from specified Schools have been established by E.T.W. Dodd (1974), R.T. Hawes (1968), and C.R. Picken (1945). Help for pupils in straitened circumstances is available from a variety of sources, notably the St Katherine Foundation set up in 1970, but also from earlier bequests such as that of Thomas Arno (1937). Arno left his residuary estate, after providing annuities to members of his family, to the Company upon trust for various broadly defined charitable objects, including the assistance of pupils at the Company's Schools, grants to the Schools for the benefit of the young, grants to assist young men starting in business, and donations to hospitals or other causes for the public benefit.[60]

But these are not the only charitable involvements of the Haberdashers. Almshouses continue to be maintained. The 20 at Monmouth were rebuilt on a new site in 1959, and the ten remaining units at Newland renovated in 1953. A new endowment from Miss Barbara Mabel Pinchin in 1969 intended for the benefit of poor people has supported five new almshouses at Dorking and Walmer.[61] The Jones Lectureship Charity continues to provide for a Golden Lecture, now one a year, and for the augmentation of clerical incomes.[62] The amalgamation of many of the smaller charities into the Haberdashers' Eleemosynary Charity has produced funds yielding £229,000 income in 1988 which are directed to 'persons in hardship', a broad category leaving the Company with much discretion as to the direction of the funds. In recent years the Company has given significant support to 'Centrepoint', Soho, a charity helping the homeless young in London by providing 16-year olds with long-stay accommodation, a new brain injury unit for children at the Royal Hospital and Home, Putney, and the Royal Surgical Aid Society's Home for the Elderly at Sevenoaks.[63]

One of the most striking transformations of the 20th century has been the broadening of the range of investments supporting the charities. The change can be summarised in terms of the achievement of a more even balance between land and securities, and a shift away from agricultural and residential properties to commercial properties. The William Jones' Grammar School Foundation may serve as an example. In the 1860s the bulk of the Jones charity's income had derived from the residential properties at Hatcham together with small estates in Staffordshire and Kent. The gross rental accounted for no less than £2,522 14s. 10d. or 90 per cent of total receipts of £2,799 7s. 4d., the remainder being accounted for by dividends on consols. In 1953 rents still predominated in the gross income of the Grammar School Foundation, providing £40,639 (93 per cent) as compared with £3,124 in dividends. By 1990, however, the picture was very different: rents provided £1.1m (52 per cent) and dividends and interest payments £1.029m. It is present Company policy to aim for a rough 50:50 asset balance between realty and personalty in the pattern of its charitable investments. Moreover, the portfolio of properties held by the charity looks very different from the early 20th century. There are only 30 houses left in the Company's possession on the Hatcham estate. The residential properties have increasingly become a liability because of the effects of rent controls, the burdens of

65. The Most Reverend and Right Honourable Archbishop Michael Ramsey, Liveryman
Honoris Causa, delivering the Golden Lecture on 24 October 1974, when he took as his
theme 'Religion and Morality Today'.

rates, and the cost of repairing houses often put up in the latter quarter of the 19th
century. In 1953 the gross rents amounted to £40,639: of this £5,376 was spent on
repairs, £5,645 on rates, and £6,209 on insurance. By the early 1970s some of the
properties were showing a near-negative return, and a policy of selling them off was
implemented. In 1974, £1.1m was raised in sales of the less desirable residential
properties to Lewisham Borough Council. The policy was accelerated in 1980 with
the establishment of the Property Committtee. The charity's income is derived
increasingly from offices such as Hamersley House in the City purchased in 1959, and
from the mix of commercial warehouses, retail shops, and offices in the Company's
Charitable Property Pool.[64]

The Company's agricultural properties have been another of the casualties of the
20th century. The farm at Pitley in Essex was sold in 1919, the farms in Kent that
had formed part of the Aske charity in 1950–1, and the Knighton estate in 1957.[65]

66. Map of the Hatcham (now more commonly known as New Cross) estate, c.1931, with housing development complete.

Income from agricultural holdings suffered from the cost of repairs on the change of tenancies, and in the inter-war years from the general downward pressure on farmers' profits which led to demands for rent reductions. Thus reviews of rents on some of the farms comprising the Knighton estate in 1933–4 resulted in reductions in rents of up to 30 per cent. The advantages that sales of agricultural property could bring to the finances of charities is demonstrated by the fact that in the first full financial year after the sale of the Knighton estate in 1958–9 the surplus income of the Adams charity rose from £400 to £2,935.[66]

The management of the Company's property was much improved with the establishment of the Property Committee in 1980. This has pursued the policy of selling off residential property, broadening the portfolio of Company investments, and managing the property in such a way as to maximise the income and maintain capital values. At about the same time the regulations under which charities could borrow from the capital funds (typically for building purposes) were changed. Under the former rules, as policed by the Charity Commissioners, the charities were obliged to repay over 30 years those monies they had borrowed by the assignment of a specified piece of stock on a fixed interest return to a recoupment fund. These rules were found to be unnecessarily restrictive not least because rises in the value of the assigned stock meant that the recoupment might become 'overpaid'. Under the new rules established by a committee chaired by Mr C.I. Bostock and authorised by the Charity Commissioners, each of the four Schools at Monmouth and Elstree is allowed to borrow up to 10 per cent of the underlying funds of the respective Jones and Aske charities, making no interest payment in the first year, and in subsequent years (up to a maximum of 15) repaying the loan, the repayment being indexed according to the Retail Price Index of the previous year. These rules, now known as the 'Bostock Rules', allow for much greater flexibility in borrowing for capital projects. Another recent development has been the establishment in 1989 of the Charities Property Pool. The intention is that in the future all the Company's significant charities will have an interest in the Property Pool giving them greater long-term stability than the Stock Exchange can guarantee.[67]

The Company's history in the later 20th century is therefore a story both of change, and of considerable continuities with the past. The Company is still governed according to a constitution which developed in the medieval and early modern periods, although the Court of Assistants is backed up by a greater range of professional advice, and its decision-making structures have become more elaborate with the proliferation of committees. Admission to the Company is still by the conventional routes of apprenticeship, redemption, and patrimony, but the character of the membership has drastically changed: there are no longer any representatives of haberdashery on the Livery which is now a bastion of the professional classes. As the trade has retreated, so the charitable aspects of the Company have advanced. The Company's major charities remain those established in the 16th and 17th centuries, and much of the Assistants' time is still taken up with the problems of the trusts established by Thomas Aldersey, William Jones, William Adams, and Robert Aske. But the character of those trusts has changed remarkably with the remodelling of charities through successive Charity Commission schemes and government Education Acts. Nowhere are the changes more dramatic than in the case of the Aske charity. In place of the Hospital for 20 old men and the boarding school for 20 boys established by Aske, the charity now supports two independent schools at Elstree, and a C.T.C. at Hatcham, as well as making a contribution to the Haberdashers' Eleemosynary Fund with wider charitable purposes. The state's involvement has dramatically increased, but the Company has jealously guarded the distinctive character of its Schools, and recent developments suggest some recovery in the autonomy of the institutions the Company supports. How secure that achievement will be, however, still depends to a large degree on forces beyond the Haberdashers' control, as the lesson of the Company's 20th-century history is the critical importance of the character of the party in power at Westminster in its affairs.

Appendix I

List of Master and Wardens, 1582–1990

A name in italics indicates a replacement for a man dying in office. The name of the Master is given in the first line for each year; the names of his Wardens appear on the following line.

1582 Sir Thomas Blanck
Clement Kelke   Francis Dod   Richard Brabourne   Mr Crymes
        Anselm Becket

1583 Thomas Smythe
William Whitmore   Thomas Allyn   Richard Gourney   William Cowper
        William Stone

1584 Henry Billingsley
John Tailor   Henry Beecher   Simon Bourman   Robert Tailor

1585 Sir Nicholas Woodrofe
William Stone   Thomas Bramley   Robert Woodrofe   Philip Smith

1586 Sir George Barne
Henry Beecher   John Garrard   Edmund Bressie   Thomas Rose

1587 Sir George Bond
Thomas Bramley   Richard Brabourne   Rowland Elrington   John Stone

1588 Thomas Smythe
John Garrard   Robert Tailor   John Graunge   William Awder

1589 Richard Gourney
Simon Bourman   Philip Smith   William Bond   William Beecher

1590 Henry Billingsley
Robert Tailor   Edmund Bressie   Leonard Mylnes   Edward Palmer

1591 William Rider
Philip Smith   John Stone   John Chaloner   Richard Arnold

1592 John Garrard
Edmund Bressie   William Arnold   Giles Crowch   Thomas Bowcher

1593 Robert Tailor
John Stone   William Bond   Thomas Lowe   Florence Caldwell

1594 Thomas Lowe
William Awder   William Beecher   Thomas Smythe   James Cullimore

1595 Henry Billingsley
William Bond   Edward Palmer   Francis Barne   Owen Morgan

1596 Richard Gourney
William Beecher   John Chaloner   Walter Fytchet   Walter Cade

1597 William Rider
Edward Palmer   Florence Caldwell   Walter Cade   Edward Osborne

1598 Christopher Hoddesdon Richard Arnold	Thomas Smythe	Nicholas Cotson	Thomas Hickman
1599 Thomas Smythe Thomas Webb	Francis Barne	Leonard White	John Susan
1600 Sir William Rider James Collymore	Owen Morgan	William Romeney	Robert Offley
1601 Sir John Garrard Francis Barne	Matthias Dolman	Martin Bond	Edward Quarles
1602 Thomas Lowe Owen Morgan	Edward Osborne	Edward Brooke	Roger Jeston
1603 Sir William Romeney Matthias Dolman	Nicholas Cotson	Edward Rider	Thomas Clerke
1604 Sir Thomas Lowe Edward Osborne	Thomas Hickman	John Cooke	Thomas Billingsley
1605 Sir Henry Billingsley *Sir John Garrard* Nicholas Cotson	Robert Offley	Edward Skegges	William Grave
1606 Sir William Rider Thomas Hickman	Martin Bond	George Smith	William Webb
1607 Sir John Garrard Robert Offley	Edward Quarles	Lancelot Peacock	William Burges
1608 Sir Thomas Lowe Martin Bond	Roger Jeston	Samuel Hare	Thomas Parradyne
1609 Sir William Romeney Edward Quarles	Thomas Clarke	Martin Smith	Thomas Allyn
1610 Francis Jones Roger Jeston	William Grove	Hugh Bullocke	Richard Fenn
1611 Sir John Garrard Thomas Clark	William Webb	William Bowcher	Richard Stratford *William Freeman*
1612 Sir Thomas Lowe William Grave	George Smith	William Sansome	John Davies
1613 Francis Jones William Webb	Lancelot Peacock	William Palmer	Edmund Traves
1614 Sir John Garrard George Smith	Thomas Parradyne	Francis Lodge	Leonard Parker
1615 Sir Thomas Lowe Lancelot Peacock	Samuel Hare	Thomas Ivatt	William Acourt
1616 Sir Francis Jones Thomas Parradyne	Thomas Allen *Hugh Bullock*	William Harrison	Hugh Hamersley
1617 Sir John Garrard Samuel Hare	Richard Fenn	Richard Rudd	Humphrey Slaney

1618 Sir Thomas Lowe Richard Fenn	William Freeman	William Palmer	Henry Robinson
1619 Hugh Hamersley William Freeman *John Davies*	John Davies *William Palmer*	Henry Haselfoot	Thomas Hukeley
1620 Sir Francis Jones William Palmer	Thomas Ivatt	Henry Wood	George Whitmore *Jeremy Smith*
1621 George Whitmore Thomas Ivatt	William Acourt	Edward White	Thomas Ball
1622 Nicholas Rainton William Acourt	Richard Rud	John Hawes	Everard Fawkener
1623 Robert Offley Richard Rud *Humphrey Slaney*	Humphrey Slaney *William Palmer*	Robert Jeffreys	Thomas Wilmer
1624 Martin Bond William Palmer	Henry Haselfoot	Richard Wilcox	Thomas Harris
1625 Richard Fenn Henry Haselfoot	Henry Wood	Nicholas Dickens	Thomas Hick
1626 William Palmer Henry Wood	Jeremy Smith	John Hewitt	Thomas Tiler
1627 Sir Hugh Hamersley Edmund White	Thomas Ashton	John Palmer	John Waller
1628 Thomas Ivatt *William Acourt* John Hawes	Henry Andrewes	Robert Hudson	Samuel Aldersey
1629 Robert Jeffreys Thomas Ashton	Thomas Harris	Humphrey Lee	John Stourton
1630 Humphrey Slaney Henry Andrewes	Nicholas Dickens	Humphrey Berrington	John Bowater
1631 Sir George Whitmore Nicholas Dickens	John Waller	George Harwood	Randolph Crew
1632 Sir Nicholas Rainton John Waller	Robert Hudson	Thomas Hall	Hugh Powell *John Graves*
1633 Henry Andrewes Robert Hudson	Edmund Page	Thomas Eyans	Richard Leigh
1634 Robert Hudson Edmund Page	Humphrey Lee	William Taylor	William Berkeley
1635 George Monoux Humphrey Lee	John Stourton	Thomas Shingler	John Goodwin
1636 Nicholas Dickens John Stourton	John Bowater	Thomas Man	Jarvice Smithson

1637 Sir Richard Fenn Humphrey Berrington	Simon Edmonds	Anthony Biddulph	George Ricketts
1638 Humphrey Lee John Bowater *John Elwes*	Thomas Stephens	Henry Hickford	John Knight
1639 Thomas Stone Simon Edmonds	John Offley	John Broome	Simon Willimott
1640 Thomas Man John Trott	Joseph Graves	Joas Croppenburgh	Robert Fenn
1641 Richard Leigh William Taylor	William Berkeley	William Thompson	George Cornish
1642 John Fowke William Berkeley	Anthony Biddulph	John Perch	John Helmes
1643 William Berkeley Anthony Biddulph	Henry Hickford	Richard Mawditt	John Bradley
1644 Simon Edmonds William Taylor	John Broome	Hillary Mempris	William Adams
1645 Randolph Crew Henry Hickford	Simon Willimott	Henry Harwell	Richard Young
1646 John Stourton John Broome	Robert Fenn	Thomas Alcocke	Tobias Dixon
1647 Humphrey Berrington Simon Willimott	George Cornish	Thomas Arnold	William Wiburd
1648 William Taylor Robert Fenn	John Perch	Humphrey Gold	Lawrence Brinley
1649 Hillary Mempris George Cornish	John Helmes	John Greene	John Roberts
1650 William Bond John Perch	Richard Mawditt	William Hobson	Owen Rowe
1651 Robert Fenn John Helmes	John Bradley	Walter Boothby	John Benthall
1652 John Fowke John Bradley	Henry Harwell	Thomas Gee	Michael Jones
1653 Henry Hickford Henry Harwell	Richard Young	James Story	Francis Woolley
1654 George Cornish Richard Young	William Wiberd	Jeremiah Sambrooke	Robert Crawley
1655 Thomas Barnes William Wiberd	Humphrey Gold	Thomas Blackall	Robert Osbolston
1656 Hugh Smithson Humphrey Gold	Lawrence Brinley	David Rogers	William Pitchford
1657 Thomas Bromefield Lawrence Brinley	John Greene	Edmund White	John King

1658 John Lawrence John Greene	Owen Rowe	Henry Tooley	James Stephens
1659 Thomas Arnold Owen Rowe *Thomas Gee*	Thomas Gee *Michael Jones*	John Dickins	Philip Owen
1660 Walter Boothby Jeremiah Sambrooke	Robert Crawley	Francis Heath	James Herbert
1661 Daniel Andrews Robert Crawley	Robert Osbolston	William Daniell	Alexander Wilding
1662 Humphrey Primate Robert Osbolston	John King	Thomas Paul	Alexander Pollington
1663 William Justice John King	Philip Owen	Anthony Dowse	John Mascall
1664 Sir John Lawrence William Daniell	Francis Heath	Hugh Radcliffe	Thomas Roche
1665 George Arnold *Sir Arthur Ingram* Francis Heath	Alexander Wilding	Peter Smith	Robert Deane *John Hind*
1666 Thomas Hayford William Daniell	Thomas Paul	Anthony Gibbon *Robert Wilding*	John Tiler
1667 Thomas Walker Alexander Wilding	Alexander Pollington	Ralph Gate	Daniel Farrington
1668 Richard Chaundler Thomas Paul	Anthony Dowse	John White	Ralph Gale
1669 Francis Towneley Alexander Pollington	John Mascall	Richard Wynn	Edmund Page
1670 Robert Wilding Anthony Dowse	Hugh Radcliffe	Alexander Hatchett	Randolph Isaackson
1671 Sir Thomas Player John Mascall	Thomas Roche	Edward Dearmer	John Athey
1672 Richard Wynn Hugh Radcliffe	Peter Smith	Nicholas Smith	John Freestone
1673 Hugh Radcliffe Edmund Page	Alexander Hatchett	John Kirkham	Robert Biddulph
1674 Edmund Page Alexander Hatchett	Randolph Isaackson	John Mills	John Duncombe
1675 Alexander Hatchett Randolph Isaackson	Edward Dearmer	Samuel Howard	Richard Baker
1676 Sir Charles Rich *Sir John Lawrence* Edward Dearmer	John Athey	Gabriel Whitley	Anthony Dansie *Arthur Art*

1677 Sir Thomas Player John Athey	Nicholas Smith	George Petty	Richard Dayrell
1678 Daniel Andrewes Nicholas Smith	John Kirkham	Thomas Carew	Richard Wheeler
1679 Arthur Baron John Kirkham	John Mills	John Martin	Edward Smith
1680 Henry Cornish John Mills	John Duncombe	William Nott	George French
1681 Henry Cornish John Duncombe	Samuel Howard	Robert Chaplin	Thomas Allen
1682 Richard Chandler Samuel Howard	Richard Baker	Gideon Awnsham	Edmund Farrington
1683 Sir Peter Daniell Richard Baker	Gabriel Whitley	Charles Hellowes	Richard Steele
1684 Robert Aske Richard Dayrell	John Martin	Robert Littlebury	John Bennet
1685 Sir Thomas Vernon John Martin	William Nott	Thomas Bates	John Perris
1686 Anthony Sturt William Nott	Robert Chaplin	Robert Curtis	John Bland
1687 Robert Boddington Gabriel Whitley	Thomas Carew	Robert Belson	John Waterworth
1688 Robert Boddington Thomas Carew	Edward Smith	Peter Mortimer	Mr. Ambler
1689 Sir Peter Daniell Robert Chaplin	Thomas Allen	Michael Watts	Valentine Houseman
1690 Sir Richard Levett Thomas Allen	Edmund Farrington	Jerome Clutterbuck	Robert Raworth
1691 Sir Richard Levett Edmund Farrington	Richard Steele	Charles Cutts	John Sindrey
1692 John Chauncy Richard Steele	Robert Littlebury	John Martin	James Nelthrope
1693 Peter White Robert Littlebury	Joseph Bennett	John Longland	Jacob Bell
1694 Major William Richardson Joseph Bennett	John Perris	Thomas Lownes	Joseph Alart
1695 Major William Richardson John Perris	Robert Curtis	Richard Colinson	John Gumley
1696 Major William Richardson Robert Curtis	John Bland	Henry Hatley	Thomas Carpenter

1697 Edward de Chaire John Bland	Michael Watts	William Sherwine	Alexander Pollington
1698 John Turvin Michael Watts	Valentine Houseman	Richard Venner	Henry Noble
1699 Nicholas Smith Robert Raworth	Charles Cutts	Thomas Gatton	John Pardoe
1700 Robert Hiscock John Martin	John Longland	Arthur Marshall	Edward Round
1701 Thomas Allen John Longland	Joseph Martin	William Clinch	John Banks
1702 Thomas Allen Joseph Martin	John Gumley	Jeremy Ives	William Hunt
1703 Maurice Moseley John Gumley	Thomas Carpenter	Thomas Blewer	Daniel Williamson
1704 Micajah Perry Alexander Pollington	Henry Noble	John Eakins	Henry Wheatley
1705 Micajah Perry Edward Round	John Banks	Thomas Barnes	Nicholas Moore
1706 John Billers John Banks	Jeremy Ives	Nicholas Burnell	Richard Meriwether
1707 John Baker Jeremy Ives	William Hunt	Samuel Fulk	William Thead
1708 Sir Robert Dunckley William Hunt	Daniel Williamson	Thomas Parry	John Jackson
1709 William Lewen Daniel Williamson	Christopher Blower	James Dodd	Thomas Trammell
1710 Thomas Bishop Christopher Blower	Henry Wheatley	George Moult	Joseph Reynardson
1711 Edmund Skinner Henry Wheatley	Capt. Thomas Barnes	Henry Cornish	Henry Lovelace
1712 John Barroby Capt. Thomas Barnes	Nicholas Burnell	Christopher Towes	William Christopher
1713 Sir Francis Forbes Nicholas Burnell	Richard Meriwether	Thomas Dodd	Gwynet Freeman
1714 Edward Round Richard Meriwether	George Moult	Benjamin Harvey	William Buckle
1715 Sir Harcourt Master George Moult	Joseph Reynardson	John Jenkins	John Hatley
1716 Sir John Eyles Joseph Reynardson	Henry Cornish	Francis Eagleton	John Stubbing
1717 John Banks Christopher Towes	William Christopher	Robert Haddock	Thomas Piggott

1718	Joseph Brooksbank			
	William Christopher	Thomas Dodd	Francis West	Matthew Tyndale
1719	Sir George Caswall			
	John Jenkins	Gwynet Freeman	Augustine Bryan	Samuel Roberts
1720	William Billers			
	John Jenkins	Major John Hatley	William Wyld	John Rideout
1721	Thomas Stiles			
	Major John Hatley	Thomas Piggott	George Waylett	Hanbury Walthall
1722	John Keble			
	Thomas Piggott	Francis West	Francis Seagood	Roger Lacy
1723	John Mayhew			
	Francis West	Augustine Bryan	John Berkeley	Samuel Harris
1724	Sir Joseph Eyles			
	Major John Hatley	John Rideout	John Heron	Thomas Phillips
1725	Samuel Cox			
	John Rideout	Hanbury Walthall	Richard Tidswell	Robert Alsop
1726	Abraham Perrot			
	Hanbury Walthall	Francis Seagood	William Unett	William Dovee
1727	Micajah Perry			
	Francis Seagood	Roger Lacy	Philip Morris	Charles Price
1728	Henry Hankey			
	Roger Lacy	John Berkeley	Jacob Bell	Thomas Blowen
1729	Thomas Sandford			
	John Berkeley	Samuel Harris	Thomas Smith	John Madden
				Thomas Sontley
1730	Robert Alsop			
	Samuel Harris	John Heron	William Haynes	James Pitt
1731	Robert Alsop			
	John Heron	Philip Morris	George Smith	James Pitt
1732	Stephen Ashby			
	Philip Morris	Charles Price	Jasper Hale	Samuel Thompson
1733	William Poston			
	Charles Price	Thomas Blowen	William West	Job Wilks
1734	William Roberts			
	Thomas Blowen	Thomas Poulley	Thomas Elton	Thomas Alen
1735	George Arnold			
	Thomas Sontley	John Rutty	Joseph Watson	John Harrison
1736	Francis Seagood			
	John Rutty	Jasper Hale	Joseph Dyer	Robert Dingley
1737	Sir Joseph Hankey			
	Jasper Hale	Samuel Thompson	Thomas Small	Thomas Wells
1738	Thomas Lingood			
	Samuel Thompson	Job Wilks	Peter Harding	John Pocock

1739 Thomas Knapp Job Wilks	Thomas Elton	Thomas Stratton	Thomas Powell
1740 Sir George Champion Thomas Elton	Thomas Alen	George Moody	John Michael Harnigh
1741 Charles Egerton Joseph Watson	John Harrison	Walter Hayter	Matthias Dupont
1742 John Bloss John Harrison	Thomas Wells	Basil Foster	Charles Collins
1743 Zachariah Craddock Thomas Wells	Thomas Powell	Thomas Sharp	Jasper Hale
1744 Sir James Creed Thomas Powell	Walter Hayter	Thomas Curryer	Abraham Whetland
1745 Sir Thomas Hankey Walter Hayter	Basil Foster	Peter Roberts	Nathaniel Adams
1746 Richard Peters *Samuel Richards* Basil Foster	Thomas Sharpe *Jasper Hale*	Joseph Gifford	John Dennis
1747 Isaac Dove Thomas Curryer	Abraham Whetland	James Edwards	William Mackerness
1748 Joseph Goodman Thomas Curryer	Peter Roberts	Samuel Crispe	William Wheatley
1749 Thomas Tyndale Peter Roberts	Nathaniel Adams	William Franklin	Thomas Loach
1750 Thomas Turner Nathaniel Adams	Joseph Gifford	Gabriel Small	Thomas Milward
1751 Thomas Harrison Joseph Gifford	William Mackerness	Edward Dymoke	Thomas Hynde
1752 Simon Foster William Mackerness	Samuel Crispe	James Bwye	William Bridgeman
1753 John Pensax Samuel Crispe	Thomas Leach	Hugh Hopley	Benjamin Atkins
1754 William Woolley Thomas Leach	Gabriel Small	William Wintle	William Hose
1755 John Payne Gabriel Small	Thomas Milward	Samuel Littlebury	John Sturges
1756 William Bowden Thomas Milward	Edward Dymoke	Benjamin Sherwill	Joseph Martin
1757 Nicholas Crispe Edward Dymoke	James Bwye	Richard Whiten	John Crowder
1758 James Wilkes James Bwye	Hugh Hopley	John Darsent	Timothy Cockshutt

1759 David Morris Hugh Hopley	William Hose	Christopher Cotterell	Nicholas Cox
1760 Lewis Jones William Hose	Thomas Piggott	Arthur Nash	John Rose
1761 William Cracroft Thomas Piggott	Benjamin Sherwill	John Hall	Nathaniel Hedges
1762 John Hitchcock Benjamin Sherwill	Richard Whiten	Peter Devisme	John Saffory
1763 Stracey Till Richard Whiten	John Dargent	John Drinkwater	John Stanton
1764 James Bwye John Dargent	Arthur Nash	Joseph Reynardson	David Delavau
1765 James Sayer Arthur Nash	John Rose	Lewis Dymocke	William Chelson
1766 Thomas Spicer John Rose	Nathaniel Hedges	Edward Hippisley	Timothy Walker
1767 Richard Whiten Nathaniel Hedges	Peter Devisme	John Wathen	William Marshall
1768 John Dargent Peter Devisme	John Saffory	Samuel Lowe	Samuel Hartley
1769 Robert Vincent John Saffory	John Drinkwater	Clement Corderoy	Samuel Taylor
1770 Nathaniel Hedges John Drinkwater	David Delavau	Joseph Balmer	Samuel Holland
1771 Charles Powell David Delavau	Edward Hippisley	Samuel Wallis	William Chancellor
1772 John Saffory Edward Hippisley	Timothy Walker	Benjamin Hawes	George Barber
1773 John Shipman Timothy Walker	William Marshall	Peter Pope	Joseph Downes
1774 John Yerbury William Marshall	Samuel Lowe	John Whitehead	John Bateman
1775 Edward Hippisley Clement Corderoy	Joseph Balmer	Edward Bridgen	Peter Nicholas
1776 William Marshall Joseph Balmer	Samuel Wallis	John Galpine	William Clare
1777 John Rogers William Chancellor	Benjamin Hawes	Joseph Waites	Thomas Walton
1778 Joseph Malpas Samuel Wallis	George Barber	George Rutt	Joseph Braint
1779 Clement Corderoy Benjamin Hawes	Peter Pope	W. Pickard	W. Belch

1780 John Marlar George Barber	John Whitehead *Edward Bridgen*	Thomas Matson	John Stratton
1781 Joseph Balmer Peter Cope	Peter N. Frisquett *John Galpine*	K. Bond	Stephen Yates
1782 James Roberts Edward Bridgen	William Clare	John Grigory	John Pepper
1783 John Milward John Galpine	Joseph Waite	Christopher Cotterell	Edward Henshaw
1784 Thomas Skinner William Clare	Thomas Walton	John Jackson	Richard Harris
1785 Sir Benjamin Hammett Joseph Waite	Joseph Braint	John Ashby	William Milward
1786 Peter Pope Thomas Walton	Thomas Matson	Richard Watts	James Carey
1787 John Galpine Joseph Braint	John Stratton	Benjamin S. Bradbury	John Cowley
1788 Thomas Walton Thomas Matson	Stephen Yates	O. Olney	Robert Bromfield
1789 Joseph Braint John Stratton	John Gregory	William Shrubb	Henry Cundell
1790 John Stratton Stephen Yates	John Pepper	William Wigan	Richard Brabant
1791 Stephen Yates J. Gregory *John Pepper*	Christopher Cotterell *Richard Harris*	Edward Beale	Thomas Brooks
1792 John Pepper Richard Harris	John Ashby	Joseph Philpot	W. Robinson *Joseph Munday*
1793 Stephen Langston John Ashby	William Milward	Robert Morris	J. Huntley
1794 John Baker William Milward	Richard Watts	Philip James	James Marshall
1795 William Langston Richard Watts	Benjamin S. Bradbury	Joseph Newberry	Richard Till
1796 Thomas Russell Benjamin S. Bradbury	William Shrubb	H. Adams	T. Stevenson
1797 David Dean William Shrubb	Richard Brabant	G. Urling	James Ayres
1798 Richard Watts Richard Brabant	Thomas Brookes	W. Shermer	G. Peacock

1799 Benjamin S. Bradbury Thomas Brookes	Joseph Philpot	Hugh Bantock	Charles Birkhead
1800 William Shrubb Joseph Philpot	Joseph Munday	William Thurbin	Richard West
1801 Henry Malpas Joseph Munday	Robert Morris	James Delegal	Edward Colebatch
1802 Richard Brabant Robert Morris	Philip James	James Vincent	Jerome W. Knapp
1803 John Brooksby Philip James	Joseph Newberry	John Gardner	Benjamin Blakesley
1804 Thomas Brooks James Marshall	Richard Till	Thomas Ovey	Joseph Newberry
1805 Joseph Philpot Joseph Newberry	James Ayres	John Spiller	Robert Edmonds
1806 Joseph Munday James Ayres	Hugh Bantock	John Killick	William S. Hall
1807 Philip James Hugh Bantock	Charles Birkhead	James Clark	Samuel Spencer
1808 Joseph Newberry Charles Birkhead	William Thurbin	John Holt	William Creak
1809 Thomas Dyke William Thurbin	James Delegal	John Bickerstaff	Samuel Tidswell
1810 Richard Till James Delegal	Edward Colebatch	William Edmonds	Thomas Playfair
1811 James Ayres Edward Colebatch	Jerome W. Knapp	Joseph F. Vandercom	George Browne
1812 Edward Colebatch Jerome W. Knapp	James Vincent	Richard Townend	William Thompson
1813 Jerome W. Knapp James Vincent	John Gardner	William Land	John Iselton
1814 Sir Ludford Harvey John Gardner	Benjamin Blakesley	Priest Shrubb	Samuel Keeble
1815 James Vincent John Newby	Robert Edmonds	Richard Langford	Thomas C. Eysham
1816 Benjamin Blakesley Robert Edmonds	William S. Hall	John Shepherd	John Staton
1817 John Newby William S. Hall	James Clark	Samuel Butler	William Coates
1818 Robert Edmonds James Clark	Samuel Spencer	John Stracey	Benjamin Hawes
1819 William S. Hall Samuel Spencer	William Creak	William Bedford	Joshua Johnston

1820 Samuel Spencer William Creak	Samuel Tidswell	Shadrach Mulcock	William King
1821 William Creak Samuel Tidswell	William Edmonds	Thomas King	Thomas Holbrook
1822 Samuel Tidswell William Edmonds	Joseph F. Vandercom	John Wilson	Joseph Weatherley
1823 John Jacks William Land	Priest Shrubb	Benjamin Blakesley	Francis Moorhouse
1824 John Dyke Priest Shrubb	Richard Langford	Richard Armstrong	John Stapp
1825 Joseph F. Vandercom Richard Langford	Thomas C. Eysham	John Buckee	Thomas Allan
1826 William Land Thomas C. Eysham	John Staton	John Joyner	John W. Liddiard
1827 John Hoffmann John Staton	Samuel Butler	James D. Capel	Thomas Howell
1828 Richard Langford Samuel Butler	John Stracey	Thomas Pattison	James Law Jones
1829 John Staton John Stracey	William Coates	George Haines	Samuel Stuart
1830 Samuel Butler William Coates	Benjamin Hawes	David Price	Elisha Wilson
1831 John Stracey Benjamin Hawes	Joshua Johnston	Samuel Osborn	John Roberts
1832 William Coates Joshua Johnston	Shadrach Mulcock	Thomas Marshall	William Knott
1833 Benjamin Hawes William Bedford	William King	John S. Engelhart	James Gutteridge
1834 Daniel Austin William King	Thomas Holbrook	James Stevenson	John W. Upward
1835 Joshua Johnston Shadrach Mulcock	Joseph Weatherley	Thomas West	Richard Edmonds
1836 William King Joseph Weatherley	Francis Moorhouse	John Dean	Hercules Paynter
1837 Shadrach Mulcock *John Stapp* John Stapp *Thomas Allan*	Thomas Allan *John W. Liddiard*	William Harris	Edward Eagleton
1838 Thomas Allan John W. Liddiard	James D. Capel	Brodie A. McGhie	Samuel Wickens
1839 John W. Liddiard James D. Capel	Thomas Howell	Samuel F. Stallard	Richard Till

1840 James D. Capel Thomas Howell	Thomas Pattison	William H. Wood	John Watherston
1841 Thomas Howell Thomas Pattison	James L. Jones	Edward C. Bracebridge	Benjamin Wilson
1842 Thomas Pattison James L. Jones	Samuel Stuart	Thomas Wilson	John C. Joyner
1843 James Law Jones Samuel Stuart	Thomas Marshall	Benjamin Wilson	Samuel Hall
1844 Samuel Stuart Thomas Marshall	William Knott	Charles Halson	Thomas Morris
1845 Thomas Marshall William Knott	John S. Englehart	Josiah J. Luntley	Robert Carter
1846 William Knott John S. Englehart	John W. Upward	William Francis	Thomas Groves
1847 John S. Englehart John W. Upward	John Dean	Charles T. Holcombe	Thomas Townend
1848 John W. Upward John Dean	William Harris	John Killick	Charles Godwin
1849 John Dean William Harris	Edward Eagleton	John Eagleton	George Haines
1850 William Harris Edward Eagleton	Thomas West	John S. Cuthbert	John Pearce
1851 Edward Eagleton Thomas West	Richard Till	William B. Simpson	Benjamin Edginton
1852 Richard Till William H. Wood	Jeremiah Pilcher	William Malpas	Thomas W. Cuthbert
1853 William H. Wood Jeremiah Pilcher	Edward C. Bracebridge	George Keen	Samuel O. Haines *John Phillips*
1854 Jeremiah Pilcher Edward C. Bracebridge	Benjamin Wilson	Drew Wood	James D. Capel
1855 Edward C. Bracebridge Benjamin Wilson	Samuel Hall	James M. Barnard	Richard A. Coward
1856 Benjamin Wilson Samuel Hall	Josiah J. Luntley	Matthew W. Johnson	John R. Cuthbert
1857 Samuel Hall Josiah J. Luntley *Robert Carter*	Robert Carter *Thomas Groves*	George J. Donne	Thomas Goddard
1858 Robert Carter Thomas Groves	John Killick	Samuel Tidswell	William Hawes
1859 Thomas Groves John Killick	John S. Cuthbert	Francis Sherriff	Thomas Higgs
1860 John Killick John S. Cuthbert	George Haines	John Haines	John Hincken

1861 John S. Cuthbert George Haines	John Pearce	Charles D. Dandy	John Betham
1862 John Pearce William B. Simpson	Benjamin Edgington	William H. Skyring	James Wilson
1863 William B. Simpson Benjamin Edgington	Drew Wood	William H. Mullens	John H. Gosling
1864 Benjamin Edgington Drew Wood	Matthew W. Johnson	James Warren	John Brown
1865 Drew Wood Matthew W. Johnson	John R. Cuthbert	Thos. W. Jones	Henry D. Smith
1866 M.W. Johnson John R. Cuthbert	G.J. Donne	R.H. Townend	G.N. Langley
1867 John R. Cuthbert G.J. Donne	W. Hawes	J.H. Eagleton	C. Wallis Hoffman *Revd. Prebendary Mackenzie*
1868 G.J. Donne W. Hawes	T. Higgs	A.J. Keen	C. Wilson
1869 W. Hawes T. Higgs	W.H. Skyring	W. Liddiard	W. Hale
1870 T. Higgs W.H. Skyring	D.H. Stone	J.A. Archer	F.G.G Goddard *W.H. Baigent*
1871 W.H. Skyring D.H. Stone, Ald.	J.H. Gosling	B. Burnell	J.D. Pilcher
1872 D.H. Stone, Ald. J.H. Gosling	John Brown	J.P. Jones	T.W. Sampson
1873 John Brown W.J.R. Cotton, Ald.	R.H. Townend	T.W. Plummer	A. Francis
1874 W.J.R. Cotton, Ald. R.H. Townend	G.N. Langley	David W. Dean	E. Eagleton
1875 R.H. Townend G.N. Langley	Revd. Prebendary Mackenzie	T.E. Phillips	C.J. Philips
1876 G.N. Langley Revd. Prebendary Mackenzie	A.J. Keen	Thomas Groves	Benjamin Field
1877 Revd. Prebendary Mackenzie A.J. Keen	J.A. Archer	W. Groves	W. Morris
1878 A.J. Keen J.A. Archer	W.H. Baigent	T. Morris	J.H. Allen
1879 J.A. Archer W.H. Baigent	B. Burnell	J. Bolton	E. Saxton

1880 W.H. Baigent B. Burnell	D.W. Dean	H.H. Allan	J.G. Pilcher
1881 B. Burnell D.W. Dean	Alderman Sir F. Wyatt Truscott	H.W. Carter	T. Townend
1882 D.W. Dean *G.J. Donne* Sir F. Wyatt Truscott	E. Eagleton	Revd. W.R. Capel	E.S. Tudor
1883 Sir F.W. Truscott E. Eagleton	T.E. Phillips	A. Slater	Revd. C.N. Edgington
1884 E. Eagleton T.E. Phillips	C.J. Phillips	W.F. Pilcher	A.P Townend
1885 T.E. Phillips C.J. Phillips	Wm. Groves	Revd. E. Pope	W.H. Potter
1886 C.J. Phillips Wm. Groves	Wm. Morris	H.D. Pilcher	W.H. Holman
1887 Wm. Groves Wm. Morris	Major Bolton	J.A. Hunt	S. Harman
1888 Major Bolton Edward Saxton	H.W. Carter	W. Fox Hawes	E. H. Simpson
1889 Edward Saxton H.W. Carter	T. Townend	W. Tudor	C. Skipper
1890 H.W. Carter T. Townend	E.S. Tudor	O.S. Tudor	J.D. Gregory
1891 T. Townend E.S. Tudor	A. Slater	J.S. Pearce	J. Weatherly
1892 E.S Tudor A. Slater	Revd. C.N. Edgington	H. Chester	H.D. Wood
1893 A. Slater Revd. C.N. Edgington	Sir D. Evans	A. Field	J. E. Turner
1894 Revd. C.N. Edgington Sir D. Evans	Revd. E. Pope	M.S. Pilcher	S. Warren
1895 Sir D. Evans Revd. E. Pope	W. H. Potter	W. Langley	E.A. Baylis
1896 Revd. E. Pope W.H. Potter	J.A. Hunt	A. Toovey	H.C. Pilcher
1897 W.H. Potter J.A. Hunt	W.F. Hawes	C.E. Layton	R.M. Cuthbert

1898 J.A. Hunt W.F. Hawes	W. Tudor	J.B. Hilditch	E.S. Saxton
1899 W.F. Hawes W. Tudor	O.S. Tudor	S. Osborn	A. Shand
1900 W. Tudor O.S. Tudor	J.D. Gregory	G.T. Pilcher	W.B. Whitmore
1901 O.S. Tudor J.D Gregory	J.S Pearce	J.A. Keen	H.L. Florence
1902 J.D. Gregory J.S. Pearce	H.D. Wood	E.B. Florence	F.W. Imbert-Terry
1903 J.S. Pearce H.D. Wood *A. Field*	A. Field *M.S. Pilcher*	P. Saxton	A.T. Hawes
1904 A. Field M.S. Pilcher	S. Warren	A. Toovey	W. Donne
1905 M.S. Pilcher S. Warren	W. Langley	Revd. S.W. Tidswell	Major T. Lay
1906 S. Warren W. Langley	E.A. Baylis	Cmdr. A.R.A. Stock	Revd. Preb H.P. Prosser
1907 W. Langley E.A. Baylis	C.E. Layton* *J.B. Hilditch*	A. Young	H.Allan
1908 E.A. Baylis J.B. Hilditch	S. Osborn	Col. H.B. Mortimer	F.J. Whitmore
1909 J.B. Hilditch S. Osborn	Sir G.W. Truscott	Cyril Plummer	Lewis G. Mortimer
1910 S. Osborn Sir G.W. Truscott	Sir J.C. Bell	Herbert Young	Henry H.Young
1911 Sir G.W. Truscott Sir J.C. Bell	J.A. Keen	Holcombe Ingleby	N.B. Morris
1912 Sir J.C. Bell J.A. Keen	H.L. Florence	W. Newton Dunn	Revd. G.S. Pownall
1913 J.A. Keen H.L. Florence	E.B. Florence	E. Bird	Revd. F.H. Stock
1914 H.L. Florence E.B. Florence	F.W. Imbert-Terry	Revd. H. Alban Williams	John W. Carr
1915 E.B. Florence F.W. Imbert-Terry	P. Saxton	H. Sanders Clark	C.B. Wright
1916 F.W. Imbert-Terry P. Saxton	A. Travers Hawes	Revd. H.S. Cronin	E.F. Donne
1917 P. Saxton A.T. Hawes	Capt. A.R.A. Stock	J.H.W. Pilcher	H.L. Stephenson

* Resigned through ill health

Year				
1918	A.T. Hawes			
	Capt. A.R.A. Stock	Revd. Preb. H.P. Prosser	C.H. Austin	P.D. Tuckett
1919	Capt. A.R.A. Stock			
	Revd. Preb. H.P. Prosser	Henry Allan	Harry Tudor	J. Perkins
1920	Revd. Preb. H.P. Prosser			
	Henry Allan	Col. H.B. Mortimer	H.F. Moseley	E.G. Simpson
1921	Henry Allan			
	Col. H.B. Mortimer	F.J. Whitmore	Lt.Col. C.M. Crompton Roberts	F.W. Carter
1922	Col. H.B. Mortimer			
	F.J. Whitmore	Cyril Plummer	R.L. Carter	Capt. A.O. Goodrich
1923	F.J. Whitmore			
	Cyril Plummer	Major H.H. Young	Major E.A. Dodd	H. Francis
1924	Cyril Plummer			
	Major H.H. Young	Col. and Ald. Sir C.C. Wakefield	G.W. Wollaston	R.R. Johnson
1925	Major H.H. Young			
	Col. and Ald. Sir C.C. Wakefield	N.B. Morris	R.H. Powell	J.G. Harris
1926	Col. and Ald. Sir C.C. Wakefield			
	N.B. Morris	Revd. H. Alban Williams	H.H. Gregory	S.H. Warren
1927	N.B. Morris			
	Revd. H. Alban Williams	Dr. J. Walter Carr	R.R.L. James	R.H. Wilkinson
1928	Revd. H. Alban Williams			
	Dr. J. Walter Carr	H.S. Sanders-Clark	J.W. Warren	C.E. Fletcher
1929	Dr. J. Walter Carr			
	H.S. Sanders-Clark	C.B. Wright	F.E. Tudor	B. Barker
1930	H.S. Sanders-Clark			
	C.B. Wright	J.H.W. Pilcher	Mr. Ald and Sheriff Maurice Jenks	A.A. Potter
1931	C.B. Wright			
	J.H.W. Pilcher	E.F. Donne	P. Saxton	J.T. Ash
1932	J.H.W. Pilcher			
	E.F. Donne	H.L. Stephenson	H.F. Moseley	E.H. Potter
1933	E.F. Donne			
	H.L. Stephenson	H.F. Moseley	S.H. Warren	E.D. Gregory

1934 H. L. Stephenson H.F. Moseley	E. Graham Simpson	H.Francis	Col. Wm. Reid Glover
1935 H.R.H. Prince Arthur of Connaught H.F. Moseley, Deputy Master E. Graham Simpson	The Rt. Hon. Lord Ebbisham	E.D. Gregory	J.E. Cooper
1936 E. Graham Simpson Ald. the Rt. Hon. Lord Ebbisham	F.W. Carter	H.H. Gregory	A.W.C. Hamsher
1937 Ald. the Lord Ebbisham F.W. Carter	R.L. Carter	E.A. Last-Smith	W.K. Warren
1938 F.W. Carter R.L. Carter	Major E.A. Dodd	Major J. Bamford Smith	Major W.E. Cook
1939 R.L. Carter Major E.A. Dodd	Ald. Sir Maurice Jenks	W.R. Wilkin	R.L. Moreton
1940 Major E.A. Dodd Ald. Sir Maurice Jenks	Sir Gerald W. Wollaston	Stephen Bird	Revd. Canon T.G. Edwards
1941 Ald. Sir Maurice Jenks Sir G. Wollaston	R.H. Powell	F.P. Coates	W.F. Dyer
1942 Sir G. Wollaston R.H. Powell	J. Gibson Harris	Bernard Elliott	Dr. D.B.I. Hallett
1943 R.H. Powell J. Gibson Harris	C.E. Fletcher	Lt. Com. A.F. Inglefield	Revd. H.S. Sard
1944 J. Gibson Harris C.E. Fletcher	F.E. Tudor	W.B. Franklin	B.G. Donne
1945 C.E Fletcher F.E. Tudor	R.R.L. James	P.C. Bull	A.S. Warren
1946 F.E. Tudor R.R.L. James	E.H. Potter	R.W. Foot	Major H.E.D Elliott
1947 R.R.L James E.H. Potter	Col. W.R. Glover	S.M. Pettitt	C.G. Gardner
1948 E.H. Potter Col. W.R. Glover	A.W.C. Hamsher	Col. K.H.A. Gross	E.T.W. Dodd
1949 Col. W.R. Glover A.W.C. Hamsher	E.A. Last-Smith	Lt.Col. C.W. Cronin	R.S. Blundell
1950 A.W.C. Hamsher E.A. Last-Smith	Lt.Col. J. Bamford Smith	J.B. Perkins	R.T. Hawes

1951 E.A. Last-Smith Lt.Col. J. Bamford Smith	W.R. Wilkin	Revd. A.W.G. Cope	The Rt. Hon. Lord Moynihan
1952 Lt.Col. J. Bamford Smith R.L. Moreton	W.F. Dyer	J.G. Carr	P.E.M. Shaw
1953 R.L. Moreton W.F. Dyer	Ald. Sir F.M. Wells	M.O. Sheffield	R.E. Brook
1954 W.F. Dyer Ald. Sir Frederick M. Wells	B. Elliott	Lt.Col. I.F. Bowater	P.B. Powell
1955 Ald. Sir Frederick Wells Bernard Elliott	Dr. D.B.I Hallett	Lt.Col. F.S. Bird	G.T. Bentley
1956 Bernard Elliott W.B. Franklin	P.C. Bull	G.S. Inglefield	H.W. Wollaston
1957 W.B Franklin P.C. Bull	C.G. Gardner	Vice-Admiral J.S.C. Salter	G. Bracewell Smith
1958 P.C. Bull C.G. Gardner	E.T.W Dodd	The Rt. Hon. The Lord Moynihan	P.E.M. Shaw
1959 C.G. Gardner E.T.W. Dodd	R.S. Blundell	J.G. Carr	M.O. Sheffield
1960 E.T.W. Dodd R.S. Blundell	Revd. A.W.G. Cope	R.E. Brook	Lt.Col and Ald. I.F. Bowater
1961 R.S. Blundell Revd. A.W.G. Cope	The Rt. Hon. The Lord Moynihan	P.B. Powell	F.S. Bird
1962 Revd. A.W.G. Cope The Rt. Hon. The Lord Moynihan	P.E.M. Shaw	G.T. Bentley	Col. and Ald. Sir Cullum Welch
1963 The Rt. Hon. The Lord Moynihan P.E.M Shaw	R.E. Brook	H.W. Wollaston	Vice-Admiral J.S.C. Salter
1964 P.E.M. Shaw and E.A. Last-Smith R.E. Brook	Col. and Ald. Sir Cullum Welch	G. Bracewell Smith	R.E. Liddiard
1965 R.E. Brook Col. and Ald. Sir Cullum Welch	J.G. Carr	R.E. Liddiard	R. Wakeford
1966 Col and Ald. Sir Cullum Welch Lt.Col. and Ald. Sir Ian Bowater	R.T. Hawes	R. Wakeford	Sir Richard Jenks

1967 Lt.Col. and Ald. Sir Ian Bowater R.T. Hawes	P.B. Powell	Sir Richard Jenks	F.H.W. Bedford
1968 R.T. Hawes P.B. Powell	Vice-Admiral J.S.C. Salter	T.C.S. Cope	G.R.R. Brown
1969 P.B. Powell Vice-Admiral J.S.C. Salter	G.T. Bentley	G.R.R. Brown	D.A.H. Sime
1970 Vice-Admiral J.S.C. Salter G.T. Bentley	F.S. Bird	D.A.H. Sime	K.M. Leach
1971 Ald. Sir Gilbert Inglefield F.S. Bird	G.R.R. Brown	K.M. Leach	Major-Gen. Sir John Bates
1972 F.S. Bird G.R.R. Brown	H.W. Wollaston	Major-Gen. Sir John Bates	C.I. Bostock
1973 G.T. Bentley H.W. Wollaston	D.A.H. Sime	H.C. Quitman	M.E. Bathurst
1974 H.W. Wollaston D.A.H. Sime	Sir Guy Bracewell Smith	W.A. Twiston Davies	I.S.B Crosse
1975 D.A.H. Sime Sir Guy Bracewell Smith	R.E. Liddiard	G.L. Bourne	J. Denza
1976 D.A.H. Sime R.E. Liddiard	Major-Gen. Sir John Bates	M.W.D. Northcott	G.R. Fox
1977 R.E. Liddiard Major-Gen. Sir John Bates	H.C. Quitman	M.A.B. Jenks	M.L. Hall
1978 Major-Gen. Sir John Bates H.C. Quitman	M.E. Bathurst	P.C.F. Warren	J.R. Welch
1979 H.C. Quitman M.E. Bathurst	W.A. Twiston-Davies	Sir John Welch	R.J.P. Jenks
1980 M.E. Bathurst W.A. Twiston-Davies	I.S.B. Crosse	R.J.P. Jenks	B.E. Sturgess
1981 W.A. Twiston-Davies I.S.B. Crosse	C.I. Bostock	B.E. Sturgess	A.D. Pilcher
1982 I.S.B. Crosse C.I. Bostock	G.L. Bourne	O.M.W. Swingland	D.G.C. Inglefield

1983	C.I. Bostock			
	G.L. Bourne	M.W.D. Northcott	D.G.C. Inglefield	P.W. Bedford
1984	G.L. Bourne			
	M.W.D. Northcott	G.R. Fox	P.W. Bedford	B.E. Shawcross
1985	M.W.D. Northcott			
	G.R. Fox	O.M.W. Swingland	B.E. Shawcross	B.C. Gothard
1986	G.R. Fox			
	O.M.W. Swingland	M.A.B. Jenks	B.C. Gothard	M.D.G. Wheldon
1987	O.M.W. Swingland			
	M.A.B. Jenks	J. Denza	D.E.K. Elliot	N.K.S. Wills
1988	M.A.B. Jenks			
	Sir John Welch	B.E. Shawcross	N.K.S. Wills	H.N. Lund
1989	D.A.H. Sime			
	Sir John Welch	D.E.K. Elliot	H.N. Lund	The Hon. L.B. Hacking
1990	Sir John Welch			
	D.E.K. Elliot	P.W. Bedford	The Hon. L.B. Hacking	Dr. C.J.T. Bateman

Appendix II

List of Clerks to the Haberdashers' Company

before 1582–1602	Lambert Osbolston
1602–1646	Basil Nicholl
1646–1652	Richard Nicholl
1652–1654	Thomas Conn
1654–1664	Robert Blayley
1664–1666	Alexander Brome
1666–1684	Robert Blayley
1684–1697	John Mould
1697–1708	Richard Stace
1708–1729	John Marsh
1729–1739	Jerome Knapp
1739–1741	Thomas Rutherford
1741–1754	Fotherly Baker
1754–1790	Jerome Knapp
1790–1825	Thomas George Knapp
1825–1843	Hambly Knapp
1843–1849	William Nelson Beechey
1849–1876	John Curtis
1876–1907	James Hamilton Townend
1907–1930	John Eagleton
1931–1950	Guy Tryon Eagleton
1950–1966	Cmmdr. Harry Prevett, O.B.E., R.N.
1966–1983	Cmmdr. William Ronald Miller, O.B.E., R.N.
1983-	Capt. Michael Ernest Barrow, D.S.O., R.N.

Appendix IIIa

The Company's Plate
(by Charles Truman)

Silver is a unique medium in the decorative arts. Until the early years of this century its value as wrought plate was directly linked to the value of the coinage of the realm, and indeed plate was frequently used as a substitute for specie. In addition silver is infinitely recyclable, and so plate which had become outmoded could be returned to the goldsmith to be melted and remade in fashionable forms. Thus a magnificent display of plate not only identified the wealth of the owner, it indicated his taste, in the modern plate, and his sense of history from the historic plate that he possessed.

The Haberdashers' Company still boasts a handsome quantity of plate which can be categorised in three groups. The first is the historic plate acquired by the Company before about 1730. This comprises the finest of the Company's silver and is therefore dealt with here in the greatest depth. The other two distinct categories of plate are each the products of single workshops: the silver by Omar Ramsden made between 1908 and 1934 and the silver and gold by Gerald Benney which has been acquired since 1956.

The history of the Company's collection, in common with most other City companies, can be read as a catalogue of past glories. Since there is no record of the Company's plate before 1633 it is impossible to determine the nature of the Company's plate before that date.[1] The evidence of wills provides a limited insight into the type of silver that the Company would have owned. William Page, who died in 1501, left the Company a standing cup of the value of £4,[2] and Ellis Draper bequeathed a gilt cup 'with a St Katherine wheel in the bottom of it' in his will dated 16 July 1527.[3] However the 1639 inventory contains no gifts of plate made before about 1560 which suggests that the Haberdashers' Company, like other City institutions was forced to sell much of its medieval plate to meet the military demands of the Crown at that time. A later bequest to the Company had also disappeared by 1639; a 'graven gilt ale cup . . . for a token of remembrance' from John Peacock in 1573.[4] It is possible that the Company had to contribute to the enforced loan made to Charles I in 1627 but no record of the sale of plate to meet the cost is recorded in the Court minutes. However in 1639 a committee was appointed to examine the Company's plate and not only have what was broken mended, but exchange pieces which were considered old fashioned or no longer useful for 'that which is more necessary'. A further disposal of plate was ordered by the Court of Assistants on the recommendation of a committee established on 14 April 1643[6] to view the Company's plate and to sell what they thought was least useful to ease the Company's financial difficulties caused by the demands of the Parliamentary war effort. Silver to the value of £726 9s. 2d. was sold to Mr. Viner, goldsmith,[7] presumably Robert Viner (or Vyner) (d.1688), subsequently goldsmith to Charles II, or a relative. In 1693 the Wardens disposed of further 'useless plate',[8] replacing it with more fashionable pieces, and a similar exercise was carried out in 1714.[9] However at the Civil War sale of plate the Court of Assistants stressed that 'it is to be remembered that the weight and also the Armes Marks letters and words which were upon those severall parcells of plate soe sould are to be sett and engraven upon the new plate which hereafter

1. G.L., MS 15866/1 fo. 279
2. P.R.O., PROB 11/13, fo. 20ᵛ
3. P.R.O., PROB 11/24, fo. 175
4. P.R.O., PROB 11/55, fo. 215ᵛ
5. G.L., MS 15842/1, fo. 303
6. G.L., MS 15842/1, fo. 315ᵛ
7. G.L., MS 15866/1, fo. 424
8. G.L., MS 15866/7, fo.
9. G.L., MS 15842/4, fo. 248

shalbe bought in lieu of them for the perpetuall memory of the donors of the same parcells so sold'. In consequence it is sometimes possible to trace gifts of plate through its various forms to pieces which survive today.

The account of the Wardens on St Katherine's Day 1639 shows the Company's plate at its most abundant. There was no less than 1,800 ozs. of gilt plate and over 1,600 ozs. of parcel-gilt or white plate. In common with other Stuart inventories, the plate described principally comprised cups, salts and spoons. There were, for example, 17 silver-gilt standing cups of which 15 had covers, 18 silver-gilt salts, two gilt ewers and basins, and three white sets, two voyders for clearing the table, a very large number of wine and beer cups (called bowls) together with some five dozen spoons.

The cup was the principal vessel of display, more common than the grander ewer and basin, but nonetheless held in the highest esteem. Such vessels were used not solely on the sideboard but for wine and beer at the table and even that spiced sugary wine concoction known as Hippocras which was considered one of the greatest luxuries. However, whilst it may have been that more than one guest shared a cup, and the custom of toasting guests was prevalent, it seems that much of the ritual drinking in City companies today has its origins no earlier than in the last century.

The standing salt was the most important piece of plate on the table. An early source instructs 'Set your salt on the right side where your souveraine shall sytte and at every ende of ye table set a salte sellar . . . and when your souveraynes table is thus arrayed, cover all the boards with salts, trenchers and cuppes'.[10] The lesser or trencher salts, originally pieces of bread with salt piled on, were scattered at random amongst the diners.

Perhaps curiously the Company's plate never seems to have included silver trenchers or plates, or saucers, and while spoons were clearly provided, a guest would have been expected to bring his own knife and a fork if he were so moved to bother with one. Indeed the Company was wont to hire the necessary flatware for banquets and dinners up until the end of the 18th century,[11] which presumably explains why so much of its routine domestic plate dates from the 19th century or later.

By 1649–50 this large quantity of silver had been savagely reduced to just under 450 ozs. of gilt plate and 410 ozs. of parcel gilt and white plate[12] almost all through the sale to 'Mr. Viner, goldsmith' in April 1643. Amongst the most important plate lost to the Company was 'One nest (set) of bowles with a Cover' weighing 81 ozs. 15dwts. made from a bequest of Robert Offley on 9 April 1596 of 40 marks,[13] all five ewers and basins, the larger of the two voyders, 13 gilt and five white salts and 14 gilt standing cups. All that remained were four gilt standing cups and covers, five gilt salts, but each without their covers and 24 gilt spoons together with a dozen white spoons 'with the image of St Katherine', a voyder weighing 112 ozs. 15 dwts., four nests of wine bowls (probably sets of three each), a small wine bowl, a nest of beer bowls and four further beer bowls. Only the salt given by Sir Hugh Hamersley in 1636, the standing cup from Thomas Ivatt in 1629, both now missing their covers, and two of the three 'beere bowles' from Edward White of 1634 are still in the Company's collection. Of these, the Hamersley Salt is without question the most important. Made in 1595 by a maker who has been tentatively identified as T. Newton,[14] it is one of the greatest pieces of English Mannerist silver. The salt is formed as a column chased around the body with a scene from Ovid's *Metamorphoses*. The subject is the Silver Age (Book I, line 144ff) which followed the Golden Age in the history of the world. Ovid writes 'After Saturn had been banished to the dark land of death, and the world came under Jove's sway, the silver race came in, lower in scale than gold but of greater worth than yellow brass. In that age men first sought shelter in houses . . . Then were the first seeds sown in long furrows and bullocks groaned beneath heavy yokes'. The chasing graphically illustrates this with three heroic figures labouring in the fields whilst a mother sits with her children beneath a rudimentary shelter. The subject would have been easily recognisable to any educated man at the time since it is frequently engraved in illustrated editions of Ovid in the 16th century, and may suggest that either the salt was originally not gilt, or that the goldsmith was giving a subtle hint that the piece was silver-gilt rather than gold.

10. Winkin de Worde, *A Boke of Kervynge* (1508)
11. G.L., MS 15871, Feast Accounts
12. G.L., MS 15866/1, fo. 723
13. P.R.O., PROB 11/87, fo. 230
14. Ian Pickford, *Jackson's English Goldsmiths* (Woodbridge, 1989), p. 103

The quality of the chasing is so fine, and evidently taken from Continental models that is tempting to suggest that the craftsman responsible was an immigrant from Germany or the Low Countries. Indeed the similarity of the borders to that on a bowl made in Amsterdam in 1606 and the comparable quality of the chasing to that on a salt by Geerart de Rasnier of 1580–1 has been noted elsewhere.[15] The Hamersley Salt was originally supplied with a cover, presumably a dome supported on scrolling brackets and probably with a vase or figure finial, and weighed in total 61 ozs. The cover was amongst the plate sold to Mr. Viner in 1642–3 when it was perhaps either damaged or considered unfashionable since most of the covers for the other salts were sold at that date.

Despite the loss of its cover the Hamersley Salt is still the heaviest Tudor salt to have survived, although the Company possessed two heavier examples. One, the gift of Richard Smith weighed 68 ozs. 5 dwts. in 1639 was sold in 1642–3, while the other, the gift of Sir William Romeney weighed 64 ozs. in 1639. The cover was sold in 1642–3 but the salt was still in the Company's collection in 1694 after some of the old plate had been judged useless.[17] Clearly it did not survive the conversion of old plate in 1714, since in the inventory of 1732 the gift of Sir William Romeney had been combined with the silver from salts given by Josias Hamo, Thomas Alcock and Henry Woodfull and made into a 'kettle, chaffingdish and lamp' weighing 100 ozs. 19 dwts. which is sadly no longer amongst the Company's plate.[18]

The other major piece to have survived the Civil War and the vagaries of taste is the cup of 1629, by the anonymous maker using the initials RB over a mullet, given by Thomas Ivatt. This standing cup, which also originally had a cover, is recorded in the Company's collection in 1633. Of typical form for the period, the bowl of the cup is chased with the arms of the City of London, the Company's arms and those of the Ivatt supported by winged demi-figures, between cartouches chased in the Auricular style enclosing scenes from the apocryphal Book of Tobit: Tobias and the great fish, Tobias and Sarah at prayer with the Archangel Raphael in the background and Tobias healing his father's sight. The cover seems to have disappeared sometime between 1649 and 1694, when the piece is listed at its present weight of 28 ozs. However, the presence of a similar cup, by the same maker, given to St John's Church, Hampstead in 1747, may well give an accurate idea of what the original cover was like.[19] The cover of the Hampstead example is domed and chased with foliage and flowers which surprisingly do not match the decoration elsewhere on the cup. Above this is a squat cylindrical element bordered by the same ovolo moulding as that on the foot and which supports an openwork pyramid on four demi-figure brackets, and surmounted by a sphere on which stands a classical warrior holding a spear and shield. Such covered cups, known today as steeple cups, survive from the 50 years or so following 1590 although it is clear from inventories that the form was produced at least as early as 1560.

The only other pieces to have survived from the early inventory are two of the 'nest of beere bowles' given by Edward White in 1634. The nest clearly originally comprised three cups, and a comparison of the weights of the extant pieces also confirms that they were intended for beer rather than forming part of the nest of wine bowls given by the same donor. As might be expected the beer bowls at 38 ozs. 15 dwts. were substantially larger than the wine bowls which weighed only 22 ozs. The weight of the beer bowls was repeated in the Company's inventory of 1732, when incidentally their number is also given as three, but the wine bowls had been converted into a candlestick, presumably identical in form to the Aldersey candlestick of 1714, also made from melting wine bowls, and still in the collection. Indeed from the description and weight of the White cups it is possible to distinguish the different sizes of cups for beer and wine which should make classification of the types easier in future. Like the White cups, the three beer bowls given by Symon Willimott in 1648 and first recorded in the following year together with a tankard, now only survive as two although all three bowls are recorded in 1732. The fate of the tankard is a mystery. Possibly one of two mentioned without a donor in 1694, it was

15. Philippa Glanville, *Silver in Tudor and Early Stuart England* (1990), pp. 159, 280, 291
16. G.L., MS 15866/1, fo. 424
17. G.L., MS 15866/7, fo. A
18. G.L., MS 15866/9, fo. 73
19. Philippa Glanville, op. cit. p. 160

probably refashioned in 1714, as were the tankards given by Hugh Smithson and Robert Barnes mentioned in the 1694 inventory but which survive today as a pair of footed salvers.

Much more problematic is the history of the splendid standing cup of 1637. Today referred to as the Company's Cup it probably originally had a cover. Assuming that with the cover it would have weighed approximately 60 ozs., there are two cups in the 1639–40 Accounts of the Wardens which survived the sale of plate in 1643 and which correspond in weight. One was given by Sir George Barnes and the other by Sir William Garrard. However the 1637 cup is not only engraved with the Company's arms but also with those probably of Hudson, although the absence of tincturing makes a firm identification impossible. It seems very likely that the cup was presented to the Company by Robert Hudson who was Master in 1635 or perhaps made in commemoration of his year of office. However there appears to be no gift of plate from Hudson and the cup is not recorded in the Company's collection until 1732 when no mention is made of its provenance.

Another example of plate with a mixed history is the 'Bell salte with a trencher salt with a cover' mentioned in the 1639 inventory as the gift of Thomas Somers. The cover was sold in 1642–3 but the Bell salt appears to have survived until at least 1694 when it was described as 'One Guilt Salte'. In 1714 it was combined with a salt weighing 27 ozs. given by Zacchariah Poplar and converted into a coffee pot, now missing.

The 'Three nests of wine bowles, white' recorded as the gift of John Wyberd in 1639 were sold to Mr. Viner three years later, but his gift has been memorialised in the inscription on the Monteith of 1714. The acquisition of another Monteith by the Company some 20 years earlier shows how the Court was aware of the changes in fashion in eating and drinking. The Monteith was apparently introduced in 1683, when Anthony à Wood wrote in his diary, 'This year in the summer time came up a new vessel or bason notched at the brim to let vessels hang there by the foot, so that the body or drinking place might land in the water to cool them. Such a bason was called a Monteigh from a fantastical Scot called Monsieur Monteigh who at that time, or a little before wore the bottom of his cloak so notched'.[20] It is clear that the Wyberd Monteith was made to match the earlier example.

In 1649 Thomas Stone, Master in 1639, presented the Company with a pair of handsome silver-gilt cups. Both have shallow domed feet, baluster stems and matted cylindrical bowls, and are of a form found in several other Livery Companies. No mention is made in the 1649 inventory of covers to the cups, but when they are listed in the Wardens' accounts of 1694 their weight had decreased by nearly 20 ozs., and both, like others in the Company's collection are now equipped with Victorian replacements.

One of the most generous gifts to the Company in the 17th century was a bequest from Thomas Arnold, Master in 1659, of £50 to be spent on plate. His executor, George Arnold, commissioned the two flagons of 1670 which bear the family name.[21] Certainly the absence of silver pouring vessels, particularly for beer, since the levies of the 1640s must have led to the use of less fitting vessels such as stoneware bottles or leather blackjacks. The flagon form is rarely found in secular buffets, however, their survival being principally among Protestant altar plate. But the sheer size of the Arnold flagons would have made them unwieldy when full and their use for purely decorative purposes cannot be excluded. Apart from two staff heads of uncertain date, the only other survival of the Company's plate from the 17th century is a bargemaster's badge, unmarked but dated 1689. It is chased with the Company's arms and has been mounted in wood as a double snuff-box by Garrards in 1865–6.

Of the 18th century plate not already mentioned is a fine George I silver-gilt cup made from a gift of plate weighing 31 ozs. 18dwts. from Hugh Ratcliffe senior. Since there is no apparent reference to a gift from Mr. Ratcliffe of the correct weight in the Wardens' Accounts before that of 1732, it must be assumed that the gift was made between 1694 and 1714 when the cup was made. The piece is in a style not usually associated with the early years of the 18th century and must be considered a remarkable example of Georgian historicism. Also of interest are the two salvers of 1714, each on trumpet feet, which would have been used for bringing glasses to the table from the sideboard, and would have been particularly necessary since the vessels would be dripping with water from the

20. Michael Clayton, *The Collector's Dictionary of the Silver and Gold of Great Britain and North America* (1971) p. 180
21. G.L., MS 15842/2, fo. 158[v-r]

Company's recently acquired monteiths. Both the salvers were made from gifts of tankards from Thomas Barnes and Hugh Smithson, who were successive Masters in 1655 and 1656.

Mention should also be made of the use of the Company's plate outside the Hall. In the 16th and 17th centuries it was normal for the Company to lend plate to members of the Company who became Lord Mayor, and sometimes to those who became Sheriffs also. Indeed in the 1670s the Company even lent plate to Sheriffs who were not free of the Haberdashers, but in 1676 it was decided to discontinue this practice because the silver 'is hurt broken and some part thereof may be in danger to be lost' and loans of plate were restricted to Lord Mayors and Sheriffs free of the Company. During the 19th century plate was loaned to the City Corporation for special occasions. The most notable of these were the visit of the Shah of Persia in 1873, the International Municipal Entertainment of 1875, and the visit of the Prince of Wales to the City on his return from India.[22]

For nearly two hundred years following the 'Order for useless plate to be changed for something convenient and useful, with regard to respective benefactors' on 1 December 1714, the Company's acquisition of plate was relatively slow and artistically unimpressive. However in 1909 the Company began an association with one of the best-known silversmiths of the 20th century, Omar Ramsden. Born in Sheffield in 1873, the son of a manufacturer of silver and electroplated flatware, Ramsden attended evening classes at the Sheffield School of Art. In 1893 he moved to London where he studied at the Royal College of Art. There he developed his skill as a modeller, although he never mastered the craft of goldsmithing. In 1897, or possibly the following year he entered into a partnership with Alwyn Carr, a fellow Yorkshireman, and together they set up a workshop at the Stamford Bridge Studios, Chelsea. They employed two goldsmiths, Walter Andrews and Leonard Burt, and a chaser, A. E. Ulyett. In 1914 Carr volunteered for the army but Ramsden stayed at home, profiting, it is said, from the many commissions available during the First World War. Either way, the partnership was dissolved on Carr's return home and Ramsden's business flourished from a workshop, St Dunstan's, named after the patron saint of goldsmiths, in Seymour Place, London, SW10. During the 1920s and 1930s only special commissions were raised by hand. Rather, a hammered finish was applied to commercially produced blanks bought in Birmingham, where casts were also made by R. Owen & Co. Other work, such as gilding was also farmed out despite the fact that there were some 20 assistants employed in the workshop, including the goldsmith Leslie Durbin who was apprenticed to Ramsden in 1929. Given this combination of a large workforce and Birmingham outworkers, the inscription found on many pieces 'Omar Ramsden me Fecit' may seem somewhat oversimplified.[23]

The earliest pieces by Ramsden acquired by the Company were two salts of silver-gilt commissioned by Samuel Osborn, Master in 1910, and struck with the makers' mark of Ramsden and Carr and the London hall-marks for 1909–10. These are clearly modelled on the Hamersley Salt, although the drum is chased with heraldic motifs rather than a scene from Ovid. It is evident from these and other pieces in the collection that Ramsden was allowed direct access to the Company's plate. However it was the patronage of the Florence family that was responsible for some of the grandest of the Ramsden silver. 1914 and 1915 saw successive members of the family as Masters of the Company. To celebrate his Mastership, Lieut. Col. Henry Florence commissioned the huge basin by Ramsden and Carr in 1915 and the following year Ernest Florence commemorated his term with the impressive silver-gilt cup and cover based in form at least on English cups of the late 15th century. This cup which was not made until 1924 is incidentally the only piece of plate to be engraved with the arms of the Company as granted by Roger Legh, Clarenceaux, in 1446. Also in 1924 E. B. Florence presented The Haberdashers' Company Golf Challenge Cup, again by Omar Ramsden. This cup is modelled on two earlier cups in the Company's collection. The foot and stem are derived from the Ivatt Cup of 1629, while the bowl is adapted from that of the Company's Cup of 1637. A silver-gilt statuette of St Katherine denotes a further link between the Haberdashers and the firm of Ramsden. The piece was commissioned in 1935 by John Eagleton, the Company's Clerk from 1907 until 1930. The surviving Ramsden archive now preserved in the Library of the Worshipful Company of Goldsmiths, suggests that another commission from Eagleton might have gone astray. In the Costs of Orders Book for 14 July 1923 to 12 November 1932 is the record of the 'Eagleton Haberdashers Bowl' made by Ulyet, Wright, Coles and Best and

---

22. G.L., MS 15842/1, passim and 15842/16, pp. 209, 351, 415
23. Peter Canon Brooks, *Omar Ramsden* (Birmingham)

completed on 28 May 1927. Perhaps the piece was a personal commemorative since it is not to be found amongst the Company's plate. There are several other examples of silver from the Ramsden workshops which are treated below.

More remarkable in many ways is the Haberdashers' Company's patronage of one of England's leading contemporary goldsmiths, Gerald Benney. Born in Hull in 1930, Benney was brought up in the world of art schools. He enrolled at Brighton College where his father was Principal, and also studied at Eric Gill's Catholic Guild of St Joseph and St Dominic. He later went to the Royal College of Art under the tutelage of Robert Goodden, and where he subsequently became Professor of Silversmithing and Jewellery. He also studied ecclesiastical metalwork under Dunstan Pruden. In 1957 he was appointed designer to the manufacturing goldsmiths, Viners of Sheffield, and two years later he was commissioned by Sir Basil Spence to provide the altar plate for the new Coventry Cathedral. In 1964 Benney bought Beenham House in Berkshire and developed his 'trade-mark' the textured silver surface which has a considerable side benefit of not showing finger marks. In 1971 he was appointed to the Faculty of Royal Designers for Industry and two years later was honoured with a retrospective exhibition at Goldsmiths' Hall.[24] Apart from many City Companies, Gerald Benney ranks among his clients the late Shah of Persia, the Corporation of the City of Reading, Leicester and Southampton Universities, the Institute of Chartered Accountants and the Archbishops of Canterbury and Philadelphia. In addition he holds warrants from Her Majesty The Queen, the Duke of Edinburgh, Queen Elizabeth, the Queen Mother and the Prince of Wales. Although actively involved with gold-smithing today, Prof. Benney is pursuing a second career as a painter.

A surprisingly bold and early commission was to celebrate the opening of the new Hall in 1956. Benney produced an elegantly fluted covered cup, a traditional concept but made entirely in the idiom of the 1950s. A cup in gold for use of the Master, presented by Sir Richard Jenks, and a goblet presented by Commander Prevett for the use of the Clerk, in 1966 heralded the commissioning of several similar vessels for the Court. In the following year a pair of two-light candelabra were bought from Gerald Benney from a bequest to the Company from P. E. M. Shaw, Master in 1964–5, and a pair of claret jugs were commissioned in 1973 by P. B. Powell, Master in 1969–70, and F. S. Bird, Master in 1972–3.

The vicissitudes of the Haberdashers' Company plate during the Civil War, and through subsequent changes of taste demonstrate the role of silver in the history of a city organisation, which could equally well be applied to private owners although their possessions are frequently less well documented. Their dogged retention of old plate, particularly the Hamersley Salt and the Ivatt Cup, indicates the Company's sense of history whilst their later commissions show their sense of taste and patronage. But above all the collection of silver and silver-gilt demonstrates the Company's wealth, confidence and stability.

24. London, Goldsmiths' Hall, *Gerald Benney* (1973)

Appendix IIIb

Chronological Catalogue of the Principal Pieces of Plate

Historic Plate

The Hamersley Salt
An Elizabeth I silver-gilt standing salt on circular domed base, cast with lobes and a band of ovolo moulding and embossed and chased with a frieze of figures in rural and family pursuits, the drum chased with The Silver Age, after a description in Ovid's *Metamorphoses* (Book I, line 144ff), a man ploughing with an ox, while others till the soil, and a woman sits with her two children by a fire beneath a shelter, bordered above and below by ropework, the convex capital chased with birds, foliage and flowers on a matted ground, beneath a further band of ovolo and lobes, the upper surface engraved 'The Guift of Sr Hugh Hamersley Kt and Alderman of London 1636', the detachable salt well with ovolo and guilloche borders, London, 1595–6, maker's mark TN over a cinquefoil in a shaped shield (Ian Pickford, *Jackson's Gold and Silver Marks*, 1989, p. 103).

Height: 8¼ ins.
Weight: 42 ozs. 5 dwts.
Literature: Philippa Glanville, *Silver in Tudor and Early Stuart England*, (1990), pp. 159, 280, 291.
Sir Charles Jackson, *History of English Plate*, (2 vols, 1916), I. 197–8, figs. 211 and 212
Exhibited: London, Burlington Fine Arts Club, 1901, No. F.7
London, Goldsmiths' Hall, 1951, No. 58

Formerly with a cover of 18 ozs. 10 dwts. sold to Mr. Viner, goldsmith, by order of the Court of Assistants, 1642–3; some splits to chasing; regilt.

The Ivatt Cup
A Charles I standing cup on circular trumpet foot with cast borders of ovolo moulding and chased with foliage and shells, the knopped stem with two floral mereses, and with traces of brackets on the knop, the flaring bowl chased with female demi-figures holding the arms of the City of London, the Company and Ivatt, between auricular cartouches enclosing scenes from the Book of Tobit: Tobias and the great fish, Tobias and Sarah at prayer with the Archangel Raphael in the background and Tobias healing his father's sight, engraved 'The Guift of Thomas Ivatt deceased Anº Dom.1629', London, 1629–30, maker's mark RB over a mullet in a shaped shield.

Height: 12 ins.
Weight: 27 ozs.
Literature: Philippa Glanville, *Silver in Tudor and Early Stuart England* (1990) p. 160
Exhibited: London, Burlington Fine Arts Club, 1901, No. F.3
London, Goldsmiths' Hall, 1951, No. 89
Brussels, Europalia, L'Orfèvrerie de la Cité de Londres, 1975, No. 35

Originally supplied with a cover, probably with an openwork steeple, which weighed 12 ozs. 5 dwts. which survived the 1642–3 sale of plate but had been lost or disposed of by 1694–5.

The White Cups
A pair of Charles I beer cups, each on a shallow conical foot, with baluster stem and bucket-shaped bowl, engraved 'The gift of Edward White Esquier, 1634', London, 1634–5, maker's mark WS over a pellet.

Height: 7¾ ins.
Weight: 25 ozs. 5dwts.

Originally part of 'One nest of beere bowles, white' which weighed 38 ozs. 15 dwts (Accounts of the Wardens, 1639–40). All three cups survived until at least 1732, and the fate of the third cup is apparently unrecorded.

The Company's Cup
A Charles I silver-gilt standing cup, the trumpet foot cast with ovolo borders and chased with foliage, the stem with a knop between two mereses and with three grotesque brackets, the bowl chased with foliage and strapwork and pounced with the Company's arms and those of Hudson(?), and with the inscription 'Fides ex Caritas Agens Valet', London, 1637–8, maker's mark PP a crescent above and below.

Height: 16¼ ins.
Weight: 46 ozs.

The arms would appear to be those of Hudson, although the absence of tincturing makes a positive identification difficult. Robert Hudson was Master in 1635 and it would seem most likely that the cup was a gift to the Company from him. However, there is no corresponding cup in the Accounts of the Wardens (even allowing for the fact that the cup originally had a lid and would therefore have weighed approximately 60 ozs. in total), until the piece was included in the inventory of 1732, the inscription being specifically mentioned.

The Willimot Cups
A pair of Charles I beer cups, each on shallow conical foot, with baluster stem and bucket-shaped bowl, engraved 'The Gift of Symon Wilimot haberdasher to the Worshipful Company of Haberdashers 1648', London, 1648–9, maker's mark illegible.

Height: 7¼ ins.
Weight: 27 ozs.
Exhibited: London, Goldsmiths' Hall, 1951, No. 100

Originally part of 'One nest of Beere bolles' which were recorded with a tankard in the Accounts of the Wardens, 1649–50, weighing a total of 69 ozs. 10 dwts., and subsequently in the Wardens' Accounts for 1694 and 1732 without the tankard at 40 ozs. 15 dwts. All three cups survived until at least 1732, and the fate of the third cup is apparently unrecorded.

The Stone Cups
A pair of Commonwealth silver-gilt standing cups, each on domed moulded foot decorated with a band of matting, the baluster stem chased with foliage and bucket-shaped matted bowl, engraved with the arms of Stone, and the inscription 'The Guift of Thomas Stone Esq', London, 1649–50, maker's mark an orb.

Height: 11½ ins.
Weight: 65 ozs.

Probably originally supplied with covers, since in the Accounts of the Wardens for 1649–50 their weight is given a 82 ozs. 5 dwts. and by 1694 the weight had been reduced to 62 ozs. 15 dwts. However no mention of covers appears in the earlier inventory.

The Arnold Flagons
A pair of Charles II flagons, each on moulded flaring foot, the plain slightly tapering cylindrical bodies engraved with the arms of Arnold within a foliate cartouche and the inscription 'The gift of Tho Arnold Esq 1670', with scrolling handle, the cushion moulded cover with crested thumbpiece pierced with a heart, London, 1670–1, maker's mark II.

Height: 15¾ ins.
Weight: 178 ozs.

The Smithson Tankard
A Charles II plain cylindrical tankard on moulded domed foot, with a moulded band to the body and engraved with the arms of Smithson and the Company and the inscription 'The Gift of Sr. Hugh Smithson of Stanwicke in ye County of Yorke, Kt & Barronett one of ye Assistants of this Company 20 Jan^ry Anno 1670', with plain domed cover engraved with the crest of Smithson and with scroll handle and couchant lion thumbpiece, by Thomas Jenkins, London, 1672–3.

Height: 8¼ ins.
Weight: 46 ozs.

This would appear to be one of two tankards given by Hugh Smithson, Master in 1756. The other, lighter example was recorded in 1694–5, but had been converted into a salver by 1714 (see below).

The Company's Monteith
A William and Mary monteith on circular spirally gadrooned foot, the hemispherical body chased with scrolls and foliage and engraved with the Company's arms and crest, the notched rim with foliate scroll between cherubs' heads, and with lion's mask drop handles, engraved under the foot 'The Haberdashers Company 58 = 15', by Francis Garthorne, London, 1693–4.

Diameter: 13½ ins.
Weight: 57 ozs.
Literature: Georgina Lee, *English Silver Monteith Bowls* (1978) No. 50

The Ratcliffe Cup
A George I silver-gilt standing cup on moulded trumpet foot with baluster stem and bell-shaped bowl with moulding to the body, engraved with the Company's arms and crest each in a Baroque cartouche, and inscribed under the base 'Applied hereto 31 = 18 the Gift of Mr. Hugh Ratcliffe sen^r 33 = 12', London, 1714–15, maker's mark illegible.

Height: 13¼ ins.
Weight: 33 ozs.

A gift of a salver from Mr. Radcliffe weighing 59 ozs. is recorded in the 1694 inventory but this would appear to be too heavy for the piece of plate, weighing 31 ozs. 18 dwts., referred to in the inscription under the base of the cup.

The Smithson and Barnes Salvers
A pair of George I salvers, each on moulded trumpet foot, with moulded borders and engraved with the Company's arms and crest, one engraved beneath 'Applied hereto 35 = 0 the Gift of Hugh Smithson Esq. 36 = 15' and the other 'Applied hereto 35 = 15 the Gift of Thomas Barnes Esq. 36 = 19', London, 1714–15, maker's mark illegible.

Diameter: 12¼ ins.
Weight: 71 ozs.

The inscriptions on these salvers indicate that they were made from the gifts of tankards of the weights specified givein by Thomas Barnes and Hugh Smithson, Masters in 1655 and 1656, which are recorded in the 1694 inventory.

The Aldersey Candlestick
A George I octagonal candlestick on faceted domed base with octagonal baluster stem and faceted moulded socket, engraved with the Company's arms, and inscribed under the base '21 = 8 Applied hereto 21 = 2 ye gift of Mr Aldersey', by Robert Timbrell and Joseph Bell, London, 1714–15.

Height: 12 ins.
Weight: 20 ozs.

This candlestick was made from the gift of 'One nest of wine bowls' from Samuel Aldersey and recorded in the Accounts of the Wardens in 1639–40, 1649–50, and presumably amongst the 21 wine bowls listed together in 1694. According to the 1732 inventory there were originally four sticks made.

Associated Three-light Candle Branches

Associated three-light candle branches, with central octagonal section, and scrolling knopped branches, with plain moulded drip pans and cylindrical sockets, one pan inscribed 'Ex dono Issac Pyke Anno 1724', by Richard Watts, London, *c.*1724, Britannia Standard mark struck four times.

Weight: 28 ozs.
The only set of candle branches recorded in 1732.
Literature: Michael Clayton, *The Collector's Dictionary of the Silver and Gold of Great Britain and North America*, (2nd ed. 1985), p. 51
Exhibited: London, Goldsmiths' Hall, 1926, Plate XXXIV
London, Goldsmiths' Hall, 1951, No. 201

The Wyberd Monteith

A George I monteith on circular spirally gadrooned foot, the hemispherical body chased with scrolls and foliage and engraved with the Company's arms and crest, the notched rim with foliate scrolls between cherub's heads, and with lion's mask drop handles, engraved under the foot 'Applied hereto 64 = 6 the Gift of Mr. John Wyberd 65 = 13', by Robert Timbrell, London, 1714–15.

Diameter: 13 ins.
Weight: 64 ozs.

Made to match the Company's Monteith of 1693–4, and memorialising the gift of 'Three nests of wine bowles, white' from John Wiburd (*sic*) recorded in the Wardens' Accounts for 1639–40 but sold to Mr. Viner, goldsmith, in 1642–3.

The Wakefield Cup

A George III two handled cup and cover, on moulded foot chased with water leaves, and with fluted trumpet stem, the partly fluted body with bands of scrolling foliage and swags of fruiting vine with an oval relief of infant Bacchantes, and another oval reserve later engraved with the arms of Wakefield and the Company, with leaf-capped scroll handles, the cover chased with a border of scrolling foliage and water leaves and with cone finial and later engraved 'The Gift of Col. and Alderman Sir Charles Cheers Wakefield Bart. C.B.E. Lord Mayor 1915–16 Master of the Company 1926–7' by William Holmes, London, 1788–9.

Height: 17½ ins.
Weight: 73 ozs.

The Hawes Warwick Vase

A George IV silver-gilt Warwick Vase on square base, the body cast and applied with Bacchanalian masks, lion's pelts, thyrsi, foliage and trailing vines, with vine tendril handles and egg and dart everted rim, by Paul Storr, London, 1821–2, mounted on a square plinth, engraved with a dedicatory inscription to William Hawes dated 1851, by Barnard Brothers, London, 1830–1.

Height: 15½ ins.
Exhibited: Brussels, Europalea, L'Orfèvrerie de la Cité de Londres (1975) No. 35
Vancouver, Centennial Museum, *Treasures of London* (1977)

The Dodd Warwick Vase

An Edward VII Warwick Vase of similar form, the base inscribed 'This replica of the Warwick Vase was given to the Haberdashers' Company by Major E. A. Dodd T. D. Past Master in commemoration of the 500th Anniversary of its charter of incorporation granted by King Henry VI 3 June 1448' and the arms of Dodd and the Company and 'Master Richard Redfern Lechmere James Esq. Wardens Ernest Harold Potter Esq, Stanley Marcus Pettit Esq, Col. William Reid Glover C.M.G., D.S.O.,

T.D., J.P. Charles Graham Gardner Esq. M.C., Guy Eagleton Clerk', London, 1909–10, maker's mark of Pairpoint Brothers overstriking another.

Weight: 11½ ozs.

Double Snuff-Box
A silver-gilt and wood double snuff-box, the cover formed from a bargemaster's badge chased with the Company's arms within a wreath, and two reserves engraved 'Thomas Carew, Edward Smith 1689' and 'Peter Mortimer, William Ambler, Wardens'. and engraved within '1865 Benjamin Edgington Esq. Master, Drew Woods Esq. Matthew Warton Johnson Esq. James Warren Esq. John Brown Esq. Wardens' and 'Goldsmiths' Hall, 1 March 1866. This box weighing 31 ozs. 0 dwt. was made to receive a chased silver shield of unknown Assay' with plain wooden base, by Garrard & Co., London, 1865–6.

Length: 9½ ins.

The Charles Arnold Cup
An Edward VII standing cup and cover, on trumpet foot chased with honeysuckle, with knopped stem and flaring bowl chased with foliage and flowers on a matted ground and set with four cabochons of lapis lazuli, the domed cover chased with stylised foliage and with onion finial, engraved 'Gilbert Marks 1902', by Gilbert Marks, London, 1901–2.

Height: 16½ ins.
Weight: 39 ozs 10 dwts.

The Gift of Charles Arnold 1958

The Master's Badge
A jewelled and enamelled gold cartouche-shaped, modelled as the Company's arms, set with rubies, sapphires and diamonds, supported by white gold goats and flanked by figures of St Katherine each holding a ruby set wheel, above a diamond set ribbon enamelled in blue inscribed 'Serve and obey', above diamond strapwork and swags of gold roses, the whole surmounted by a white and yellow gold helmet with the Company's crest enamelled in flesh tones and set with emeralds, bordered by further diamond strapwork, inscribed on the back, 'Provided by the Haberdashers' Company for the Master A.D. 1875. The Right Hon. W. J. R. Cotton, Lord Mayor of London, M. C. and Senior Representative of the City, Master'.

*c.*1875
3¾ ins. high

The silver of Omar Ramsden and Alwyn Carr

The Blundell Mustard and Pepper
An Edward VII capstan-shaped mustard pot, the upper section chased with foliage, and with fruit and flower brackets, with domed cover, the scroll handle with wirework thumbpiece, engraved under the base 'Omar Ramsden et Alwyn Carr me fecerunt' and later 'The Gift of Richard Sutherland Blundell, Master 1961–2' and a matching pepper caster with pierced cover, similarly engraved, by Omar Ramsden and Alwyn Carr, London, 1908–10.

Height: Mustard – 4¾ ins., pepper – 4¼ ins.
Weight: 15 ozs.

The Osborn Salts
A pair of Edward VII silver-gilt drum salts, each on domed foot cast with an ovolo border and chased with foliage, the drum chased with the Company's arms, motto and supporters, and the arms and motto of Osborn, beneath a further band of foliage, and around the salt well a border of ovolo and the inscription 'The Gift of S. Osborn Esq of the Haberdashers' Company 1910–11' and engraved

under the base 'Omar Ramsden et Alwyn Carr me Fecerunt', by Omar Ramsden and Alwyn Carr, London, 1909–10.

Height: 6½ ins.
Weight: 48 ozs.

These salts were clearly modelled on the Hamersley Salt to which Ramsden and Carr presumably had access.

The Col. H. L. Florence Basin
A George V massive circular basin, with plain moulded border, chased around with foliage and flowers, and the arms, crest and motto of Florence, the well chased with the inscription 'I was wrought for the Haberdashers' Company by command of Lieut. Col. Henry Louis Florence T.D. to commemorate his Mastership A.S. MCMXIV-XV' the raised print chased with waves and the Company's arms, crest, motto and supporters, the base engraved 'Omar Ramsden et Alwyn Carr me Fecerunt', by Omar Ramsden and Alwyn Carr, London, 1915–16.

Diameter: 24 ins.

The E. B. Florence Cup
A George V silver-gilt standing cup and cover, the moulded foot applied with a band of foliage and Tudor roses, the trumpet stem with interlaced rose collar, the double ogee bowl engraved with the first and second grant of the Company's arms and the arms of Florence and the inscription 'I was wrought for the Worshipful Company of Haberdashers by Command of Ernest Louis Florence to mark his year of office as Master in the years of our Lord 1915 and 1916', the domed cover with a border of shields engraved with the arms of the City of London and heraldic devices and the mottoes of the Company and Florence, with the finial formed as St Katherine, by Omar Ramsden, London, 1924–5.

Height: 21 ins.
Weight: 88 ozs.

The Haberdashers' Company Golf Challenge Cup
A George V silver-gilt standing cup, on trumpet foot cast with a border of ovolo and foliage, and chased with foliage and scrolls, the knopped stem set with two mereses and three brackets, the bowl chased with foliage and engraved with the arms of the Company and Florence and the inscription 'I was wrought for the Worshipful Company of Haberdashers by command of Ernest B. Florence, Past Master June 1924', by Omar Ramsden, London, 1924–5, on silver and silver-gilt mounted plinth engraved with names and dates.

Height: 13⅝ ins.
Weight: 45 ozs. 10 dwts.

The foot and stem of this cup is based on that of the Ivatt Cup while the bowl follows the form of the Company's Cup.

The Tuckett Casters
Three George V hexagonal sugar casters each on trumpet foot chased with the inscription 'The Gift of Phillip Debell Tuckett Liveryman and Assistant Nov. 1933' and with stepped tapering bodies engraved with the Company's arms, and with pierced detachable covers, by Omar Ramsden, London, one 1930–1, and two 1933–4.

Height: 8½ ins.
Weight: 48 ozs.

Three George V octagonal sugar casters, each on stepped foot, the vase-shaped bodies engraved with the Company's arms, and with detachable domed pierced covers, each engraved with the same inscription as the preceeding, and engraved under the foot 'Omar Ramsden me fecit', by Omar Ramsden, London, one 1933–4, two 1934–5.

Height: 9 ins.
Weight: 52 ozs.

The Eagleton St Katherine Figure
A George V silver-gilt figure of St Katherine, the square base engraved 'Omar Ramsden me fecit', on silver mounted ebonised socle inscribed 'St Katherine, Patron of the Company, Virgin and Martyr' with the Company's arms and 'The Gift of John Eagleton, Liveryman 1882. Clerk of the Company 1907 to 1930 and thereafter a member of the Court of Assistants', by Omar Ramsden, London, 1935–6.

Height: 12¾ ins.

Silver and gold by Gerald Benney

A Standing Cup and Cover
An Elizabeth II standing cup and cover on plain circular foot engraved 'Commissioned by the Worshipful Company of Haberdashers to Commemorate the Opening of Haberdashers Hall on 28 June 1956', the slightly tapering cylindrical stem and funnel-shaped bowl chased with flutes, the conical cover similarly fluted, and engraved with the Company's arms, with ball finial, engraved under the foot 'Des and made by Gerald Benney', by Gerald Benney, London, 1956–7.

Height: 19¾ ins.
Weight: 50 ozs.

The Jenks Cup
An Elizabeth II gold goblet on square foot with textured border engraved 'The Gift of Sir Richard Jenks, Assistant 1966, for the use of the Master' and the crest of Jenks, with polished cylindrical stem and textured bowl, engraved with the Company's arms, by Gerald Benney, London, 1966–7. 18 carat.

Height: 6¾ ins.
Weight: 18 ozs.

An Elizabeth II smaller similar gold cup engraved under the base 'A replica of the Master's cup, Haberdashers' Company', by Gerald Benney, London, 1967–8. 18 carat.

Height: 5 ins.
Weight: 9 ozs.

An Elizabeth II silver-gilt cup, similar, engraved 'The Gift of the Haberdashers' Company to Col. and Ald. Sir Cullum Welch, Bt., O.B.E., M.C., Master 1966–7', by Gerald Benney, London, 1967–8.

Height: 6¾ ins.
Weight: 14 ozs.

An Elizabeth II goblet, on plain polished foot and stem, engraved 'The Gift of Commander Harry Prevett, O.B.E., R.N. Clerk 1950–66 for the use of the Clerk', the textured cylindrical bowl engraved with the Company's arms, by Gerald Benney, London, 1966–7.

Four Elizabeth II goblets each on circular polished foot, with textured cylindrical bowls engraved with the Company's arms, and each with a dedicatory inscription dated 1967 relating to Mr. K. M. Leach, Mr. R. T. Hawes, Col. Sir Cullum Welch and Major C. H. K. Fisher, by Gerald Benney, London, 1967–8. And three similar by Gerald Benney, London, 1977–8 and 1978–9.

Height: 5 ins.
Weight: 73 ozs.

A pair of Elizabeth II two light candelabra each on rectangular base, with the central depression supporting a textured column, engraved with the Company's arms, with a polished collar and two branches with cylindrical textured sockets and detachable polished nozzles, with an octagonal pyramid between, and engraved under the base 'These candelabra were commissioned in 1967 from Gerald

Benney, Silversmith, using a bequest of the late P. E. M. Shaw, Master of the Company, 1964–5' and stamped 'Gerald Benney, London', by Gerald Benney, London, 1967–8.

Height: 25 ins.
Weight: 168 ozs.

An Elizabeth II goblet on plain polished circular foot, engraved 'Presented by the Haberdashers' Company to Vice Admiral J. S. C. Salter, Master 1970–1', the textured cylindrical bowl engraved with the Company's arms, by Gerald Benney, London, 1970–1.

Height: 5 ins.
Weight: 7 ozs.

An Elizabeth II plain slightly flaring cylindrical textured beaker, engraved 'G. T. B. 1974', by Gerald Benney, London, 1971–2.

Height: 4 ins.
Weight: 7 ozs.

A pair of Elizabeth II claret jugs, each of textured flask form, engraved with the Company's arms, with polished scroll handle and flaring neck, one engraved 'Given by Patrick Boileau Powell A. F. C. Master 1969–70' and the other 'Given by Fraser Stephen Bird, T. D. Master 1972–3', the bases stamped 'Gerald Benney, London', by Gerald Benney, London, 1973–4.

Height: 12⅛ ins.
Weight: 68 ozs.

Appendix IV

The Company's Minor Charities

Charity	Object
William Adams' Corpus Christi Exhibition Established by agreement, dated 1 April 1958, under the Scheme of the Adams' Newport Charity dated 8 December 1909.	Scholarships for pupils educated at Adams' Grammar School, nominated by the Headmaster.
William Adams' Eleemosynary Charity Governed by an Order of the Charity Commissioners dated 25 July 1963, supplemented by a Scheme dated 10 November 1965 and an Order dated 16 November 1979	Covering the cost of repairs and insurance of the Charity's property, and other administrative expenses.
Thomas Aldersey's Charity Established by letter patent dated 2 January 1594.	The net income is allocated in fixed proportion between the Preacher and Vicar of Bunbury, the Aldersey Educational Charity (q.v.), and the poor of Bunbury; the Company's poor receive £6 p.a.
Thomas Aldersey's, Educational Charity Established under a scheme dated 26 April 1935	The net income is paid to the school managers. From 1965 £200 p.a. was set aside for repairs and the balance paid annually to the School Managers; from 1977 the sum for repairs was increased to £350 p.a.
Thomas Arno Bequest By his will Thomas Arno, who died 30 May 1937, established a trust for his widow, his grandchildren and their children. The residue of the income after providing for these annuities was to be paid to the Bequest, which was also the residuary legatee.	Assisting boys and girls whilst at or after leaving the Company's schools, and grants to these schools for the benefit of young people; grants to poor Freemen and Liverymen or their relations or other poor deserving persons; starting or assisting young men being British

subjects in business;
donations or subscriptions
to hospitals, convalescent
homes and other institutions
or other purposes for public
benefit.

John Banks' Trust
Established by the will and
deed of appointment dated 21
March 1717 of John Banks
(Master 1717).

Annual payments to the
Congregational Chapel in
Bethnal Green Road, 10
inhabitants of the parish
of St Saviour, Southwark,
10 inhabitants of the parish
of St Mary, Battersea, and the
Preacher and Sexton of St
Lawrence Jewry; pensions to
the Company's poor payable
under the original will are
now governed by a Scheme dated
13 April 1972 which provides
that pensioners shall be poor
Company Freemen and their
widows.

The Barker Trust
The late Miss Phyllis Barker
bequeathed her residuary
estate to the St Catherine
Foundation (q.v.) in memory
of her father, Benjamin
Barker (Liveryman 1902).

Martha Barrett's Charity
Established by will dated 25
September 1584.

Annuities for the poor of the
parishes of Isleworth and
Totteridge, Middlesex.

Olive Blair's Charity
Established by the will of
Olive Blair (a member of the
staff of Haberdashers' Aske's
Hatcham Girls' School, 1916-
1950) who died on 8 April
1961.

Silver brooches for the three
Head Girls of the Hatcham
Girls' School annually, and
a contribution towards
refreshments for the school's
staff on Foundation Day; the
residue is used for the
benefit of the Hatcham Girls'
School and the Haberdashers'
Aske's Girls' School at Elstree.

Buckland's Charity
Established by the will dated
22 August 1573 of Richard
Buckland (Freeman 1532)

An annuity for the parish of
Shepperton.

Lady Burghley's Charity
Established in 1583 by an endowment of £200 given by Lady Mildred Burghley (wife of Lord Burghley, Treasurer to Queen Elizabeth).

An annuity for the parish of Cheshunt, Hertfordshire.

The Henry Chester Bequest
Established by will dated 14 February 1898 of Henry Chester (Third Warden 1892).

An annuity for Guys Hospital.

Frances Clarke's Charity
Established in 1608 by an endowment of £200 given Mrs. Frances Clarke.

An exhibition at Christ Church, Oxford, and another at any college at Cambridge.

R. S. Cochrane Bequest
Established by will dated 9 July 1984 of Reginald Cochrane (a pupil of Haberdashers' Aske's Hatcham Boys' School 1909-1915).

Scholarships in metallurgy, material sciences, electronics or medicine for scholars of the Hatcham Boys' School at universities or institutions of higher education.

J. E. Cooper Charity
Established by trust deed, dated 15 August 1960, and endowed from the residue of the estate of the late John Cooper (Assistant).

Covering one year's costs for any person undergoing a course of education or travel outside the United Kingdom or Ireland; the Company can give preference to Liverymen or their children or grandchildren.

Culverwell's Charity
Established by will dated 22 October 1569 of Nicholas Culverwell.

Awards for two preachers studying divinity at Christ's College, Cambridge and Magdalen College, Oxford, nominated by the Bishop of London.

Curtis Scholarship
Endowed in July 1874 by John Curtis (Assistant, previously Clerk 1849-1876)

A scholarship for a child or grandchild of a Company Liveryman, tenable at any secondary school approved by trustees, for a period of three years; the award is now made to the child obtaining the highest marks in the

annual examinations for the
Haberdashers' Aske's
Exhibitions.

E. A. Dodd Trust
Established by trust deed
dated 24 April 1974, by E. T.
W. Dodd (Master, 1960) in
memory of his father, the late
Major E. A. Dodd (Master
1940).

Awards to ex-pupils of the
Aske's Hatcham Schools for
study to become retail
jewellers, silversmiths,
goldsmiths, or members of the
Gemmological Association of
Great Britain; in the absence
of suitable applicants, the
trustees have discretion to
make awards for courses in
art or other charitable
purposes.

Dyson Memorial Fund
Established by a trust deed
dated 22 February 1965, and
endowed by subscription from
former pupils and colleagues
in memory of Miss E. G. Dyson
(Headmistress of Haberdashers'
Aske's Hatcham Girls' School
1943-8).

Relief of poverty amongst
girls attending Haberdashers'
Aske's Hatcham Girls School,
their parents, and girls who
have attended the school.

E. B. Florence Trust
Endowed in 1933 by Miss E. E.
Florence (sister of Mr. E. B.
Florence, Master 1915).

Income is divided equally
between pensioners
benefiting from the Banks'
Charity (q.v.).

Freeman's Charity
Endowed by Mrs. Elizabeth
Freeman in 1630.

An annuity for the poor of
of the parish of Aspenden,
Hertfordshire.

Haberdashers' Donations Trust
Endowment from the residue of
the estate of W. F. Dyer
(Master 1954), supplemented by
a covenanted donation of
£3,000 p.a. from the
Haberdashers' Company.

The Haberdashers' Company Eleemosynary Charity
Established by a Scheme dated
17 May 1978, which
consolidated a number of
Charities mostly dating from
the 16th and 17th centuries:
Robert Aske's Eleemosynary,

Grants to those in need, hardship
or distress; two thirds of
the income can be applied
to Freemen of the Company
or the City of London and
their wives and children.

Thomas Barnes, Robert
Boddington and Edmund Boulter,
William Bond, William Cleave,
the Haberdashers' Consolidated
Charities for the Poor (which
had consisted of the charities
of Sir George Barne, Richard
Buckland, Thomas Cleave,
George French, Joseph Holden,
Thomas Huntlowe, Thomas
Johnson, William Jones, Robert
Offley, Mary Paradyne, Dame
Rebecca Romeney, Henry Somer,
Thomas Arnold, Thomas
Carpenter, and Sir Stephen
Peacock), Edmund Hammond, John
Hobby, Sir Nicholas Rainton,
the Loan Fund Bearing Interest
(which had consisted of the
charities of John Whyte,
Thomas Bowcher, Richard
Gourney, Dame Mary Ramsay,
Mary Monox, Catherine Hall,
John Howes and Clement Kelke),
Anne Whitmore, Martha Wood and
William Henry Wood.

Edmund Hammond's Charity (Blakeney)
Endowed by Edmund Hammond   The income of the Charity is
(Freeman 1598) by will dated   now paid to the incumbent as
25 February 1639; the   contribution towards his
advowsons of the Rectory of   expenses.
Awre and the Chapelry of
Blakeney, in Gloucestershire,
were purchased.

(See Appendix V, The Company's
Advowsons)

Haslefoot's Charity
Established by deed dated 22   Annuities to Company Freemen,
August 1646, and endowed by   St Thomas' Hospital, St
Henry Haslefoot (Freeman 1583)   Bartholomew's Hospital, and
                                   the City and Metropolitan
                                   Welfare Charity.

Hatcham Schools' Centenary Scholarship
Established by trust deed   An annual scholarship (awarded
1 May 1975 to commemorate   alternately to boys and girls) for a
the centenary of the founding   school leaver who is going on
of the Hatcham Schools.   to any place of higher education.

R. T. Hawes Memorial Scholarships
Established by trust deed
dated 22 March 1984, and
endowed by Mr. R. T. Hawes
(Master 1968).

Annual scholarships for a boy
or boys at one or more of the
Company's schools towards the
cost of education while at
school; preference is given
to boys intending to make
a career in insurance.

Hutchinson and Gournay Scholarship Fund
Established by will dated 19
August 1575 of John Hutchinson
(Freeman 1539) and will dated
1596 of Richard Gournay
(Master 1589 and 1596); the
foundation is now governed by
the Haberdashers' Company Loan
Fund Bearing Interest Scheme
Confirmation Act 1912, and the
Scheme dated 31 January 1980.

Assistance for students of
divinity at Oxford or
Cambridge.

Jeston's Charity
Established by will dated 2
April 1622 of Roger Jeston
(Freeman 1575); now governed
by a Scheme dated 6 April 1897
(as amended by a varying
Scheme dated 20 October 1966).

An exhibition at Trinity
College, Cambridge; other
beneficiaries are poor hatmakers,
poor clergymen, the parish of
Lambeth, St Thomas' Hospital
St Bartholomew's Hospital,
the poor of the parish of
Kinver in Staffordshire,
and poor Freemen of the
Company and of the City of
London.

The Jones Lectureship Charity
Endowed by William Jones in
1614, the Charity is now
governed by a Scheme dated 3
July 1953 (as amended by a
varying Scheme dated 22
February 1957 and further
varying Schemes dated 28
August 1974 and 31 October
1984).

A stipend for a Jones'
Lecturer (or Lecturers) to
deliver a sermon (or course
of sermons) in a church in
the City of London; stipends
for Jones' Preachers, who
must be incumbents of
parishes within 10 miles
of Haberdashers' Hall.

K. M. Leach Trust
Established by deed of trust
dated 21 October 1969, and
endowed by Mr. Kenneth Leach
(Assistant).

Assisting charitable
foundations at the Trustees'
absolute discretion (in
practice the income is made
available in grants to pupils
or former pupils of Adams'

Grammar School, or used for
special projects at the
school excluding buildings;
the Christopher Nash Memorial
Scholarship.

Loan Funds without Interest
An amalgamation of several
endowments from Company
members and others, now
governed by the Regulation
made in the Court of Chancery
in 1834.

Interest free loans for poor
Company Freemen.

Northcott Travelling Scholarships
Established by trust deed
dated 8 September 1959, and
endowed by Commander Walter
Northcott.

Travelling scholarships for
pupils of King's College
School Wimbledon,
Haberdashers' Aske's School,
and University College
(Senior) School.

Nunn Trust
Established following the sale
of 'Oakdene', Bunbury.

Donations towards the
expenses of Vicars of Bunbury
(past or present) incurred
generally speaking in the
discharge of their duties.

Robert Offley's Charity
Established by will, dated 9
April 1596 of Robert Offley
(Freeman 1585).

A scholarship tenable at the
Universities of Oxford and
Cambridge by the
Haberdashers' Company and the
Corporation of Chester; no
scholarships have been
awarded since 1973, but part
of the annual income is used
to augment Nicholas
Culverwell's Charity (q.v.).

Paradine's Charity
Established by indenture dated
4 September 1629 and endowed
by Mrs. Mary Paradine.

Annual grants to four poor
preachers.

Picken's Bequest
Established by will, dated 1
December 1945 of Charles
Picken.

A scholarship in pharmacy
for a boy attending Adams'
Grammar School, paid through
the Pharmaceutical Society
of Great Britain.

Pinchin Foundation
Established by trust deed

Grants or loans to poor

dated 14 April 1969, and
endowed by Miss Barbara
Pinchin.

Powell Travelling Bursaries
Established by trust deed
dated 18 August 1982, and
endowed by Mr. P. B. Powell
(Master 1969)

deserving people, and other
charitable purposes.

A bursary for a sixth form
pupil at Monmouth School or
Monmouth School for Girls in
his or her last year at
school, or to an ex-pupil
who has left within the
previous twelve months, to
cover all or part of the
costs of an educational trip
outside the British Isles.
The bursary is awarded
alternately to boys and
girls.

Henry Paul Prosser Trust
Established by the will of
Constance Prosser, who died 18
October 1967.

Augmenting the annual payments
under Jeston's Charity (q.v.) to
poor Church of England
clergymen, or their wives
and children.

Lady Romeney's Charity
Established by Dame Rebecca
Romeney (widow of Sir William
Romeney, Master 1603 and 1609)
by indenture dated 4 September
1629.

Four exhibitions for divinity
students; two at Emmanuel
College, Cambridge and two
at Sidney Sussex College,
Cambridge.

St Catherine Foundation
(including the Barker Trust)
Established by trust deed
dated 23 September 1970.

Assistance for pupils
attending fee-paying schools,
usually those in their final
year(s) at school who would
otherwise have to leave
before sitting public
examinations.

Shingler's Charity
Established by indenture dated
22 March 1617 by Thomas
Shingler (Freeman 1603).

An annuity for the poor of
Rugby.

Simon Stuart Scholarship
Endowed in 1980.

An annual bursary for a boy
attending the Haberdashers'
Aske's School.

Trotman's Charity
Established by will dated 30

October 1663 of Throckmorton
Trotman, the charity is now
adminstered as two separate
charities:

Trotman 'A' Educational Charity
Governed by a Scheme dated 28
March 1912 (as amended by
varying Schemes dated 16 May
1966 and 30 June 1969).

(a)   senior exhibitions
tenable at universities
and other colleges
of further education.
(b)   junior exhibitions tenable
at secondary schools or other
educational institutions.

2. *Trotman 'B' Non-Educational Charity*
Established by a Scheme dated
10th July 1937.

the income is distributed
proportionately to the
Company's poor, St John's
Church Hoton, St Giles
and St Luke's joint
parochial charities, the
parish of Cam, the Rector
of Dursley and a preacher
appointed by the Company.

Lady Weld's Charity
Established by the will of
Dame Mary Weld dated 12
February 1624 under which the
following livings were purchases:

The income is paid annually
to Chertsey church.

Vicarage of Albrighton, Shropshire
Vicarage of Bitteswell,
Leicestershire
Vicarge of Chertsey, Surrey
Vicarage of Diseworth,
Leicestershire
Perpetual Curacy of Leiston, Suffolk
Vicarage of Wigston Magna,
Leicestershire.

See Appendix V, The Company's
Advowsons

Richard Wynne's Charity
Established in 1679 by the
endowment of Richard Wynne
(Master 1672).

The income is divided equally
between the parish of Chad
Parochial Trustees and
apprenticing a Freeman's
son; by a Scheme dated
2 November 1950, the
apprentice's award can be
used to assist a Freeman's
son by way of further education

Appendix V

The Company's Advowsons

The Company holds the patronage of 11 livings, administered under four separate charities. The churches range from pre-Conquest foundations to Victorian parishes designed to cope with the spiritual needs of the expanding London suburbs; they are all very different in character. In many cases, either the patronage or the right of presentation is shared with other institutions.

1. *Thomas Aldersey's Charity*
Bunbury (Diocese of Chester)
The Company was appointed patron of this benefice in 1594 under the will of Thomas Aldersey, as part of an ambitious concept for local provision which included the foundation of Bunbury School and financial security for the parish. The diocese is currently planning an amalgamation with the living of Tilstone Fearnal.

The Revd. D. R. Marr, who was appointed in 1987 and was also Rural Dean of Malpas, resigned through ill health at Easter 1991.

2. *Edmund Hammond's Charity* Awre and Blakeney (Diocese of Gloucester)
Edmund Hammond bequeathed £1,000 to the Company in 1639 to buy rectories or parsonages impropriate in fee simple. The Company received the legacy in 1652, and in 1657 paid £1,400 for the rectory of Awre and chaplaincy of Blakeney. In 1952, the livings were joined as the united benefice of Awre and Blakeney. In 1982, they were further joined with Newnham to create the benefice of Newnham with Awre and Blakeney. As a result, the right of presentation is exercised alternately by the Company and the Bishop of Gloucester.

The Revd. G. A. Satterly, who was appointed in 1973, moved on to Instow with Westleigh (Diocese of Exeter) in 1990. It is the Bishop of Gloucester's turn to present to the benefice.

3. *Lady Weld's Charity*
Dame Mary Weld bequeathed £2,000 to the Merchant Taylors' Company in 1624, to buy rectories or parsonages, impropriate in fee simple; the Merchant Taylors refused the trust, which passed to the Haberdashers' Company, and the legacy was first paid in 1630.

Lady Weld ordered the payment of a maximum two thirds of the annual profits of the livings in stipends, while the remaining third was to be saved until another £2,000 had accumulated. At this point, the entire annual profits could be paid over to the ministers, and the Company was to start the process of buying impropriations again, setting up an eternal cycle of benefaction. The trustees were to render accounts to Christ's Hospital. By a Chancery Court order in 1708 the Governors of Christ's Hospital were given alternate right of presentation, with the agreement of all parties. Consequently nomination is shared, but presentations are always made under the seal of the Company as patrons.

(i) *Wigston Magna (Diocese of Leicester)*
Wigston Magna was acquired for £560 in 1631.
The vicar is the Revd. E. J. Green, who was nominated by Christ's Hospital in 1973

(ii) *Leiston (Diocese of St Edmundsbury and Ipswich*
Leiston was bought for £550 in 1631. The vicar is the Revd. D. C. Lowe, who was nominated by Christ's Hospital in 1986.

(iii) *Bitteswell (Diocese of Leicester)*
Bitteswell was purchased for £870 in 1632.

In 1988, the Bishop suspended presentation to the living for three years pending consultation on a proposed team ministry. The Revd. J. Blackhouse was licensed as priest-in-charge in 1989.

(iv) *Albrighton (Diocese of Lichfield)*
Albrighton was acquired for £830 in 1665. The vicar is the Revd. R. B. Balkwill, who is also Rural Dean of Shifnal, and was appointed by the Company in 1982.

(v) *Diseworth (Diocese of Leicester)*
Diseworth was purchased for £660 in 1666. In 1978 it was amalgamated with Long Whatton, and in 1983 both were combined with Hathern to produce the new benefice of Hathern, Long Whatton and Diseworth. The right of presentation is exercised in turn by the Lord Chancellor (on behalf of the Crown), the Company (or Christ's Hospital), and the Bishop of Leicester. A further merger with Belton and Osgathorpe is likely. The vicar, who is based at Hathern, is the Revd. S. Samuel who was nominated by Christ's Hospital in 1982.

(vi) *Chertsey (Diocese of Guildford)*
Chertsey was bought for £2,650 in 1819. The vicar is the Revd. Canon D. L. H. Head, who was appointed by Christ's Hospital in 1982 and installed as an Honorary Canon of Guildford Cathedral in 1984.

4. *The Jones Lectureship Charity*
In 1866, the site of three houses owned by the charity in Size Lane were required for the construction of a new street running from the Embankment at Blackfriars Bridge to Mansion House. The Metropolitan Board of Works paid £29,000 in compensation, which was invested in 3 per cent consols. The dividend was expected to yield a considerable increase of income over the old rents, and the charity was expanded to include three London parishes which received substantial grants. The Company consequently received the advowsons, either whole or in part.

(i) *All Saints', Hatcham Park (Diocese of Southwark)* In 1870 the Company agreed to give £1,500 towards the completion of the church. The Company holds a one-third share in the patronage, which is exercised jointly with the Hyndman Bounty Trust.
The vicar is Fr. O. J. Beament, who was appointed by the Company in 1974.

(ii) *St Catherine's, Hatcham (Diocese of Southwark)*
The Company gave over £19,000 to build this parish church which was consecrated in 1894 and stands opposite Haberdashers' Aske's Hatcham School for Boys. The Company is sole patron. The vicar is the Revd. M. N. A. Torry, who was appointed in 1988.

(iii) *St John the Baptist, Hoxton (Diocese of London)*
In 1870–1, the Company voted a total of £4,000 towards purchasing the site and building the church of St Peter's, Hoxton. St Peter's subsequently merged with the older parish of St John's, and the Company had a half share in the patronage which was exercised in turn with the Archdeacon of Hackney. St Johns' amalgamated with Christ Church, Hoxton in the early 1950s, and the living continued under alternate presentation. In 1988, St John's formed a team ministry as part of the new benefice of St Leonard Shoreditch and St John the Baptist, Hoxton. The right of presentation is exercised by a patronage board consisting of the Company, the Bishop of London and the Archdeacon of Hackney. The Revd. M. Macnaughton was installed as Team Vicar in 1990.

Appendix VI

A Note on the Value of Money

Although many historians have attempted to construct indices of the cost of living, the results are notoriously unreliable. Most cover only short periods: the exception, the Phelps Brown and Hopkins index, covering the period 1264–1954, suffers from its failure to incorporate key elements of family budgets such as rent, and from the regionally specific nature of the data behind it. Nor are indices based on supposed working class budgets applicable to an institution such as the Haberdashers' Company, for salaries, building costs, and legal fees (key components of Company expenditure) changed at different rates to foodstuffs. Nevertheless, decennial averages taken from the Phelps Brown and Hopkins index for the period 1300–1920 are reproduced below in order to give a rough idea of changes in the cost of living; for the period from 1915 figures from the retail price index are given.

The Phelps Brown and Hopkins Index (Base, 1451–75 = 100)

1300–9	99
1310–9	142
1320–9	123
1330–9	107
1340–9	96
1350–9	129
1360–9	142
1370–9	131
1380–9	108
1390–9	109
1400–9	110
1410–9	113
1420–9	104
1430–9	115
1440–9	101
1450–9	99
1460–9	104
1470–9	94
1480–9	116
1490–9	101
1500–9	104
1510–9	110
1520–9	148
1530–9	155
1540–9	192
1550–9	289
1560–9	279
1570–9	315
1580–9	357
1590–9	472
1600–9	475
1610–9	528
1620–9	516
1630–9	616

1640–9	617
1650–9	636
1660–9	646
1670–9	615
1680–9	577
1690–9	647
1700–9	591
1710–9	663
1720–9	608
1730–9	553
1740–9	599
1750–9	628
1760–9	704
1770–9	805
1780–9	824
1790–9	998
1800–9	1474
1810–9	1601
1820–9	1221
1830–9	1146
1840–9	1136
1850–9	1154
1860–9	1267
1870–9	1330
1880–9	1059
1890–9	965
1900–9	1007
1910–9	1483

Retail Price Index, 1915–1990 (Base Jan. 1987 = 100)

1915–9	6.3
1920–9	6.7
1930–9	5.4
1940–9	7.4
1950–9	10.7
1960–9	14.7
1970–4	22.3
1975–9	45.4
1980–4	79.4
1985	94.6
1986	97.8
1987	101.9
1988	108.8
1989	116.4
1990	126.5

Source: L. Munby, *How Much Is That Worth?* (Chichester, 1989)

Notes

Notes for Chapter 1

1. *Memorials of London and London Life in the Thirteenth, Fourteenth, and Fifteenth Centuries*, ed. H.T. Riley (1868), pp. 422–3.
2. C.W. and P. Cunnington, *Handbook of English Medieval Costume* (2nd. edn., 1969), p. 83; C.W. and P. Cunnington, *Handbook of English Costume in the Sixteenth Century* (2nd. edn., 1970), pp. 23, 94; G. Egan and F. Pritchard, *Medieval Finds from Excavations in London, 3: Dress Accessories, c.1150-c.1450* (H.M.S.O., forthcoming, 1991).
3. *C.L.B.D.*, pp. 35–178; *C.P.M.R., 1364–1381*, pp. xxxii-xxxiii.
4. *C.L.B.A.*, pp. 15–16; *Two Early London Subsidy Rolls*, ed. E. Ekwall (Lund, 1951), pp. 109, 223, 316; *Calendar of Wills Proved and Enrolled in the Court of Husting, London, A.D. 1258 – A.D. 1688*, ed. R.R. Sharpe (2 vols., 1889–90), I. 130–1.
5. S. Thrupp, 'The Grocers of London: A Study of Distributive Trade', in *Studies in English Foreign Trade in the Fifteenth Century*, ed. E. Power and M.M. Postan (1933), pp. 268, 284; *C.P.M.R., 1381–1412*, pp. 224–7; D. Keene, *Survey of Medieval Winchester* (2 vols., 1985), I. 320.
6. S.M. Newton, *Fashion in the Age of the Black Prince: A Study of the Years 1340 to 1365* (Woodbridge, 1980), pp. 3–5; M. Scott, *A Visual History of Costume: the Fourteenth and Fifteenth Centuries* (1986), pp. 16–17; Cunnington and Cunnington, *English Medieval Costume*.
7. *Cronica Johannis de Reading et Anonym. Cantuariensis, 1346–1367*, ed. J. Tait (Manchester, 1914), p. 88, cited by Newton op.cit., p. 9. Cf. ibid., pp. 53–4.
8. Ibid. pp. 14–18; Egan and Pritchard, *Dress Accessories*.
9. Ibid.
10. C. Dyer, *Standards of Living in the Later Middle Ages: Social Change in England, c.1200–1520* (Cambridge, 1989), chs. VI-VIII; N.B. Harte, 'State Control of Dress and Social Change in Pre-Industrial England', in *Trade, Government, and Economy in Pre-Industrial England: Essays Presented to F.J. Fisher*, ed. A.H. John and D.C. Coleman (1976), pp. 132–65, esp. at pp. 134–5, 138, 141; *S.R.*, 37 Ed. III c. 15.
11. Egan and Pritchard, *Dress Accessories*.
12. Riley, *Memorials*, pp. 354–5.
13. S. Thrupp, *The Merchant Class of Medieval London* (1948), p. 3; S. Rappaport, *Worlds Within Worlds: Structures of Life in Sixteenth-Century London* (Cambridge, 1989), pp. 32–6.
14. *C.L.B.E.*, p. 13; G. Norton, *Commentaries on the History, Constitution, and Chartered Franchises of the City of London* (1869), p. 334.
15. *C.P.M.R., 1364–1381*, p. xxxvii.
16. Thrupp, 'Grocers', pp. 261, 282–4; P.R.O., C1/66/345; *C.L.B.K.*, pp. 109, 144, 213, 233, 234, 327, 347–8.
17. *C.L.R.O.*, MC1/2/5.
18. G. Unwin, *The Gilds and Companies of London* (1908), pp. 85, 88–9, 107; *C.L.B.D.*, p. 271; *Memorials*, ed. Riley, pp. 239–40.
19. *C.L.B.D.*, pp. 271–3; *C.L.B.E.*, p. 87; *Placita de Quo Warranto Temporibus Edw. I, II, and III* (1818), p. 451.
20. E.M. Carus-Wilson, 'An Industrial Revolution of the Thirteenth Century', in her *Medieval Merchant Venturers* (1954), pp. 183–210; Riley, *Memorials*, pp. 402–4, 529, 558–9, 667; *C.P.M.R., 1364–1381*, pp. 230, 233.
21. *C.L.B.I.*, pp. 176–7, 181; C.L.R.O., Jour. 1, fo. 16v.

22. C.L.R.O., Jour. 3, fo. 73v; P.R.O., SC8/307/15336. I am grateful to Dr. C.M. Barron for the latter reference.

23. C.M. Barron, 'The Parish Fraternities of Medieval London', in *The Church in Pre-Reformation Society*, ed. C. Harper-Bill and C.M. Barron (1985), pp. 14–17; Unwin, *Gilds and Companies*, pp. 93–109; E. Veale, *The Fur Trade in the Later Middle Ages* (Oxford, 1966), pp. 105–115.

24. J. Stow, *A Survey of London*, ed. C.L. Kingsford (2 vols., Oxford, 1908), I. 81; *Early London Subsidy Rolls*, ed. Ekwall, pp. 311–17.

25. P.R.O., C47/41/200; *C.L.B.H.*, pp. 43, 250; H.F. Westlake, *The Parish Guilds of Medieval England* (1919), p. 183. I am extremely grateful to Dr C.M. Barron for these references, and for the suggestion of the link between the Haberdashers and this fraternity.

26. D. Attwater, *A Dictionary of Saints* (1965), pp. 209–10; D.H. Farmer, *The Oxford Dictionary of Saints* (Oxford, 1978), pp. 69–70.

Notes for Chapter 2

1. Thrupp, *Merchant Class*, pp. 378–86; P.R.O., E179/251//15B; below, p. 18.

2. *C.P.R., 1446–52*, p. 164; Unwin, *Gilds and Companies*, pp. 158–63; S.R., 15 HVI c. 6; R. Griffiths, *The Reign of Henry VI* (1981), pp. 142–4, 167–71, 551–61, 790–5.

3. G.L., MS 15874, pp. 24–7; *The British Atlas of Historic Towns, Vol. III: The City of London*, ed. M.D. Lobel (Oxford, 1989), pp. 80, 94, 99; Stow, *Survey of London*, I. 298.

4. G.L., MS 15874, p. 25; *English Medieval Architects: A Biographical Dictionary Down to 1550*, ed. J. Harvey (1984), p. 333; Unwin, *Gilds and Companies*, pp. 176–87.

5. G.L., MS 15868, fos. 27, 63v, 125, 146, 207.

6. G.L., MS 15842/1, fo. 303; Stow, *Survey of London*, I. 304–5; *Parliamentary Papers*, 1824.XIII. 189.

7. B.L., Harleian MS 6363, fo. 20.

8. Haberdashers' Hall, 1446 grant of arms; Notes by Peter de Vere Beauclerk-Dewar, former Falkland Pursuivant Extraordinary, on Heraldry of Haberdashers; G.L., MSS 15866/1, inventories; 15869.

9. Thrupp, *Merchant Class*, pp. 14–16, 29, 42–3; Unwin, *Gilds and Companies*, p. 166; Veale, *Fur Trade*, p. 105.

10. A.B. Beaven, *The Aldermen of the City of London* (2 vols., 1908–13), II. 14, 16, 19; Thrupp, *Merchant Class*, pp. 322, 324, 373.

11. G.L., MS 9171/5, fos. 395v–7v; below, pp. 32, 34, 37.

12. Unwin, *Gilds and Companies*, pp. 166–8; idem, *Industrial Organization in the Sixteenth and Seventeenth Centuries* (Oxford, 1904), pp. 81–4; *C.P.R., 1494–1509*, pp. 243, 261; C.L.R.O., Rep. 1, fos. 33v, 75, 75v; below, pp. 57, 66.

13. Haberdashers' Hall, 1502 grant of arms; notes by Peter de Vere Beauclerk-Dewar on Company Heraldry; Thrupp, *Merchant Class*, p. 40.

14. *The Charters of the Merchant Taylors' Company*, ed. F.M. Fry and R.T.D. Sayle (1937), pp. 34–9; H. Miller, 'London and Parliament in the Reign of Henry VIII', *Bulletin of the Institute of Historical Research*, 25 (1962), 130–9.

15. *Letters and Papers, Foreign and Domestic, of the Reign of Henry VIII*, ed. J.S. Brewer et. al. (21 vols., 1862–1910), I. pt.i. 355; C.L.R.O., Rep. 1, fo. 118v; Rep. 2, fo. 110.

16. F.F. Foster, *The Politics of Stability: A Portrait of the Rulers of Elizabethan London* (1977), pp. 44–5; Beaven, *Aldermen*, I. 330–1; II. xlvi. The order of precedence is Mercers, Grocers, Drapers, Fishmongers, Goldsmiths, Skinners, Merchant Tailors, Haberdashers, Salters, Ironmongers, Vintners, and Clothworkers.

17. Rappaport, *Worlds Within Worlds*, p. 393; I.W. Archer, 'Governors and Governed in Late Sixteenth Century London, *c.* 1560–1603: Studies in the Achievement of Stability' (Oxford D. Phil. thesis, 1988), pp. 127–30; G.D. Ramsay, 'The Recruitment and Fortunes of some London Freemen in the Mid-Sixteenth Century', *Economic History Review*, second series, 31 (1978), 532; G.L., MS 15857.

18. Rappaport, *Worlds Within Worlds*, pp. 47–9; Thrupp, 'Grocers', pp. 255–6; T.F. Reddaway, *The Early History of the Goldsmiths' Company, 1327–1509* (1975), pp. 121, 155; Haberdashers' Hall, ordinances of 1505.

19. E.M. Carus-Wilson and O. Coleman, *England's Export Trade, 1275–1547* (Oxford, 1963), pp. 124–5, 140–1; J.L. Bolton, *The Medieval English Economy, 1150–1500* (1980), pp. 290–300.

20. E. Power, 'The Wool Trade in the Fifteenth Century', in *English Trade*, ed. Power and Postan; *The Overseas Trade of London: Exchequer Customs Accounts, 1480–1*, ed. H.S. Cobb (London Record Society, XXVII, 1990), p. 165; P.R.O., E159/236, recorda, Hilary, m.23. I am grateful to Dr W. Childs for the latter reference. Cf. B.L., Additional MS 48082, fo. 126.

21. E.M. Carus-Wilson, 'The Origins and Early Development of the Merchant Adventurers' Organisation', in her *Medieval Merchant Venturers*, pp. 143–82. The representatives of the Haberdashers recorded at the general courts in the reign of Henry VII were Henry Somer, Robert Aldernes, William Jeffery, Richard Wethir, John Auncell, Richard Aubrey, Thomas Billesdon, Henry Wynger, Nicholas Nyandezer, and William Page: *Acts of Court of the Mercers' Company, 1453–1527*, ed. L. Lyell and F.D. Watney (Cambridge, 1936).

22. *Customs Accounts, 1480–1*, ed. Cobb; P. Ramsey, 'The Merchant Adventurers Organisation in the Early Sixteenth Century' (Oxford D. Phil., 1965).

23. W. Childs, *Anglo-Castilian Trade in the Later Middle Ages* (Manchester, 1978), pp. 184, 187, 189–90.

24. P. Ramsey, *Tudor Economic Problems* (1968), p. 48; G.D. Ramsay, 'Victorian Historiography and the Guilds of London: the Report of the Royal Commission on the Livery Companies of London, 1884', *London Journal*, 10 (1984), 159; B.L. Harleian MS 6363, fo. 20.

25. Ramsey, *Tudor Economic Problems*, p. 64; P.R.O., PROB11/9, fo. 228; E179/251/15B. William Marler was assessed at £1,200 and John Hardy at £1,000.

26. *T.E.D.*, III. 111: G.R. Elton, *Reform and Reformation: England, 1509–1558* (1977), pp. 158–9, 164–5.

27. *A Discourse of the Commonweal of this Realm of England*, ed. E. Lamond (Cambridge, 1893), p. 64; Elton, *Reform and Reformation*, pp. 320–5.

28. *Discourse*, ed. Lamond, pp. 63, 91, 130; *T.E.D.*, III. 111.

29. J. Thirsk, *Economic Policy and Projects: the Development of a Consumer Society in Early Modern England* (Oxford, 1978), pp. 12–17, 78–83; *T.E.D.*, I. 327.

30. *S.R.*, 5 Eliz. I c. 7; Thirsk, *Economic Policy and Projects*, p. 81.

31. *Rotuli Parliamentorum* (6 vols., 1767–77), V. 506–7; *S.R.*, II. 495–6; Exchequer Customs Accounts, ed. Cobb, pp. xxxiii, xxxvi–xxxvii; C. Ross, *Edward IV* (1974), pp. 359–60. The pinners were involved with other crafts in securing the legislation of 1464 as the payment of 26s. 8d. to 'Barette Coteler and his fellowship for the wele of our crafte and þe suyte at Westminster': B.L. Egerton MS 1142, fo. 14v.

32. P.R.O. E122/71/8. I am very grateful to Dr. V. Harding for the loan of her transcript of this document. Cf. N.S.B. Gras, *The Early English Customs System* (Cambridge, Mass., 1918), p. 509.

33. *Exchequer Customs Accounts, 1480–1*, ed. Cobb.

34. *The Port and Trade of Early Elizabethan London*, ed. B. Dietz (London Record Society, VIII, 1972), esp. at pp. 152–5. It should be pointed out that some haberdashery wares (e.g. combs, inkhorns, and thimbles) were not included in the 1559–60 listing.

35. *Port and Trade*, ed. Dietz; T.S. Willan, *The Muscovy Merchants of 1555* (Manchester, 1953), p. 117; *C.P.R., 1553*, p. 392.

36. P.R.O., PROB2/15.

37. E. Veale, 'Craftsmen and the Economy of London in the Fourteenth Century', in R. Holt and G. Rosser, *The English Medieval Town: A Reader in English Urban History, 1200–1540* (1990), p. 130; P.R.O., E154/2/7; D.C. Coleman, *The British Paper Industry, 1495–1860: A Study in Industrial Growth* (Oxford, 1958), chs. I-III.

38. C.L.R.O., MC1/56/190; A. Fraser, *A History of Toys* (1966).

39. P.R.O., PROB2/15; C.L.R.O., MC1/56/190; MC1/19/90; D. Davis, *A History of Shopping* (1966), pp. 100–1.

40. Thirsk, *Economic Policy and Projects*; M. Spufford, *The Great Reclothing of Rural England: Petty Chapmen and their Wares in the Seventeenth Century* (1984).

41. C. Dyer, *Standards of Living in the Later Middle Ages*, p. 49. Aristocratic demand in later medieval London is the subject of a current research project by Dr C.M. Barron.

42. W.A.M. 12163, fo. 13. I am grateful to Dr C.M. Barron for this reference.

43. Thirsk, *Economic Policy and Projects*, p. 78.

44. P. Erondell, *The French Garden* (1605).
45. *The Paston Letters*, ed. J. Gairdner (3 vols., 1872–5), I. 83, 236–7, 254; *The Lisle Letters: An Abridgement*, ed. M. St. Clare Byrne (1983), pp. 67, 235, 236, 239, 240. For Tailor, see P.R.O., E101/421/16.
46. *The Canterbury Tales*, ed. A.C. Crawley (Everyman edn., 1958), General Prologue, lines 233–4; Spufford, *Great Reclothing*, pp. 88, 89, 94, 100, 103.
47. Bolton, *Medieval English Economy*, pp. 266, 273, 282, 286, 319; Dyer, *Standards of Living*, chs. VI-VIII; *Exchequer Customs Accounts, 1480–1*, ed. Cobb, pp. xxvii-xxviii.
48. Thrupp, 'Grocers', p. 281; W.C. Hazlitt, *A Select Collection of Old English Plays* (1874), I. 349–50; Spufford, *Great Reclothing*, pp. 69, 70, 72, 76, 78–80, 158–60, 172–7.
49. Thrupp, 'Grocers', pp. 273–6.

Notes for Chapter 3

1. Haberdashers' Hall, ordinances of 1505.
2. Ibid.
3. P.R.O., PROB 11/9, fo. 228; 31, fo. 123v; G.L., MS 9171/10, fo. 187.
4. P.R.O., PROB 11/13, fo. 108.
5. *London and Middlesex Chantry Certificate, 1548*, ed. C.J. Kitching (London Record Society, XVI, 1980), p. 91.
6. The following remarks are based on a survey of haberdasher wills for the period 1470–1540: P.R.O., PROB 11; G.L., MSS 9171/6–11. See also J.J. Scarisbrick, *The Reformation and the English People* (1984), chs. I-II; C. Harper-Bill, *The Pre-Reformation Church in England* (1989).
7. P.R.O., PROB 11/27, fo. 270Av; PROB 11/31, fo. 229v; G.L., MSS 9171/6, fo. 373; 9171/8, fo. 48v.
8. P.R.O., PROB 11/9, fo. 228.
9. Ibid.
10. P.R.O., PROB 11/25, fo. 263; PROB 11/28, fo. 153; G.L., MS 9171/7, fo. 45.
11. P.R.O., PROB 11/9, fo. 228.
12. G.L., MS 9171/6, fo. 154v.
13. Barron, 'Parish Fraternities of Medieval London', pp. 13–37.
14. Chaucer, *Canterbury Tales*, General Prologue, lines 361–4.
15. P.R.O., PROB 11/27, fo. 188.
16. G.L., MSS 9171/6, fos. 243, 373; 9171/7, fos. 55, 87; 9171/8, fo. 45; 9171/9, fo. 139; 9171/10, fos. 55v; 124v; P.R.O., PROB 11/9, fo. 177; PROB 11/13, fos. 20v, 108; PROB 11/23, fo. 90v; PROB 11/25, fo. 263; PROB 11/27, fo. 188.
17. P.R.O., PROB 11/24, fos. 156, 175; PROB 11/31, fo. 123v; Barron, 'Parish Fraternities', p. 19.
18. Barron, 'Parish Fraternities', p. 32; P.R.O., PROB 11/25, fo. 263; PROB 11/28, fo. 61; G.L., MS 9171/10, fo. 27.
19. G.L., MSS 9171/6, fos. 154v; 9171/8, fos. 45, 204.
20. P.R.O., PROB 11/10, fo. 223; PROB 11/24, fo. 175.
21. *S.R.*, 1 Ed. VI c. 14; A. Kreider, *English Chantries: the Road to Dissolution* (Cambridge, Mass., 1979), pp. 187–208.
22. *C.P.R.*, *Edward VI*, II. 102–12; S. Brigden, *London and the Reformation* (Oxford, 1989), pp. 390, 391.
23. Haberdashers' Hall, ordinances of 1505, charter of 1578.
24. Haberdashers' Hall, grants of arms, 1446 and 1502.
25. G.L., MS 15868, fo. 8.
26. G.L., MS 15839.
27. Below, pp. 140–1.
28. Brigden, *London and the Reformation*, pp. 338, 412; P.R.O., PROB 11/28, fo. 61 (Thomas Cherell); PROB 11/30, fos. 104v(Thomas Huntlowe), 225v(John Simpson), 262 (Thomas Marbury); PROB 11/43, fo. 315 (Nicholas Spackman).
29. *Letters and Papers*, XVII.102.
30. Brigden, *London and the Reformation*, pp. 380–92, 411–16, 483–6, 628–32.
31. P.R.O., PROB 11/29, fos. 140v, 156v; PROB 11/30, fo. 104v.

32. P.R.O., PROB 11/26, fo. 88v; PROB 11/27, fos. 160v, 267.
33. R. Grafton, *Chronicles* (2 vols.; 1809), II. 523.
34. P.R.O., PROB 11/82, fo. 210v; Archer, *Pursuit of Stability*, pp. 251–4.
35. P.R.O., PROB 11/69, fo. 127v.
36. P.R.O., PROB 11/89, fo. 268.
37. N. Tyacke, *The Fortunes of English Puritanism, 1603–1640* (Friends of Dr Williams' Library Forty-Fourth Lecture, 1990), pp. 5–10; D. Williams, 'London Puritanism: the Haberdashers' Company', *Church History*, 32 (1963), 1–24; below, pp. 80–2.
38. P.R.O., PROB 11/52–55; 83–90; G.L., MSS 9051/3–5; 9171/15–16, 18; 25626/2–3; W.P.L., Will Registers Elsam and Bracy.
39. C.L.R.O., Rep. 12, fos. 324, 327v, 330, 337v, 344.
40. C.L.R.O., Rep. 15, fos. 356, 385r–v.
41. G.L., MS 15866/1.
42. *Parliamentary Papers*, 1824.XIII. 188–232.
43. G.L., MS 15842/1, fos. 8v, 12v, 18, 20, 36v, 69, 95, 101.
44. Ibid. fos. 139v, 178v, 180, 187v–8.
45. Ibid. fo. 162.
46. Below, pp. 76–7.
47. G.L., MS 15866/1, inventories.
48. G.L., MS 15868, fos. 146, 151v, 156, 164v, 170v, 181, 185.
49. G.L., MS 15839.
50. *The Ordre of my Lorde Mayor, the Aldermen & the Shiriffes for their Metings and Wearynge of Apparell Throughout the Yeare* (1568).
51. Stow, *A Survey of London*, I. 167–8.
52. G.L., MS 15866/1, acct. for 1633–4; D. Cressy, *Bonfires and Bells: National Memory and the Protestant Calendar in Elizabethan and Stuart England* (1989).
53. G.L., MS 15839.
54. P.R.O., PROB 11/43, fo. 315.
55. Dp. Co., Rep. C, pp. 192, 201.
56. P.R.O., PROB 11/46, fo. 302.
57. P.R.O., PROB 11/57, fo. 70.
58. G.L., MS 15866/1, inventories.
59. Below, chs. V-VI.

Notes for Chapter 4

1. Haberdashers' Hall, ordinances of 1505; G.L., MS 15839.
2. G.L., MS 15842/1, fos. 230v, 314v; Beaven, *Aldermen*, II. 47–65.
3. G.L., MS 15842/1, fos. 248v, 271.
4. G.L., MSS 15845, 15860/1–2.
5. G.L., MS 15842/1, fo. 268.
6. G.L., MSS 15839; 15866/1.
7. G.L., MSS 15839; 15842/1, *passim*.
8. G.L., MS 15842/1, analysis of attendances for 1641.
9. G.L., MS 15839.
10. G.L., MSS 15839; 15866/1; 15842/1, fos. 236v–7, 263v, 264, 270v–1.
11. Haberdashers' Hall, ordinances of 1505; G.L., MS 15839.
12. G.L., MS 15842/1, fos. 263, 282v, 290.
13. G.L., MS 15842/1, fos. 234, 282v; 15866/1, accts. for 1633–4 and 1635–6.
14. For identity of Assistants see *The Members of the City Companies in 1641*, ed. T.C. Dale (Society of Genealogists, 2 vols., 1934), I. 230–68; G.L., MSS 15860/1–2.
15. G.L., MS 15845; P.R.O., PROB 11/25, fo. 263; PROB 11/27, fo. 160v; *The Visitation of London*, ed. J.J. Chester and J.L. Howard (2 vols., 1880–3).
16. G.L., MS 15860/2, 27 Mar. 1604.

17. G.L., MS 15845.
18. T.K. Rabb, *Enterprise and Empire* (Cambridge, Mass., 1967); R. Brenner, 'Commercial Change and Political Conflict: the Merchant Community in Civil War London' (Princeton Ph. D., 1970).
19. R. Ashton, *The City and the Court, 1603–1643* (Cambridge, 1979), pp. 140, 147–8; V. Pearl, *London and the Outbreak of the Puritan Revolution* (Oxford, 1960), pp. 304–5.
20. Brenner, 'Commercial Change', pp. 34, 46, 92–3, 101, 104, 175, 215, 280–1, 398, 440–2.
21. Pearl, *London and the Outbreak*, pp. 306–7, 313, 316–20; Brenner, 'Commercial Change', pp. 369–70, 386, 397–8, 401–2, 410–411, 440–2; idem, 'The Civil War Politics of London's Merchant Community', *Past and Present*, 58 (1973), 53–107.
22. P.R.O., SP 12/20/63.
23. P.R.O., REQ2/394/22; REQ2/259/64.
24. G.L. Gomme (ed.), 'The Names and Trades of those Houses that were Burnt upon the Bridge', *The Gentleman's Magazine Library English Topography*, 15 (1904), 308–9; G.L., MS 15842/1, fo. 216.
25. G.L., MS 15842/1, fos. 162v, 165, 167, 168v, 169v, 173v, 176, 182v, 213v, 226.
26. G.L., MS 15842/1, fo. 239v.
27. G.L., MS 15842/1, fos. 182, 237, 269.
28. G.L., MSS 15839; 15868; 15842/1, fos. 275, 281.
29. G.L., MS 15868. The dinner was held in 1601, 1602, 1605, 1607, 1609, 1610, 1613, 1616, 1619, 1623, 1628, 1633, and 1640.
30. G.L., MS 15842/1, fo. 217v.
31. G.L., MS 15842/1, fo. 241v.
32. G.L., MS 15866/1.
33. G.L., MS 15866/1, acct. for 1635–6.
34. G.L., MSS 15866/1; 15868; 15839.
35. G.L., MS 15866/1, acct. for 1635–6.
36. G.L., MS 15842/1, fos. 192v, 202, 242v, 279v.
37. G.L., MSS 15839.
38. G.L., MS 15842/1, fos. 181v, 182, 187v, 189, 190v, 193v, 194, 195v, 199v, 203, 210v, 215, 247v.
39. P. Cain, 'Robert Smith and the Reform of the Archives of the City of London, 1580–1623', *London Journal*, 13 (1987–8), 3–16; G.L., MS 15842/1, fo. 158.
40. G.L., MSS 15866/1; 15868; 15839; earnings for fees calculated from apprentice bindings, freedom admissions, and Livery admissions, 1600–40.
41. G.L., MS 15842/1, fo. 194.
42. G.L., MS 15842/1, fo. 137v, 158, 200v, 256v, 258r-v.
43. G.L.R.O., HI/ST/A1/3, fos. 179v, 180v; C.L.R.O., Rep. 20, fo. 131; Rep. 22, fo. 399v.
44. G.L.R.O., HI/ST/A1/4, fo. 177.
45. G.L., MS 15842/1, fo. 158.

Notes for Chapter 5

1. C. Phythian-Adams, *Desolation of a City: Coventry and the Urban Crisis of the Late Middle Ages* (Cambridge, 1979), p. 217; R.H. Morris, *Chester in the Plantagenet and Tudor Reigns* (Chester, n.d.), pp. 316–7, 435–6; I. Leadam, *Select Cases Before the King's Council in the Star Chamber Commonly Called the Court of Star Chamber, vol. II, A.D. 1509–1544*, (Selden Society, XXV, 1911), pp. 268–9; P. Clark, ' "The Ramoth-Gilead of the Good": Urban Change and Political Radicalism at Gloucester, 1540–1640', in *The English Commonwealth, 1547–1640*, ed. P. Clark, A.G.R. Smith and N. Tyacke (Leicester, 1979), p. 171.
2. *Discourse of the Common Weal*, ed. Lamond, pp. 125–6; J. Stow, *The Annales or a General Chronicle Continued by Edmund Howes* (1631), p. 870; Cunnington and Cunnington, *English Medieval Costume*, pp. 33–4, 62–6, 87–9, 111–17, 125–31, 147–50, 161–5; Cunnington and Cunnington, *Costume in the Sixteenth Century*, pp. 40–8, 70–84, 131–41, 172–9; above, p. 23 on imports of hats. For discussion of feltmaking techniques, see M. Sonenscher, *The Hatters of Eighteenth-Century France* (1987), pp. 20–5.
3. *Port and Trade*, ed. Dietz, p. 153.

4. *S.R.*, 3 Henry VIII c. 15, 21 Henry VIII c. 9; C.L.R.O., Rep. 5, fos. 82v–3; Jour. 13, fos. 189–90, 254–5.

5. *Discourse*, ed. Lamond, pp. 67, 172; *C.J.*, I. 5, 6, 26, 30, 31; *S.R.*, 1 Mary st.2 c.11.

6. *S.R.*, 8 Eliz I c. 11, 13 Eliz. I c. 19, 39 Eliz I c. 18; *C.J.*, I. 76–7.

7. M. C. Linthicum, *Costume in the Drama of Shakespeare and his Contemporaries* (Oxford, 1936), p. 225; *Love's Labour's Lost*, V. ii. 283; *The Dutch Courtesan*, III. iii. 27.

8. C.L.R.O., Rep. 18, fos. 147, 170; *Historical Manuscripts Commission, Hatfield House*, V. 296; *Calendar of Patent Rolls, Elizabeth I, 1575–8*, pp. 8–9; F.A. Youngs, *The Proclamations of the Tudor Queens* (Cambridge, 1976), pp. 148–51.

9. Cf. the earlier account by Unwin, *Industrial Organization*, pp. 129–35, 159–64.

10. G.L., MS 15838; C.L.R.O., Letter Book 'S', fo. 93v; A. Pettegree, *Foreign Protestant Communities in Sixteenth-Century London* (Oxford, 1986), p. 147.

11. I. Scouloudi, 'Alien Immigration and Alien Communities in London, 1558–1640' (London M. Sc., 1933); *Returns of Aliens Dwelling in the City and Suburbs of London*, ed. R.E.G. and E.F. Kirk (Huguenot Society Publications, X, 4 vols., 1900–8), III. 362–70, 425–33; *Returns of Strangers in the Metropolis, 1593, 1627, 1635, 1639*, ed. I. Scouloudi (Huguenot Society Publications, LVII, 1985), pp. 131, 148.

12. *Proceedings in the Parliaments of Elizabeth I, 1559–81*, ed. T.E. Hartley (Leicester, 1981), p. 539; G.L., MS 15842/1, fo. 8; *S.R.*, 1 Ja I c. 17.

13. C.L.R.O., Rep. 13, fos. 504v, 508.

14. Merchant-Tailors' Company, C.M. I, p. 759; II, fos. 12v, 15; III, fos. 4v–5v, 5v–6; C.L.R.O., Rep. 18, fos. 433, 438v; Rep. 19, fo. 59v.

15. Clothworkers' Company, C.M. II, fos. 214, 219v, 237v; G.L., MS 14346/1, fo. 122.

16. J. Boulton, *Neighbourhood and Society: a London Suburb in the Seventeenth Century* (Cambridge, 1987), pp. 70–1; C.L.R.O., Jour. 32, fo. 84.

17. *C.J.*, I. 89, 108, 114, 129; *Proceedings*, ed. Hartley, pp. 218, 482, 537, 539; Trinity College, Dublin MS N. 2. 12, fos. 82, 89v; S. D'Ewes, *The Journals of All the Parliaments During the Reign of Queen Elizabeth* (1682), pp. 654, 658, 680; G.L., MS 15842/1, fos. 12v, 119v.

18. G.L., MS 15842/1, fos. 1, 52v; B.L., Lansdowne MSS 38/4–5, fos. 11–17.

19. G.L., MS 6117, pp. 48–50.

20. B.L., Lansdowne MSS 24/7; 28/29.

21. G.L., MS 6117, pp. 46–7, 51–3.

22. B.L., Lansdowne MSS 28/28, 30–1, fos. 65–66, 69–71; 29/22–26, 27, fos. 52–59v, 61.

23. G.L., MS 15842/1, fos. 17v, 108v, 111v.

24. B.L., Lansdowne MS 29/25, fo. 57v.

25. B.L., Lansdowne MS 28/28, fo. 65.

26. C.L.R.O., Rep. 22, fos. 251v–2, 267r–v; G.L., MSS 15842/1, fos. 83, 83v; 6117, pp. 51–3.

27. G.L., MS 15842/1, fos. 52v, 55r–v, 83, 119v, 121.

28. P.R.O., C66/1640, mm. 1–5.

29. G.L., MS 15842/1, fo. 141.

30. *C.J.*, I. 194; P.R.O., STAC 8/141/20; G.L., MS 15842/1, fo. 182.

31. C.L.R.O., Rep. 26, fos. 256, 547, 553; Rep. 27, fos. 7, 62, 72, 182v; Rep. 28, fo. 107; Rep. 30, fos. 97, 101v–2, 245v–6v; Rep. 31, fos. 45r–v, 431; Rep. 32, fo. 19v; Rep. 33, fos. 343, 354v–5; Jour. 27, fo. 144v; Jour. 28, fo. 293v; Remembrancia III, no. 77; G.L., MS 15842/1, fo. 190.

32. C.L.R.O., Rep. 36, fo. 233; Jour. 32, fos. 75v–8, 83v–4v; G.L., MS 15842/1, fos. 216, 228.

33. *Calendar of State Papers Domestic, 1639–40*, pp. 335, 344–5, 370.

34. C.L.R.O., Rep. 60, fos. 103, 187, 193–8.

35. G.L., MS 15842/1, fos. 175, 237, 346.

Notes for Chapter 6

1. This and the following paragraphs are based upon the following sources: *Parliamentary Papers*, 1824.XIII. 188–232; G.L., MSS 15866/1–3; 15860/1. See also W.K. Jordan, *The Charities of London, 1480–1660: the Aspirations and Achievements of the Urban Society* (1960); W.M. Warlow, *A History of the Charities of William Jones at Monmouth and Newland* (Bristol, 1899); J.R. Meredith, *Adams' Grammar*

School, Newport, 1656–1956: A Short History (Newport, 1956); D. Williams, 'London Puritanism: the Haberdashers' Company', *Church History*, 32, (1963), 1–24.

2. P.R.O., PROB 11/126, fo. 408.

3. Sample of London wills discussed in Archer, 'Governors and Governed, pp. 218–233; C.L.R.O., Common Serjeant's Book, I.

4. P.R.O., PROB 11/93, fo. 68; PROB 11/126, fo. 408; PROB 11/189, fo. 9; PROB 11/197, fo. 222; PROB 11/305, fo. 239.

5. G.L., MSS 15842/1, fos. 102, 208v; 361; 15842/2, fos. 43, 52.

6. *Parliamentary Papers*, 1824.XIII. 188–232, *passim*; G.L., MSS 15842/1, fos. 174v, 283, 286, 324; 15842/2, fos. 88, 163.

7. Williams 'London Puritanism', pp. 2–7; *The Seconde Parte of a Register*, ed. A. Peel (2 vols., Cambridge, 1915), II. 219–21; *The Spending of the Money of Robert Nowell*, ed. A.B. Grosart (1877), pp. 102, 104, 228; C.L.R.O., Rep. 18, fo. 398v; Archer, 'Governors and Governed', pp. 318–25; P.R.O., PROB 11/93, fo. 68.

8. Williams 'London Puritanism', pp. 7–15; P.R.O., PROB 11/126, fo. 408; P. Seaver, *The Puritan Lectureships: The Politics of Religious Dissent, 1560–1662* (Stanford, 1970), *passim* for Egerton and Sedgwick; H.R. Trevor-Roper, *Archbishop Laud, 1573–1645* (1940), pp. 244–57; G.L., MS 15842/1, fos. 192v, 200v.

9. Williams 'London Puritanism', pp. 15–16.

10. V. Pearl, *London and the Outbreak of the Puritan Revolution: City Government and National Politics, 1625–43* (Oxford, 1961), pp. 304–5; P.R.O., P.C.C., 129 Twisse; Seaver, *Puritan Lectureships, passim,* for Culverwell and Hardy.

11. P.R.O., PROB 11/305, fo. 209; *D.N.B.* for Horton.

12. P.R.O., PROB 11/189, fo. 9; *D.N.B.* for Downham, Potter and Hammond.

13. P.R.O., PROB 11/316, fo. 219.

14. W. Perkins, *Works* (1605), p. 862; T. Lever, *A Fruitfull Sermon . . . in Poules Church* (1550), sig. B iii; T. Horton, *The Unrighteous Mammon Exchanged for True Riches* (1661); A. Willet, *Synopsis Papismi* (1634), p. 1219; W.K. Jordan, *Philanthropy in England, 1480–1660: A Study of the Changing Pattern of English Social Aspirations* (1959), pp. 155–239; M. Todd, *Christian Humanism and the Puritan Social Order* (Cambridge, 1987), ch. V.

15. C. Hill, 'Puritans and "the Dark Corners of the Land" ', *Transactions of the Royal Historical Society*, fifth series, 13 (1963), 77–102; J.S. Morrill, *Cheshire, 1630–1660: County Government and Society During the English Revolution* (Oxford, 1974), p. 18; K. Kissack, *Monmouth: the Making of a County Town* (1975), pp. 31–6; P. Collinson, *The Religion of Protestants: the Church in English Society, 1559–1625* (Oxford, 1982), p. 93.

16. G.L., MS 15842/1, fos. 201v, 354.

17. Ibid. fos. 193v, 215v, 225, 232.

18. Ibid. fos. 247, 325, 326v, 334.

19. Ibid. fos. 154v, 207v, 214, 231; W. Hinde, *A Faithfull Remonstrance of the Holy Life and Happy Death of John Bruen of Bruen-Stapleford in the County of Chester Esquire* (1641).

20. G.L., MS 15842/1, fos. 257v, 326v, 327, 330v.

21. Ibid. fo. 276v; T. Worthington Barlow, *Cheshire: its Historical and Literary Associations* (Manchester, 1855), pp. 150–189.

22. Williams 'London Puritanism', pp. 5–6.

23. *Parliamentary Papers*, 1824.XIII. 188–232.

24. G.L., MS 15842/1, fo. 158v; *Parliamentary Papers*, 1824.XIII. 190, 192, 198, 216.

25. G.L., MSS 15842/1, fos. 182v, 184v–5, 185r–v, 186, 187v, 188r–v, 190; 15897.

26. Ibid. fos. 203, 210v, 216, 216v, 221v, 223v, 225v, 226v, 227v, 229, 229v, 230, 234, 238, 239, 243v.

27. Ibid. fo. 194.

28. Warlow, *Monmouth and Newland*, pp. 52–3.

29. G.L., MS 15842/1, fos. 338v–9.

30. G.L., MS 15842/2, fos. 144, 150, 151v.

31. Ibid. fos. 43r–v, 147.

32. G.L., MSS 15842/1, fos. 351v, 352; 15842/2, fo. 4.

33. *Meredith, Adams' Grammar School*, pp. 8–9.
34. G.L., MS 15842/1, fos. 327, 331, 334v, 352; 15842/1, fo. 80.
35. Ibid. fos. 43r-v, 81v.
36. G.L., MSS 15842/1, fos. 276, 276v, 280; 15842/2, fos. 15, 20, 25, 43v, 79v, 81v, 83r-v, 84v.
37. G.L., MS 15842/1, fos. 203, 210v, 215v.
38. Ibid., fos. 340v, 343r-v, 347.
39. G.L., MS 15842/2, fos. 56, 93v, 100v, 105, 107, 107v–8, 109r-v, 110v.
40. Ibid. fos. 110v–1, 123, 165r-v; 15842/3, pp. 1, 4, 11.
41. G.L., MS 15842/3, pp. 152–3, 159, 161–2, 174, 180; P.R.O. C5/441/108.
42. G.L., MS 15842/3, pp. 161, 183, 184–5, 188, 189–90, 198, 199; P.R.O., C5/441/108.
43. G.L., MS 15842/3, pp. 218, 223, 242, 245, 247.
44. G.L., MS 15842/2, fo. 81v.
45. Ibid. fos. 129v, 131v, 133v, 136, 137r-v; 15842/3, pp. 13, 52–3, 185.
46. G.L., MSS 15842/1, fo. 334; 15842/2, fos. 55v, 66, 98v, 105v, 107, 109r-v.
47. Ibid. fo. 123v.

Notes for Chapter 7

1. G.L., MS 15842/6, pp. 127–36.
2. G.L., MS 15842/1, fos. 304, 304v, 311r-v, 316v–17.
3. Ibid. fo. 315v; G.L., MS 15866/1, fo. 424.
4. G.L., MSS 15842/1, fos. 318A, 323, 335, 344, 347v; 15866/1, 1642–3 acct.
5. G.L., MSS 15842/1, fos. 327v, 339v, 340v, 344v, 347v, 350v; 15842/2, fo. 10.
6. G.L., MSS 15842/1, fos. 349v–50, 350r-v; 15842/2, fo. 56v.
7. G.L., MS 15842/2, fo. 86v.
8. Ibid. fo. 101v.
9. Ibid. fos. 32v, 57r-v.
10. *The Shorter Pepys*, ed. R. Latham (1986), pp. 659–72; G.L., MS 15842/2. fo. 131v.
11. G.L., MS 15842/2, fos. 133v, 135, 135v, 143, 149v–50.
12. Ibid. fos. 100, 139v, 141, 143, 145v; *A Biographical Dictionary of British Architects, 1600–1840*, ed. H. Colvin (1978), pp. 459–60. The idea that Wren designed the Hall is mythical pace J. Elmes, *The Life and Times of Sir Christopher Wren* (1829), p. 431 and Prevett, *Short Description*, p. 11.
13. G.L., MSS 15842/2, fos. 153, 157v, 159, 159v; 15842/3, pp. 6, 18, 63, 102–3, 187, 212, 217, 218, 219, 232, 253; 15866/6, pp. 49, 55–6.
14. G.L., MSS 15842/2, fos. 138v, 143v; 15842/3, pp. 23, 32; *The Fire Court*, ed. P.E. Jones (2 vols., 1966–70), II. 87–8. Cf. ibid., I. 23–4, 47.
15. C.G.A. Clay, *Economic Expansion and Social Change: England, 1500–1700* (2 vols., Cambridge, 1984), I. 91; G.L., MS 15842/3, pp. 8, 258, 294, 305.
16. G.L., MS 15842/2, fo. 161.
17. G.L., MSS 15842/2, fos. 149v–50, 151, 159, 162, 164v, 165v; 15842/3, p. 2.
18. G.L., MSS 15842/3, pp. 4, 6, 19–20, 53–4, 58, 64, 67, 134, 150, 164, 171, 203; 15870.
19. G.L., MSS 15842/2, fos. 160, 165v; 15842/3, pp. 30, 37, 40–1, 43, 79–80.
20. G.L., MSS 15842/2, fo. 160; 15842/3, pp. 20, 136, 142, 165, 180, 183.
21. G.L., MS 15842/3, pp. 60, 64, 65, 68–73.
22. Ibid. pp. 82–3, 84, 89–90, 91.
23. Ibid. pp. 61, 86, 94, 96, 102, 103, 107, 156; G.L., MSS 15866/5, fos. 45, 56, 70; 15866/6, fo. 8v.
24. G.L., MS 15842/3, pp. 250, 297; *Parliamentary Papers*, 1824.XIII. 190, 196, 198.
25. P.R.O., PROB 11/136, fo. 219; G.L., MS 15842/2, fo. 153; *Parliamentary Papers*, 1824.XIII. 221–2.
26. G.L., MS 15842/3, pp. 539–40.
27. Ibid. pp. 191–2.
28. Ibid. pp. 363, 388, 396–8, 404, 406.
29. G.L., MS 15842/5, pp. 431–4.
30. G.L., MSS 15842/5, pp. 380, 442, 450, 460, 473, 493, 501; 15842/6, pp. 2, 42, 89.
31. G.L., MS 15842/6, pp. 112, 127–36, 142–6.

32. Ibid. pp. 137–8, 140, 142–6, 157–8, 161, 166, 178, 193–4, 198, 330–1, 350, 390–1; *Parliamentary Papers*, 1824.XIII. 229–30.

33. J.R. Kellett, 'The Breakdown of Guild and Corporation Control over the Handicraft and Retail Trades of London', *Economic History Review*, 2nd series, 10 (1957–8), 381–94; P. Earle, *The Making of the English Middle Class: Business, Society, and Family Life in London, 1660–1730* (1989), p. 252; G.L., MS 15860/8.

34. R. Finlay and B. Shearer, 'Population Growth and Suburban Expansion', in *London, 1500–1700: the Making of the Metropolis*, ed. A.L. Beier and R. Finlay (1986), p. 45.

35. G.L., MS 15842/1, fo. 346.

36. 15842/3, pp. 154, 607–8.

37. P. Langford, *A Polite and Commercial People: England, 1727–1783* (Oxford, 1989), pp. 99–101; G.L., MS 15842/6, pp. 288, 292. Other groups hiring the Hall were the Society for the Propagation of Religious Knowledge and the Society of the Free and Accepted Masons: G.L., MS 15842/6, pp. 164, 350–1.

38. R. Campbell, *The London Tradesman* (1747).

39. G.L., MS 15842/3, p. 301.

40. G.L., MS 15842/4, p. 84.

41. G.L., MSS 15866/7–9.

42. G.L., MS 15842/3, pp. 495–6, 496–7, 500.

43. G.L., MSS 15842/3, p. 499; 15842/5, pp. 75, 284, 377; 15842/6, pp. 12, 332, 333.

44. G.L., MSS 15842/3, pp. 68–73, 394; 15842/5, p. 419.

45. G.L., MSS 15842/4, p. 111; 15842/5, pp. 187–8.

46. G.L., MS 15842/5, p. 283.

47. G.L., MS 15842/6, pp. 142–6.

48. G.L., MSS 15842/3, pp. 165, 180, 184, 197, 198, 304, 399; 15866/6, pp. 15, 26, 37.

49. G.L., MS 15842/3, p. 410.

50. Ibid. pp. 459, 495.

51. G.L., MS 15842/5, p. 337.

52. Ibid. pp. 285, 287, 290.

53. G.L., MSS 15842/3–4 for relevant years.

54. G.L., MS 15842/3, pp. 544–62, passim.

55. G.L., MSS 15842/3, pp. 603–7; 15842/4, pp. 35–56, 174–90.

56. G.L., MS 15842/3, p. 554.

57. G.L., MSS 15842/4, pp. 44–5, 69; 15842/7, p. 11.

58. G.L., MSS 15842/6, pp. 170–1, 310–11; 15854/1.

59. G.L., MSS 15842/5, pp. 71, 178–9, 255, 282, 305; 15842/6, pp. 80, 93, 94.

60. G.L., MS 15842/6, p. 364.

61. Ibid. p. 116.

62. G.L., MSS 15842/4, pp. 146, 189; 15842/5, p. 268; 15842/6, pp. 116, 310–11; W. Le Hardy, *The Worshipful Company of Haberdashers. The Descriptive Class List of Records* (1954), pp. 10–11.

63. G.L., MSS 15842/4, p. 111; 15842/5, pp. 282, 285, 389, 398; 15842/6, p. 147.

64. G.L., MS 15842/3, p. 535.

65. G.L., MSS 15842/4, pp. 103, 111, 140; 15842/5, pp. 259, 422.

66. G.L., MS 15842/6, pp. 127–36.

Notes for Chapter 8

1. *Parliamentary Papers*, 1819.X. 286–96; *Parliamentary Papers*, 1824.XIII. 225–30; J.R. Meredith, *The Foundation and Early History of Aske's Hospital at Hoxton, 1689–1754* (1964), pp. 8, 84–5.

2. Meredith, *Aske's Hospital*, pp. 14–15, 30, 40–2, 52–3, 58.

3. Ibid. pp. 16–19.

4. Ibid. pp. 19–23.

5. Ibid. pp. 54–5.

6. Ibid. pp. 43–5.

7. Ibid. pp. 45–6, 48–9.

8. Ibid. pp. 45–6, 49.

9. G.L., MSS 15866/6–7.

10. Above, pp. 93–4; G.L., MS 15866/6, fos. 6, 17, 28, 39, 59, 63, 86, 136, 147, 158.

11. G.L., MS 15866/7, fos. 127–9.

12. Ibid. fos. 106v, 107–8.

13. G.L., MS 15842/3, p. 376; 15866/7, fos. 39v, 51.

14. G.L., MS 15866/7, fos. 17, 40, 108.

15. G.L., MSS 15866/6–7.

16. Above, pp. 92–3; G.L., MSS 15842/3, pp. 347, 349, 533; 15842/4, p. 46.

17. G.L., MS 15842/3, pp. 532–3, 552.

18. Ibid. pp. 396–8, 405.

19. Ibid. pp. 357, 381, 463, 506, 521, 525, 526, 533, 535.

20. G.L., MS 15842/4, pp. 42, 46–7, 56.

21. G.L., MSS 15842/5, pp. 416, 473, 493, 501, 612; 15842/6, pp. 168, 170, 206, 224–6, 230, 244, 253, 257–8, 361, 395–6, 404, 407–8, 412–4, 430; *Parliamentary Papers*, 1824.XIII. 218–19.

22. Meredith, *Aske's Hospital*, pp. 47–8.

23. G.L., MSS 15843/1, pp. 33–46, 128, 129–30, 130–3; 15866/6, fo.95.

24. G.L., MSS 15842/3, pp. 549, 591; 15842/4, pp. 36, 124–5.

25. G.L., MSS 15842/4, pp. 103, 111; 15842/5, p. 259; 15843/1, pp. 1–32.

26. *Parliamentary Papers*, 1821.XII. 422–3.

27. Above, p. 95; G.L., MS 15842/3, pp. 477, 525, 532, 543, 559, 563, 567, 576, 593; P.R.O., C5/223/31; *H.M.C. House of Lords*, V. 152–3; *L.J.*, XVII. 178, 251; *The Company of Haberdashers, Appellants; the Attorney General and the Poor of Newland Respondents; the Respondents' Case* (1703); (1702) 2 Bro. P.C. 370, *1 English Reports*, 1003–4; Warlow, *Monmouth and Newland*, pp. 59–63.

28. G.L., MS 15842/4, pp. 113–14, 239, 241–2.

29. G.L., MS 15842/5, pp. 277, 278, 315; Warlow, *Monmouth and Newland*, pp. 64–5.

30. G.L., MSS 15866/7, fos. 153, 178v, 202, 226; 15866/8, p. 6.

31. Warlow, *Monmouth and Newland*, p. 69.

32. G.L., MSS 15842/6, pp. 64–5, 15843/1, pp. 281–5.

33. G.L., MSS 15842/3, pp. 557; 15842/5, p. 140; 15842/6, pp. 174, 372; 15843/1, pp. 269–73; 15843/2, pp. 90–103.

34. G.L., MSS 15842/6, pp. 36, 41; 15843/1, pp. 176–87.

35. G.L., MSS 15842/3, p. 568; 15842/5, p. 140; 15843/1, pp. 269–73; Meredith, *Adams' Grammar School*, pp. 10–11.

36. G.L., MS 15842/5, p. 412.

37. G.L., MSS 15843/1, pp. 176–87; 15843/2, pp. 34–44; Warlow, *Monmouth and Newland*, pp. 168–9.

38. G.L., MS 15843/1, pp. 269–73.

39. *Parliamentary Papers*, 1821.XII. 423–4; G.L., MSS 15843/2, pp. 90–3, 121–2, 148, 263–4; 15843/3, pp. 194–6, 197–8. For revisionist assessments of the 18th-century grammar school, see R.S. Tompson, *Classics or Charity? The Dilemma of the Eighteenth-Century Grammar School* (Manchester, 1971).

40. G.L., MS 15842/3, pp. 380–1.

41. G.L., MS 15842/4, pp. 99–100.

42. G.L., MS 15842/5, pp. 334, 404.

43. G.L., MS 15842/6, p. 91.

44. G.L., MS 15866/6, fos. 17, 39.

45. G.L., MSS 15842/6, pp. 69, 74, 91; 15843/1, p. 400; 15843/2, pp. 37–8; Warlow, *Monmouth and Newland*, pp. 166–7, 169–71.

46. G.L., MSS 15842/3, pp. 379, 382, 390, 498, 512, 598, 600; 15843/1, pp. 58–76.

47. G.L., MSS 15842/3, pp. 333, 524, 556, 559; 15842/4, pp. 64–5.

48. G.L., MS 15842/3, pp. 474, 475.

49. G.L., MS 15843/1, pp. 151–2, 163, 188.

50. Ibid. p. 184.

51. Above, pp. 96–7; G.L., MSS 15842/5, pp. 295–6; 15842/6, pp. 275–8; 15843/6, pp. 31–7; 15843/7, pp. 33–56.
52. *Parliamentary Papers*, 1821.XII. 423–4.
53. Ibid; G.L., MSS 15843/2, pp. 121–2, 148, 191, 206, 244–5, 255–67, 311, 312; 15843/3, pp. 279–84.
54. Warlow, *Monmouth and Newland*, pp. 63, 65, 69.
55. *Parliamentary Papers*, 1824.XIII. 203–5; Warlow, *Monmouth and Newland*, p. 67.
56. G.L.,MS 15843/6, pp. 204–8.
57. G.L., MS 15843/1, pp. 65, 73–4, 142, 146, 148–53, 171.
58. G.L., MSS 15866/11, 1767–8 acct., p. 18, 1770–1 acct., p. 18; 15843/1, pp. 163, 171, 174.
59. G.L., MSS 15866/11, 1768–9 acct., p. 20, 1769–70 acct., pp. 19, 20, 1772–3 acct., p. 22; 15843/1, pp. 169–70, 171–2, 197–201, 230–2, 236, 273, 322–3.

Notes for Chapter 9

1. G.L., MS 15842/1, fo. 69v.
2. R. Withington, *English Pageantry: An Historical Outline* (2 vols., New York, 1926); D.M. Bergeron, *English Civic Pageantry, 1558–1642* (1971); *Lord Mayor's Pageants of the Merchant Taylors' Company*, ed. R.T.D. Sayle (1937), pp. 2–3; *Calendar of State Papers, Venetian*, XV.58–63; *A Calendar of Dramatic Records in the Books of the Livery Companies of London, 1485–1640*, ed. J. Robertson and D.J. Gordon (Malone Society Collections, III, 1958), pp. 54–5, 57–8, 61–8, 100, 111–12, 120–2, 125; J. Tatham, *London's Triumphs Celebrated* (1664); G.L., MS 15869.
3. G.L., MS 15842/2, fo. 7v.
4. G.L., MS 15842/1, fos. 32v, 119, 119v, 218, 248; *Calendar of State Papers, Venetian*, XV.58–63; *Calendar of Dramatic Records*, p. 66.
5. T. King, 'The Haberdashers' Company of London, 1602–42' (Univ. of Oxford B.A. dissertation, copy on deposit at Haberdashers' Hall), p. 33; Rappaport, *Worlds Within Worlds*, pp. 232–4, 389–91.
6. Rappaport, *Worlds Within Worlds*, p. 234; G.L., MSS 15868, fos. 146, 156, 164v, 170v, 181, 185, 207; 15842/4, p. 265; 15866/5, fos. 7, 38; 15866/6, fos. 26, 72, 83, 106.
7. P.R.O., PROB11/13, fo. 20v; PROB11/29, fo. 140v; G.L., MSS 9171/9, fo. 104; 9171/12, fo. 53.
8. Rappaport, *Worlds Within Worlds*, pp. 311–15; T. King, 'Haberdashers' Company', p. 33.
9. Bridewell Court Book, I, fos. 32, 50v, 59, 60v, 67v.
10. Ibid. fos. 33, 53v–4, 64v, 69r–v, 96v–7v.
11. G.L., MS 15842/1, fos. 9v, 10, 18, 22.
12. Ibid. fos. 9v, 18.
13. Rappaport, *Worlds Within Worlds*, pp. 32–6; Archer, Pursuit of Stability, pp. 74–5.
14. Above, pp. 68–71.
15. G.L., MSS 15839; 15866/1; 15842/1, fos. 245v, 334; 15842/3, pp. 465–6.
16. G.L., MS 15842/1, fos. 162v, 191v; 15842/2, fo. 58.
17. G.L., MS 15842/1, fo. 61v.
18. *T.E.D.*, II.60.
19. G.L., MSS 15839; 15866/1, 1633–4 acct., 15842/1, fo. 162v, 241r–v, 244, 260v.
20. G.L., MSS 15842/1, fos. 278v–9; 15842/2, fo. 61v.
21. G.L., MSS 15842/1, fos. 241r–v, 244, 263; 15866/1.
22. Drapers' Hall, Feast Accounts; Archer, *Pursuit of Stability*, pp. 116–18.
23. B.L., Lansdowne MS 16/72; *John Isham, Mercer and Merchant Adventurer: Two Account Books of a London Merchant in the Reign of Elizabeth I*, ed. G.D. Ramsay (Northamptonshire Record Society XXI, 1962), pp. lxx-lxxiii.
24. G.L., MS 15842/1, fos. 174, 187, 253.
25. Archer, *Pursuit of Stability*, p. 117.
26. G.L., MS 15842/1, fos. 180, 186v, 235v, 250.
27. G.L., MSS 15842/1, fo. 268; 15842/2, fo. 59r–v; 15842/3, p. 166.
28. G.L., MS 15868.
29. Ibid.; Archer, 'Governors and Governed', pp. 127–30.
30. G.L., MSS 15842/1, fos. 25, 31, 37v, 42v, 47v, 78v; 15842/2, fos. 10v, 75; 15868.

31. Archer, *Pursuit of Stability*, pp. 198–9.

32. G.L., MS 15842/1, fos. 219v, 222.

33. Ibid. fos. 241r-v, 242, 244v, 245v, 248v, 289, 289v.

34. G.L., MSS 15842/1, fos. 334, 343; 15842/2, fo. 61v.

35. G.L., MSS 15842/2, fos. 153v, 159; 15842/3, pp. 45, 46, 47, 63.

36. G.L., MS 15842/3, pp. 351, 497, 517, 524.

37. G.L., MSS 15842/3, pp. 45, 333, 334–5; 15842/4, pp. 44–5, 69.

38. G.L., MS 15871.

39. Ibid.; above, pp. 96–7.

40. Archer, *Pursuit of Stability*, pp. 120–4.

41. *Parliamentary Papers*, 1824.XIII. 189; G.L., MS 15842/1, fo. 303; above, pp. 72–3.

42. G.L., MS 15842/1, fos. 18v, 25v, 166v, 215v, 292, 295v, 343.

43. G.L., MS 15842/1, fo. 175.

44. G.L., MS 15842/6, fos. 404, 431.

45. G.L., MS 15842/1, fos. 23v, 24v, 25, 38, 166v, 174v, 203v.

46. G.L., MSS 15842/1, fos. 193, 200, 222v, 303; 15842/2, fo. 88v.

47. *Parliamentary Papers*, 1824.XIII. 217–8; above, pp. 72–3, 105.

48. *Parliamentary Papers*, 1819.X. 286–96; *Parliamentary Papers*, 1824.XIII. 209–10, 216, 217–18, 225.

49. G.L., MSS 15842/1, fos. 189, 292, 315; 15842/2, fo. 25; 15842/3, pp. 417, 433; 15842/5, p. 312.

50. G.L., MS 15842/1, fos. 147v, 151v.

51. G.L., MS 15842/3, pp. 151, 276.

52. G.L., MS 15842/3, pp. 431, 435, 437, 439; Meredith, *Aske's Hospital*, pp. 32–5.

53. *The Ordre of my Lorde Mayor, the Aldermen & the Shiriffes for their Metinges and Wearynge of Apparell Throughout the Yeare* (1568); G.L., MS 15839; Haberdashers' Hall, 1505 ordinances, fo. 7; P.R.O., PROB11.

54. G.L., MS 15842/1, fos. 22v, 26v, 53v, 69v, 90v, 126v–7, 156v, 161.

Notes for Chapter 10

1. G.L., MS 15842/1, fos. 134, 141v, 265v.

2. Tatham, *London's Triumphs Celebrated*; E. Settle, *The Triumphs of London for the Inauguration of Sir Richard Levett* (1699); J. Squire, *Tres Irenae Trophaea. Or the Tryumphes of Peace . . .* (1620); J. Heywood, *Londini Artium & Scientiarum Scaturigo: or, London's Fountaine of Arts and Sciences* (1630); idem, *London's Ius Honorarium* (1631).

3. G.L., MS 15869.

4. E.W. Ives, *Anne Boleyn* (1986), pp. 215–18; C.L.R.O., Rep. 2, fo. 70v; Rep. 9, fo. 2.

5. C.L.R.O., Rep. 13, fos. 69, 70v, 76v, 79v.

6. G.L., MS 15866/1, 1640–1 acct.; J. Taylor, *England's Comfort and London's Joy* (1641).

7. *Ordre of my Lorde Mayor*; G.L., MS 15866/1.

8. G.L., MS 15842/3, p. 180.

9. Haberdashers' Hall, Contract for building of barge.

10. G.L., MS 15869

11. G.L., MS 15842/1, fo. 119; Tatham, *London's Triumphs Celebrated*.

12. Tatham, *London's Triumphs Celebrated*.

13. Ibid.; Settle, *Triumphs of London*.

14. Tatham, *London's Triumphs Celebrated*.

15. Beaven, *Aldermen*.

16. R.M. Benbow, *Index of London Citizens Involved in City Government, 1558–1603* (typescript on deposit at Centre for Metropolitan History, London).

17. B.R. Masters, *The Chamberlain of the City of London, 1237–1987* (1988), pp. 23–4; Foster, *Politics of Stability*, p. 188.

18. C.L.R.O., Rep. 24, fos. 124v–6v.

19. C.L.R.O., Rep. 11, fos. 486, 487v; Rep. 12, fos. 395v, 408v; Brigden, *London and the Reformation*, pp. 169, 493, 494, 515, 534, 595.

20. C.L.R.O., Jour. 18, fos. 57, 57v–60, 62v, 66; Rep. 15, fos. 108, 109, 110v, 113, 115, 116; Clothwork-
    ers' Hall, Quarter Wardens' Accts., 1561–2, fo. 7r-v; Drapers' Hall, Wardens' Accts., 1562–3, fos.
    5v–8; G.L., MSS 11588/1, fos. 68, 69r-v; 5174/2, fos. 105v–6.
21. C.L.R.O., Jour. 19, fos. 407–8, 417v; Jour. 20, fos. 391, 394v–8, 410v, 414; Jour. 21, fos. 19, 21,
    45v, 50v, 52v, 421v, 426–7, 436v; G.L., MS 15842/1, fo. 17; B.L., Lansdowne MS 44/47.
22. C.L.R.O., Rep. 20, fo. 90.
23. C.L.R.O., Jour. 24, fos. 105r-v, 147r-v.
24. G.L., MS 15842/1, fos. 313, 314v.
25. G.L., MS 15842/2, fos. 122v, 128v.
26. G.L., MS 15842/3, p. 354.
27. N.S.B. Gras, *The Evolution of the English Corn Market from the Twelfth to the Eighteenth Century* (Cam-
    bridge, Mass., 1915), chs. III-IV; S. Thrupp, *A Short History of the Worshipful Company of Bakers*
    (1934), ch. V; C.L.R.O., Rep. 14, fo. 350v; Jour. 20, fos. 440v–2, 444–6.
28. C.L.R.O., Rep. 3, fos. 18v, 39v, 155r-v; Rep. 20, fos. 393v, 439; Jour. 11, fo. 260v.
29. Above, pp. 63–4.
30. C.L.R.O., Rep. 10, fo. 243v; Rep. 15, fo. 177v; Rep. 19, fo. 45v.
31. Above, pp. 17–18; Miller, 'London and Parliament', pp. 130–9.
32. C.L.R.O., Rep. 15, fo. 451; Rep.16, fo. 159v; Rep. 20, fos. 316, 332v; Rep. 23, fo. 395v.
33. G.L., MS 15842/1, fo. 217.
34. M. James, 'At a Crossroads of a Political Culture: the Essex Revolt, 1601', in his *Society, Politics
    and Culture: Studies in Early Modern England* (Cambridge, 1986), pp. 448, 449, 451–2; *The House of
    Commons, 1558–1603*, ed. P.W. Hasler (3 vols., 1981), III. 406–8; *D.N.B.*; Pearl, *London and the
    Outbreak*, pp. 306–7.
35. G.L., MS 15842/1, fo. 192v.
36. B.L., Lansdowne MSS 38/17–29; 114/13; C.L.R.O., Jour. 22, fo. 142v; G.L., MS 15842/1, fos. 2,
    4, 7v, 8v, 13v, 14, 15, 16, 17v, 20v; C.J. Kitching, 'The Quest for Concealed Lands', *Transactions
    of the Royal Historical Society*, 5th series, 24 (1984), 63–78.
37. *C.P.R., 1575–8*, p. 11; P.R.O., C66/1448, mm. 35–7; C.L.R.O., Rep. 23, fos. 560v, 570v; Rep. 24,
    fos. 349–50; G.L., MS 15842/1, fos. 87, 98v, 102v *Acts of the Privy Council of England*, ed. J.R. Dasent
    (32 vols., 1890–1907), XXX. 614–5.
38. J.S. Curl, *The Londonderry Plantation, 1609–1914* (Chichester, 1986), pp. 22–39, 314–19.
39. James, 'Crossroads'.
40. Brenner, 'Commercial Change', pp. 292, 293, 296, 321–2, 384, 398, 440; Pearl, *London and the
    Outbreak*, pp. 313, 316–20, 306–7.
41. Above, pp. 51–2.
42. Brenner, 'Commercial Change', pp. 356, 384, 397, 398, 410–11; Pearl, *London and the Outbreak*, pp.
    316–20.
43. Pearl, *London and the Outbreak*, pp. 316–20.
44. G.L., MS 15842/2, fos. 72v, 73–4, 80, 92.
45. *The House of Commons, 1660–1690*, ed. B.D. Henning (3 vols., 1983), III. 250–2; *The Rulers of London,
    1660–1689: A Biographical Record of the Aldermen and Common Councilmen of the City of London*, ed. J.R.
    Woodhead (London and Middlesex Archaeological Society, 1965), p. 131; Masters, *Chamberlain*,
    pp. 48–9; G.S. de Krey, 'London Radicals and Revolutionary Politics, 1675–1683', in *The Politics
    of Religion in Restoration England*, ed. T. Harris, P. Seaward, and M. Goldie (1990), pp. 137–8, 157.
46. *Rulers of London*, ed. Woodhead, p. 52; K.H.D. Haley, *The First Earl of Shaftesbury* (Oxford, 1968),
    pp. 703–4; T. Harris, *London Crowds in the Reign of Charles II: Propaganda and Politics from the Restoration
    until the Exclusion Crisis* (Cambridge, 1987), p. 185.
47. G.L., MSS 15842/3, pp. 270, 271–2, 276, 279; 15841, pp. 19–37; 15866/6, pp. 72, 83; Meredith,
    Aske's Hospital, pp. 84–5.
48. G.L., MS 15841; Prevett, *Short Description*, pp. 8–9; W.A. Speck, *Reluctant Revolutionaries: Englishmen
    and the Revolution of 1688* (Oxford, 1988), chs. III-IV.
49. *D.N.B.*; G.L., MS 15842/3, pp. 5, 58–9, 135.
50. Haley, *Shaftesbury*, pp. 694–5.
51. *A List of the Poll of the Severall Companies of London for a Lord Mayor for the Year Ensuing* (1682); G.S.

de Krey, *A Fractured Society: the Politics of London in the First Age of Party, 1688–1715* (Oxford, 1985), pp. 167–70.

52. *The Poll of the Liverymen of the City of London* (1710); *An Account of the Election of Members of Parliament for the City of London in the Year 1727* (1728); N. Rogers, *Whigs and Cities: Popular Politics in the Age of Walpole and Pitt* (Oxford, 1989), ch. I; Rogers, *Whigs and Cities*, pp. 32, 158.
53. G.L., MSS 15842/4, p. 259; 15842/5, pp. 28–9, 53, 63; Rogers, *Whigs and Cities*, pp. 32, 158.
54. G.L., MS 15842/5, pp. 63, 91, 107; *The House of Commons, 1714–45*, ed. R. Sedgwick (2 vols., 1970), I. 534–5; II. 21; Rogers, *Whigs and Cities*, pp. 32, 51, 63–4, 137, 140, 158.

Notes for Chapter 11

1. G.L., MS 15843/5, pp. 87, 94–6, 138–9, 174.
2. G.L., MSS 15843/4, pp. 584–7; 15843/7, pp. 58–60, 136–40; 15843/8, pp. 79–80.
3. G.L., MS 15843/7, pp. 8–11.
4. G.L., MSS 15843/5, pp. 298, 304; 15843/7, pp. 133–5, 173–4.
5. J. Read, 'The Manor of Hatcham: Aspects of its Development, 1600–1900' (Diploma of History thesis, University of London, 1973), pp. 12–17; R. Thatcher, *Hatcham and Telegraph Hill: An Historical Sketch* (Lewisham Local History Society, 1982), pp. 2–3.
6. Read, 'Manor of Hatcham', pp. 24–8; *Parliamentary Papers*, 1884.XXXIX, pt. IV, pp. 461–2, 465.
7. Read, 'Manor of Hatcham', pp. 33–43; *Parliamentary Papers*, 1884.XXXIX, pt. IV, pp. 460–1, 465, 469–70; Warlow, *Monmouth and Newland*, p. 68.
8. G.L., MS 15851/1, pp. 226–9, 244–6, 259–61, 282, 299–300, 306–7.
9. G.L., MS 15843/9, pp. 47–65.
10. Ibid.; Le Hardy, *Guide*, pp. 8–9, 11, 56.
11. G.L., MSS 15851/1–2.
12. G.L., MSS 15843/9, pp. 571–4; 15852/2.
13. G.L., MS 15843/9, pp. 96–100; Haberdashers' Hall, Compendium; *A Manual for the Use of the Court of Assistants of the Haberdashers' Company, Being an Abridgement of their Compendium* (1828).
14. G.L., MS 15843/9, pp. 47–65.
15. G.L., MS 15843/9, pp. 47–65, 512–16.
16. G.L., MS 15843/9, pp. 117–18, 512–16, 571–4; *Parliamentary Papers*, 1884. XXXIX, pt. II, p. 480.
17. G.L., MS 15843/10, pp. 68–74.
18. G.L., MS 15843/9, pp. 47–65, 300–9.
19. G.L., MSS 15843/9, pp. 512–16; 15843/10, pp.68–74; *Parliamentary Papers*, 1884., XXXIX, pt. II, p. 480.
20. G.L., MS 15843/10, pp. 68–74.
21. G.L., MSS 15843/7, pp. 426–9; 15843/9, pp. 118, 316–22.
22. *Parliamentary Papers*, 1884.XXXIX, pt. II, pp. 480–1; L.E. Ingarfield and M.B. Alexander, *Haberdashers' Aske's Hatcham Boys' School: A Short History*, p. 3; G.L., MSS 15843/9, pp. 563–8; 15849/6, pp. 35–8, 461–3.
23. *Parliamentary Papers*, 1884.XXXIX, pt. II, pp. 480–1.
24. *Parliamentary Papers*, 1837.XXV. 301; *Parliamentary Papers*, 1884.XXXIX, pt. II, p. 479; G.L., MSS 15843/6, pp. 328–30; 15857/2.
25. *Parliamentary Papers*, 1837.XXV. 301; *Parliamentary Papers*, 1884.XXXIX, pt. II, p. 479; G.L., MS 15857/2.
26. G.T. Eagleton, 'The Eagletons of Wakerley, Eltham', typescript in possession of Mr B.C. Gothard. I am grateful to Mr Gothard both for the loan of this typescript, and for sharing with me his own recollections of the Eagleton family.
27. *A List of the Master, Wardens, Assistants, and Liverymen of the Worshipful Company of Haberdashers* (1837); Armstrong, 'The Use of Information about Occupation'.
28. G.L., MSS 15866/13; 15843/6, pp. 2–14, 27; *Parliamentary Papers*, 1884.XXXIX, pt. II, pp. 511–16; *Abstract of British Historical Statistics*, ed. B.R. Mitchell (1988), pp. 737–8.
29. D. Owen, *English Philanthropy, 1660–1960* (1965), p. 285.
30. E.W. Brayley, *Londiniana, or Reminiscences of the British Metropolis* (4 vols., 1829), IV. 151–2.

31. G.L., MSS 15843/5, pp. 131–4, 253–4; 15843/6, pp. 310; 15843/7, pp. 557–9.
32. G.L., MS 15843/5, pp. 46–50, 51–2, 57, 65–71, 72–3, 131–4, 148–50.
33. G.L., MS 15843/8, pp. 176, 187, 199, 200, 504; Elmes, *Wren*, p. 431.
34. G.L., MS 15843/9, pp. 370–84.
35. G.L., MS 15843/9, pp. 441–3, 465–8, 469–70, 471–5.
36. G.L., MS 15843/9, pp. 499–500; 'The Worshipful Company of Haberdashers', *The Builder*, 1 Sept. 1916.
37. G.L., MSS 15871; 15844/6, pp. 299–300, 324, 325, 332, 344–5.
38. G.L., MS 15844/7, pp. 16, 72, 88, 89, 282; Haberdashers' Hall, Luff Collection of programmes and menus.
39. G.L., MSS 15842/15, pp. 259, 382, 388; 15844/9, pp. 176, 177.
40. Haberdashers' Hall, Luff Collection; G.L., MSS 15842/16, pp. 44, 62, 119, 150; 15842/17, p. 526; 15844/9, pp. 248, 258, 283, 288, 318, 460; 15844/10, p. 414.
41. G.L., MSS 15843/9, pp. 96–100; 15844/9, pp. 214, 241, 272, 330, 453, 455.
42. G.L., MSS 15842/16, p. 508; 15842/17, p. 526.
43. G.L., MS 15842/16, pp. 110, 314.
44. G.L., MSS 15842/15, pp. 590, 602, 605; 15842/16, pp. 51, 117, 119, 202, 259, 416, 472, 514, 581; 15851/1, pp. 353–4, 355–6, 357, 362, 363, 365, 367, 373.
45. *Parliamentary Papers*, 1884.XXXIX, pt. II, pp. 511–16; G.L., MSS 15844/9, pp. 24, 255, 258, 318; 15851/1, p. 365.
46. *Parliamentary Papers*, 1884.XXXIX, pt. II, p. 478.
47. G.L., MSS 15842/14, pp. 35, 70, 211, 236.
48. G.L., MS 15842/15, p. 104; Haberdashers' Hall, Luff Collection; *The City Press*, 3 Dec. 1904. Cf. ibid. 19 Dec. 1874, 9 Dec. 1882.
49. *The City Press*, 19 Dec. 1874.
50. Withington, *English Pageantry*, II. 117, 118, 119–20.
51. Beaven, *Aldermen* II. 146–54.
52. G.L., MSS 15842/16, pp. 302, 373; 15842/17, pp. 18, 292; 15844/9, pp. 381–5; Haberdashers' Hall, Court of Wardens, 1898–1917, pp. 197, 200, 202, 223, 229; *The City Press*, 6 Nov. 1875, 13 Nov. 1875, 7 Nov. 1874.
53. G.L., Civic Entertainments Collection, 9 Nov. 1875, 9 Nov. 1891, 9 Nov. 1907, 9 Nov. 1908; Withington, *English Pageantry*, II. 122, 133–5; D. Cannadine, 'The Context, Performance, and Meaning of Ritual: the British Monarchy and the Invention of Tradition, c. 1820–1977', in *The Invention of Tradition*, ed. E. Hobsbawm and T. Ranger (Cambridge, 1983), pp. 120–38.
54. G.L., MS 15842/16, pp. 100, 102, 259.
55. G.L., MSS 15842/16, pp. 195, 201, 206–8; 15844/9, p. 334; Ingarfield and Alexander, *Hatcham Boys' School*, p. 4.
56. G.L., MSS 15842/16, pp. 93, 575; 15842/17, pp. 213, 214.
57. *3 Hansard*, CCXXIX, cols. 1117–1138, 1142; J.F.B. Firth, *Municipal London* (1876), ch. III.
58. Above, pp. 173–4; L.B.S., *The City Livery Companies and Their Corporate Property* (1885), pp. 49–50.
59. L.B.S, *City Livery Companies*, p. 51; *Parliamentary Papers*, 1884.XXXIX, pt. II, p. 479.
60. *Parliamentary Papers*, 1884.XXXIX, pt. II, pp. 462–71.
61. Above, p. 163; G.L., MS 15843/9, pp. 512–16.
62. *Parliamentary Papers*, 1884.XXXIX, pt. II, p. 479; G.L., MS 15849/2, pp. 41, 252.
63. *Parliamentary Papers*, 1884.XXXIX, pt. II, pp. 511–16; G.L., MS 15849/5, pp. 418–26; 15849/7, p. 127.
64. *Parliamentary Papers*, 1884.XXXIX, pt. II, pp. 511–16; *Crockford's Clerical Directory* (1876); G.L., MS 15849/6, pp. 213–17, 218–20, 221–4, 225–7, 228–30, 238–40.
65. J. Lang, *City and Guilds of London Institute Centenary, 1878–1978* (1978), pp. 1–18; above, pp. 167–8.
66. I.G. Doolittle, *The City of London and its Livery Companies* (Dorchester, 1982), pp. 21–7; *Parliamentary Papers*, 1837.XXV. 22–4, 299–302; G.L., MS 15842/12, pp. 11, 29, 34.
67. Doolittle, *City of London*, pp. 37–50.
68. Ibid. pp. 53–63; G.L., MSS 15842/14, pp. 248–50; 15843/9, pp. 389, 404; *Who's Who of British Members of Parliament*, ed. S.M. Stenton and F.M. Lees (4 vols, 1976–9), I. 263.

69. Doolittle, *City of London*, pp. 63–8; G.L., MS 15842/14, pp. 388–9, 412–13, 414–15, 543–4.

70. Doolittle, *City of London*, pp. 71–88.

71. Ibid. pp. 92–5; *3 Hansard*, CCXXIX, cols. 1117–1138; Firth, *Municipal London*; G.L., MS 15842/16, p. 420.

72. *3 Hansard* CCXXIX, cols. 1139–42; *Who's Who of British Members of Parliament*, I. 91–2.

73. Doolittle, *City of London*, pp. 95–9; Owen, *English Philanthropy*, pp. 284–9; *Parliamentary Papers*, 1884.XXXIX; Ramsay, 'Victorian Historiography'.

74. G.L., MSS 15853, pp. 13–14, 18, 20; 15842/17, pp. 10–11, 17, 54, 114.

75. Doolittle, *City of London*, pp. 99–100.

76. Ibid. pp. 100–101; G.L., MSS 15853, p. 26; 15842/17, pp. 271, 276, 289, 327, 347; E. Bristow, 'The Liberty and Property Defence League and Individualism', *Historical Journal*, 18 (1975), 761–89.

77. Dollittle, *City of London*, pp. 101–2; Owen, *English Philanthropy*, pp. 289–90.

Notes for Chapter 12

1. *Parliamentary Papers*, 1819.X. 289-93; *Parliamentary Papers*, 1821.XII. 423-4; *Parliamentary Papers*, 1824.XII. 203-5; *Parliamentary Papers*, 1884.XXXIX, pt. IV, pp. 421-2, 436-40, 460-1; Meredith, *Adams' Grammar School*, pp. 42-3, 56, 58-9.

2. G.L., MSS 15843/4, pp. 469-70, 510-14, 526-8, 540; 15843/6, pp. 166-8, 245-7.

3. G.L., MSS 15843/4, pp. 516-17; 15843/5, pp. 534-5, 591-2; 15843/6, pp. 57-8, 243-4; *Parliamentary Papers*, 1819.X. 290.

4. G.L., MSS 15843/6, pp. 543, 598-604; 15843/8, pp. 145-7.

5. G.L., MS 15843/5, pp. 408-10, 420-1; 15843/7, pp. 311-14, 331-6.

6. Meredith, *Adams' Grammar School*, p. 24; G.L., MSS 15843/5, pp. 110-13, 200-02, 263-8, 376-8; 15843/6, pp. 103-12; 15843/8, pp. 48-55; 15881, pp. 61-2.

7. G.L., MS 15899, pp. 8-9.

8. *Parliamentary Papers*, 1821.XII. 423; G.L., MSS 15849/1, pp. 204-5; 15843/6, pp. 204-8, 232-3.

9. Ward, *Monmouth School*, p.13.

10. Ibid. p. 14; Kissack, *Monmouth*, p. 164; G.L., MS 15843/6, pp. 522-34; 15843/8, pp. 542-53.

11. G.L., MS 15849/1, pp. 45-65, 71-92.

12. Kissack, *Monmouth*, p. 164; G.L., MS 15843/6, pp. 522-34; 15843/8, pp. 542-53.

13. Kissack, *Monmouth*, ch. III.

14. G.L., MSS 15843/6, pp. 522-34; 15843/8, pp. 542-53, 575-84; Owen, *English Philanthropy*, pp. 248-9.

15. G.L., MS 15843/8, pp. 542-53, 575-84.

16. G.L., MSS 15843/9, pp. 1-6; 15849/1, pp. 16-19, 178-80; 15899, pp. 49-64, 112-14; (1828) 3 Russ. 530, *38 English Reports*, 674-7. For an argument that Chancery practice was flexible, and that Eldon's intentions were rather more liberal than subsequent interpretations of his judgment suggested, see R.S. Tompson, *Classics or Charity?*, pp. 116-24.

17. G.L., MSS 15843/8, pp. 575-84; 15843/9, pp. 1-6; 15899, pp. 79-83, 97-100.

18. Kissack, *Monmouth*, p. 165; G.L., MS 15849/1, pp. 125-39, 159-61.

19. G.L., MS 15849/1, pp. 45-65, 71-92, 93-9.

20. Above, pp. 160–3; G.L., MS 15843/8, pp. 575-84.

21. G.L., MS 15849/2, pp. 42-87.

22. G.L., MS 15849/1, pp. 231-4, 242-5, 298-306.

23. Owen, *English Philanthropy*, pp. 84-5, 182-97.

24. G.L., MS 15843/6, pp. 402-3; 15843/7, pp. 329-30.

25. G.L., MS 15843/8, pp. 111-14, 294-341, 379-503, 505-15, 534-5; *Parliamentary Papers*, 1819.X. 289-93; *Parliamentary Papers*, 1821.XII. 423-4; *Parliamentary Papers*, 1824.XII. 188-292; R. Tompson, *The Charity Commission and the Age of Reform* (1979).

26. *Parliamentary Papers*, 1884.XXXIX, pt. IV, p. 437; G.L., MSS 15843/8, pp. 362-70, 564-7; 15843/9, pp. 34-41; *A Biographical Dictionary of British Architects, 1600-1840*, pp. 705-6.

27. G.L., MS 15843/9, pp. 28-33.

28. G.L., MS 15843/9, pp. 145-6, 147-50, 152-5; 15849/1, pp. 296-7, 298-306; *Parliamentary Papers*, 1884.XXXIX, pt. IV, pp. 440-1.
29. G.L., MSS 15849/1, pp. 322-45, 352-9, 360-77; 15849/2, pp. 1-4, 42-87; 15849/4, pp. 327-34; 15843/9, pp. 409-38.
30. Warlow, *Monmouth and Newland*, pp. 377-86; G.L., MSS 15849/4, pp. 91-112; 15843/9, pp. 444-64.
31. G.L., MSS 15849/4, pp. 40-6; 15849/5, pp. 63-4, 70-81.
32. G.L., MS 15849/1, pp. 322-45.
33. Warlow, *Monmouth and Newland*, pp. 367-86; G.L., MSS 15849/3, pp. 40-6; 15849/4, pp. 91-112, 342-75.
34. G.L., MSS 15881, pp. 122-5; 15843/5, pp. 77-8; 15849/1, pp. 296-7, 307-13.
35. G.L., MSS 15849/1, pp. 378-87; 15849/2, pp. 42-87, 143-7, 148-61, 252-7.
36. G.L., MS 15849/3, pp. 313-17, 320-2, 324-30.
37. G.L., MS 15849/4, pp. 252-61, 292-9, 327-34; *Parliamentary Papers*, 1867-8.XXVIII, pt. XIV, pp. 21-7; *Parliamentary Papers*, 1884.XXXIX, pt. IV, pp. 431-5; D. Allsobrook, *Schools for the Shires: the Reform of Middle-Class Education in Mid-Victorian England* (Manchester, 1986), pp. 85-6.
38. Owen, *English Philanthropy*, p. 191.
39. Ibid. pp. 199-200; G.L., MSS 15842/13, pp. 37, 46-7, 111-12, 121, 136, 384, 397; 15843/9, pp. 323-5, 326-9; 15849/4, pp. 35-9.
40. *3 Hansard*, LXXXVI, 733.
41. Owen, *English Philanthropy*, pp. 202-8, 249-50.
42. Ibid. pp. 250-1; Allsobrook, *Schools for the Shires*, ch. VIII; G. Sutherland, 'Secondary Education: the Education of the Middle Classes', in *Government and Society in Nineteenth-Century Britain*, ed. C. Fox et al. (Truro, 1977), pp. 139, 142-3, 145-6.
43. *Parliamentary Papers*, 1867-8.XXVIII, pt. XII, pp. 297-305; *Parliamentary Papers*, 1867-8.XXVIII, pt. XVI, pp. 25-32.
44. Owen, *English Philanthropy*, pp. 251-3; P.H.J.H. Gosden, *The Development of Educational Administration in England and Wales* (Oxford, 1966), pp. 59-62.
45. Owen, *English Philanthropy*, pp. 253-5; Gosden, *Educational Administration*, pp. 62-5.
46. G.L., MSS 15849/6, pp. 87-92; 15851/1.
47. Owen, *English Philanthropy*, pp. 257-8; Allsobrook, *Schools for the Shires*, ch. X; *British Parliamentary Election Results, 1832-1885*, ed. F.W.S. Craig (2nd. edn., Aldershot, 1989), pp. 4-6.
48. Allsobrook, *Schools for the Shires*, pp. 196-7; *Parliamentary Papers*, 1884.XXXIX, pt. IV, p. 464; *Gladstone's Speeches*, ed. A. Tilney Bassett (1911), p. 339; G.L., MS 15849/5, pp. 332-58.
49. *Parliamentary Papers*, 1867-8.XXVIII, pt. XVI, pp. 26-7.
50. *Parliamentary Papers*, 1884.XXXIX, pt. IV, pp. 465-9.
51. G.L., MS 15849/5, pp. 332-58, 465-9; *Parliamentary Papers*, 1867-8.XXVIII, pt. XVI, pp. 27-9.
52. G.L., MS 15843/9, pp. 593-4.
53. G.L., MSS 15849/5, pp. 446-8, 449-51; 15849/6, pp. 1-4, 43-8.
54. *Parliamentary Papers*, 1884.XXXIX, pt. IV, pp. 442-51.
55. G.L., MS 15849/5, pp. 213-19, 220-1, 224-5, 226-33, 253-9; *Parliamentary Papers*, 1884.XXXIX, pt. IV, p. 441.
56. G.L., MSS 15849/5, pp. 326-7, 383-94, 471-4, 475-7, 478-9; 15849/6, pp. 7-10.
57. G.L., MS 15843/9, pp. 545-52.
58. G.L., MS 15849/6, pp. 120-2, 125-6, 127; 15843/9, pp. 589-92.
59. G.L., MS 15852/1, pp. 14-19, 20-3, 24-9, 30, 31-2, 33-5, 36-7, 47-51, 53-4, 55-6, 57-9, 60-1, 62-4; *Parliamentary Papers*, 1884.XXXIX, pt. IV, pp. 442-51.
60. J. Wigley, *A Short History of the Haberdashers' Aske's School, Elstree* (Elstree, 1984), pp. 7-8; Ingarfield and Alexander, *Hatcham Boys' School*, pp. 3-4, 7, 43. For the subsequent move of the Boys' and Girls' Schools at Hoxton to Hampstead and Acton respectively between 1898 and 1901, see Wigley, *Short History*, pp. 8-9.
61. *Parliamentary Papers*, 1884.XXXIX, pt. IV, pp. 424-30; G.L., MSS 15852/1, pp. 10-12, 39-40, 41-4, 45-6, 77-8, 79-80, 81-2, 83, 84-5, 86, 87-8; 15849/6, pp. 378-81.
62. L. Wynne Evans, 'The Evolution of Welsh Educational Structure and Administration, 1881-1921', in *Studies in the Government and Control of Education Since 1860* (History of Education Society, 1970),

pp. 51-5; *A Manual for the Private Use of the Court of Assistants of the Haberdashers' Company, London* (1954), pp. 83-6; Monmouth Grammar School, Abstract of Accounts, 1893; Monmouth School for Girls, Abstract of Accounts, 1898; G.L., MS 15852/1, pp. 278-81, 284-5, 306-7, 310-12.

63. G.L., MS 15852/1, pp. 197-200, 216-17; T. Morgan, *Monmouthshire Education, 1889-1974* (1988), pp. 39-40.

64. G.L., MS 15852/1, pp. 270-2, 278-81, 292-3, 315-17, 324-7; Haberdashers' Hall, Endowed Schools Committee, 1894-1913, pp. 53-4.

65. G.L., MS 15852/1, pp. 286-9, 310-12, 321-2, Haberdashers' Hall, Endowed Schools Committee, 1894-1913, pp. 6, 11-13, 19-21, 59-60; *Monmouthshire Beacon*, 3 Dec. 1897.

66. G.L., MS 15852/1, pp. 315-17, 319-20, 327-9; Haberdashers' Hall, Endowed Schools Committee, 1894-1913, pp. 18, 19-21, 59-60.

67. *Parliamentary Papers*, 1884.XXXIX, pt. IV, pp. 470-3; Manual (1954), pp. 104-5.

68. *Manual* (1954), pp. 59, 61, 62.

Notes for Chapter 13

1. *List of the Court and Livery of the Worshipful Company of Haberdashers* (1937); *Members of the Worshipful Company of Haberdashers* (1990).

2. *Members* (1990); Haberdashers' Hall, Freedom and Apprenticeship Registers.

3. Haberdashers' Hall, Court of Wardens, 1960; 1962; 1969; 1972; 1973; 1979; Court of Assistants, 1961.

4. Haberdashers' Hall, Minute Book, 1940-4, pp. 480, 492; Court of Wardens, 1960; 1964; 1966; Members (1990).

5. *Standing Orders*; Haberdashers' Hall, Court of Assistants, 1961; 1973; 1975; 1980; 1981; *Master's Newsletter*, 1981.

6. *Standing Orders*, pp. 12-14; Haberdashers' Hall, Minute Book, 1926-31, pp. 595-6.

7. Haberdashers' Hall, Court of Assistants, 1958.

8. Haberdashers' Hall, Minute Book, 1926-31, p. 156; Minute Book, 1948-50, pp. 139-40; Court of Assistants, 1958; 1969.

9. Haberdashers' Hall, Minute Book, 1926-31, pp. 249, 423-4, 462-4, 484-5, 500-1; Minute Book, 1937-40, pp. 2-3; Minute Book, 1940-4, pp. 224, 254-5, 461-2; Minute Book, 1944-8, p. 73; Court of Assistants, 1958; *Standing Orders*, p.12; *Members* (1990).

10. *Standing Orders* (1990), pp. 15-17.

11. Haberdashers' Hall, Minute Book, 1917-20, pp. 16-18, 272, 345.

12. Haberdashers' Hall, Minute Book, 1917-20, pp. 423, 483, 495, 523-4, 627; Minute Book, 1920-6, pp. 144, 217, 236, 284-5, 431, 540.

13. Haberdashers' Hall, Minute Book, 1937-40, pp. 327, 356, 394, 407, 423, 449; Minute Book, 1940-4, pp. 169, 278-9, 492.

14. Haberdashers' Hall, Minute Book, 1944-8, pp. 122, 128-9; Minute Book, 1948-50, pp. 163, 308-9, 425-6, 439, 459-61; Court of Assistants, 12 Feb. 1952.

15. Haberdashers' Hall, Minute Book, 1920-6, p. 144; Minute Book, 1934-7, pp. 146, 274-5; Minute Book, 1937-40, pp. 140, 208.

16. Haberdashers' Hall, Minute Book, 1944-8, pp. 483-4; Court of Assistants, 1960; 1961; 1964; 1969; 1975; 1978; 1980; *Masters' Newsletters*, 1970, 1971.

17. Haberdashers' Hall, Minute Book, 1948-50, p. 224; Court of Assistants, 11 Nov. 1952.

18. Haberdashers' Hall, Court of Wardens, 1964; Court of Assistants, 1976; *Masters' Newsletters*, 1971, 1985. At this and at numerous other points in this chapter I have relied heavily on interviews with Captain M.E. Barrow, the present Clerk to the Company.

19. Annual Calendar issued with Company Diary.

20. Haberdashers' Hall, Minute Book, 1920-6, p. 362; Minute Book, 1931-4, pp. 123, 474; Minute Book, 1934-7, p. 36.

21. Haberdashers' Hall, Court of Wardens, 5 Mar. 1951, 3 July 1951; *Master's Newsletter*, 1970.

22. *D.N.B.*; Haberdashers' Hall, Minute Book, 1934-7, p. 160; Court of Assistants, 10 Nov. 1954; Court of Wardens, 4 Jan. 1955; Court of Assistants, 1966.

23. Haberdashers' Hall, Minute Book, 1926-31, p. 355; Minute Book, 1931-4, p. 77; Minute Book, 1934-7, pp. 269, 349; Ward, *Monmouth School*, p. 32; Ingarfield and Alexander, *Hatcham Boys' School*, p. 25; *Masters' Newsletters, passim.*

24. Haberdashers' Hall, Minute Book, 1920-6, pp. 178, 306; Minute Book, 1934-7, p. 69.

25. Haberdashers' Hall, Minute Book, 1934-7, pp. 146, 174; *Master's Newsletter*, 1977.

26. Haberdashers' Hall, Minute Book, 1934-7, pp. 402, 414; Court of Wardens, 16 Jan. 1953, 3 Mar. 1953; Court of Assistants, 12 May 1953, 16 June 1953, 14 July 1953, 15 Sep. 1953.

27. Haberdashers' Hall, Minute Book, 1937-40, pp. 154, 197, 288, 332, 452; Minute Book, 1940-4, pp. 94, 424; Minute Book, 1944-8, p. 64.

28. Haberdashers' Hall, Court of Wardens, 7 Jan. 1953, 10 Dec. 1957; *Masters' Newsletters*, 1977, 1984, 1986, 1988; Programme for Services Dinner, 10 Apr. 1991.

29. Haberdashers' Hall, Minute Book, 1940-4, p. 435; Minute Book, 1944-8, pp. 6, 30-1, 53, 65-6, 97-8, 107-9; Court of Wardens, 1980; *Master's Newsletter*, 1980; Members (1990).

30. Haberdashers' Hall, Minute Book, 1940-4, pp. 30, 32.

31. Haberdashers' Hall, Minute Book, 1937-40, p. 297; Minute Book, 1940-4, pp. 194-5, 223.

32. Haberdashers' Hall, Minute Book, 1944-8, pp. 349, 401-2, 447; Minute Book, 1948-50, pp. 133-5; Court of Assistants, Apr. 1952; Planning Committee, 4 Feb. 1953, 11 Mar. 1953, 16 Mar. 1954, 21 Apr. 1954, 8 July 1954, 14 Oct. 1954, 11 Jan. 1955, 29 Mar. 1955, 22 Nov. 1955; Finance Committee, 16 Nov. 1955; Prevett, *Short Description*, pp. 11-12.

33. Haberdashers' Hall, Court of Assistants, 1980.

34. *Master's Newsletter*, 1976; ex. inf. Clerk.

35. Ex. inf. Clerk.

36. Curtis, *History of Education*, pp. 345-6; Haberdashers' Hall, Minute Book, 1917-20, pp. 473-4, 529, 554-5, 698-9; Minute Book, 1920-6, pp. 20-2; Ingarfield and Alexander, *Hatcham Boys' School*, p. 21.

37. Haberdashers' Hall, Minute Book, 1920-6, p. 651; Minute Book, 1926-31, pp. 57-8, 61, 68-9, 72, 113-5, 127-8, 130, 185, 197-9, 202-3, 232, 238-42; Ingarfield and Alexander, *Hatcham Boys' School*, pp. 22-3.

38. *Manual* (1954), pp. 86-8; Ward, *Monmouth School*, pp. 26, 28.

39. Haberdashers' Hall, Minute Book, 1920-6, pp. 650-1; Minute Book, 1926-31, pp. 128-9, 138-9, 164, 196-7, 305-6, 470, 569-70.

40. Haberdashers' Hall, Minute Book, 1931-4, pp. 167, 209, 242, 261, 304; Minute Book, 1934-7, p.9.

41. Haberdashers' Hall, Minute Book, 1920-6, pp. 699-700; Minute Book, 1926-31, pp. 47, 57, 185-6, 232; Meredith, *Adams' Grammar School*, p. 20.

42. Haberdashers' Hall, Minute Book, 1934-7, p. 488, Minute Book, 1937-40, pp. 6-7, 93-4, 125, 127, 156, 170; Meredith, *Adams' Grammar School*, p. 20.

43. Curtis, *History of Education*, pp. 383-4, 389.

44. Haberdashers' Hall, Minute Book, 1940-4, pp. 486, 496-7.

45. Ingarfield and Alexander, *Hatcham Boys' School*, pp. 27-8; *Manual* (1954), p. 42; Haberdashers' Hall, Minute Book, 1944-8, pp. 183-4, 382.

46. Haberdashers' Hall, Minute Book, 1944-8, pp. 185-6, 331-2, 352-3, 360-1, 364; Minute Book, 1948-50, pp. 13, 126, 155, 416; *Manual* (1954), p. 28.

47. Haberdashers' Hall, Minute Book, 1944-8, pp. 5, 183-4; Minute Book, 1948-50, pp. 155-7, 413-16; Endowed Schools Committee, 31 May 1951; *Manual* (1954), pp. 88-9.

48. Haberdashers' Hall, Minute Book, 1944-8, pp. 183-4; Court of Assistants, 8 Dec. 1953, 16 Mar. 1954, 13 Dec. 1955; Wigley, *Haberdashers' Aske's Elstree*, pp. 12-13; *Masters' Newsletters*, 1971, 1974.

49. *Masters' Newsletters*, 1970, 1976, 1977, 1985.

50. *Hatcham Tercentenary: A Literary Review of the Hatcham Schools*, ed. R.M. Hills (1990), pp. 34-6; Masters' Newsletters, 1975, 1976.

51. *Masters' Newsletters*, 1971, 1972, 1973, 1974, 1975.

52. Ibid. 1977, 1978, 1979, 1980, 1981, 1982.

53. Ibid. 1987, 1988.

54. Ibid. 1980, 1987.

55. Ibid. 1989, 1990; ex. inf. Clerk.

56. *The Economist*, 14 July 1990; *The Financial Times*, 25 June 1990; *Hansard*, Written Answers, 6/7 Mar. 1991.
57. C. Kay, *Times Educational Supplement*, 23 Nov. 1990.
58. Hansard, 23 Mar. 1990; *The Independent*, 24 Feb. 1990; 17 May 1990.
59. *Masters' Newsletters*, 1973, 1976, 1987.
60. *Manual* (1988), pp. 8-9, 16, 20, 29, 31, 32.
61. *Manual* (1954), pp. 102-3; *Manual* (1988), pp. 27-8, 31.
62. *Manual* (1988), p. 28.
63. Ibid. pp. 18-19; *Masters' Newsletters*, 1987, 1989, 1990.
64. *Parliamentary Papers*, 1884.XXXXIX, pt. IV, pp. 460-2; *Manual* (1954), pp. 90, 92-7; *Manual* (1988), pp. 23-7; Haberdashers' Hall, Court of Assistants, 1974; *Master's Newsletter*, 1981; ex. inf. Clerk.
65. Haberdashers' Hall, Minute Book, 1917-20, pp. 457, 551-2; Manual (1954), p. 40; Haberdashers' Hall, Court of Assistants, 8 Jan. 1957, 25 Apr. 1957; Finance Committee, 4 Dec. 1957.
66. *Manual* (1954), pp. 22-5; Haberdashers' Hall, Finance Committee, 1959.
67. Ex. inf. Past Master Bostock and Clerk.

Bibliography

1: MANUSCRIPT SOURCES

The records of the Haberdashers' Company are discussed by W. Le Hardy, *The Worshipful Company of Haberdashers. The Descriptive Class List of Records* (1954), a copy of which is available for consultation in the Guildhall Library Manuscripts Department. The records themselves are divided between the Guildhall and the Company's Hall in Staining Lane. Most pre–1900 records are kept at the Guildhall; most thereafter at the Hall. The list below is not a comprehensive survey of the archive, for which readers should consult Le Hardy. It simply represents those documents found most useful in the writing of the present volume.

THE RECORDS OF THE HABERDASHERS' COMPANY

Records Stored at Guildhall Library (G.L., MSS)

15841	Letters Patent to Haberdashers, 1685, with Documents on Company in James II's Reign
15838	Ordinances of the Hatmakers, 1501 and 1511
15839	Ordinances of the Haberdashers, 1629
15840	Ordinances of the Haberdashers, 1675
15842/1–18	Minutes of the Court of Assistants, 1583–1892
15844/1–10	Minutes of the Court of Wardens, 1725–1898
15887/1–6	Minutes of the Hoxton Committee, 1695–1874
15849/1–7	Minutes of the Charities Committee, 1827–1904
15850/1–11	Minutes of the Estates Committee, 1827–1900
15845	Committee Minute Book, 1689–97
15846	Minutes of Grand and Select Committees, 1811–27
15847	Minutes of Survey Committee, 1811–25
15881	Minutes of the Adams Committee, 1812–26
15889	Minutes of the Kent Committee, 1812–27
15899	Minutes of the Jones Committee, 1814–25
15848	Rough Committee Minute Book, 1820–7
15851/1–2	Special Committee Minutes, 1854–1901
15900	Minutes of the New Cross Estates Committee, 1858–9
15852/1	Minutes of the Endowed Schools Committee, 1870–94
15853	Minutes of the Guilds Committee, 1880–94
15843/1–11	Report Books, 1760–1897
15876/1–2	Report of the Select Committee of 1757
15866/1–13	Accounts of the Wardens and Clerk, 1633–1807
15868	Accounts of the Wardens of the Yeomanry, 1600–61
15869	Accounts for Lord Mayors' Triumphs, 1604, 1620, 1627, 1631, 1632, 1664, and 1699
15870	Accounts of the Rebuilding of the Hall, 1667–76
15888	Accounts of Aske's Hospital, 1696–1761
15903/1–2	Accounts of Lady Weld's Charity, 1630–1826
15854/1–3	Accounts for Attendance at Courts and Committees, 1723–1825
15871	Accounts for Dinners, 1729–1825
15874	Memoranda Book, relating to Company properties, commenced c. 1600
15876	Memoranda Book, being an Account of State of Company in 1657

15877   Memoranda Book, being an Account of Charities, c. 1731
15873   Will Book, 1535–1908
15875   Register of Benefactions, 1607
15885   Memoranda Relating to Aldersey's Charity
15897   Memoranda Relating to Jones' Charity
15898/1–3   Statutes for Monmouth and Newland Charities
15879   Statutes for Newport Charity
15886/1–3   Statutes for Aske's Hospital
15880   Memoranda Relating to Adams Charity, 1657
15882   Visitors' Book for Adams Charity, 1806–27
15883/1–2   Surveys of Knighton Estate, 1782 and 1804
15901   Visitors' Book for Trotman School, 1827–99
15902   Admissions Register for Trotman School, 1844–99
15890   Hoxton Hospital Inventory, 1831
15891/1–3   Hoxton Hospital Visitation Books, 1835–74
15892   Hoxton Hospital, Reports of Chaplain, 1854–72
15860/1–10   Registers of Apprentice Bindings, 1583–1967
15864/1–5   Index to Apprentice Bindings, 1690–1967
15857/1–3   Registers of Freedom Admissions, 1526–1967
15858/1–2   Index to Freedom Admissions, 1642–1967
15855/1–2   Lists of Courts and Committees, 1787–1940

Records Stored at Haberdashers' Hall
        Letters Patent to Haberdashers, 1448
        Letters Patent to Haberdashers, 1498
        Letters Patent to Haberdashers, 1502
        Letters Patent to Haberdashers, 1510
        Letters Patent to Haberdashers, 1558
        Letters Patent to Haberdashers, 1578
        Letters Patent to Haberdashers, 1685
        Letters Patent to Haberdashers, 1935
        Ordinances of the Haberdashers, 1505
        Grant of Arms to Haberdashers, 1446
        Grant of Arms to Haberdashers, 1503
        Grant of Crest and Supporters to Haberdashers, 1570

  Minutes of Court of Assistants, 1892–1916 (2 vols.)
  Minutes of Court of Wardens, 1898–1917 (1 vol.)
  Minutes of Charities Committee, 1904–17 (1 vol.)
  Minutes of Estates Committee, 1900–17 (2 vols.)
  Minutes of the Finance Committee, 1827–1916 (5 vols.)
  Minutes of the Endowed Schools Committee, 1894–1917 (2 vols.)

From 1917 the minutes of the various Courts and Committees are gathered together in individual volumes.

  Maps and Plans of Company estates and properties as listed by Le Hardy, *Descriptive List*, pp. 59–63.
  G.F. Luff Collection of programmes, menus and invitations

OTHER MANUSCRIPT SOURCES

Guildhall Library, London
9051/1–5   Archdeaconry Court of London, Will Registers, 1363–1604

9171/1–19	Commissary Court of London, Will Registers, 1374–1603
5174/2	Bakers' Company, Wardens' Accounts, 1548–86
6117	Curriers' Company, Memorandum Book
14346/1	Curriers' Company, Wardens' Accounts, 1557–94
11588/1	Grocers' Company, Court Minutes, 1556–91

Merchant Tailors' Company Records (microfilms at Guildhall)
C.M. I-III   Court Minutes, 1562–1601

Bridewell Court Book, vol. I, Apr. 1559-June 1562, microfilm on deposit at Guildhall Library

Corporation of London Records Office
                        Repertories of the Court of Aldermen
                        Journals of the Court of Common Council
                        Letter Books
                        Remembrancia
                        Mayor's Court, Original Bills
                        Common Serjeant's Book, vol. I

Greater London Records Office
H1/ST/A1/3–4   St Thomas' Hospital, Court Minutes, 1568–1608

Drapers' Company
W.A.   Wardens' Accounts, bundles for each year separately foliated
                           Feast Accounts, 1563–1602
Clothworkers' Company
C.M. II   Court Minutes, 1558–81
Q.W.A.   Quarter Wardens' Accounts, bundles for each year separately foliated

Westminster Abbey Muniments
12163

British Library
                        Additional Manuscripts
                        Cotton Manuscripts
                        Egerton Manuscripts
                        Lansdowne Manuscripts

Public Record Office
C1   Chancery, Proceedings
C5   Chancery, Proceedings
C66   Chancery, Patent Rolls
E122   Exchequer, Customs Accounts
E159   Exchequer, King's Remembrancer, Memoranda Rolls
E179   Exchequer, King's Remembrancer, Lay Subsidies
PROB 2   Prerogative Court of Canterbury, Inventories
PROB 11   Prerogative Court of Canterbury, Will Registers
REQ2   Court of Requests, Elizabeth I
SC8   Ancient Petitions
SP12   State Papers Domestic, Elizabeth I
STAC8   Court of Star Chamber, James I

2: WORKS OF REFERENCE

Abstract of British Historical Statistics, ed. B.R. Mitchell (1988)
The Aldermen of the City of London, ed. A.B. Beaven (2 vols., 1908–13)

A Biographical Dictionary of British Architects, 1600–1840, ed. H. Colvin (1978)

The British Atlas of Historic Towns, Vol. III: The City of London, ed. M.D. Lobel (Oxford, 1989)

British Parliamentary Election Results, 1832–1885, ed. F.W.S. Craig (2nd edn., Aldershot, 1989)

Calamy Revised, Being a Revision of Edmund Calamy's Account of the Ministers and Others Ejected and Silenced, 1660–2, ed. A.G. Mathews (2nd edn., Oxford, 1988)

Crockford's Clerical Directory

Dictionary of National Biography

A Dictionary of Saints, ed. D. Attwater (1965)

English Medieval Architects: A Biographical Dictionary Down to 1550, ed. J. Harvey (1984)

The History of Parliament

The House of Commons, 1509–1558, ed. S.T. Bindoff (3 vols., 1982)

The House of Commons, 1558–1603, ed. P.W. Hasler (3 vols., 1981)

The House of Commons, 1660–1690, ed. B.D. Henning (3 vols., 1983)

The House of Commons, 1714–1745, ed. R. Sedgwick (2 vols., 1970)

Index of London Citizens Involved in City Government, 1558–1603, compiled by R.M. Benbow (unpublished typescript on deposit at Centre for Metropolitan History, London)

The Oxford Dictionary of Saints, ed. D.H. Farmer (Oxford, 1978)

The Rulers of London, 1660–1689: A Biographical Record of the Aldermen and Common Councilmen of the City of London, ed. J.R. Woodhead (London and Middlesex Archaeological Society, 1965)

Who Was Who

Who's Who of British Members of Parliament, ed. M. Stenton and S. Lees (4 vols., 1976–9)

3: PRINTED PRIMARY SOURCES

An Account of the Election of Members of Parliament for the City of London in the Year 1727 (1728)

Acts of Court of the Mercers' Company, 1453–1527, ed. L. Lyell and F.D. Watney (Cambridge, 1936)

Amman, J., *Panoplia Omnium Illiberalium Mechanicarum aut Sedentarium Artium Genera Continens* (1568)

Blakesley, G.H., *The London Companies Commission: A Comment on the Majority Report* (1885)

Brayley, E.W., *Londiniana, or Reminiscences of the British Metropolis* (4 vols., 1829)

Calendar of Dramatic Records in the Books of the Livery Companies of London, 1485–1640, ed. J. Robertson and D.J. Gordon (Malone Society Collections, III, 1958)

Calendar of Letter Books Preserved Among the Archives of the Corporation of the City of London, 1275–1498, ed. R.R. Sharpe (11 vols., 1899–1912)

Calendar of Letters and Papers Foreign and Domestic, Henry VIII, ed. J.S. Brewer, J. Gairdner, and R.H. Brodie (H.M.S.O., 1862–1932)

Calendar of Patent Rolls (H.M.S.O., 1901-)

Calendar of Plea and Memoranda Rolls Preserved Among the Archives of the City of London, ed. A.H. Thomas (vols I–IV) and P.E. Jones (vols. V–VI) (6 vols., Cambridge, 1926–61)

Calendar of State Papers, Domestic (1856-)

Calendar of State Papers, Venetian, vol. XV, ed. A.B. Hinds (1909)

Calendar of Wills Proved and Enrolled in the Court of Husting, London, A.D. 1258 - A.D. 1688, ed. R.R. Sharpe (2 vols., 1889–90)

Campbell, R., *The London Tradesman* (1747)

Chaucer, G., *The Canterbury Tales*, ed. A.C. Crawley (1958)

The Charters of the Merchant Taylors' Company, ed. F.M. Fry and R.T.D. Sayle (1937)

The City Press

The Company of Haberdashers, Appellants; the Attorney General and the Poor of Newland Respondents; the Respondents' Case (1703)

Cronica Johannis de Reading et Anonym Cantuariensis, 1346–1367, ed. J. Tait (Manchester, 1914)

The Daily Post Extraordinary, Tuesday April 9, 1734: A List of Persons Who Have Poll'd for Mr William Selwin

Dale, T.C. (ed.), *The Members of the City Companies in 1641* (Society of Genealogists, 2 vols., 1934)

D'Ewes, S., *The Journals of All the Parliaments During the Reign of Queen Elizabeth* (1682)

De Worde, Winkin, *A Boke of Kervynge* (1508)

A Discourse of the Commonweal of this Realm of England, ed. E. Lamond (Cambridge, 1895)

Ditchfield, P.H., *The City Companies of London and Their Good Works* (1904)

Two Early London Subsidy Rolls, ed. E. Ekwall (Lund, 1951)

The Economist

English Reports

Erondell, P., *The French Garden* (1605)

Fawcet, S., *A Seasonable Sermon for These Troublesome Times Preached to the Companie of Haberdashers* (1641)

The Financial Times

Firth, J.F.B., *Municipal London* (1876)

Gomme, G.L. (ed.), 'The Names and Trades of Those Houses that Were Burnt Upon the Bridge', *The Gentleman's Magazine Library English Topography*, 15 (1904), 308–9

Grafton, R., *Chronicles* (2 vols., 1809)

Hansard

Heywood, T., *London's Ius Honorarium* (1631)

Heywood, T. *Londini Artium & Scientiarum Scaturigo: or, London's Fountaine of Arts and Sciences* (1632)

Heywood, T., *Londini Speculum: Or, London's Mirror, Exprest in Sundry Triumphs . . . at the Initiation of . . . Richard Fenn, into the Mairalty . . .* (1637)

Hinde, W., *A Faithfull Remonstrance of the Holy Life and Happy Death of John Bruen of Bruen Stapleford in the County of Chester Esquire* (1641)

Historical Manuscripts Commission:

Hatfield House (24 vols., 1883–1976)

House of Lords, new series (12 vols., 1900–77)

Horton, T., *Unrighteous Mammon Exchanged for True Riches* (1661)

The Independent

John Isham, Mercer and Merchant Adventurer: Two Account Books of a London Merchant in the Reign of Elizabeth I, ed. G.D. Ramsay (Northamptonshire Record Society, XXI, 1962)

P.E. Jones (ed.), *The Fire Court: Calendar to the Judgments and Decrees of the Court of Judicature Appointed to Determine Differences Between Landlords and Tenants as to Rebuilding After the Great Fire* (2 vols., 1966–70)

Journals of the House of Commons

Journals of the House of Lords

L.B.S., *The City Livery Companies and Their Corporate Property* (1885)

Leslie, J.H., 'A Survey or Muster of the Armed and Trained Companies of London, 1588 and 1599', *Journal of the Society of Army Historical Research*, 4 (1925), 62–71

Lever, T., *A Fruitfull Sermon . . . in Poules Churche* (1550)

The Lisle Letters: An Abridgement, ed. M. St Clare Byrne (1983)

A List of the Conventicles or Unlawfull Meetings Within the City of London (1683)

List of the Court and Livery of the Worshipful Company of Haberdashers (1933)

A List of the Master, Wardens, Assistants, and Liverymen of the Worshipful Company of Haberdashers (1837)

A List of the Poll of the Severall Companies of London for a Lord Mayor the Year Ensuing (1682)

London and Middlesex Chantry Certificate, 1548, ed. C.J. Kitching (London Record Society, XVI, 1980)

A Manual for the Use of the Court of Assistants of the Haberdashers' Company, Being an Abridgement of their Compendium (1828)

A Manual for the Private Use of the Court of Assistants of the Haberdashers' Company, London (1850)

A Manual for the Private Use of the Court of Assistants of the Haberdashers' Company, London (1876)

A Manual for the Private Use of the Court of Assistants of the Haberdashers' Company, London (1901)

A Manual for the Private Use of the Court of Assistants of the Haberdashers' Company, London (1954)

A Manual for the Private Use of the Court of Assistants of the Haberdashers' Company, London (1988)

Masters' Newsletters to the Wardens, Court of Assistants, and Liverymen of the Worshipful Company of Haberdashers (1969-)

Members of the Worshipful Company of Haberdashers (1990)

Memorials of London and London Life in the Thirteenth, Fourteenth, and Fifteenth Centuries, ed. H.T. Riley (1868)

The Monmouthshire Beacon

Norton, G., *Commentaries on the History, Constitution, and Chartered Franchises of the City of London* (1869)

'Observations on the Judges of the Court of Chancery and the Practice and Delays Complained in that Court', *Edinburgh Review*, 39 (1823), 246–59

The Ordre of my Lorde Mayor, the Aldermen, & the Shiriffes for Their Metings and Wearynge of Apparell Throughout the Yeare (1568)

The Overseas Trade of London: Exchequer Customs Accounts, 1480–1, ed. H.S. Cobb (London Record Society, XXVII, 1990)

Parliamentary Papers —

1819.X: Second Report of the Commissioners for Inquiring Concerning Charities

1821.XII: Fifth Report of the Commissioners for Inquiring Concerning Charities

1824.XIII: Further Report (10) of the Commissioners for Inquiring Concerning Charities

1837.XXV: Second Report of Commissioners of Inquiry into the Municipal Corporations of England and Wales

1867–8.XXVIII: Report of Her Majesty's Commissioners Appointed to Inquire into the Education Given in Schools not Contained Within Her Majesty's Two Former Commissions (Taunton Report)

1884.XXXIX: City of London Livery Companies Commission: Report and Appendix, in 5 parts

The Paston Letters, ed. J. Gairdner (3 vols., 1872–5)

The Shorter Pepys, ed. R. Latham (1986)

Perkins, W., *Works*, (1605)

Placita de Quo Warranto Temporibus Edw. I, II, et III (1818)

The Poll of the Liverymen of the City of London (1710)

The Port and Trade of Early Elizabethan London, ed. B. Dietz (London Record Society, VIII, 1972)

Proceedings in the Parliaments of Elizabeth I, 1559–1581, ed. T.E. Hartley (Leicester, 1981)

Returns of Aliens Dwelling in the City and Suburbs of London, ed. R.E.G. and E.F. Kirk (Huguenot Society Publications, X, 4 vols., 1900–08)

Returns of Strangers in the Metropolis, 1593, 1627, 1635, 1639, ed. I. Scouloudi (Huguenot Society Publications, LVII, 1985)

Rotuli Parliamentorum (6 vols., 1767–77)

The Seconde Parte of a Register, ed. A. Peel (2 vols., Cambridge, 1915)

Select Cases Before the King's Council in the Star Chamber Commonly Called the Court of Star Chamber, vol 2: A.D. 1509 - A.D. 1544 (Selden Society, XXV, 1911)

A Select Collection of Old English Plays, ed. W.C. Hazlitt (1874)

Settle, E., *The Triumphs of London, for the Inauguration of . . . Sir Richard Levett* (1699)

The Spending of the Money of Robert Nowell, ed. A.B. Grosart (1877)

Squire, J., *Tres Irenae Trophaea. Or, the Tryumphes of Peace. That Celebrated the Solemnity of . . . Sir Francis Jones . . . on his Inauguration to the Maioraltie of London* (1620)

The Standing Orders of the Worshipful Company of Haberdashers Adopted by the Court Pursuant to the Company's Charter and Bye-Laws (1986)

Statutes of the Realm

Stow, J., *A Survey of London*, ed. C.L. Kingsford (2 vols., Oxford, 1908)

Stow, J., *The Annales or a Generall Chronicle Continued by Edmund Howes* (1631)

Tatham, J., *London's Triumphs Celebrated . . . in Honour of . . . Sir John Lawrence* (1664)

The Times Educational Supplement

Tudor Economic Documents, ed. R.H. Tawney and E. Power (3 vols., 1924)

The Visitation of London, ed. J.J. Howard and J.L. Chester (2 vols., 1880–3)

Willet, A., *Synopsis Papismi* (1634)

4: SECONDARY WORKS

Alford, B.W.E., and Barker, T.C., *A History of the Carpenters' Company* (1968)

Allsobrook, D.I., *Schools for the Shires: the Reform of Middle-Class Education in Mid-Victorian England* (Manchester, 1986)

Archer, I.W., *The Pursuit of Stability: Social Relations in Elizabethan London* (Cambridge, 1991)

Armstrong, W.A., 'The Use of Information About Occupation', in *Nineteenth-Century Society: Essays in the Use of Quantitative Methods for Social Data*, ed. E.A. Wrigley (Cambridge, 1972), pp. 191–310

Ashton, R., *The City and the Court, 1603–1643* (Cambridge, 1979)

Aylmer, G., *The King's Servants: the Civil Service of Charles I, 1625–1642* (1961)

Barlow, T. Worthington, *Cheshire: its Historical and Literary Associations* (Manchester, 1865)

Barron, C.M., 'The Parish Fraternities of Medieval London', in *The Church in Pre-Reformation Society: Essays in Honour of F.R.H. du Boulay*, ed. C.M. Barron and C. Harper-Bill (1985), pp. 13–37

Barron, C.M., 'London and Parliament in the Lancastrian Period', *Parliamentary History*, 9 (1990), 343–67

Bassett, A. Tilney, *Gladstone's Speeches* (1916)

Bergeron, D.W., *English Civic Pageantry, 1558–1642* (1971)

Bolton, J.L., *The Medieval English Economy, 1150–1500* (1980)

Boulton, J.P., *Neighbourhood and Society: A London Suburb in the Seventeenth Century* (Cambridge, 1987)

Brenner, R., 'The Civil War Politics of London's Merchant Community', *Past and Present*, 57 (1973), 53–107

Brigden, S., *London and the Reformation* (Oxford, 1989)

Bristow, E. 'The Liberty and Property Defence League and Individualism', *Historical Journal*, 18 (1975), 761–89

Bromley, J., and Wagner, A.R., *The Armorial Bearings of the Guilds of London* (1960)

Brooks, P.C., *Omar Ramsden* (Birmingham, 1980)

Cain, P., 'Robert Smith and the Reform of the Archives of the City of London, 1580–1623', *London Journal*, 13 (1987–8), 3–16

Cannadine, D., 'The Context, Performance, and Meaning of Ritual: the British Monarchy and the Invention of Tradition, c. 1820–1977', in *The Invention of Tradition*, ed. E. Hobsbawm and T. Ranger (Cambridge, 1983), pp. 101–64

Carus-Wilson, E.M., *Medieval Merchant Venturers* (1954)

Carus-Wilson, E.M., and Coleman, O., *England's Export Trade, 1275–1547* (Oxford, 1963)

Childs, W., *Anglo-Castilian Trade in the Later Middle Ages* (Manchester, 1978)

Clark, P., '"The Ramoth-Gilead of the Good": Urban Change and Political Radicalism at Gloucester, 1540–1640', in *The English Commonwealth, 1547–1640*, ed. P. Clark, A.G.R. Smith, and N. Tyacke (Leicester, 1979), pp. 167–87

Clay, C.G.A., *Economic Expansion and Social Change: England, 1500–1700* (2 vols., Cambridge, 1984)

Clayton, M., *The Collector's Dictionary of the Silver and Gold of Great Britain and North America* (2nd. edn, 1985)

Coleman, D.C., *The British Paper Industry, 1495–1860: A Study in Industrial Growth* (Oxford, 1958)

Collinson, P., *The Religion of Protestants: the Church in English Society, 1559–1625* (Oxford, 1982)

Coulter, J., 'The Browning House at New Cross', *Browning Society Notes*, 15: 2–3 (1985–6), 2–19

Crawford, A., *A History of the Vintners' Company* (1977)

Cressy, D., *Bonfires and Bells: National Memory and the Protestant Calendar in Elizabethan and Stuart England* (1989)

Cunnington, C.W. and P., *Handbook of English Medieval Costume* (2nd edn., 1969)

Cunnington, C.W. and P., *Handbook of British Costume in the Sixteenth Century* (2nd edn., 1970)

Curl, J.S., *The Londonderry Plantation, 1609–1914* (1986)

Curtis, S.J., *History of Education in Great Britain* (7th. edn., 1967)

Davis, D., *A History of Shopping* (1966)

De Krey, G.S., *A Fractured Society: the Politics of London in the First Age of Party, 1688–1715* (Oxford, 1985)

De Krey, G.S., 'London Radicals and Revolutionary Politics, 1675–1683', in *The Politics of Religion in Restoration England*, ed. T. Harris, P. Seaward, and M. Goldie (1990), pp. 133–62

Doolittle, I.G., *The City of London and its Livery Companies* (Dorchester, 1982)

Dyer, C. *Standards of Living in the Later Middle Ages: Social Change in England, c.1200–1520* (Cambridge, 1989)

Earle, P., *The Making of the English Middle Class: Business, Society, and Family Life in London, 1660–1730* (1989)

Egan, G., and Pritchard, F., *Medieval Finds from Excavations in London, 3: Dress Accessories, c.1150–c.1450* (H.M.S.O., 1991)

Elmes, J., *The Life and Times of Sir Christopher Wren* (1829)

Elton, G.R., *Reform and Reformation: England, 1509–1558* (1977)

Finlay, R., and Shearer, B., 'Population Growth and Suburban Expansion', in *London, 1500–1700: the Making of the Metropolis*, ed. A.L. Beier and R. Finlay (1986), pp. 37–59

Fletcher, S., *Feminists and Bureaucrats: A Study in the Development of Girls' Education in the Nineteenth Century*, (Cambridge, 1980)

Foster, F.F., *The Politics of Stability: A Portrait of the Rulers of Elizabethan London* (1977)

Fraser, A., *A History of Toys* (1966)

Girtin, T., *The Golden Ram: A Narrative History of the Clothworkers' Company, 1528–1958* (1958)

Glanville, P., *Silver in Tudor and Early Stuart England* (1990)

Glover, E., *A History of the Ironmongers' Company* (1991)

Goldsmiths' Hall, *Gerald Benney* (1973)

Gosden, P.H.J.H., *The Development of Educational Administration in England and Wales* (Oxford, 1966)

Gras, N.S.B., *The Evolution of the English Corn Market from the Twelfth to the Eighteenth Century* (Cambridge, Mass., 1915)

Gras, N.S.B., *The Early English Customs System* (Cambridge, Mass., 1918)

Grassby, R., 'The Personal Wealth of the Business Community in Seventeenth-Century England', *Economic History Review*, 2nd series, 23, (1970), 220–34

Griffiths, R., *The Reign of Henry VI* (1981)

Haley, K.H.D., *The First Earl of Shaftesbury* (Oxford, 1968)

Harper-Bill, C., *The Pre-Reformation Church in England* (1989)

Harris, T., *London Crowds in the Reign of Charles II: Propaganda and Politics from the Restoration until the Exclusion Crisis* (Cambridge, 1987)

Harte, N., 'State Control of Dress and Social Change in Pre-Industrial England', in *Trade, Government, and Economy in Pre-Industrial England: Essays Presented to F.J. Fisher*, ed. P. Corfield et. al. (1976), pp. 132–65

Herbert, W., *The History of the Twelve Great Livery Companies of London* (2 vols., 1834–7)

Hill, C., 'Puritans and the "Dark Corners of the Land" ', *Transactions of the Royal Historical Society*, 5th series, 13 (1963), 77–102

Hills, R.M. (ed.), *Hatcham Tercentenary: A Literary Review of the Hatcham Schools* (1990)

Ingarfield, L.E., and Alexander, M.B., *Haberdashers' Aske's Hatcham Boys' School: A Short History* (1985)

Ives, E.W., *Anne Boleyn* (1986)

Jackson, C., *A History of English Plate* (2 vols., 1916)

James, M., 'At a Crossroads of a Political Culture; the Essex Revolt, 1601' in his *Society, Politics and Culture: Studies in Early Modern England* (Cambridge, 1986), pp. 416–65

Johnson, A.H., *A History of the Worshipful Company of Drapers of London* (5 vols., 1914–22)

Jones, P.E., *The Butchers of London: A History of the Worshipful Company of Butchers of the City of London* (1976)

Jordan, W.K., *The Charities of London, 1480–1660: the Aspirations and Achievements of the Urban Society* (1960)

Kahl, W.F., 'Apprenticeship and the Freedom of the London Livery Companies, 1690–1750', *Guildhall Miscellany*, 7 (1956), 17–20

Keene, D., *Survey of Medieval Winchester* (2 vols., 1985)

Kellett, J.R., 'The Breakdown of Guild and Corporation Control over the Handicraft and Retail Trades of London', *Economic History Review*, 2nd series, 10 (1957–8), 381–94

Kissack, K., *Monmouth: the Making of a County Town* (1975)

Kitching, C.J., 'The Quest for Concealed Lands', *Transactions of the Royal Historical Society*, 5th series, 24 (1974), 63–78

Kreider, A., *English Chantries: the Road to Dissolution* (Cambridge, Mass., 1979)

Lang, J., *City and Guilds of London Institute Centenary, 1878–1978* (1978)

Lang, R.G., 'Social Origins and Social Aspirations of Jacobean London Merchants', *Economic History Review*, second series, 27 (1974), 28–47

Langford, P., *A Polite and Commercial People: England, 1727–1783* (Oxford, 1989)

Lee, G., *English Silver Monteith Bowls* (1978)

Linthicum, M.C., *Costume in the Drama of Shakespeare and his Contemporaries* (Oxford, 1936)

Masters, B.R., *The Chamberlain of the City of London, 1237–1987* (1988)

Meredith, J.R., *Adams' Grammar School, Newport, 1656–1956: A Short History* (Newport, 1956)

Meredith, J.R., *The Foundation and Early History of Aske's Hospital at Hoxton, 1689–1755* (1964)

Miller, H., 'London and Parliament in the Reign of Henry VIII', *Bulletin of the Institute of Historical Research*, 35 (1962), 128–49

Morgan, T., *Monmouthshire Education, 1889–1974* (Old Cwmbran, 1988)

Morrill, J.S., *Cheshire, 1603–1660: County Government and Society During the English Revolution* (Oxford, 1974)

Morris, R.H., *Chester in the Plantagenet and Tudor Reigns* (Chester, n.d.)

Munby, L., *How Much is That Worth?* (British Association for Local History, Chichester, 1989)

Newton, S.M., *Fashion in the Age of the Black Prince: A Study of the Years 1340 to 1365* (Woodbridge, 1980)

Owen, D., *English Philanthropy, 1660–1960* (1965)

Pearl, V., *London and the Outbreak of the Puritan Revolution* (Oxford, 1960)

Pettegree, A., *Foreign Protestant Communities in Sixteenth-Century London* (Oxford, 1986)

Phythian-Adams, C., *Desolation of a City: Coventry and the Urban Crisis of the Late Middle Ages* (Cambridge, 1979)

Pickford, I., *Jackson's English Goldsmiths* (Woodbridge, 1989)

Power, E., 'The Wool Trade in the Fifteenth Century', in *English Trade in the Fifteenth Century*, ed. E. Power and M.M. Postan (Cambridge, 1933)

Rabb, T.K., *Enterprise and Empire* (Cambridge, Mass, 1967)

Ramsay, G.D., 'The Recruitment and Fortunes of Some London Freemen in the Mid-Sixteenth Century', *Economic History Review*, 2nd series, 31 (1978), 526–40

Ramsay, G.D., 'Victorian Historiography and the Guilds of London: the Report of the Royal Commission on the Livery Companies of London, 1884', *London Journal*, 10 (1984), 155–66

Ramsey, P., *Tudor Economic Problems* (1968)

Rappaport, S., *Worlds Within Worlds: Structures of Life in Sixteenth-Century London* (Cambridge, 1989)

Reddaway, T.F., *The Early History of the Goldsmiths' Company, 1327–1509*, (1975)

Rogers, N., *Whigs and Cities: Popular Politics in the Age of Walpole and Pitt* (Oxford, 1989)

Ross, C., *Edward IV* (1974)

Scarisbrick, J.J., *The Reformation and the English People* (Oxford, 1984)

Scott, M., *A Visual History of Costume; the Fifteenth and Sixteenth Centuries* (1986)

Seaver, P., *The Puritan Lectureships: the Politics of Religious Dissent, 1560–1662* (Stanford, 1970)

Skeat, W.W., '"Haberdasher"', *The Academy*, 72 (1907), 513–14

Sonenscher, M., *The Hatters of Eighteenth-Century France* (1987)

Speck, W., *Reluctant Revolutionaries: Englishmen and the Revolution of 1688* (Oxford, 1988)

Spufford, M., *The Great Reclothing of Rural England: Petty Chapmen and their Wares in the Seventeenth Century* (1984)

Sutherland, G., 'Secondary Education: the Education of the Middle Classes', in *Government and Society in Nineteenth-Century Britain*, ed. C. Fox et al. (Truro, 1977), pp. 137–66

Swanson, H., *Medieval Artisans: An Urban Class in Late Medieval England* (Oxford, 1989)

Thatcher, R., *Hatcham and Telegraph Hill: An Historical Sketch* (Lewisham Local History Society, 1982)

Thirsk, J., *Economic Policy and Projects: the Development of a Consumer Society in Early Modern England* (Oxford, 1978)

Thrupp, S., 'The Grocers of London: A Study of Distributive Trade', in *English Foreign Trade in the Fifteenth Century*, ed. E. Power and M.M. Postan (1933)

Thrupp, S., *The Merchant Class of Medieval London* (1948)

Todd, M., *Christian Humanism and the Puritan Social Order* (Cambridge, 1987)

Tompson, R., *Classics or Charity? The Dilemma of the Eighteenth-Century Grammar School* (Manchester, 1971)

Tompson, R., *The Charity Commission and the Age of Reform* (1979)

Trevor-Roper, H.R., *Archbishop Laud, 1573–1645* (1940)

Turner, M., 'The Land Tax, Land, and Property: Old Debates and New Horizons', in *Land and Property; the English Land Tax, 1692–1832*, ed. M. Turner and D. Mills (Gloucester, 1986)

Tyacke, N., *The Fortunes of English Puritanism, 1603–1640* (Friends of Dr Williams' Library Forty-Fourth Lecture, 1990)

Unwin, G., *Industrial Organisation in the Sixteenth and Seventeenth Centuries* (Oxford, 1904)

Unwin, G., *The Gilds and Companies of London* (1908)

Veale, E., *The Fur Trade in the Later Middle Ages* (Oxford, 1966)

Veale, E., 'Craftsmen and the Economy of London in the Fourteenth Century' in *The English Medieval Town: A Reader in English Urban History, 1200–1540*, ed. R. Holt and G. Rosser (1990)

Ward, H.A., *Monmouth School, 1614–1964: An Outline History* (1964)

Warlow, W.M., *A History of the Charities of William Jones at Monmouth and Newland* (Bristol, 1899)

Westlake, H.F., *The Parish Guilds of Medieval England* (1919)

Whetham, E.H., *The Agrarian History of England and Wales, Vol VIII, 1914–1939* (Cambridge, 1978)

Wigley, J., *A Short History of the Haberdashers' Aske's School, Elstree* (Elstree, 1984)

Willan, T.S., *The Muscovy Merchants of 1555* (Manchester, 1953)

Williams, D., 'London Puritanism: the Haberdashers' Company', *Church History*, 32 (1963), 1–24

Withington, R., *English Pageantry; An Historical Outline* (2 vols., New York, 1926)

Wynne Evans, L., 'The Evolution of Welsh Educational Structure and Administration, 1881–1921', in *Studies in the Government and Control of Education Since 1860* (History of Education Society, 1970), pp. 43–67

Youngs, F.A., *The Proclamations of the Tudor Queens* (Cambridge, 1976)

5: UNPUBLISHED SECONDARY SOURCES

Archer, I.W., 'Governors and Governed in Late Sixteenth-Century London, *c.*1560–1603: Studies in the Achievement of Stability' (Oxford D.Phil, 1988)

Brenner, R., 'Commercial Change and Political Conflict: the Merchant Community in Civil War London' (Princeton Ph.D., 1970)

Eagleton, G.T., 'The Eagletons of Wakerley, Eltham', typescript in possession of Mr B.C. Gothard

Elliott, V.B., 'Mobility and Marriage in Pre-Industrial England' (Cambridge Ph.D., 1978)

Howells, P.E., 'The Hospital at Hoxton of the Foundation of Robert Aske Esq, 1695–1864', typescript on deposit at Haberdashers' Hall

King, T., 'The Haberdashers' Company of London, 1602–42' (Univ. of Oxford B.A. thesis, n.d.), copy on deposit at Haberdashers' Hall

Ramsey, P., 'The Merchant Adventurers' Organization in the Early Sixteenth Century' (Oxford D.Phil., 1963)

Read, J., 'The Manor of Hatcham: Aspects of its Development, 1600–1900' (Dip. Hist. thesis, Univ. of London, 1973), copy on deposit at Lewisham Archives and Local History Department

Scouloudi, I., 'Alien Immigration and Alien Communities in London, 1558–1640' (London M.Sc., 1933)

Index